Frommer's®

W9-DHT-717

Los Cabos & Baja

2nd Edition

by Emily Hughey Quinn

Here's what the critics say about Frommer's:

"Amazingly easy to use. Very portable, very complete."

—Booklist

"Detailed, accurate, and easy-to-read information for all price ranges."
—Glamour Magazine

"Hotel information is close to encyclopedic."

—Des Moines Sunday Register

"Frommer's Guides have a way of giving you a real feel for a place."
—Knight Ridder Newspapers

BICENTENNIAL
1807
WILEY
2007
BICENTENNIAL

Wiley Publishing, Inc.

About the Author

Born and raised on the Kansas prairie, nothing was more alarming to **Emily Hughey Quinn** than being surrounded by salt water on three sides. She moved to Los Cabos, Mexico, in 2003 after launching *Cabo Living* magazine and falling for the man of her dreams, an avid free diver and spearfisherman who not only introduced her to the bliss of freediving, but also kept her freezer full of fish for nearly 4 years. Emily's travel articles on Mexico have appeared in *Luxury Golf & Travel*, *Cabo Living*, *Méxican Pacific*, and *Luxury Living* magazines.

Published by:

Wiley Publishing, Inc.

111 River St.
Hoboken, NJ 07030-5774

ISBN: 978-0-470-14603-3

Editor: Stephen Bassman
Production Editor: Michael Brumitt
Cartographer: Anton Crane
Photo Editor: Richard Fox
Anniversary Logo Design: Richard Pacifico
Production by Wiley Indianapolis Composition Services

Front cover photo: Kayaking toward a natural arch
Back cover photo: A Boojum tree and a Cardon cactus in Desierto Central, Baja

For information on our other products and services or to obtain technical support, please contact our Customer Care Department within the U.S. at 800/762-2974, outside the U.S. at 317/572-3993 or fax 317/572-4002.

Wiley also publishes its books in a variety of electronic formats. Some content that appears in print may not be available in electronic formats.

Manufactured in the United States of America

5 4 3 2 1

Contents

List of Maps

This book is dedicated to Brian, Therese Drillien, Lucila DiNucci, India Wood, Marina Verdugo, Warren Gibson, José Alonso, Alicia Chávez, Alejandro Olea, Jim, Cate Edwards, Mónica Medina, Kim Clapham, Amy Thomas, Sheila Vaananen, Amy Abbott, Sigra, and all the others who may or may not realize the depths of their contribution to my love for Mexico, to my exploration of the land and culture, and to my particular appreciation for the complexities of Southern Baja.

Acknowledgments

A huge thanks to my husband, Brian Quinn who—in his magnanimous, unconditional way—gave me the opportunity to dedicate 6 months to flying, driving, and writing about the peninsula we love so much. Thanks also to Rick Hughey, my dad and "research assistant," and to my sister, Andrea, for always picking up her phone. And, of course, to my friend and predecessor, Lynne Bairstow, whose meticulous planning, astute observations, and darn good writing in the first edition gave me a wonderful springboard from which to blaze my own trails.

—Emily Hughey Quinn

An Invitation to the Reader

In researching this book, we discovered many wonderful places—hotels, restaurants, shops, and more. We're sure you'll find others. Please tell us about them, so we can share the information with your fellow travelers in upcoming editions. If you were disappointed with a recommendation, we'd love to know that, too. Please write to:

Frommer's Los Cabos & Baja, 2nd Edition
Wiley Publishing, Inc. • 111 River St. • Hoboken, NJ 07030-5774

An Additional Note

Please be advised that travel information is subject to change at any time—and this is especially true of prices. We therefore suggest that you write or call ahead for confirmation when making your travel plans. The authors, editors, and publisher cannot be held responsible for the experiences of readers while traveling. Your safety is important to us, however, so we encourage you to stay alert and be aware of your surroundings. Keep a close eye on cameras, purses, and wallets, all favorite targets of thieves and pickpockets.

Frommer's Star Ratings, Icons & Abbreviations

Every hotel, restaurant, and attraction listing in this guide has been ranked for quality, value, service, amenities, and special features using a **star-rating system.** In country, state, and regional guides, we also rate towns and regions to help you narrow down your choices and budget your time accordingly. Hotels and restaurants are rated on a scale of zero (recommended) to three stars (exceptional). Attractions, shopping, nightlife, towns, and regions are rated according to the following scale: zero stars (recommended), one star (highly recommended), two stars (very highly recommended), and three stars (must-see).

In addition to the star-rating system, we also use **seven feature icons** that point you to the great deals, in-the-know advice, and unique experiences that separate travelers from tourists. Throughout the book, look for:

Finds	Special finds—those places only insiders know about
Fun Fact	Fun facts—details that make travelers more informed and their trips more fun
Kids	Best bets for kids and advice for the whole family
Moments	Special moments—those experiences that memories are made of
Overrated	Places or experiences not worth your time or money
Tips	Insider tips—great ways to save time and money
Value	Great values—where to get the best deals

The following **abbreviations** are used for credit cards:

AE	American Express	DISC	Discover	V	Visa
DC	Diners Club	MC	MasterCard		

Frommers.com

Now that you have this guidebook to help you plan a great trip, visit our website at **www. frommers.com** for additional travel information on more than 3,600 destinations. We update features regularly to give you instant access to the most current trip-planning information available. At Frommers.com, you'll find scoops on the best airfares, lodging rates, and car rental bargains. You can even book your travel online through our reliable travel booking partners. Other popular features include:

- Online updates of our most popular guidebooks
- Vacation sweepstakes and contest giveaways
- Newsletters highlighting the hottest travel trends
- Online travel message boards with featured travel discussions

The Best of Los Cabos & Baja

It was May of my senior year in college when I found out I was going to Los Cabos for the first time. A publisher in my hometown dreamed up a magazine called *Cabo Living* and hired me—with my stockpile of youthful ambition—to be the editor. All I really knew about Cabo was that Debbie Hunt, the dating-service-crazed redhead in Cameron Crowe's movie, *Singles* (1992), buys a plane ticket to Cabo, meets an enticing divorcé when she lands, he likes her earrings, they fall in love, and she plans to move there with him if she can get a job at the local TV station. (Aside: There is no local TV station in Cabo, Cameron Crowe.)

I had nothing in common with Debbie Hunt—I was a suburban-bred Kansan barely out of school and she was a grunge-era Seattleite making her way in the world—but I suddenly considered her a kindred spirit. I had reached near Hollywood status because I was going to Cabo, this glamorous and mysterious beachy paradise someone was paying me to explore.

My friend, India, calls Los Cabos "a real cooker," by which she means all experiences here are amplified. India's theory—as I interpret it—is that because Los Cabos is surrounded by water on three sides, desert moonscape all around, and mountains to the north, energy in general has nowhere to diffuse, so it swirls around Baja's tip, making things happen with extra gusto. Couples fall in love, couples separate, old friends reunite, careers take off, careers tank, people evolve, deep friendships take root, healing occurs, and Debbie Hunt meets her sugar daddy, all in the blink of an eye.

Having begun my own career, experienced moments I still can't believe, and met my beau for life (not to mention a few soul sisters) in Los Cabos, I think India may be right. Above all, its breathtaking landscape, luxurious resorts, delectable restaurants, opulent real estate, and ceaseless adventure make Los Cabos a real cooker.

The funny thing about Baja, though, is that everyone believes his or her area is the peninsula's seat of, well, everything. In my travels, I've heard countless declarations from "best sunset" to "best marlin fishing" and "best surf break" to "best taco" in La Paz, San Felipe, Ensenada, Loreto, and more. And you could drink for weeks if you tried downing every "best margarita in Baja." Like a true Land's Endophile, for a short time, I believed Los Cabos represented the best of Baja, mostly for its magical "cooker" aspect, and because I felt that no other place could hold all the promise and paradox so ubiquitous at Baja's tip.

A little exploring early on proved me—and everyone else who swears his peninsular plot is the best ever—completely wrong. No matter where I go in Baja, I meet people with their own unique "cooker" stories, elaborate and unexpected tales of how they ended up here, how they realized their life's dream, how they fell in love, how they overcame unbelievable obstacles. Baja—from top to bottom—is brimming with the stuff of legends: horticulturist turned flamenco guitarist, near-death cancer patient turned vibrant survivor, high school dropout turned real estate mogul, former drug trafficker turned yogi, off-road racer turned businessman, ski filmmaker turned land developer, pregnant teenager turned CEO, Olympic coach turned surf junkie, covert government agent turned fisherman, and more.

Beyond all the beautiful things to do and see in Baja—and there are many, as you'll find if you read on—the most important thing to do in Baja is be. Travel itineraries and the suggestions I provide in this book are useful, but please be open to the subtle currents of life, and if you feel the sudden urge to turn right instead of left, walk instead of drive, say "gracias" instead of "thank you," do it. When you vacation in a "real cooker" like Baja, even the subtlest currents may be leading you to the stuff of legends. I think Debbie Hunt would vouch for that.

1 The Most Unforgettable Travel Experiences

- **Harvest Festival in the Valle de Guadalupe:** Mexico's wine country comes alive in true fiesta style each year, late August to early September, during this annual wine festival. The celebrations combine wine tastings with parties, concerts, blessings of the grapes, and other events. See p. 156.

- **Exploring Baja's Missions:** From the late 17th through the 19th centuries, Jesuit, Franciscan, and Dominican friars founded a succession of missions in Baja California. The missions were part of the many institutions that the Spanish crown used to colonize the territories of "Nuevo España." Explore one or several along the "Camino Real Misionero." See p. 125.

- **Arts Festival in Todos Santos:** Although Todos Santos is filled with a creative, artistic ambience at any time of year, it reaches a peak each February during the annual Arts Festival. Held since the early 1990s, the festival continues to grow in popularity and content. See p. 95.

- **Feria de San José:** Those nostalgic for the traveling carnivals of old will find just the sensory overload they've been missing in the litigious U.S. For 1 full week at the end of March, the carnival comes to downtown San José del Cabo in celebration of San José Day. With it come endless booths of spicy food and full-service bars, rickety rides, housewares hawkers, shooting and dart games you're never supposed to win, live *banda* music, a Palenque tent with organized cockfights, and even a house of mirrors. It's my favorite week of the year. See p. 61.

- **Foxploration!:** When the 1997 movie *Titanic* was filmed here, at a seaside soundstage created for the production of the movie, Hollywood turned its attention to Rosarito Beach for even more moviemaking. The original production facility has been turned into an interactive museum and entertainment center that brings into focus the art of moviemaking and special effects, especially those made along Baja's coastline. See p. 163.

- **Bullfights in Tijuana:** No matter what your opinion of bullfighting may be, the pastime is an undeniable part of the sporting culture of Mexico, drawing from its Spanish heritage. Considered among the best venues for watching this sport in North America, Tijuana's dual bullrings feature top matadors in their contests against bulls. The season runs from May to September. See p. 157.

- **Cave Paintings of Central Baja:** Primitive rock paintings on the walls of caves in central Baja are the only examples of this type of art on the North American continent. Their origin remains a mystery, and researchers say they could date back as far as 10,000 years, created during the Prehistoric Age. Regardless of who created them, or when they were created, the colorful, mystical murals are impressive. The journey to reach them is also an adventure in itself. See "Baja's Cave Paintings: An Exploration of the Mysterious" on p. 126.

- **Carnaval in La Paz:** The best Carnaval (or Mardi Gras) party in Baja takes place in La Paz, where round-the-clock revelries take place just prior to Lent. The oceanfront *malecón* is the site of most of the festivities as this generally tranquil town swings into party mode. See p. 101.

2 The Best Beach Vacations

- **Los Cabos Corridor:** Dramatic rock formations and crashing waves mix with wide stretches of soft sand and rolling surf breaks here. This stretch of coast is also home to some of Mexico's most luxurious resorts, verdant golf greens, and crowd-free surf breaks. Start at Playa Palmilla in San José del Cabo and work your way down to the famed Playa de Amor at Land's End in Cabo San Lucas. Some beaches here are more suitable for contemplation than for swimming, which isn't all bad. See chapter 4.

- **Los Barriles:** The gentle, sleepy-town feel of this blossoming East-Cape fishing village is just the start of why this place is magical. Sweeping beaches, accommodations that feel luxurious despite friendly price tags, a thriving expat artist community, a handful of truly delectable eateries, and all the fish in the sea make Los Barriles a must for the beach-bound vacationer. See p. 94.

- **La Paz:** If you want time to stop in its tracks, this town—the capital city of Baja Sur—offers slow-paced beach life at its best. Most accommodations are modest, inexpensive inns, with a few unique, well-appointed places tossed in. Follow the scent of ocean-going adventure in the air or just follow the breeze to myriad sandy beaches. In La Paz, no one expects anything of you, allowing you to pave your own way to underwater vistas and offshore islands or shallow snorkels and comfy beach chairs. See chapter 5.

- **Loreto:** Once the center of the Jesuit mission movement in Baja, Loreto is both a town of historical interest as well as a naturalist's dream. Offshore islands provide abundant opportunities for kayaking, snorkeling, diving, and exploring, and the beaches to the south of town are downright dreamy. If you tire of the big blue, there are plenty of inland explorations nearby as well. See chapter 6.

- **Rosarito to Ensenada:** Northern Baja's beach towns may be primarily known for attracting a rowdy party crowd on weekends, but regardless of whether you're here for the revelry, you'll also find this stretch of coast ideal for great surfing and dramatic diving. See chapter 7.

3 The Best Museums

- **Museo Histórico Comunitario:** It's a little-known fact that this region—now known as Mexico's wine country—was originally settled by Russian immigrants who were granted political asylum by Mexico in the early 1900s. A tribute to these pioneers of grape cultivation in the area, this small but intriguing museum tells the story of this curious time. An adjacent restaurant serves traditional Russian food. See p. 178.

- **Museo de las Misiones, Loreto:** The missionaries who came to Baja in the 17th through 19th centuries did more than work on converting the local populations to Christianity. This museum features a complete collection of historical and anthropological exhibits pertaining to the Baja peninsula, and includes the zoological studies and scientific writings of the friars. It also documents the contribution of these missions to the demise of indigenous cultures. See p. 125.

- **Museo de Antropología (Anthropology Museum), La Paz:** If you can't make it to see the actual cave paintings of central Baja, this museum has large, although faded, photographs of them along with a number of exhibits on various topics concerning the geology and history of Baja California. See p. 108.

- **Serpentarium, La Paz:** Reptiles are the star of this mostly open-air natural museum that offers plenty of opportunities to get up close and personal with the snakes, iguanas, lizards, crocodiles, and other reptilians of Baja. Children seem especially happy to explore here. See p. 110.

- **Museo Regional de Historia, Mulegé:** It's not so much this museum that fascinates me; it's more about the fact that it was once a state penitentiary that allowed its inmates to leave during the day—on the condition they return at dusk! For some reason, escape attempts were rare in this honor-system prison. The museum details the operation of this unique entity and the town of Mulegé. See p. 139.

- **Museo de Cera, Tijuana:** Many of the 90 figures in this wax museum are creepy, but it's hard not to be fascinated by the eclectic mix of personalities memorialized in wax that range from Aztec warriors and Dominican friars to Bill Clinton and Whoopi Goldberg. Don't miss the Chamber of Horrors. See p. 153.

- **Museo de las Identidades Mexicanas (Museum of Mexican Identities), Tijuana:** Located inside the Centro Cultural Tijuana, this permanent collection of artifacts from pre-Hispanic through modern times displays the gamut of Mexican historical and cultural influences, leaving visitors with a better understanding of this complex society. See p. 154.

4 The Best Outdoor Adventures

- **Whale-Watching in Magdalena Bay:** Few sights are as awe inspiring as watching whales in their natural habitat, and few places in the world can offer as complete an experience as Mexico's Baja peninsula, especially in Magdalena Bay in the El Vizcaíno Biosphere Reserve. The various protected bays and lagoons in this area on the Pacific coast are the preferred winter waters for migrating gray whales as they journey south to mate and give birth to their calves. See chapter 6.

- **Surfing the Baja Coastline:** Northern Baja has the perfect combination of perpetual right-breaking waves and cheap places to stay, not to mention the legendary Killers Break at Todos Santos Island, while Southern Baja guarantees premium waves and worry-free beach camping year round. See chapters 4 and 7.

- **Kayaking the Islands off Loreto:** The offshore islands and inlets surrounding Loreto are a kayaker's paradise, and numerous outfitters are equipped to take you on day trips or overnight kayak excursions. Especially popular is exploring Isla del Carmen, a mostly inaccessible and private island just offshore. See chapter 6.

- **Freediving and Spearfishing off La Paz:** Gliding beneath the water on a deep breath alone—without a heavy scuba tank or bubbles—is as liberating as it gets. And, if regular fishing bores you, a deep breath is the first step to your hand-picked catch. Test your spear-gun shot underwater against the sea's pelagic predators. Tour companies offer freediving and spear-fishing instruction; and in the reefs, seamounts, and blue water surrounding La Paz, you never know what may swim by. See chapter 5.

- **Golf in Los Cabos:** Los Cabos has evolved as one of the world's top golf destinations. It currently has seven courses open to challenge golfers and several more under construction. The destination master plan calls for a total of 207 holes of play. In addition to the championship design, quality, and exquisite desert-and-sea scenery of these courses, Cabo offers very reliable weather. The ample and intriguing variety of courses challenges golfers of all levels. See chapter 4.

- **Exploring the Caves in Central Baja:** The goal of a trip to these caves is to see the mysterious cave paintings that potentially date back to the Prehistoric Age, but, in itself, the journey to the caves in Central Baja is a fascinating adventure. Depending on your destination, treks can be mildly challenging to difficult. These treks will take you through the canyons, crossing streams, and up challenging climbs. In many protected areas, access is allowed only with an authorized guide. The caves are in the San Francisco de la Sierra and Santa Martha mountains in Central Baja. See chapter 6.

- **Sportfishing in Los Cabos:** You're as likely to reel in the big one here as anywhere in the world, where bringing in a 45-kilogram (100-lb.) marlin is considered routine. The Sea of Cortez has an abundance of fighting fish, and easy access to the Pacific provides opportunities for stellar sportfishing in all seasons. Among your likely catches are sailfish, wahoo, tuna, and the famed marlin, in black, blue, and striped varieties. See chapter 4.

- **Hiking the National Parks of Northern Baja:** In northern Baja, several national parks provide ample opportunities for hiking, camping, climbing, and other explorations. Among the most notable is the **Parque Nacional Constitución de 1857,** a 5,000-hectare (12,350-acre) preserve, at an altitude that averages 1,200m (3,936 ft.), and, contrary to what you may expect in Mexico, has a large lake in an alpine setting. In the **Parque Nacional Sierra San Pedro Mártir,** you'll find the Picacho del Diablo (Devil's Peak), a mountain with a summit at 3,095m (10,152 ft.) from which you can see both oceans and an immense stretch of land. See chapter 7.

5 The Best Places to Get Away from It All

- **Rancho La Puerta:** In 1940, well before resort spas were the rage—or even an acceptable form of vacationing—Rancho La Puerta opened its doors. It was called a "health camp" then, and today it is considered a pioneer of the modern spa and fitness movement. In the more than 50 years it's been in operation, it has consistently been at the cutting edge of promoting health and wellness. It emphasizes a mind/body/spirit philosophy in one of the most relaxing and pristine settings you can imagine. For those looking to get away from it all in search of your best self, this is the place. See p. 162.

- **Cabo Pulmo:** It's only a 37km (60-mile) drive from the Los Cabos airport to Cabo Pulmo, yet if the mounded Sierra de La Laguna peaks weren't a dead giveaway for Baja, you could be in the South Pacific. Swaying in the shade of a *palapa*-roofed bungalow fronting the Sea of Cortez, you won't care where you are—you just won't want to leave. The coral reef itself is a sight to behold, but the real attraction is the flourishing sea life in this protected marine park. The underwater world is ideal for washing away earthly cares, and extensive hiking/mountain-biking trails loop through the mountains, for those who prefer the peace of the desert. See chapter 4.

- **Camping near Loreto:** The beautiful succession of tranquil coves and beaches bordering Loreto makes for a few great places to set up camp. Once settled you can kayak the coast, explore the desert, hike a hill, or just hold court on the sand. See chapter 6.

- **Punta Colorada, East Cape:** Baja's East Cape is close enough to the bustle of Los Cabos that you can drift as far away as you want while being close enough to do lunch or dinner in San José. Punta Colorada is a classically stark Baja escape steeped in a culture of fishing, hiking, bird watching, beach combing, and, more than anything, just being. See chapter 4.

- **Valle de Guadalupe:** Mexico's wine country bears little resemblance to the tourism-oriented wineries of Northern California. Here you'll find plenty of peace and quiet in the midst of acres of vineyards. A couple of small inns welcome visitors who want to stop and smell the grapes—or vintages produced here. And, its eclectic history makes exploring the area a treat. See chapter 7.

- **El Santuario:** This resort's location, 40km (25 miles) south of Loreto on pristine Ensenada Blanca Bay, makes it far away from most everything, but you won't miss a thing. Nestled in rolling sand dunes, six small *palapa*-topped casitas are located throughout the property, allowing for privacy in the stillness of this sustainable eco-retreat. All meals—mostly vegetarian—and a host of activities are included in the rate. Therapy sessions based on the mind-body connection also are available with one of the owners, a renowned psychotherapist from California. See p. 129.

- **Posada La Poza:** On its own, a visit to Todos Santos feels worlds away—especially from the crowds of Los Cabos—but nestled beside a quiet lagoon that borders the Pacific is Posada La Poza. This gracious boutique retreat, awash in desert colors, birdsong, and meticulous detail, will take you even farther into your own reverie. See chapter 4.

6 The Best Shopping

Some tips on bargaining: Although haggling over prices in markets is expected and part of the fun, don't try to browbeat the vendor or bad-mouth the goods. Vendors won't bargain with people they consider disrespectful unless they are desperate to make a sale, and in the resort areas of Baja, unless it's an open-air market, the prices in stores are fixed, so bargaining is not an option. Nevertheless, it never hurts to ask. For best results, be insistent but friendly.

- **Carved Furniture in Rosarito:** Rosarito Beach's Bulevar Benito Juárez has become known for its selection of shops featuring ornately carved wooden furniture. Comparing the offerings has become easy, with so many options in one central location. See p. 164.
- **Art in Todos Santos:** Whether it's oil on canvas, pottery, or weavings, you'll find very high-quality original works of art in this cultural community. The annual Arts Festival, held every February, brings an even greater selection of works to choose from. See p. 94.
- **Homemade candy in San Bartolo:** The unassuming stand at the curve in Highway 1, between La Paz and Los Cabos, is home to mind-blowing macaroons made of *cajeta* (caramel made from goat's milk) and rough-hewn coconut thick and fresh from the grove in the valley below. Buy it by the truckload, if you can. Fresh fig jam and *cajeta* caramels are other worthy reasons to stop. See p. 100.
- **Ibarra's Pottery, La Paz:** Not only can you shop for hand-painted tiles, tableware, and decorative pottery here, but you can also watch it being made. Each piece offered for sale in this popular shop is individually made. See p. 111.
- **San José's boutiques:** As San José del Cabo becomes increasingly gentrified, so does its shopping experience. In southern Baja, the best boutiques and shops offering clothing, jewelry, and decorative items for the home are found within the lovely colonial buildings in this tree-lined town. See p. 63.
- **Avenida Revolución in Tijuana:** This rowdy drive is shopping central for the entire Baja peninsula. The most popular items offered here are electronics, traditional Mexican souvenirs, T-shirts, and prescription medicines (sans prescription). See p. 158.
- **Mercado de Artesanías, Tijuana:** For a more authentic and spirited marketplace atmosphere to pick up your colorful sombrero or serape, head to this collection of more than 200 stalls in Tijuana, where bargaining is both accepted and expected. You'll also find pottery, clothing, and crafts from throughout Mexico. See p. 158.
- **Duty-Free in Cabo San Lucas:** Fine jewelry, watches, perfumes, and cosmetics are offered at duty-free prices in Cabo's UltraFemme store, the largest duty-free shop in Mexico. See p. 85.

7 The Hottest Nightlife

Although, as expected, Cabo San Lucas is home to much of Baja's nightlife, that resort city isn't the only place to have a good time after dark. Along the northern Pacific coast, beachside dance floors with live bands and extended happy hours in seaside bars dominate the nightlife. Here are some of my favorite hot spots:

- **Nikki Beach, Los Cabos:** The global haven of the hip has recently arrived in Cabo San Lucas, on the beachfront of the new ME Cabo resort on Médano Beach. Lounge on oversize beds draped in white, day or night, while sipping colorful cocktails and watching the beautiful people groove to music spun by the worlds' hottest DJs. See p. 91.
- **Tijuana's Avenida Revolución:** This street ranks among the world's most

famous—or infamous—for night-time carousing. "La Revo," as it's commonly known, is probably the single most-common introduction tourists have to Mexico, though it offers only a glimmer of the country's wealth of attractions. No matter the night, you're likely to find a party atmosphere here on par with the best of a Mardi Gras celebration in full swing. Bring plenty of aspirin for the next morning—as overindulgence is the norm. See chapter 7.

- **Locals bars in Loreto:** In Loreto, "nightlife" starts well before sun-down. A couple draft beers at Del Borracho, which closes at sunset, will jumpstart the afternoon. Then, roll

into Augie's Bar & Bait Shop around 4pm, take a seat at the bar, and wait for the rowdy barrage of friendly expats to join you for half-priced drinks till 7pm. Chances are, you'll make a few friends and end up coming back for more the next day. See chapter 6.

- **Beach Bars of Rosarito and Ensenada:** It doesn't have to be spring break in Rosarito or Ensenada to find a similar let-loose party atmosphere here. The favored spot is Papas & Beer, which has a location in both of these beach towns. And both regularly draw a young and spirited crowd for endless-summer–style fun. See chapter 7.

8 The Most Luxurious Hotels

- **Las Ventanas al Paraíso** (Los Cabos Corridor; ☎ **888/525-0483** in the U.S., or 624/144-0300; www.las ventanas.com): Understated luxury by the sea, Las Ventanas perfectly melds desert landscapes and sophisticated pampering in this elegant, yet intimate, resort. Special extras such as telescopes, fireplaces, private pools, and rooftop terraces, make each suite a slice of heaven. Their seaside infinity pool is one of my favorite places in the world, helped, in no small part, by the exceptional service offered by the resort's pool butlers. See p. 70.

- **Esperanza** (Los Cabos Corridor; ☎ **866/331-2226** in the U.S., or 624/145-6400; www.esperanzaresort.com): A creation of the famed Auberge Resorts group, this dramatically designed resort, set on a bluff overlooking two small coves, feels more like a collection of villas than a hotel. Hallmarks are its exceptional spa,

award-winning restaurant, yoga studio, and impeccable service. See p. 70.

- **Posada de las Flores** (Loreto; ☎ **877/245-2860** in the U.S., or 613/135-1162; www.posadadelasflores.com): The best of old-world style and modern luxury meet in this historic building on Loreto's main square. A rooftop pool, lavish linens, and detailed service are matched by location, charm, and ambience. See p. 129.

- **Casa Natalie** (Ensenada; ☎ **888/562-8254** in the U.S., or 646/174-7373; www.casanatalie.com): Stillness and comfort are the marks of this modern boutique resort, which opened a little more than a year ago. Neutral colors contrast the blue of the ocean, cozy nooks await peace seekers, the rooms are some of the best in Baja, and an overall atmosphere of unpretentious luxury ensures a divine experience. See p. 172.

9 The Best Budget Inns

- **Cabo Inn** (Cabo San Lucas; © 619/ 819-2727 in the U.S., or 624/143- 0819; www.caboinnhotel.com): This former bordello is the best budget inn in the area. Rooms are small but extra clean and invitingly decorated, amenities are generous, and the owner/managers are friendly and helpful. Ideally located, close to town and near the marina, the inn caters to sportfishers. See p. 87.
- **Hotel Mediterrane** (La Paz; © 612/ 125-1195; www.hotelmed.com): Mixing Mexican with Mediterranean decor details, the result here is a stylish, economical inn. The location near the *malecón* means you're close to everything. The on-site Trattoria

La Pazta restaurant is one of La Paz's best. See p. 112.
- **La Damiana Inn** (Loreto; © 613/ 135-0356; www.ladamianainn.com): This charming inn, crafted from a century-old family home, is a cozy, well-appointed hideaway perfect for couples, families, and solo travelers alike. The friendly service can't be topped. See p. 130.
- **Hotel Hacienda Mulegé** (Mulegé; © 615/153-0021): Right in the heart of Mulegé, this former 18th-century hacienda is a comfortable and value-priced place to stay, complete with a small shaded pool and popular bar. See p. 140.

10 The Best Unique Inns

- **Casa Natalia** (San José del Cabo; © 888/277-3814 in the U.S., or 624/142-5100; www.casanatalia. com): This renovated historic home, now a masterfully crafted inn, is an oasis of palms, waterfalls, and flowers set against the desert landscape. Each room and suite is an artful combination of modern architecture and traditional Mexican touches. The restaurant is the hottest in town. See p. 64.
- **Hotel California** (Todos Santos; © 612/145-0525 or 612/145-0522): After undergoing a complete renovation in 2003, the Hotel California has emerged as the hippest place to stay in the area. Jewel-tone rooms and a profusion of candles and eclectic accents make this a study in creative style. Although you can check out anytime you like, chances are you won't want to after being lured in by the inviting

pool area and the popular La Coronela Restaurant and Bar. See p. 96.
- **La Villa del Valle** (Valle de Guadalupe; © 649/183-9249; www. lavilladelvalle.com): The six rooms of this charming inn, flanked by lavender fields, make for casual respite in the middle of Ensenada wine country. Plus, a garden teeming with chef-ready produce and fresh herbs ensures every meal is the freshest in the valley. See p. 180.
- **Punta Chivato** (north of Mulegé at Punta Chivato; © 615/153-0188; www.posadadelasflores.com): Enjoy the 3 hectares (7½ acres) of desert landscape and tranquil, private beach that come with a stay in the large and beautifully decorated suites and guest rooms here. Meals are included, as are a host of light activities. There's even a private airstrip to make it more accessible. See p. 139.

11 The Best Dining Experiences

In this section, best doesn't necessarily mean most luxurious. Although some of the restaurants listed here are fancy affairs, others are simple places to get fine, authentic Mexican cuisine.

- **Las Guacamayas** (San José del Cabo; ℂ 624/172-6162): Nothing is more Mexican than tacos, and the tacos at Las Guacamayas reign supreme. Take your pick from pastor, *huitlacoche,* squash blossoms, and more. Whatever you order, this hole-in-the-wall will rock your world. See p. 68.

- **Laja** (Valle de Guadalupe; ℂ 646/155-2556): This lovely adobe-and-stone gourmet restaurant has become a reason in and of itself to visit Mexico's wine country. A daily fixed menu of four to eight courses is prepared, regularly drawing a crowd and winning mounting accolades. See p. 180.

- **Café Santa Fe** (Todos Santos; ℂ 612/145-0300): Excellent northern Italian cuisine prepared in the exhibition kitchen of this gracious cafe has been a driving factor in drawing people to Todos Santos over the past decade. Enjoying lunch here in the flower-filled courtyard is a particularly wonderful way to pass an afternoon. See p. 97.

- **Mi Cocina** (San José del Cabo; ℂ 624/142-5100; www.casanatalia.com/dining.cfm): It could be the creative menu, the captivating garden setting, or even the hibiscus-infused martinis, but whatever the reason, Mi Cocina, at Casa Natalia, is one of the best dining experiences in Los Cabos. See p. 67.

- **The Mulegé Pig Roast** (Mulegé): Regardless of where you stay in Mulegé, if it's Saturday, you won't want to miss the pig roast at the Hotel Serenidad. As they say here, it's more than a pig, it's a party; and it's the must-do tourist activity in town, one in which the pig is roasted Polynesian style, in a palm-lined open pit, for hours while guests enjoy libations. See p. 140.

- **El Boleo** (Santa Rosalía; ℂ 615/152-0310): Throughout Mexico, bakeries offer a small version of the French baguette known as *bolíos,* and it's not far fetched to wonder if the name derives from this bakery, in Santa Rosalía. This bakery has been operating since the late 1800s when the French Compañía de Boleo obtained a 99-year lease from the Mexican government to operate the area's copper mines in exchange for creating employment opportunities. Of course, the French executives running the operation needed their bread, which continues to be addictive to this day. While the bolíos are good, the sweet breads, namely the pitahaya, are out of this world. See p. 142.

- **Cien Años** (Tijuana; ℂ 664/633-3900): One of the finest gourmet Mexican restaurants in Baja, Cien Años will intrigue even the most adventurous of diners, with regional specialties that may include garlicky ant eggs or buttery *guisanos* (cactus worms). See p. 161.

- **Don Emiliano** (San José del Cabo; ℂ 624/142-0266): Farm-fresh ingredients laced with Mexican tradition are Don Emiliano's masterpieces. Modern takes on classic favorites, such as *chile en nogada* with a sherried cream sauce and lemon atole with candied pumpkin, emerge from the kitchen in radiant glory. There's always a special menu tailored to the season, and the regular menu combines the likes of locally made cheeses with roasted tomatillos and dried hibiscus flowers with beef tenderloin. This is by far Los Cabos's best sampling of *alta cocina* Mexicana. See p. 67.

- **Lobster in Puerto Nuevo** (Puerto Nuevo): It seems almost every restaurant or simple shack serving food in this tiny seaside town has locally caught lobster on the menu—and there's good reason why. It's fresh, and it's delicious. The Puerto Nuevo way of serving it is grilled and accompanied with fresh tortillas, salsa, limes, beans, and rice, and the price is just over $10, making it well worth a stop in this town. See p. 50.

2

Planning Your Trip to Los Cabos & Baja

A little planning can make the difference between a good trip and a great trip. When should you go? What's the best way to get there? How much should you plan on spending? What festivals or special events will be taking place during your visit? What safety or health precautions are advised? I'll answer these and other questions for you in this chapter. In addition to these basics, I highly recommend taking a little time to learn about the culture and traditions of Mexico and the Baja. The more you understand this paradoxical land, the more likely you'll be to turn simply getting away for a few days into the vacation of a lifetime. See appendix A for more details.

1 Baja California at a Glance

Baja California is a place of complementary contrasts: hot desert and cool ocean, manicured golf greens and craggy mountains, glistening resorts and frontier land. The Baja peninsula is part of Mexico—and yet it is not. Attached to the mainland United States and separated from the rest of Mexico by the Sea of Cortez (also called the Gulf of California), the Baja peninsula is longer than Italy, stretching 1,410km (874 miles) from Mexico's northernmost city of Tijuana to Cabo San Lucas at its southern tip. Volcanic uplifting created the craggy desertscape you see today. Whole forests of cardoon cactus, spiky elephant trees, and spindly ocotillo bushes populate the raw, untamed landscape.

Culturally and geographically, Baja is set apart from mainland Mexico, and it remained isolated for many years. As such, Baja lays claim to a striking and peculiar blend of Mexican and American cultures, and it can't be found anywhere else in Mexico. However, tourism has touched the length of Baja, concentrating its uber-vacation powers on the southern portion, where golf, fishing, diving, and whale-watching abound. For early travelers in the '50s and '60s, great sportfishing was the first draw to Los Cabos, and it remains a lure today, although golf may have overtaken it as the principal attraction. Once accessible only by water, Baja attracted a hearty community of cruisers, fishermen, divers, and adventurers, starting in the late 1940s. By the early 1980s, the Mexican government realized the growth potential of Los Cabos and invested in new highways, airport facilities, golf courses, and modern marine facilities. Expanded air traffic and the opening of the Carretera Transpeninsular, or Transpeninsular Highway, in 1973 paved the way for the area's spectacular growth.

BAJA CALIFORNIA SUR Of the peninsula's three regions, Baja Sur is the tourism darling. The area between La Paz and Los Cabos has attracted the lion's share of attention and travelers. Twin towns with distinct personalities sit at the tip of the peninsula: **Cabo San Lucas** and **San José del Cabo.** The two Cabos are the center of accommodations and activities.

The road that connects Cabo San Lucas and San José del Cabo is the centerpiece of resort growth. Known as **the Tourist Corridor,** this stretch of four well-paved lanes offers cliff-top vistas but has little nighttime lighting, so take care when driving after dark. The area's most deluxe resorts and renowned golf courses are here, along with a collection of dramatic beaches and coves.

Although Los Cabos often feels like the southern playground of the United States' West Coast, other areas of Baja Sur can seem like the least-crowded corners of Mexico. The peninsula's **East Cape,** just northeast of San José del Cabo, has beaches, coral reefs, dive sites, hiking paths, waterfalls, and a vibe that inspires on contact. **Todos Santos,** an artistic community on the Pacific side of the coastal curve, just north of the tip, draws travelers who find that Cabo San Lucas has outgrown them. **La Paz,** the capital of Baja Sur, remains an easygoing maritime port, with an interesting assortment of small lodgings and a fascinating diversity of eco- and adventure activities.

MID-BAJA   Among the highlights of the mid-Baja region are the east coast towns of **Loreto, Mulegé,** and **Santa Rosalía.** Although they have a much richer historic and cultural heritage than Baja Sur's resort towns, they've been eclipsed by the growth of tourism infrastructure and services in the two Cabos. Owing to its breathtaking natural land- and seascape, Loreto currently stands at the center of attention of the Mexican government's promotional and investment focus, so even this quiet town is well on its way to a boom.

This area's environmental perks have made it a center for sea kayaking, sportfishing, freediving, and hiking—including excursions to view indigenous cave paintings, which UNESCO has named a World Heritage Site. This also is the place to come if you're interested in whale-watching; many tour companies operate out of Loreto and smaller neighboring towns. For more information, see "Whale-Watching in Baja: A Primer," in chapter 6.

BAJA CALIFORNIA (NORTE)

Northern Baja is officially known as Baja California. **Tijuana** has the dubious distinction of being the most visited and perhaps most misunderstood town in all of Mexico. Dog racing, free-flowing tequila, and a sin-city reputation have all been hallmarks of this classic border town, a favored resort for the party-ready jet set during Prohibition. New cultural and sporting attractions, extensive shopping, and strong business growth—of the reputable kind—are helping to brighten Tijuana's image.

Tranquil **Rosarito Beach** is also reemerging as a resort town, given a boost after the movie *Titanic* was filmed here (the set is now a movie-themed amusement park). Farther down the Pacific coast is the lovely port town of **Ensenada,** also known for its prime surfing and sportfishing. The nearby vineyards of Mexico's wine country, in the Valle de Guadalupe, are a new and growing attraction, and San Felipe holds court as Northern Baja's sleepiest resort boom town.

2 Visitor Information & Maps

The **Mexico Hot Line** (© **800/44-MEXICO**) is an excellent source for general information; you can request brochures on the country and get answers to the most common questions from the exceptionally well-trained, knowledgeable staff.

More information (15,000 pages' worth) about Mexico is available on the official site of Mexico's Tourism Promotion Board, www.visitmexico.com. The U.S. Department of State (© 202/647-5225; http://travel.state.gov) offers a Consular Information Sheet on Mexico, with safety, medical, driving, and general travel information gleaned from reports by its offices in Mexico, and consistently updated. You can also request the Consular Information Sheet by fax (© 202/647-3000). The same website also provides other consular information sheets and warnings as well as "Tips for Travelers to Mexico." Another source is the Department of State's background notes series. Visit the Department of State home page (www.state.gov) for information.

The Centers for Disease Control and Prevention Hot Line (© 800/311-3435 or 404/639-3534; www.cdc.gov) is a source of medical information for travelers to Mexico and elsewhere. For travelers to Mexico and Central America, the number with recorded messages is © 877/FYI-TRIP. The toll-free fax number for requesting information is © 888/232-3299. Information is also available at www.cdc.gov/travel. The U.S. Department of State offers medical information for Americans traveling abroad and a list of air-ambulance services at http://travel.state.gov.

MEXICAN GOVERNMENT TOUR-IST BOARD   The board has offices in major North American cities, in addition to the main office in Mexico City (© 555/203-1103).

United States: Chicago (© 312/228-0517), Houston (© 713/772-2581, ext. 105, or 713/772-3819), Los Angeles (© 310/282-9112), Miami (© 786/621-2909), and New York (© 212/308-2110). The Mexican Embassy is at 1911 Pennsylvania Ave. NW, Washington, DC 20005 (© 202/728-1600).

Canada: Montreal (© 514/871-1103), Toronto (© 416/925-0704), and Vancouver (© 604/669-2845). The Embassy office is at 1500-45 O'Connor St., Ottawa (© 613/233-8988; fax 613/235-9123).

Baja's two states each have their own tourism bureaus with information for travelers. Visit www.discoverbajacalifornia.com for info on the state of Baja California in English, and visit the Spanish-language site, www.bcs.gob.mx, and click the "turismo" link for information on Baja California Sur.

3 Entry Requirements

PASSPORTS

For information on how to get a passport, go to "Passports" in the "Fast Facts" section of this chapter—the websites listed provide downloadable passport applications as well as the current fees for processing passport applications. For an up-to-date, country-by-country listing of passport requirements around the world, go to the "Foreign Entry Requirement" Web page of the U.S. Department of State at http://travel.state.gov.

Note: Children under 18 traveling without parents or with only one parent must have a notarized letter from the absent parent(s) authorizing the travel.

VISAS

For information on obtaining Mexican visas, visit www.sre.gob.mx/english/services/visasforeigners.htm, which has information in English, or go straight to the source, the Instituto Nacional de Migración at www.inm.gob.mx/pagina_ingles/principal-ingles.asp.

MEDICAL REQUIREMENTS

There currently are no medical requirements for traveling to Mexico. For information on health and medicine during your trip, see "Health," p. 24.

CUSTOMS
WHAT YOU CAN BRING INTO MEXICO
When you enter Mexico, Customs officials will be tolerant as long as you have no illegal drugs, firearms, excessive electronic equipment, or heaps of clothing with the tags still on. The underlying guideline is: Don't bring anything that looks as if it's meant to be resold in Mexico.

You're allowed to bring in two cartons of cigarettes or 50 cigars, plus 1 kilogram (2.2 lb.) of smoking tobacco; two 1-liter bottles of wine or hard liquor, and 12 rolls of film. A laptop computer, camera equipment, and sports equipment that could feasibly be used during your stay also are allowed.

WHAT YOU CAN TAKE HOME FROM MEXICO
You're allowed to take $800 worth of merchandise duty-free, including 2 liters of alcoholic beverages and household effects not for resale (furniture, carpets, tableware, linens, and similar household furnishings). Beyond the $800 limit, you'll be charged a flat rate of 4% duty on the next $1,000 of purchases. Fine art is duty-free and no produce or agricultural products from Mexico are allowed into the U.S.

U.S. Citizens: For specifics on what you can bring back and the corresponding fees, download the invaluable free pamphlet *Know Before You Go* online at **www.cbp.gov**. (Click on "Travel," and then click on "Know Before You Go! Online Brochure.") Or contact the U.S. Customs & Border Protection (CBP), 1300 Pennsylvania Ave. NW, Washington, DC 20229 (© **877/287-8667**), and request the pamphlet.

Canadian Citizens: For a clear summary of Canadian rules, write for the booklet *I Declare,* issued by the Canada Border Services Agency (© **800/461-9999** in Canada, or 204/983-3500; www.cbsa-asfc.gc.ca).

U.K. Citizens: For information, contact HM Customs & Excise at © **0845/010-9000** (from outside the U.K., 020/8929-0152), or consult their website at **www.hmce.gov.uk**.

Australian Citizens: A helpful brochure available from Australian consulates or Customs offices is *Know Before You Go.* For more information, call the Australian Customs Service at © **1300/363-263,** or log on to **www.customs.gov.au**.

New Zealand Citizens: Most questions are answered in a free pamphlet available at New Zealand consulates and Customs offices: *New Zealand Customs Guide for Travellers, Notice no. 4.* For more information, contact New Zealand Customs, The Customhouse, 17–21 Whitmore St., Box 2218, Wellington (© **04/473-6099** or 0800/428-786; www.customs.govt.nz).

4 When to Go

High season on the Baja peninsula begins around December 20 and continues to Easter. In the South, winter is the best time for warm-but-not-hot weather; snorkeling and diving; and for visiting the missions, mountains, and historic sites that dot the interior of the peninsula. The Pacific side generally is a few degrees cooler year round and Sea of Cortez towns in mid-Baja can be warmer and cooler than their Southern Baja counterparts in summer and winter, respectively. Book well in advance if you plan to be in Los Cabos around the holidays or Spring Break and be prepared to pay premium rates close to Thanksgiving, Christmas, and the New Year.

Low season begins the day after Easter and continues to mid-December; during low season, prices may drop 20% to 50%.

The weather in Baja, land of extremes, can be unpredictable. Baja California's weather runs the gamut from cold to hot, windy to still, sunny to overcast, and dry to humid at any given moment in time. It can be sizzling hot in summer and cold and windy in winter—so windy that fishing and other nautical expeditions may be grounded for a few days. And it can be completely different in the north of the peninsula than it is in the south. Although winter is often warm enough for wetsuit-free watersports—especially in Los Cabos, south of the Tropic of Cancer—bring a wetsuit if you're a serious diver or snorkeler, as well as warmer clothes for unexpectedly chilly weather at night. Because the sea is full of life, some of which can sting your skin, it's always a good idea to wear a full-body Lycra skin, no matter the temperature of the water.

CALENDAR OF EVENTS

For an exhaustive list of events beyond those listed here, check **http://events.frommers. com**, where you'll find a searchable, up-to-the-minute roster of what's happening in cities all over the world.

Note: Banks, government offices, and many stores close on national holidays.

January

Día de Año Nuevo (New Year's Day). This national holiday is perhaps the quietest day in all of Mexico. Most people stay home or attend church on the first day of the year. All businesses are closed. In traditional indigenous communities, new tribal leaders are inaugurated with colorful ceremonies rooted in the pre-Hispanic past. January 1.

Día de los Reyes (Three Kings Day). This day commemorates the day the Three Wise Men arrived bearing gifts for the Christ Child. On this day, children receive gifts, much like the traditional Christmas gift-giving in the United States, although Santa Claus

has melded with Mexican traditions in Los Cabos. Friends and families gather to share the Rosca de Reyes, a ring-shaped cake. Inside the cake is a small doll representing the Christ Child; whoever receives the doll must host a tamales-and-*atole* party on February 2, or Dos de la Candelaria. January 6.

February

Día de la Candelaria (Candlemas). Music, dances, processions, food, and other festivities lead up to a blessing of seed and candles in a ceremony that mixes pre-Hispanic and European traditions marking the end of winter. Those who attended the Three Kings celebration reunite to share *atole* and tamales at a party hosted by the recipient of the doll found in the Rosca. February 2.

Día de la Constitución (Constitution Day). This national holiday is in honor of the current Mexican constitution, signed in 1917 as a result of the revolutionary war of 1910. It's celebrated through small parades. February 5.

Carnaval. Carnaval takes place over the 3 days before the beginning of Lent. La Paz celebrates with special zeal, and visitors enjoy a festive atmosphere and parades. The 3 days preceding Ash Wednesday.

Miércoles de Ceniza (Ash Wednesday). The start of Lent and time of abstinence, this is a day of reverence nationwide; some towns honor it with folk dancing and fairs.

March

Feria de San José. The end of March brings a weeklong party to downtown San José del Cabo, where carnival rides and games, traditional Mexican aromas, and jewelry and knickknack vendors fill the streets. San José Day is March 19.

Semana Santa (Holy Week). This week celebrates the last week in the life of Christ from Palm Sunday through Easter Sunday with somber religious processions almost nightly, spoofing of Judas, and reenactments of biblical events, plus food and craft fairs. Businesses close during this traditional week of Mexican national vacations.

If you plan on traveling to or around Mexico during Holy Week, make reservations early. Late March or April.

May

El Día del Trabajo (Labor Day). Workers' parades take place countrywide, and everything closes on this national holiday. May 1.

La Paz Foundation. This celebration observes the founding of La Paz by Cortez in 1535 and features *artesanía* exhibitions from throughout southern Baja. May 1 to 5.

Cinco de Mayo. This national holiday commemorates the defeat of the French at the Battle of Puebla. May 5.

June

Día de la Marina (Navy Day). This day is celebrated in all coastal towns, with naval parades and fireworks. June 1.

August

Fiestas de la Vendimia (Wine Harvest Festival). Ensenada's food-and-wine festival celebrates the annual harvest, with blessings, seminars, parties, and wine tastings. Call © **800/44-MEXICO** for details and schedule. Mid- to late August.

September

Día de la Independencia (Independence Day). This national holiday (Sept 16) celebrates Mexico's independence from Spain with a day of parades, picnics, and family reunions throughout the country. At 11pm on September 15, the president of Mexico gives the famous independence *grito* (shout) from the National Palace in Mexico City. At least half a million people crowd into the capital's *zócalo* (town square), and the mayor of each town across the country gives the *grito* in front of thousands in his own town square. Those who don't venture into the craziness of their main plaza to celebrate do watch the event on TV. September 15 and 16.

October

Festival Fundador. This festival celebrates the founding of the town of Todos Santos in 1723. Streets around the main plaza fill with food, games, and wandering troubadours. October 10 to 14.

Día de la Raza ("Ethnicity Day," or Columbus Day). This day commemorates the fusion of the Spanish and Mexican peoples. October 12.

November

Día de los Muertos (Day of the Dead). This national holiday (Nov 1) actually lasts for 2 days: All Saints' Day—honoring saints and deceased children—and All Souls' Day, honoring deceased adults. Relatives gather at cemeteries countrywide, carrying candles, food, flowers, and colorful decorations, and often spend the night beside graves of loved ones. Weeks before, bakers begin producing bread in the shape of mummies or round loaves decorated with bread "bones." Sugar skulls emblazoned with glitter are sold everywhere. Many days ahead, homes and churches erect altars laden with bread, fruit, flowers, candles, favorite foods, and photographs of saints and of the deceased as a way of remembering them. Traditionally, costumed children walk through the streets both nights carrying mock coffins and pumpkin lanterns, into which they expect money will be dropped. However, in Los Cabos, costumed kids are out in full force for Halloween rather than on Day of the Dead. November 1 and 2.

Día de la Revolución (Revolution Day). This national holiday commemorates the start of the Mexican Revolution in 1910 with parades, speeches, rodeos, and patriotic events. November 20.

December

Feast of the Virgin of Guadalupe. Religious processions, street fairs, dancing, fireworks, and Masses honor Mexico's patroness. It is one of the country's most moving and beautiful displays of traditional culture. The Virgin of Guadalupe, an apparition of the Virgin Mary, appeared to a young man, Juan Diego, in December 1531 on a hill near Mexico City. Her image in a cloth is on display at the Basílica de Guadalupe in Mexico City. It's customary for children to dress up as Juan Diego, wearing mustaches and red bandanas. December 12.

Christmas Posadas. On each of the 9 nights before Christmas, it's customary to reenact Mary and Joseph's search for an inn in which to have the baby Jesus. Door-to-door candlelit processions pass through cities and villages nationwide, especially Querétaro and Taxco. Hosted by businesses, community organizations, and even among friends, these take the place of the northern tradition of a Christmas party. December 15 to 24.

Navidad (Christmas). Mexicans extend this celebration and leave their jobs, often beginning 2 weeks before Christmas and continuing all the way through New Year's. Many businesses close, and resorts and hotels fill. December 23 to 25.

Víspera de Año Nuevo (New Year's Eve). As in the rest of the world, New Year's Eve in Mexico is celebrated with parties, fireworks, and plenty of noise. However, contrary to U.S. custom, Mexicans celebrate the New Year at home over a traditional dinner with their families and then hit the town after midnight. December 31.

5 Getting There

BY PLANE

The airline situation in Mexico is rapidly improving, with many new regional carriers offering scheduled service to areas previously not served. In addition to regularly scheduled service, charter service direct from U.S. cities to resorts is making Baja—and Mexico in general—more accessible.

THE MAJOR INTERNATIONAL AIRLINES The main airlines operating direct or nonstop flights from the United States to points in Baja include **Aeroméxico** (© 800/237-6639; www.aeromexico.com), **Alaska Airlines** (© 800/252-7522; www.alaskaair.com), **America West/US**

Airways (© 800/235-9292; www.usairways.com), **American Airlines** (© 800/223-5436; www.aa.com), **Continental** (© 800/537-9222; www.continental.com), **Frontier Airlines** (© 800/432-1359; www.frontierairlines.com), **Mexicana** (© 800/531-7921; www.mexicana.com), **Northwest/KLM** (© 800/225-2525; www.nwa.com), and **United** (© 800/538-2929; www.united.com). **Southwest Airlines** (© 800/435-9792; www.iflyswa.com) serves San Diego (but not Mexico).

The main departure points in North America for flights to Baja are Atlanta, Chicago, Dallas/Fort Worth, Denver,

Houston, Los Angeles, New York, Phoenix, San Diego, and San Francisco. Most domestic flights to Baja come from Mexico City.

The following airport codes apply to these Baja destinations, all of which are easy arrivals and a crowd-free experience, except at Los Cabos International Airport, which sees quite a bit more daily traffic than the others:

- Los Cabos/San José del Cabo: SJD
- Cabo San Lucas: CSL
- La Paz: LAP
- Loreto: LTO
- Tijuana: TIJ

ARRIVING AT THE AIRPORT

Throughout Baja, the procedure is fairly standard. You disembark the plane—often directly onto the tarmac—and enter the line for immigration. You will present your passport and immigration officials will provide you with a tourist visa. You will then pass to baggage claim, pick up your luggage, and pass through customs. Your luggage may be scanned, and then you'll be asked to push a button. If green, you are free to pass through, and if red, you may have your luggage searched. It's an easy process that, barring excessive crowds, takes about 15 to 20 minutes.

GETTING INTO TOWN FROM THE AIRPORT

Getting from the airport to your final destination is simple in Baja. In most airports, there is a kiosk where you can sign up for a shuttle—the economical option. Otherwise, taxis are always waiting when flights come in; so hopping a cab to your hotel or downtown is a cinch.

BY CAR

Driving is not the cheapest or most efficient way to get to Mexico, but it is the best way to see the country. Even so, you may think twice about taking your own car south of the border once you've pondered the bureaucracy involved. One option is to rent a car once you arrive and tour around a specific region. Rental cars in Mexico generally are new, clean, and well maintained. Although they're pricier than in the United States, discounts are often available for rentals of a week or longer, especially when you make arrangements online or in advance from the United States. (See "Getting Around," later in this chapter, for more details.)

If, after reading the section that follows, you have additional questions or you want to confirm the current rules, call your nearest Mexican consulate or the Mexican Government Tourist Office. Although travel insurance companies are generally helpful, they may not have the most accurate information. To check on road conditions or to get help with any travel emergency while in Mexico, call ✆ **01-800/903-9200,** or 555/250-0151 in Mexico City. English-speaking operators staff both numbers. If you plan to stay in Baja, the **Discover Baja Travel Club** is a long-standing favorite among Baja road warriors for insurance, travel tips, permits, and more (www.discover baja.com).

In addition, check with the **U.S. Department of State** (see "Visitor Information & Maps," earlier in this chapter) for warnings about dangerous driving areas.

CAR DOCUMENTS To drive your car into Mexico (even for the day), you'll need a **temporary car-importation permit,** which is granted after you provide a required list of documents (see below). The permit can be obtained through Banco del Ejército (Banjercito) officials, who have a desk, booth, or office at the Mexican Customs (aduana) building after you cross the border into Mexico.

The following strict requirements for border crossing were accurate at press time:

- **A valid driver's license,** issued outside of Mexico.
- **Current, original car registration and a copy of the original car title.** If the registration or title is in more than one name and not all the named people are traveling with you, a notarized letter from the absent person(s) authorizing use of the vehicle for the trip is required; have it ready. The registration and your credit card (see below) must be in the same name.
- **A valid international major credit card.** With a credit card, you are required to pay only a $23 car-importation fee. The credit card must be in the same name as the car registration. If you do not have a major credit card (American Express, Diners Club, MasterCard, or Visa), you must post a bond or make a deposit equal to the value of the vehicle. Check cards are not accepted.
- **Original immigration documentation.** This is either your tourist permit (FMT) or the original immigration booklet, FM2 or FM3, if you hold more permanent status.
- **A signed declaration promising to return to your country of origin with the vehicle.** Obtain this form *(Carta Promesa de Retorno)* from AAA or Sanborn's before you go, or from Banjercito officials at the border. There's no charge. The form does not stipulate that you must return by the same border entry through which you entered.
- **Temporary Importation Application.** By signing this form, you state that you are only temporarily importing the car for your personal use and will not be selling it. This is to help regulate the entry and restrict the resale of unauthorized cars and trucks. Make sure the permit is canceled when you return to the U.S.

If you receive your documentation at the border, Mexican officials will make two copies of everything and charge you for the copies. For up-to-the-minute information, a great source is the Customs office in Nuevo Laredo, or *Módulo de Importación Temporal de Automóviles, Aduana Nuevo Laredo* (© 867/712-2071).

Important reminder: Someone else may drive, but the person (or relative of the person) whose name appears on the car-importation permit must *always* be in the car. (If stopped by police, a nonregistered family member driving without the registered driver must be prepared to prove familial relationship to the registered driver—no joke.) Violation of this rule subjects the car to impoundment and the driver to imprisonment, a fine, or both. You can drive a car with foreign license plates only if you have a foreign (non-Mexican) driver's license.

MEXICAN AUTO INSURANCE

Liability auto insurance is legally required in Mexico. U.S. insurance is invalid; to be insured in Mexico, you must purchase Mexican insurance, and you must have proof of U.S. insurance to acquire it. Any party involved in an accident who has no insurance may be sent to jail and have his or her car impounded until all claims are settled. This is true even if you just drive across the border to spend the day. U.S. companies that broker Mexican insurance are commonly found at the border crossing, and several quote daily rates.

Discover Baja Travel Club, 3089 Clairemont Dr., San Diego, CA 92117 (© 800/727-2252; www.discoverbaja. com), is a great, friendly place to start. You can also buy car insurance through **Sanborn's Mexico Insurance,** P.O. Box 52840, 2009 S. 10th, McAllen, TX (© 956/686-3601; fax 800/222-0158 or 956/686-0732; www.sanbornsinsurance. com). The company has offices at all U.S. border crossings. Its policies cost the same as the competition's do, but you get legal coverage (attorney and bail bonds if needed) and a detailed mile-by-mile guide for your proposed route. Most of Sanborn's border offices are open Monday through Friday, and a few are staffed on Saturday and Sunday. **AAA** auto club also sells insurance.

RETURNING TO THE UNITED STATES WITH YOUR CAR You must return the car papers you obtained when you entered Mexico when you cross back with your car, or at some point within 180 days. (You can cross as many times as you wish within the 180 days.) If the documents aren't returned, heavy fines are imposed ($250 for each 15 days late), and your car may be impounded and confiscated or you may be jailed if you return to Mexico. You can only return the car documents to a Banjercito official on duty at the Mexican Customs building before you cross back into the United States. Some border cities have Banjercito officials on duty 24 hours a day, but others do not; some also do not have Sunday hours.

6 Money & Costs

It's always advisable to bring money in a variety of forms on a vacation: a mix of cash, credit cards, and traveler's checks. You should also exchange enough petty cash to cover airport incidentals, tipping, and transportation to your hotel before you leave home, or withdraw money upon arrival at an airport ATM.

In many international destinations, ATMs offer the best exchange rates. Avoid exchanging money at commercial exchange bureaus and hotels, which often have the highest transaction fees.

CURRENCY

The currency in Mexico is the Mexican **peso** (MXN). Paper currency comes in denominations of 20, 50, 100, 200, 500, and 1,000 pesos. Coins come in denominations of 1, 2, 5, 10, and 20 pesos, and 20 and 50 **centavos** (100 centavos = 1 peso). The current exchange rate for the U.S. dollar, and the one used in this book, is around 11 pesos; at that rate, an item that costs 11 pesos would be equivalent to US$1. (If you want the up-to-the-second conversion rate, visit www.xe.com/ucc).

Contrary to most people's ideas of Mexico, most of Baja is not cheap. On the contrary, you should expect to pay the same amount you would for such things as dinners, drinks, and taxis as you would at home; in Los Cabos, you might even spend more. The exception is mid-Baja, where tourism is still blossoming and prices may be a notch less than in the north and south.

Getting **change** can be a problem. Small-denomination bills and coins are hard to come by, so start collecting them early in your trip. Shopkeepers everywhere always seem to be out of change and small bills; that's doubly true in markets. And shops rarely accept American bills higher than $20.

Many establishments that deal with tourists, especially in coastal resort areas, quote prices in dollars. To avoid confusion, they use the abbreviations "USD" for dollars and "MXN" for pesos. All dollar equivalencies in this book were based on an exchange rate of 11 pesos per dollar.

In general, avoid carrying the U.S. $100 bill, the bill most commonly counterfeited in Mexico and therefore the most difficult to exchange, especially in smaller towns. Because small bills and coins in pesos are hard to come by in Mexico, the $1 bill is very useful for tipping. A tip of U.S. coins, which cannot be exchanged into Mexican currency, is of no value to the service provider.

Money Matters

The universal currency sign ($) is used to indicate pesos in Mexico. The use of this symbol in this book, however, denotes U.S. currency.

The bottom line on exchanging money: Ask first, and shop around. Banks generally pay the top rates, though hotels sometimes pay higher rates than banks in an effort to attract dollars.

ATMS

The easiest and best way to get cash away from home is from an ATM (automated teller machine), sometimes referred to as a "cash machine," or a "cashpoint." The **Cirrus** (© **800/424-7787;** www.master card.com) and **PLUS** (© **800/843-7587;** www.visa.com) networks span the globe. Go to your bank card's website to find ATM locations at your destination. Be sure you know your daily withdrawal limit before you depart. *Note:* Many banks impose a fee every time you use a card at another bank's ATM, and that fee can be higher for international transactions (up to $5 or more) than for domestic ones (where they're rarely more than $2). In addition, the bank from which you withdraw cash may charge its own fee. For international withdrawal fees, ask your bank.

Most ATMs in Mexico accept four-digit PIN numbers only, so if you have a five- or six-digit number, check with your bank to see if you can get a temporary four-digit number for your trip.

Note: Banks that are members of the **Global ATM Alliance** charge no transaction fees for cash withdrawals at other Alliance member ATMs; these include Bank of America, Scotiabank (Canada, Caribbean, and Mexico), Barclays (U.K. and parts of Africa), Deutsche Bank (Germany, Poland, Spain, and Italy), and BNP Paribus (France).

CREDIT CARDS

Credit cards are another safe way to carry money. They also provide a convenient record of all your expenses, and they generally offer relatively good exchange rates. You can withdraw cash advances from your credit cards at banks or ATMs but high fees make credit card cash advances a pricey way to get cash. Keep in mind that you'll pay interest from the moment of your withdrawal, even if you pay your monthly bills on time. Also, note that many banks now assess a 1% to 3% "transaction fee" on **all** charges you incur abroad (whether you're using the local currency or your native currency).

TRAVELER'S CHECKS

Traveler's checks are not the most efficient companion when traveling in Mexico. Especially in the more remote areas of Baja, it's likely a merchant won't even know what to do with it. If it's your preferred way to travel, keep in mind you may need to stick to well-traveled tourist spots, which are more likely to accept traveler's checks.

You can buy traveler's checks at most banks. They are offered in denominations of $20, $50, $100, $500, and sometimes $1,000. Generally, you'll pay a service charge ranging from 1% to 4%.

The most popular traveler's checks are offered by **American Express** (© **800/ 807-6233** or © **800/221-7282** for card holders—this number accepts collect calls, offers service in several foreign languages, and exempts AmEx gold and platinum cardholders from the 1% fee); **Visa** (© **800/732-1322**)—AAA members can obtain Visa checks for a $9.95 fee (for checks up to $1,500) at most AAA offices or by calling ✆ **866/339-3378;** and **MasterCard** (✆ **800/223-9920**).

Be sure to keep a record of the traveler's checks' serial numbers separate from your checks in the event that they are stolen or lost. You'll get a refund faster if you know the numbers.

American Express, Thomas Cook, Visa, and **MasterCard** offer **foreign currency traveler's checks,** useful if you're traveling to one country or to the Euro zone; they're accepted at locations where dollar checks may not be.

Another option is the new prepaid traveler's check cards, reloadable cards that work much like debit cards but aren't linked to your checking account. The **American Express Travelers Cheque Card,** for example, requires a minimum deposit, sets a maximum balance, and has a one-time issuance fee of $14.95. You can withdraw money from an ATM (for a fee of $2.50 per transaction, not including bank fees), and the funds can be purchased in dollars, euros, or pounds. If you lose the card, your available funds will be refunded within 24 hours.

7 Travel Insurance

The cost of travel insurance varies widely, depending on the destination, the cost and length of your trip, your age and health, and the type of trip you're taking, but expect to pay between 5% and 8% of the vacation itself. You can get estimates from various providers through **InsureMyTrip. com.** Enter your trip cost and dates, your age, and other information, for prices from more than a dozen companies.

U.K. citizens and their families who make more than one trip abroad per year may find an annual travel insurance policy works out cheaper. Check **www.money supermarket.com,** which compares prices across a wide range of providers for single- and multitrip policies.

Most big travel agents offer their own insurance and will probably try to sell you their package when you book a holiday. Think before you sign. **Britain's Consumers' Association** recommends that you insist on seeing the policy and reading the fine print before buying travel insurance. **The Association of British Insurers** (✆ **020/7600-3333;** www.abi. org.uk) gives advice by phone and publishes *Holiday Insurance,* a free guide to policy provisions and prices. You might also shop around for better deals: Try **Columbus Direct** (✆ **0870/033-9988;** www.columbusdirect.net).

TRIP-CANCELLATION INSURANCE

Trip-cancellation insurance will help retrieve your money if you have to back out of a trip or depart early, or if your travel supplier goes bankrupt. Trip cancellation traditionally covers such events as sickness, natural disasters, and Department of State advisories. The latest news in trip-cancellation insurance is the availability of **expanded hurricane coverage** and the **"any-reason"** cancellation coverage—which costs more but covers cancellations made for any reason. You won't get back 100% of your prepaid trip cost, but you'll be refunded a substantial portion. **TravelSafe** (✆ **888/885-7233;** www.travelsafe.com) offers both types of coverage. Expedia also offers any-reason cancellation coverage for its air-hotel packages.

For details, contact one of the following recommended insurers: **Access America** (✆ 866/807-3982; www.accessamerica. com); **Travel Guard International** (✆ 800/826-4919; www.travelguard. com); **Travel Insured International** (✆ 800/243-3174; www.travelinsured. com); and **Travelex Insurance Services** (✆ 888/457-4602; www.travelex-insurance.com).

MEDICAL INSURANCE

For travel overseas, most U.S. health plans (including Medicare and Medicaid) do not provide coverage, and the ones that do often require you to pay for services up front and reimburse you only after you return home.

Chances are the worst ailment you'll face in Baja is a sunburn, but it's important to know emergency health care is not Baja's strength (although even in the most remote areas, the peninsula is full of excellent doctors and healers). As a safety net, you may want to buy travel medical insurance, particularly if you're traveling to a remote or high-risk area where emergency evacuation might be necessary. If you require additional medical insurance, try **MEDEX Assistance** (✆ 410/453-6300; www.medexassist.com) or **Travel Assistance International** (✆ 800/821-2828; www.travelassistance.com; for general information on services, call the company's **Worldwide Assistance Services, Inc.,** at ✆ 800/777-8710).

Canadians should check with their provincial health plan offices or call **Health Canada** (✆ 866/225-0709; www.hc-sc.gc.ca) to find out the extent of their coverage and what documentation and receipts they must take home in case they are treated overseas.

My choice provider is Los Cabos' own **International Insurance Services,** a long-standing favorite among Southern Baja expats for health, home, and medical evacuation insurance. Personally, I like them for their prompt, professional, comprehensive, and personal service. Visit **www.caboinsurance.com** or call owner Cathie Smith at ✆ **624/143-1212** to get set up.

LOST-LUGGAGE INSURANCE

On international flights (including U.S. portions of international trips), baggage coverage is limited to approximately $9.07 per pound, up to approximately $635 per checked bag. If you plan to check items more valuable than what's covered by the standard liability, see if your homeowner's policy covers your valuables, get baggage insurance as part of your comprehensive travel-insurance package, or buy Travel Guard's "BagTrak" product.

If your luggage is lost, immediately file a lost-luggage claim at the airport, detailing the luggage contents. Most airlines require that you report delayed, damaged, or lost baggage within 4 hours of arrival. The airlines are required to deliver luggage, once found, directly to your house or destination free of charge.

8 Health

GENERAL AVAILABILITY OF HEALTH CARE

In most of Mexico's resort destinations, health care meeting U.S. standards is now available and, where it is not, air-evacuation ambulances are available. Check your insurance to see if medical evacuation is covered.

Most of the health concerns travelers to Baja face are related to the digestive system. Complications ranging from basic diarrhea to typhoid fever are more common than most travelers realize, but they can be avoided. As a general rule,

pay close attention to the food you eat while traveling, try to steer clear of the delectable taco stands that line the street, and, if you buy produce in a grocery store, soak it in a solution of water and a few drops of microdyne (available at most grocers) before eating it.

If you should encounter an ailment, prescription medicine is broadly available at Mexico pharmacies. However, be aware that you may need a copy of your prescription, or need to obtain a prescription from a local doctor. This is especially true in the border towns, such as in Tijuana,

Tips Treating & Avoiding Digestive Trouble

It's called "travelers' diarrhea" or *turista,* the Spanish word for "tourist": persistent diarrhea, often accompanied by fever, nausea, and vomiting, that used to attack many travelers to Mexico. (Some in the U.S. call this "Montezuma's revenge," but you won't hear it called that in Mexico.) Widespread improvements in infrastructure, sanitation, and education have practically eliminated this ailment, especially in well-developed resort areas such as Los Cabos. Most travelers make a habit of drinking only bottled water, which also helps to protect against unfamiliar bacteria. In resort areas, and generally throughout Mexico, only purified ice is used. If you do come down with this ailment, nothing beats Pepto Bismol, readily available in Mexico. Imodium is also available in Mexico and is used by many travelers for a quick fix. A good high-potency (or "therapeutic") vitamin supplement and even extra vitamin C can help; active-culture yogurt is good for healthy digestion.

Since dehydration can quickly become life threatening, the Public Health Service advises that you be careful to replace fluids and electrolytes (potassium, sodium, and the like) during a bout of diarrhea. Drink Pedialyte, a rehydration solution available at most Mexican pharmacies, or natural fruit juice, such as guava or apple (stay away from orange juice, which has laxative properties), with a pinch of salt added.

How to Prevent It: The U.S. Public Health Service recommends the following measures for preventing travelers' diarrhea: **Drink only purified water** (boiled water, canned or bottled beverages, beer, or wine). **Choose food carefully.** In general, avoid salads (except in first-class restaurants), uncooked vegetables, undercooked protein, and unpasteurized milk or milk products, including cheese. Choose food that is freshly cooked and still hot. In addition, something as simple as **clean hands** can go a long way toward preventing *turista.*

where many Americans have been crossing into Mexico specifically for the purpose of purchasing lower-priced prescription medicines, but it's rare for a pharmacy to require prescriptions further down the peninsula.

Contact the **International Association for Medical Assistance to Travellers** (IAMAT; ✆ **716/754-4883** or, in Canada, 416/652-0137; www.iamat.org) for tips on travel and health concerns in the countries you're visiting, and for lists of local, English-speaking doctors. The United States **Centers for Disease Control and Prevention** (✆ **800/311-3435;**

www.cdc.gov) provides up-to-date information on health hazards by region or country and offers tips on food safety. **Travel Health Online** (www.tripprep. com), sponsored by a consortium of travel medicine practitioners, may also offer helpful advice on traveling abroad. You can find listings of reliable medical clinics overseas at the **International Society of Travel Medicine** (www.istm.org).

COMMON AILMENTS
TROPICAL ILLNESSES You shouldn't be overly concerned about tropical diseases if you stay on the normal tourist

routes and don't eat street food. However, dengue fever, typhoid, parasites, and cholera do exist in Baja. Talk to your doctor or to a medical specialist in tropical diseases about precautions you should take. You can also get medical bulletins from the U.S. Department of State and the Centers for Disease Control and Prevention (see "Visitor Information & Maps," earlier). You can protect yourself by taking some simple precautions: Wash your hands before eating; don't touch your eyes unless your hands are clean; watch what you eat and drink; stay out of the ocean near arroyos (riverbeds) after a storm; don't swim in stagnant water (ponds, slow-moving rivers, or wells); and avoid mosquito bites by covering up, using repellent, and sleeping under netting.

DIETARY RED FLAGS In general, Baja is not the best place for vegans, vegetarians, or anyone who observes any kind of strict dietary regimen. Although it's possible to find stellar vegetarian options on the menu, it's not always guaranteed.

Because of its distance from mainland Mexico and the U.S., organic produce is harder to find the farther South you travel, save for in the most expensive restaurants. While Los Cabos, Todos Santos, La Paz, Ensenada, and Tijuana have their fair share of fine-dining restaurants serving organic produce, it's especially difficult to find the same in mid-Baja. Nevertheless, you'll find the produce in most restaurants is good and fresh. While traveling in Baja, as long as it's clean (and if you're eating at a clean restaurant, it probably is), the rest is a nonissue.

In terms of foods to avoid, as delicious as street food (commonly tacos, burritos, hot dogs, hamburgers, *licuados*/smoothies/*raspados,* etc.) can be, if you want your digestive system to stay intact during your trip and beyond, it's simply best to avoid them. Also, of note, salsas generally pack more heat in Mexico than in the U.S., so if you're sensitive to chiles, take it slow on your first taste.

BUGS, BITES & OTHER WILDLIFE CONCERNS Mosquitoes and gnats are prevalent along the coast. Insect repellent *(repelente contra insectos)* is a must, and it's not always available in Mexico. If you'll be in these areas and are prone to bites, bring along a repellent that contains the active ingredient DEET. Avon's Skin So Soft also works extremely well. Another good remedy to keep the mosquitoes away is to mix citronella essential oil with basil, clove, and lavender essential oils. If you're sensitive to bites, pick up some antihistamine cream from a drugstore at home.

Most readers won't ever see a scorpion *(alacrán)* and very few in Baja are deadly. Nonetheless, if one stings you, go immediately to a doctor. In Mexico you can buy scorpion toxin antidote at any drugstore. It is an injection and it costs around $25. This is a good idea if you plan to camp in a remote area where medical assistance can be several hours away.

The same goes for jellyfish stings. The ocean is its own wilderness full of creatures large and microscopic that can sting your skin. The most common name for the tiny stings you may feel while swimming is *agua mala* (bad water). After a dip into agua mala, your body may be covered in irritating red splotches or, worse, painful foot-long scars from Portuguese man-of-war tentacles, so it's highly recommended you wear a Lycra skin to protect your body from these poisons. If you do get stung, don't rub the wound. Most boat captains have vinegar on hand to pour over the affected area and ease the pain, so if you're not allergic and on your way to see a doctor, try to leave it alone and let the irritation subside on its own.

HIGH-ALTITUDE HAZARDS Unless you're scaling mountains (Picacho del Diablo reaches 3,094m/10,154 ft.), you're not likely to encounter altitude sickness in Baja, but travelers to certain regions of Mexico occasionally experience **elevation sickness,** which results from the relative lack of oxygen and the decrease in barometric pressure that characterizes high elevations (more than 1,500m/5,000 ft.). Symptoms include shortness of breath, fatigue, headache, insomnia, and even nausea. Mexico City is at 2,121m (6,957 ft.) above sea level, and mountainous points within central Baja are also at high elevations. At high elevations, it takes about 10 days to acquire the extra red blood corpuscles you need to adjust to the scarcity of oxygen. To help your body acclimate, drink plenty of fluids, avoid alcoholic beverages, and don't overexert yourself during the first few days. If you have heart or lung problems, talk to your doctor before going above 2,400m (8,000 ft.).

SUN/ELEMENTS/EXTREME WEATHER EXPOSURE The sun in Baja is powerful, so while it's important to protect yourself when traveling throughout the peninsula, it's most pertinent south of the Tropic of Cancer in the Los Cabos and East Cape regions. Sunscreen, hats, and lightweight shirts and pants can make a major difference in the long-term health of your skin, so make sun protection a priority. You should wear an SPF of 30 on your face at the very least, and remember to reapply every hour or two.

Despite boasting 350 days of sun a year, Southern Baja visitors do contend with some weather in the summer and fall. June 1 is the official start of hurricane season, and it's also when the temperatures start rising, tourism drops off, and many expats head north. Historically, hurricanes and tropical storms blow into Los Cabos, the East Cape, La Paz, and Todos Santos from August into mid-October, with September being the peak of the season. Although no deaths have occurred in recent years, among other hurricanes, Juliet wreaked havoc in Los Cabos in 2001 and Hurricane John brought severe damage to Loreto, the East Cape, and La Paz in 2006.

WHAT TO DO IF YOU GET SICK AWAY FROM HOME

For travel abroad, and certainly in Baja, you may have to pay all medical costs up front and be reimbursed later. This can be costly—especially in facilities that only accept cash—so be prepared. Medicare and Medicaid do not provide coverage for medical costs outside the U.S. Before leaving home, find out what medical services your health insurance covers. To protect yourself, consider buying medical travel insurance (see "Medical Insurance," under "Travel Insurance," above).

Most resorts have a doctor on staff, and, in Los Cabos, the best hospital is **Amerimed** (© **624/143-9671**) a 24-hour, American-standards clinic with bilingual physicians and emergency air-evacuation services; it also accepts major credit cards.

Very few health insurance plans pay for medical evacuation back to the U.S. (which can cost $10,000 and up). A number of companies offer medical evacuation services anywhere in the world. If you're ever hospitalized more than 150 miles from home, **MedjetAssist** (© **800/527-7478;** www.medjetassistance.com) will pick you up and fly you to the hospital of your choice virtually anywhere in the world in a medically equipped and staffed aircraft 24 hours day, 7 days a week. Annual memberships are $225 individual, $350 family; you can also purchase short-term memberships.

We list **hospitals** and **emergency numbers** under "Fast Facts," p. 41.

If you suffer from a chronic illness, consult your doctor before your departure. Pack **prescription medications** in your carry-on luggage, and carry them in their original containers, with pharmacy labels—otherwise they won't make it through airport security. Carry the generic name of prescription medicines, in case a local pharmacist is unfamiliar with the brand name.

9 Safety

STAYING SAFE

I have lived and traveled in Mexico for years, have never had any serious trouble, and rarely feel suspicious of anyone or any situation. You will probably feel physically safer in most Mexican cities and villages than in any comparable place at home—especially in Southern Baja, where tourism dollars mean plenty of work for locals and therefore less petty crime. However, crime in Mexico has received attention in the North American press and entertainment industry over the past several years. Many feel this unfairly exaggerates the real dangers, but it should be noted that crime rates, including taxi robberies, kidnappings, and highway carjackings, have risen in recent years—mostly on the mainland. The most severe problems have been concentrated in Mexico City, where even longtime residents will attest to the overall lack of security. Isolated incidents have also occurred in Ixtapa, Baja, and Cancún. Check the U.S. Department of State advisory before you travel for any notable hot spots.

Precautions are necessary, but travelers should be realistic. Common sense is essential. You can generally trust someone that you approach for help or directions, but be wary of anyone who approaches you offering the same. The more insistent the person is, the more cautious you should be. The crime rate, on the whole, is much lower in Mexico than in most parts of the United States, possibly owing to the fact that firearms are illegal, and the nature of crimes, in general, is less violent. Random, violent, or serial crime is essentially unheard of in Mexico. You are much more likely to meet kind and helpful Mexicans than you are to encounter those set on thievery and deceit. (See also "Emergencies" under "Fast Facts," later in this chapter.)

BRIBES & SCAMS   As is the case around the world, there are the occasional bribes and scams in Mexico, targeted at people believed to be naive—such as the telltale tourist. For years, Mexico was known as a place where bribes—called *mordidas* (bites)—were expected; however, the country is rapidly changing. Frequently, offering a bribe today, especially to a police officer, is considered an insult, and it can land you in deeper trouble.

If you believe a **bribe** is being requested, here are a few tips on dealing with the situation. Even if you speak Spanish, don't utter a word of it to Mexican officials. That way you'll appear innocent, all the while understanding every word.

When you are crossing the border, should the person who inspects your car ask for a tip, you can ignore this request—but understand that the official may suddenly decide that a complete search of your belongings is in order. If faced with a situation where you feel you're being asked for a *propina* (literally, "tip"; colloquially, "bribe"), how much should you offer? Usually $3 to $5 or the equivalent in pesos will do the trick. Many tourists have the impression that everything works better in Mexico if you "tip"; however, in reality, this only perpetuates corruption and the *mordida* attitude.

Whatever you do, **avoid impoliteness;** under no circumstances should you insult a Latin American official. Extreme politeness, even in the face of adversity, rules Mexico. In Mexico, *gringos* have a reputation for being loud and demanding. By adopting the local custom of excessive courtesy, you'll have greater success in negotiations of any kind. Stand your ground, but do it politely.

As you travel in Mexico, you may encounter several types of **scams,** which are typical throughout the world. One involves some kind of a **distraction** or feigned commotion. While your attention is diverted, a pickpocket makes a grab for your wallet. In another common scam, an **unaccompanied child** pretends to be lost and frightened and takes your hand for safety. Meanwhile the child or an accomplice plunders your pockets. A third involves **confusing currency.** A shoeshine boy, street musician, guide, or other individual might offer you a service for a price that seems reasonable—in pesos. When it comes time to pay, he or she tells you the price is in dollars, not pesos. Be very clear on the price and currency when services are involved.

DEALING WITH DISCRIMINATION

Mexico, as a whole, does not embrace political correctness, but discrimination is rarely an issue for travelers. For example, if a man is blond, he's called "guero," which, loosely translated, means "white boy." If a woman is fat, her nickname is "gorda" (fat girl). Mexicans call it like they see it, so if you are African American, you may be called "negro" (*neh*-gro); if you're southeast Asian, you may be called "hindú"; and if you have almond-shaped eyes, you are definitely "chino." No matter how erroneous or offensive it may be, the local people who say these things mean no harm. Mexicans are some of the warmest people in the world and, particularly in Baja, they welcome all colors, creeds, and sexual preferences and generally don't discriminate against anyone.

10 Specialized Travel Resources

TRAVELERS WITH DISABILITIES

Most disabilities shouldn't stop anyone from traveling. There are more options and resources out there than ever before.

Mexico may seem like one giant obstacle course to travelers in wheelchairs or on crutches. At airports, you may encounter steep stairs before finding a well-hidden elevator or escalator—if one exists—and wheelchair ramps sometimes look more like alpine ski runs. Airlines will often arrange wheelchair assistance to the baggage area. Porters are generally available to help with luggage at airports and large bus stations, once you've cleared baggage claim.

Mexican airports are upgrading their services, but it is not uncommon to board from a remote position, meaning you either descend stairs to a bus that ferries you to the plane, which you board by climbing stairs, or you walk across the tarmac to your plane and ascend the stairs. Deplaning presents the same problem in reverse.

Organizations that offer a vast range of resources and assistance to travelers with disabilities include **MossRehab** (© 800/ CALL-MOSS; www.mossresourcenet. org); the **American Foundation for the Blind** (AFB; © 800/232-5463; www. afb.org); and **SATH (Society for Accessible Travel & Hospitality;** © 212/447-7284; www.sath.org). **AirAmbulance Card.com** is now partnered with SATH and allows you to preselect top-notch hospitals in case of an emergency.

Access-Able Travel Source (© 303/ 232-2979; www.access-able.com) offers a comprehensive database on travel agents from around the world with experience in accessible travel; destination-specific access information; and links to such resources as service animals, equipment rentals, and access guides.

Many travel agencies offer customized tours and itineraries for travelers with disabilities. Among them are **Flying Wheels Travel** (© 507/451-5005; www.flying wheelstravel.com); and **Accessible**

Journeys (© 800/846-4537 or 610/521-0339; www.disabilitytravel.com).

Flying with Disability (www.flying-with-disability.org) is a comprehensive information source on airplane travel. Avis Rent a Car (© 888/879-4273) has an "Avis Access" program that offers services for customers with special travel needs. These include specially outfitted vehicles with swivel seats, spinner knobs, and hand controls; mobility scooter rentals; and accessible bus service. Be sure to reserve well in advance.

Also check out the quarterly magazine *Emerging Horizons* (www.emerging horizons.com), available by subscription ($16.95 year U.S.; $21.95 outside U.S).

The "Accessible Travel" link at Mobility-Advisor.com (www.mobility-advisor.com) offers a variety of travel resources to persons with disabilities.

British travelers should contact Holiday Care (© 0845-124-9971 in UK only; www.holidaycare.org.uk) to access a wide range of travel information and resources for those with disabilities and elderly people.

GAY & LESBIAN TRAVELERS

Mexico is a conservative country, with deeply rooted Catholic religious traditions. Public displays of same-sex affection are rare and still considered shocking for men, especially outside of urban or resort areas. Women in Mexico frequently walk hand in hand, but anything more would cross the boundary of acceptability. However, gay and lesbian travelers are generally treated with respect and should not experience any harassment, assuming they give the appropriate regard to local culture and customs. Los Cabos and La Paz, in particular, are very gay-friendly resort destinations.

The International Gay and Lesbian Travel Association (IGLTA; © 800/448-8550 or 954/776-2626; www.iglta.org) is the trade association for the gay and lesbian travel industry, and offers an online directory of gay- and lesbian-friendly travel businesses and tour operators.

Many agencies offer tours and travel itineraries specifically for gay and lesbian travelers, but you may have to dig to find Baja-specific gay and lesbian tours. Pink Pavilions (no phone; www.pinkpavilions.com) offers a search of gay- and lesbian-friendly vacation rentals. Alyson Adventures (© 800/825-9766; www.alyson adventures.com) offers gay and lesbian adventure travel tours, including a Baja-specific kayaking tour from La Paz to Loreto. Now, Voyager (© 800/255-6951; www.nowvoyager.com) is a well-known San Francisco–based gay-owned and -operated travel service. Olivia Cruises & Resorts (© 800/631-6277; www.olivia.com) charters entire resorts and ships for exclusive lesbian vacations and offers smaller group experiences for both gay and lesbian travelers.

Gay.com Travel (© 800/929-2268 or 415/644-8044; www.gay.com/travel or www.outandabout.com), is an excellent online successor to the popular *Out & About* print magazine. It provides regularly updated information about gay-owned, gay-oriented, and gay-friendly lodging, dining, sightseeing, nightlife, and shopping establishments in every important destination worldwide. British travelers should click on the "Travel" link at www.uk.gay.com for advice and gay-friendly trip ideas.

The Canadian website GayTraveler (http://gaytraveler.ca) offers ideas and advice for gay travel all over the world.

SENIOR TRAVEL

Mexico is a popular country for retirees. For decades, North Americans have been living indefinitely in Mexico by returning to the border and re-crossing with a new tourist permit every 6 months. Mexican immigration officials have caught on, and now limit the maximum time in the country to 6 months within any year.

This is to encourage even partial residents to acquire proper documentation.

Some of the most popular places for long-term stays in Baja are La Paz, Los Cabos, and Loreto. Also, northern Baja, specifically Rosarito Beach, Ensenada, and San Felipe, is experiencing a retiree real-estate boom.

Sanborn Tours, 2015 S. 10th St., McAllen, TX 78505-0519 (© **800/395-8482**), offers a "Retire in Mexico" orientation tour.

Mention the fact that you're a senior citizen when you make your travel reservations. Although most of the major U.S. airlines except America West have canceled their senior discount and coupon-book programs, many hotels still offer discounts for seniors.

Members of **AARP,** 601 E St. NW, Washington, DC 20049 (© **888/687-2277;** www.aarp.org), get discounts on hotels, airfares, and car rentals. AARP offers members a wide range of benefits, including *AARP: The Magazine* and a monthly newsletter. Anyone over 50 can join.

Many reliable agencies and organizations target the 50-plus market. **Elderhostel** (© **800/454-5768;** www.elderhostel.org) arranges worldwide study programs for those aged 55 and over. **ElderTreks** (© **800/741-7956** or 416/558-5000 outside North America; www.eldertreks.com) offers small-group tours to off-the-beaten-path or adventure-travel locations, restricted to travelers 50 and older.

Recommended publications offering travel resources and discounts for seniors include the quarterly magazine *Travel 50 & Beyond* (www.travel50andbeyond.com) and the best-selling paperback *Unbelievably Good Deals and Great Adventures That You Absolutely Can't Get Unless You're Over 50 2005–2006, 16th Edition* (McGraw-Hill), by Joann Rattner Heilman.

FAMILY TRAVEL

No culture loves children more than Mexicans, and Baja is the ideal place to introduce children to the exciting adventure of exploring a different culture. Among the best destinations for children in Mexico is La Paz (see chapter 5). The larger, moderate to luxury hotels in Los Cabos may offer kids' clubs, special daytime activity programs, or private babysitters. Few budget hotels offer these amenities.

Before leaving, you should check with your doctor to get advice on medications to take along. Disposable diapers cost about the same in Mexico but are of poorer quality. You can get Huggies and Pampers identical to the ones sold in the United States, but at a higher price. Many stores sell Gerber's baby foods. Dry cereals, powdered formulas, baby bottles, and purified water are all easily available in midsize and large cities or resorts.

Cribs, however, may present a problem—only the largest and most luxurious hotels provide them. Rollaway beds are often available for children staying in the room with parents. Child seats or high chairs at restaurants are common, and most restaurants will go out of their way to accommodate your child.

Because many travelers to Baja will rent a car, it is advisable to bring your car seat. Leasing agencies in Mexico do not rent car seats.

Every country's regulations differ, but in general children traveling abroad should have plenty of documentation on hand, particularly if they're traveling with someone other than their own parents (in which case a notarized form letter from a parent is often required). For details on entry requirements for children traveling abroad, go to the U.S. Department of State website (travel.state.gov/foreignentry reqs.html).

Tips **Advice for Female Travelers**

As a female traveling alone, I personally feel safer traveling in Mexico than in the United States. But I use the same common-sense precautions I follow traveling anywhere else in the world and am alert to what's going on around me.

Mexicans in general, and men in particular, are nosy about single travelers, especially women. If a taxi driver, waiter, or anyone else with whom you don't want to become friendly asks about your marital status, family, and so forth—and they will—my advice is to make up a set of answers (regardless of the truth): "I'm married, traveling with friends, and I have three children." Saying you are single and traveling alone may send the wrong message. U.S. television, widely viewed now in Mexico, has portrayed American single women as sexually promiscuous. Check out the award-winning website **Journeywoman** (www.journeywoman.com), a "real-life" women's travel information network where you can sign up for a free e-mail newsletter and get advice on everything from etiquette and dress to safety. Or the travel guide *Safety and Security for Women Who Travel* (Travelers' Tales, Inc.), by Sheila Swan and Peter Laufer, offers common-sense tips on safe travel.

Throughout this book, the "Kids" icon distinguishes attractions, hotels, restaurants, and other destinations that are particularly attractive and accommodating to children and families.

To locate accommodations, restaurants, and attractions that are particularly kid-friendly, refer to the "Kids" icon throughout this guide.

Recommended family travel websites include **Family Travel Forum** (www. familytravelforum.com), a comprehensive site that offers customized trip planning; **Family Travel Network** (www. familytravelnetwork.com), an online magazine providing travel tips; and **Travel WithYourKids.com** (www.travelwith yourkids.com), a comprehensive site written by parents for parents offering sound advice for long-distance and international travel with children.

11 Staying Connected

TELEPHONES

Mexico's telephone system is slowly but surely catching up with modern times. All telephone numbers have 10 digits. Every city and town that has telephone access has a two-digit (Mexico City, Monterrey, and Guadalajara) or three-digit (everywhere else) area code. In Mexico City, Monterrey, and Guadalajara, local numbers have eight digits; elsewhere, local numbers have seven digits. To place a local call, you do not need to dial the area code.

To call long distance within Mexico, the cheapest way is by using the "Ladatel" phone booths, into which you insert prepaid cards—available at most pharmacies and convenience stores. Steer clear of calling home from your hotel room, which can cost as much as $10 per minute. Instead, insert a Ladatel card (available in increments of $5, $10, $20, and $50—the $10 card is plenty for two 10-minute calls home) and dial the national long-distance code **01** before dialing the area code and then the number. Mexico's area codes *(claves)* are listed in the front of telephone directories. Area codes are listed before all phone numbers in this book. For long-distance dialing, you will often see the term "LADA," which is the automatic long-distance service offered by Telmex, Mexico's former telephone monopoly and its largest phone company. To make a person-to-person or collect call inside Mexico, dial ℂ **020.** You can also call 020 to request the correct area codes for the number and place you are calling.

Many fax numbers are also regular telephone numbers; ask whoever answers for the fax tone (*"me da tono de fax, por favor?"*). Cellular phones are very popular for small businesses in resort areas and smaller communities. To call a cellular number inside the same area code, dial 044 and then the number. To dial the cellular phone from anywhere else in Mexico, first dial 01, then the three-digit area code and the seven-digit number. To dial it from the U.S., dial 011-52, plus the three-digit area code and the seven-digit number.

To call the Baja Peninsula:
1. Dial the international access code: 011 from the U.S.; 00 from the U.K., Ireland, or New Zealand; or 0011 from Australia.
2. Dial the country code 52.
3. Dial the two- or three-digit city code and then the seven-digit number.

To make international calls: To make international calls from Baja, first dial 00 and then the country code (U.S. or Canada 1, U.K. 44, Ireland 353, Australia 61, New Zealand 64). Next you dial the area code and number. For example, if you wanted to call the British Embassy in Washington, D.C., you would dial 00-1-202-588-7800.

For directory assistance: Dial 040 if you're looking for a number inside Mexico, and dial 090 for numbers to all other countries.

For operator assistance: If you need operator assistance in making a call, dial 090 if you're trying to make an international call and 020 if you want to call a number in Mexico.

Toll-free numbers: Numbers beginning with 01-800 within Mexico are toll-free, but calling a 1-800 number in the States from Mexico is not toll-free. In fact, it costs the same as an overseas call.

Cellular phone calls: To call a cell number inside the same area code, dial 044 and then the full 10-digit number, including the city code. To dial a cellphone from anywhere else in Mexico, first dial 01, then the three-digit area code and the seven-digit number. To dial a cellphone from the U.S., dial 011-52-1, plus the three-digit area code and the seven-digit number.

CELLPHONES

The three letters that define much of the world's wireless capabilities are **GSM** (Global System for Mobile Communications), a big, seamless network that makes for easy cross-border cellphone use throughout Europe and dozens of other countries worldwide. In the U.S., T-Mobile, AT&T Wireless, and Cingular use this quasi-universal system; in Canada, Microcell and some Rogers customers are GSM, and all Europeans and most Australians use GSM. GSM phones function with a removable plastic SIM card, encoded with your phone number and account information. If your cellphone is on a GSM system, and you have a world-capable multiband phone such as many Sony Ericsson, Motorola, or Samsung models, you can make and receive calls across civilized areas around much of the globe. Just call your wireless operator and ask for "international roaming" to be activated on your account. Unfortunately, per-minute charges can be high—usually $1 to $2 in Baja.

Chances are, your cell will get service in all the major tourist zones in Baja, but if you will be traveling for an extended period of time and want to have a more economic mobile option, **renting** a phone is a good idea. While you can rent a phone from any number of overseas sites, including kiosks at airports and at car-rental agencies, we suggest renting the phone before you leave home.

Los Cabos travelers may rent phones ahead of time through **Cabo Cell** (© **624/143-5950;** www.cabocell.com. mx). The phone will be waiting at your hotel when you check in and service includes a 24/7 local personal assistant, translator, and emergency assistance. Otherwise, you may visit the office at Boulevard Lazaro Cardenas s/n, Edificio Pioneros, Local 2 in downtown Cabo San Lucas.

North Americans can rent one before leaving home from **InTouch USA** (© **800/872-7626;** www.intouchglobal. com) or **RoadPost** (© **888/290-1606** or 905/272-5665; www.roadpost.com). InTouch will also, for free, advise you on whether your existing phone will work overseas; simply call © **703/222-7161** between 9am and 4pm EST, or go to **http://intouchglobal.com/travel.htm**.

Buying a phone can be economically attractive, as Mexico has cheap prepaid cellphones available. Once you arrive at your destination, stop by a local Telcel shop and get the cheapest package; you'll probably pay less than $100 for a phone and a starter calling card. Local calls may be as low as 10¢ per minute, and incoming calls are free.

VOICE OVER INERNET PROTOCOL (VOIP)

If you have Web access while traveling, you might consider a broadband-based telephone service (in technical terms, **Voice over Internet protocol,** or **VoIP**) such as Skype (www.skype.com) or Vonage (www.vonage.com), which allows you to make free international calls if you use their services from your laptop or in a cybercafe. The people you're calling must also use the service for it to work; check the sites for details.

INTERNET/E-MAIL WITHOUT YOUR OWN COMPUTER

To find cybercafes in your destination, check **www.cybercaptive.com** and **www. cybercafe.com**. The downtown and/or tourist areas in most of Baja's primary destinations have Internet centers and cafes sprinkled every block or so. Also, most large resort and hotel chains offer access to an onsite business center. Although more expensive than most cybercafes, hotel business centers are usually quite efficient.

Most major airports have **Internet kiosks** that provide basic Web access for a per-minute fee that's usually higher than cybercafe prices. However, Baja's airports may not always be up to international standards. Check out copy shops such as **Kinko's** (FedEx Kinko's), which offers computer stations with fully loaded software (as well as Wi-Fi).

WITH YOUR OWN COMPUTER

More and more hotels, resorts, airports, cafes, and retailers are going **Wi-Fi** (wireless fidelity), becoming "hotspots" that offer free high-speed Wi-Fi access or charge a small fee for usage. Most laptops sold today have built-in wireless capability. To find public Wi-Fi hotspots at your destination, go to **www.jiwire.com**; its Hotspot Finder holds the world's largest directory of public wireless hotspots.

For dial-up access, most business-class hotels throughout the world offer dataports for laptop modems.

Wherever you go, bring a **connection kit** of the right power and phone adapters, a spare phone cord, and a spare Ethernet network cable—or find out whether your hotel supplies them to guests. Luckily, all of Mexico is on the same voltage as the United States, so just take your regular power cords.

12 Escorted General-Interest Tours

Escorted tours are structured group tours with a group leader. The price usually includes everything from airfare to hotels, meals, tours, admission costs, and local transportation.

In general, these types of escorted tours are less popular in Baja than they are in other regions of the world. However, very popular in Baja are adventure tours. (See "Special-Interest Trips" below.) If you're interested in a group tour, Los Cabos in particular has a wealth of destination-management companies that offer excellent guided tours and are able to schedule and guide your entire trip if you so choose. Visit **www.bookcabo.com** for some of the freshest tour and entertainment options in the destination.

Of note, RV caravans are popular group tours throughout Baja. **Baja and Back RV Caravan Tours** (✆ **866/782-2252**; www.bajaandback.com) offers a 28-day San Diego–to–Cabo San Lucas trip for $1,290, which includes, among other things, maps, campsite rental, 24-hour guide service, and margarita parties.

13 Special-Interest Trips

Los Cabos, with nine golf courses and growing, has become the preeminent golf destination in Mexico. However, visitors to Baja can enjoy a broad range of activities, including diving, surfing, hiking, rock climbing, mountain biking, horseback riding, wine tasting, shopping, and more.

WINERY TOURS   All the wineries in northern Baja offer tours and tastings by appointment or are open to the public, but if you'd like to tour a few in a day and let someone else handle the details, the exquisite **Casa Natalie** (✆ **888/562-8254** or 646/174-7373; www.casanatalie.com) boutique hotel in Ensenada offers winery tour and tasting excursions into the Valle de Guadalupe for $80 per person, which includes wine tastings and gourmet cheeses at four wineries. **Adobe Guadalupe** (✆ **649/631-3098** in the U.S., or 646/155-2094; www.adobe guadalupe.com) offers tours on horseback to Monte Xanic. If you're coming from San Diego and want to make a quick trip of it, **Baja California Tours** (✆ **858/454-7166**; www.bajaspecials.com) out of La Jolla, California, offers a day tour of three wineries and lunch in the Guadalupe Valley for $89. They also offer a 2-day, 1-night tour for $296. Transportation is included in the cost.

MOTORCYCLE   EXPEDITIONS Cabo **BMW Rentals,** on Lázaro Cardenas across from McDonald's in Cabo San Lucas (✆ **866/241-9899** in the U.S., or 624/143-2640), offers guided and self-guided motorcycle tours around Southern Baja. A good resource for motorcyclists in B.C.S. is the *Cabo Loop Riders Guide,* available for $25 on their website.

OUTDOOR ADVENTURE   Mexico Travel Link Ltd., Vancouver, BC, Canada (✆ **604/454-9044;** fax 604/454-9088; www.mexicotravel.net), offers travel tips plus cultural, sports, and adventure tours to Baja and other destinations.

Baja Expeditions, 2625 Garnet Ave., San Diego, CA 92109 (✆ **800/843-6967** or 858/581-3311; www.bajaex. com), offers natural-history cruises, whale-watching, sea-kayaking, camping, and scuba-diving trips out of Loreto, La Paz, and San Diego. Small groups and special itineraries are the firm's specialty.

For more than 20 years, local resident Trudi Angell has guided sea-kayaking, mountain-biking, and horseback-riding tours in the Loreto area with **Tour Baja,** P.O. Box 827, Calistoga, CA 94515

(© 800/398-6200 or 707/942-4550; fax 707/942-8017; www.tourbaja.com). She and her guides offer firsthand knowledge of the area, its natural history, and its local culture. Her company's kayaking, mountain-biking, mule-riding, pack trips, and sailing charters combine these elements with great outdoor adventures.

Natural Habitat Adventures, 2945 Center Green Court, Suite H, Boulder, CO 80301 (© 800/543-8917 or 303/449-3711; www.nathab.com), offers naturalist-led natural-history and adventure travel. Expeditions focus on whale-watching in Baja.

CULTURAL EXCURSIONS   Baja is not the overt hotbed of Mexican culture that the mainland is; here you have to dig for culture, but it's well worth it. Several tour companies with guided tours to the missions and the ancient cave paintings of mid-Baja are based in Loreto (**Arturo's Sport;** © 613/135-0766; www.arturo sport.com) and Mulegé (**Mulegé Tours;** © 615/153-0232; at the Las Casitas Hotel in downtown Mulegé). However, one of the best tours, which provides a comprehensive education on mid-Baja missions, plus a visit to the indigenous cave paintings, is **Baja Outback's** 4-day **Mission Trail Expedition** (© 624/142-9200; www.bajaoutback.com). Visit the missions in Loreto, Mulegé, La Purisma mission site (now in ruins), San Miguel, San José de Comondu, and San Javier, which were some of the first built by Spanish missionaries between 1683 and 1834. Twenty Jesuit missions, two Franciscan missions, and 11 Dominican missions make up the Baja portion of the 966km (600-mile) Camino Real ("Royal Road") mission trail, which extends into the U.S. state of California. For more information on the cave paintings, see "Baja's Cave Paintings: An Exploration of the Mysterious" in chapter 6.

SEA KAYAKING   By alternating sea-kayaking trips between Alaska and Baja for 2 decades, **Sea Trek Sea Kayaking Center** (© 415/488-1000; fax 415/488-1707; www.seatrekkayak.com) has gained an intimate knowledge of the remote coastline of Baja. Eight-day trips depart from and return to Loreto; a 12-day expedition travels from Loreto to La Paz. An optional day excursion to Bahía Magdalena for whale-watching is also available. Full boat support is provided, and no previous paddling experience is necessary.

Mountain Travel Sobek, 6420 Fairmount Ave., El Cerrito, CA 94530 (© 800/227-2384, 888/687-6235, or 510/527-8100; www.mtsobek.com), takes groups kayaking in the Sea of Cortez and whale-watching in Baja. Sobek is one of the world's leading ecotour outfitters.

Sea Kayak Adventures, 1036 Pine Ave., Coeur d'Alene, ID 83814 (© 800/616-1943 or 208/765-3116; fax 208/765-5254; www.seakayakadventures.com), features kayak trips in both the Sea of Cortez and Magdalena Bay, with a focus on whale-watching. This company has the exclusive permit to paddle Magdalena Bay's remote northern waters, and they guarantee gray whale sightings. Trips combine paddling of 4 to 5 hours per day with hiking across dunes and beaches, while nights are spent camping.

14 Getting Around

BY CAR

It's quite possible to get around without a car in Baja—especially in the tiny resort destinations—but renting a car gives you the ability to set your own itinerary for exploration and follow your whims as opposed to those of taxi and bus drivers.

Although you'll drive on the right side of the road, observe similar speed limits (listed in kilometers per hour instead of miles per hour), and see road signs that mean the same thing as they do in the United States, you'll find driving in Mexico is nothing like driving at home.

Most Mexican roads are not up to U.S. standards of smoothness, hardness, width of curve, grade of hill, or safety markings. Driving at night is dangerous—the roads are rarely lit; trucks, carts, pedestrians, and bicycles usually have no lights; and you can hit potholes, animals, rocks, dead ends, or uncrossable bridges without warning.

The spirited style of Mexican driving sometimes requires acute vision and reflexes. Be prepared for new customs, as when a truck driver flips on his left turn signal when there's not a crossroad for miles. He's probably telling you the road's clear ahead for you to pass. Flashing hazard lights on oncoming vehicles or the cars in front of you means there's something going on up ahead (animals in or near the road, a car accident, a slow-moving vehicle, etc.) and to proceed with caution. Another custom that's very important to respect is turning left. Never turn left by stopping in the middle of a highway with your left signal on. Instead, pull onto the right shoulder, wait for traffic to clear, and then proceed across the road.

GASOLINE There's one government-owned brand of gas and one gasoline station name throughout the country—**Pemex** (Petroleras Mexicanas). There are two types of gas in Mexico: *magna,* 87-octane unleaded gas, and premium 93 octane. In Mexico, fuel and oil are sold by the liter, which is slightly more than a quart (40 liters equals about 11 gal.). Many franchise Pemex stations have bathroom facilities and convenience stores—a great improvement over the old ones.

It's common practice for an attendant to fill your tank for you. I've watched many gringos hop out of their car to avert a "scam" but, rest assured, locals rarely fill their own tank. If the attendant cleans

your windshield, a small tip of 5 to 10 pesos (50¢–$1) is appropriate.

Important notes: No credit cards are currently accepted for gas purchases.

BREAKDOWNS If your car breaks down on the road, help might already be on the way. Radio-equipped green repair trucks operated by uniformed English-speaking officers patrol major highways during daylight hours. These **"Green Angels"** perform minor repairs and adjustments free, but you pay for parts and materials.

Your best guide to repair shops in Baja is a friend who knows. However, the Yellow Pages can work in a pinch. For repairs, look under "Automóviles y Camiones: Talleres de Reparación y Servicio"; auto-parts stores are under "Refacciones y Accesorios para Automóviles." To find a mechanic on the road, ask a local (because Baja is so rough on cars, most locals know a mechanic) or look for a sign that says TALLER MECANICO.

Places called *vulcanizadora* or *llantera* repair flat tires, and it is common to find them open 24 hours a day on the most traveled highways.

MINOR ACCIDENTS When possible, many Mexicans drive away from minor accidents or try to make an immediate settlement, to avoid involving the police. If the police arrive while the involved persons are still at the scene, everyone may be locked in jail until blame is assessed. In any case, you have to settle up immediately, which may take days. Foreigners who don't speak fluent Spanish are at a distinct disadvantage when trying to explain their version of the event. Three steps may help the foreigner who doesn't wish to do as the Mexicans do: If you were in your own car, notify your Mexican insurance company, whose job it is to intervene on your behalf. If you were in a rental car, notify the rental company immediately and ask how to contact the nearest adjuster. (You

See Baja by Boat: Cruising the Sea of Cortez

John Steinbeck made this journey famous, recording his observations and philosophies on a 2,500km (4,000-mile) expedition during which he collected marine specimens in the 1951 classic *The Log from the Sea of Cortez*. These days, a few companies offer small-ship cruises that leave from Los Cabos, La Paz, or Loreto and cruise around the Gulf of California for several days, an ideal way to sample the best of Baja. Any travel agent can price or book Sea of Cortez cruises.

Some of my favorite cruises can be found through **Lindblad Expeditions** (© 800/397-3348 in the U.S.; www.expeditions.com) and **Cruise West** (© 800/888-9378 or 206/441-8687 in the U.S.; fax 206/441-4757; www.cruisewest.com). Both offer multiple voyages that explore the interior Baja coast. Lindblad offers 8- to 14-day trips that explore the migrating whales and the relationship between the desert and the sea. Along the way, the ships pull into small, pristine coves where passengers can participate in nature walks, hiking, snorkeling, diving, and kayaking. Both companies include expert guides that bring together history, science, storytelling, and experience for cruisers. Small ships allow for easy maneuverability and an intimate experience; and they have all the trimmings of a luxury cruise. Prices for both Cruise West and Lindblad expeditions range from $3,490 to $7,430 per person (based on double occupancy) for a 7- to 14-day cruise; all meals and activities are included. Cruise West is oriented toward a slightly older passenger and Lindblad Expeditions caters to everyone: singles, families, and seniors. In both, there's an exceptional educational orientation aimed at learning about the areas explored, especially the regional flora and fauna. Photography-themed cruises also are available on both.

did buy insurance with the rental, right?) Finally, if all else fails, ask to contact the nearest Green Angel, who may be able to explain to officials that you are covered by insurance. See also "Mexican Auto Insurance" in "Getting There," earlier in this chapter.

CAR RENTALS You'll get the best price if you reserve a car at least a week in advance in the United States, and, unless you're renting a jeep, all companies offer automatic cars rather than manual transmissions (stick shifts). U.S. car-rental firms include **Advantage** (© 800/777-5500 in the U.S. and Canada; www.advantagerentacar.com); **Avis** (© 800/331-1084 in the U.S. and Canada; www.

avis.com), **Budget** (© 800/527-0700 in the U.S. and Canada; www.budget.com); **Budget Baja,** Baja's own service-oriented franchise with locations throughout Southern Baja (www.budgetbaja.com); **Hertz** (© 800/654-3131 in the U.S. and Canada; www.hertz.com); **National** (© 800/227-7368 in the U.S. and Canada; www.nationalcar.com); and **Thrifty** (© 800/367-2277 in the U.S. and Canada; www.thrifty.com), which often offers discounts for rentals in Mexico. For European travelers, **Kemwel Holiday Auto** (© 800/678-0678; www.kemwell.com) can arrange Mexican rentals, sometimes through other agencies, in Cabo San Lucas, La Paz, and

Tijuana. Kemwel, **Auto Europe** (888/ 223-5555; www.autoeurope.com), and some local firms have offices in Mexico City and most other large Mexican cities. You'll find rental desks at airports, all major hotels, and many travel agencies.

Cars are easy to rent if you are 21 or over and have a major credit card, valid driver's license, and passport with you. Without a credit card, you must leave a cash deposit, usually a big one. One-way rentals are usually simple to arrange but more costly.

NAVIGATING BAJA This long-and-skinny peninsula is surprisingly easy to navigate. Highway 1, or Carretera Transpeninsular, is the highway linking all major destinations in Baja—especially in Southern Baja. In Northern Baja, Highway 3 and Highway 5 are useful for getting around San Felipe, Tecate, and Ensenada; and Highway 19 takes you from Cabo San Lucas to Todos Santos in the South. Road signs are helpful and up-to-date throughout the peninsula, making it easy—if you stay on the highways—not to get lost on the many dirt roads that snake through the desert. You may encounter a military checkpoint or two if you're traveling any great lengths in Baja. Although it looks threatening (read: the checkpoints are staffed with stern 16-year-olds holding M-16s), military checkpoints are standard procedure, so let the uniformed soldiers inspect your car for drugs or agricultural products if requested, and then be on your merry way.

Be prepared for border-crossing delays of at least 45 minutes when you're heading back into the United States, and avoid crossing on a Friday afternoon, as the lines are longer then.

If you're not up to driving from destination to destination, **Aereo Calafia** (© **624/143-4302;** www.aereocalafia. com.mx) offers flights between Cabo San Lucas, La Paz, and Loreto.

BY TAXI

Taxis are the preferred way to get around in almost all the resort areas of Mexico, with the exception of Los Cabos, which is fairly spread out, and taxis are very expensive. One-way travel between Cabo San Lucas and San José del Cabo averages $40. Short trips within towns are generally charged by preset zones and are quite reasonable compared with U.S. rates. For longer trips or excursions to nearby cities, taxis can generally be hired for around $10 to $15 per hour, or for a negotiated daily rate, but it's better to find a tour operator who can offer the same price, plus a guide, water, and sometimes a meal or snack. Even drops to different destinations can be arranged. A negotiated one-way price may be much less than the cost of a rental car for a day, and service is much faster than travel by bus. For anyone who is uncomfortable driving in Mexico, this is a convenient, comfortable alternative. A bonus is that you have a Spanish-speaking person with you in case you run into any car or road trouble. Many taxi drivers speak at least some English. Your hotel can assist you with the arrangements.

BY TRAIN

Train travel is mostly unavailable in Baja, save for a rail excursion that leaves Saturday mornings and evenings from San Diego to Tecate, where brewery tours, lunch on your own, and exploration await. Organized by the **Pacific Southwest Railway Museum,** tickets cost $43 for adults and $23 for kids, and may be booked at © **619/478-9937** or **www. sdrm.org.** Dates fill up quickly, so book in advance.

BY BUS

Bus service is not as well developed in the Baja peninsula as in other parts of the country, although it is available between principal points. Travel class is generally labeled *segunda* (second), *primera* (first), and *ejecutiva* (deluxe). The deluxe buses often have fewer seats than regular buses, show movies en route, are air-conditioned, have bathrooms, and make few stops; some have complimentary refreshments.

Many run express from origin to the final destination. They are well worth the few dollars more that you'll pay. In rural areas, buses are often of the school-bus variety, with lots of local color.

15 Tips on Accommodations

Baja is a generous host offering all kinds of accommodations, from basic and comfortable to lush and luxurious, at all prices, from rock-bottom to sky-high.

MEXICO'S HOTEL RATING SYSTEM

The hotel rating system in Mexico is called "Stars and Diamonds." Hotels may qualify to earn one to five stars, or five diamonds. Many hotels that have excellent standards are not certified, but all rated hotels adhere to strict standards. The guidelines relate to service, facilities, and hygiene more than to prices.

Five-diamond hotels meet the highest requirements for rating: The beds are comfortable, bathrooms are in excellent working order, all facilities are renovated regularly, infrastructure is top-tier, and services and hygiene meet the highest international standards.

Five-star hotels usually offer similar quality, but with lower levels of service and detail in the rooms. For example, a five-star hotel may have less luxurious linens or room service during limited hours rather than 24 hours.

Four-star hotels are less expensive and more basic, but they still guarantee

cleanliness and basic services such as hot water and purified drinking water. Three-, two-, and one-star hotels are at least working to adhere to certain standards: Bathrooms are cleaned and linens are washed daily, and you can expect a minimum standard of service. Two- and one-star hotels generally provide bottled water rather than purified water.

The nonprofit organization Calidad Mexicana Certificada, A.C., known as **Calmecac** (www.calmecac.com.mx), is responsible for hotel ratings.

HOTEL CHAINS

In addition to the major international chains, you'll run across a number of less-familiar brands as you plan your trip to Mexico. They include:

- **Fiesta Americana** and **Fiesta Inn** (www.posadas.com). Part of the Mexican-owned Grupo Posadas company, these hotels set the country's midrange standard for facilities and services. They generally offer comfortable, spacious rooms and traditional Mexican hospitality. Fiesta Americana hotels offer excellent beach-resort packages. Fiesta Inn hotels are usually more business oriented. Baja's offerings

---

Finds Out-of-the-Ordinary Places to Stay

Mexico lends itself beautifully to the concept of small, private hotels in idyllic settings. They vary in style from grandiose estate to palm-thatched bungalow. **Mexico Boutique Hotels** (www.MexicoBoutiqueHotels.com) specializes in smaller places to stay with a high level of personal attention and service. Most options have less than 50 rooms, and the accommodations consist of entire villas, *casitas,* bungalows, or a combination. At press time, Baja's only Mexico Boutique Hotel offering is Casa Natalia in Los Cabos.

> **_Tips_ House-Swapping & Vacation Rentals**
>
> House-swapping is becoming a more popular and viable means of travel; you stay in their place, they stay in yours, and you both get a more authentic and personal view of a destination, the opposite of the escapist retreat many hotels offer. Try **HomeLink International** (www.homelink.org), the oldest home-swapping organization, founded in 1952, with more than 13,000 listings worldwide ($75 yearly membership). **HomeExchange.com** ($99.95 for over 17,000 listings) and **InterVac.com** ($68.88 for over 10,000 listings) are also reliable.
>
> To get the house without the swap, try the reputable **Vacation Rentals By Owner** website **www.vrbo.com/vacation-rentals/mexico**. In Los Cabos and the East Cape, look to the reputable **Earth, Sea & Sky Vacations** (© 800/745-2226; www.cabovillas.com) for the widest and best variety of rental accommodations.

include Fiesta Americana Los Cabos, the Fiesta Inn in La Paz, Fiesta Inn Mexicali, Fiesta Inn Tijuana, and the Fiesta Inn Tijuana Otay Aeropuerto.

- **Hoteles Camino Real** (www.camino real.com). The premier Mexican hotel chain, Camino Real maintains a high standard of service at its properties. Its beach hotels are traditionally on the best beaches in the area. This chain also focuses on the business market. The hotels are famous for their vivid and contrasting colors. The only Camino Real hotel in Baja is the Camino Real Tijuana.
- **Mayan Resorts** (www.mayanresorts. com.mx). One of Mexico's newest hospitality dynamos is driving some of Mexico's most well done and affordable master-planned resort communities. Mayan Resorts projects usually include a large-scale resort, ownership options ranging from fractional condominiums to full-ownership homes, a commercial center, and one or more championship golf courses. A new Mayan Palace Resort

is under construction in San José del Cabo and another property is rumored to be breaking ground on Baja's East Cape.

SURFING FOR HOTELS

In addition to the online travel-booking sites **Travelocity, Expedia, Orbitz, Priceline,** and **Hotwire,** you can book hotels through **Hotels.com, Quikbook** (www.quikbook.com), and **Travelaxe** (www.travelaxe.net).

Nonetheless, some of the hotel chains—especially in Los Cabos—have a best-rate guarantee on their website, so be sure to check the hotel's individual website before booking on a travel site.

HotelChatter.com is a daily webzine offering smart coverage and critiques of hotels worldwide. Go to **TripAdvisor. com** or **HotelShark.com** for helpful independent consumer reviews of hotels and resort properties.

It's a good idea to **get a confirmation number** and **make a printout** of any online booking transaction.

16 Etiquette & Customs

APPROPRIATE ATTIRE

Baja is one of the more casual corners of Mexico. In resort areas—remote and well traveled—pretty much anything goes. By

day, flip-flops and shorts (for men) or skirts, shorts, and sundresses (for women) are standard apparel for locals and tourists alike. If you want to blend in with the local crowd of Los Cabos, La Paz, Ensenada, and Tijuana by night, trousers and knit shirts (for men) and dresses, skirts, or trousers with heels, pumps, nice sandals, or wedges (for women) will show the right amount of respect for the dining establishment or nightclub you choose. The rest of the beach resorts are 24/7 flip-flop-and-shorts land. That said, plenty of female tourists think it's okay to cruise town in their bikini top and a sarong, and for every such woman, there's a shirtless man toting a six-pack of beer and a sunburn. In the ever-proper country of Mexico, please cover up, keep your beer in the bars, and be respectful of the town you're exploring.

GESTURES

Some gringos think it appropriate to kiss the cheek of everyone they meet in Mexico, but this happens only when you're meeting a friend of a friend, not your fishing-boat captain, an employee, the housekeeper, the gardener, the timeshare salesperson, or a new business associate. Friend-to-friend kisses occur between man and woman and woman and woman, but men always shake hands with new acquaintances. Do expect Mexicans to stand a little closer to you than your non-Latin friends; they have a much different definition of personal space than gringos do.

AVOIDING OFFENSE

Mexico social interactions are founded on extreme politeness and a complex web of social considerations that incorporate respect and prevention of shame. In fact, saying so much as "I need to leave" after an hour-long lunch may be deemed an insult to your dining companion. (It's better to say something like, "shall we go?" or the like.) Outright negativity is rare and offensive, so you'll rarely hear the word "no" from a Mexican, especially in laid-back Baja, and you will come across

as abrasive if you use it very often. Most importantly, if you're negotiating a difficult situation, never get angry. Stay as patient as possible and keep the ball in play. No matter how dire the situation seems, there's almost always a way for you to get what you want if you remain polite, courteous, and persistent in a non-confrontational way.

EATING & DRINKING

If you want to eat and drink like a local in Baja, breakfast in the morning is whenever you have time, lunch is around 2 or 3pm, coffee with friends substitutes for happy hour, dinner starts between 8 and 10pm, the nightlife kicks off around 11pm, and tacos are there to refuel after dancing and to continue the evening with friends—not to help "soak up the alcohol" before you head home. On the whole, it is shameful to appear drunk if you're Mexican, and the drinking-equals-partying attitude is a behavior brought to Mexico by gringos, not the other way around. That's not to say the alcohol doesn't flow at dinner parties and clubs, but Mexicans are much more modest about the process than most non-Latin cultures. So, if you can, try to avoid saying things like, "Dude, I am so wasted!" and drinking so much you think it's a good idea to stand on a cocktail table and try to dance like a stripper.

If you've been invited to someone's house for *la comida* (lunch, turned into a social event on a Sunday) dinner, it's considered polite to bring a bottle of wine or alcohol, but be sure you double-check with your host the actual arrival time; I often ask my friends if they mean "Gringo Time" or "Mexican Time." For example, in Baja, an 8pm dinner invitation means an 8:15pm arrival on Gringo Time and a 9pm arrival on Mexican time—at the earliest. If you're not sure, just ask your host. Once you're there, be prepared for a long cocktail hour followed by an even longer, lingering meal that takes you into the wee hours. There is never the slightest rush when dining at someone's home, so plan to stay a while and give yourself up to the *sobremesa* (conversation around the table long after the meal, usually accompanied by a bottle of wine or a little tequila).

FAST FACTS: Baja California

Abbreviations Dept. (apartments); Apdo. Postal (post office box); Av. (*Avenida;* avenue); c. (*calle;* street); Calz. (*Calzada;* boulevard). C on faucets stands for *caliente* (hot), F for *fría* (cold). PB *(planta baja)* means ground floor; most buildings count the next floor up as the first floor (1).

American Express There are American Express Travel offices in the following destinations: **Los Cabos** (© 624/142-1306; Plaza La Misión at Mijares and Paseo Finisterra, San José del Cabo, B.C.S., Mexico); **La Paz** at Viajes Perla (© **612/122-8666;** 5 de Mayo 170, B.C.S., Mexico); **Ensenada** at Damiana Viajes (© **646/174-0170;** Calle 2a no. 300-4 at corner of Obregón, Ensenada, B.C., Mexico); and **Mexicali** at KL Internacional (© **686/554-1200;** Justo Sierra and Zaragoza Sur 2089, Mexicali, B.C., Mexico).

Area Codes Tijuana, 664; Rosarito Beach, 661; Ensenada, 646; Mulegé and Santa Rosalía, 615; Loreto, 613; La Paz, 612; Todos Santos, 612; Los Cabos and East Cape, 624.

ATM Networks See "Money & Costs," p. 21.

Business Hours In general, businesses in larger cities are open between 9am and 7pm; in smaller towns many close between 2 and 4pm. Most close on Sunday. In resort areas it is common to find stores open at least in the mornings on Sunday, and for shops to stay open late, often until 8pm or even 10pm. Bank hours are Monday through Friday from 9 or 9:30am to anywhere between 3 and 7pm. Increasingly, banks open on Saturday for at least a half-day.

Currency See "Money & Costs," p. 21.

Drugstores Farmacias will sell you just about anything you want, with a prescription or without one. Most drugstores are open Monday through Saturday from 8am to 8pm. Generally, the major resort areas have one or two 24-hour pharmacies. If you are in a smaller town and need to buy medicine after normal hours, ask for the name of the nearest 24-hour pharmacy; they are becoming more common.

Electricity The electrical system in Mexico is 110 volts AC (60 cycles), as in the United States and Canada. In reality, however, it may cycle more slowly and overheat your appliances. To compensate, select a medium or low speed on hair dryers and bring a surge protector for your laptop. Many older hotels still have electrical outlets for flat two-prong plugs; you'll need an adapter for any plug with an enlarged end on one prong or with three prongs. Many better hotels have three-hole outlets (*trifásicos* in Spanish) and only a fraction of Baja's most budget hotels may require you to bring your own adapter.

Embassies & Consulates They provide valuable lists of doctors and lawyers, as well as regulations concerning marriages in Mexico. Contrary to popular belief, your embassy cannot get you out of a Mexican jail, provide postal or banking services, or fly you home when you run out of money. Consular officers can provide you with advice on most matters and problems, however. Unless otherwise noted, all embassies listed here are in Mexico City. Try the **Embassy of Australia** (© 55/1101-2200); the **Embassy of Canada** (© 624/142-4333 consulate office in San José del Cabo; 664/684-0461 in Tijuana; www.canada.org.mx); the **Embassy of New Zealand** (© 55/5283-9460; kiwimexico@compuserve.com.mx); the **Embassy of the United Kingdom** (© 555/242-8500; www.embajadabritanica. com.mx); and the **Embassy of Ireland** (© 55/5520-5803). The **Embassy of the United States** in Mexico City is at Paseo de la Reforma 305, next to the Hotel María Isabel Sheraton at the corner of Río Danubio (© 55/5080-2000 or 55/5511-9980). Visit **www.usembassy-mexico.gov** for a list of U.S. consulates in Mexico. There is a **U.S. Consulate General** in Tijuana, at Tapachula 96 (© 664/622-7400), and a consular agency in Cabo San Lucas (© 624/143-3566).

Emergencies In case of a tourist emergency, dial 065 from any phone within Mexico. No coin is needed. For police emergency numbers, call 066 or turn to "Fast Facts" in the chapters that follow. You should also contact the closest consular office in case of an emergency.

Holidays Independence Day (September 15 and 16), Christmas (December 25), Easter, and Three Kings Day (January 6) are the biggest holidays celebrated throughout all of Baja, and mainland Mexico aficionados may be surprised to find it devoid of the pomp and circumstance surrounding some of these holidays on the mainland. The only time of year that may outdo the mainland is Spring Break in Los Cabos, San Felipe, Ensenada, and Rosarito Beach. For more information on holidays, see "Calendar of Events," earlier in this chapter.

Hospitals Every embassy and consulate is prepared to recommend local doctors and dentists with good training and modern equipment; some of the doctors and dentists speak English. See the list of embassies and consulates under "Embassies & Consulates," above. Hotels with a large foreign clientele can often recommend English-speaking doctors. Almost all first-class hotels in Mexico have a doctor on site or on call. For detailed information on medical care in your destination, see the Fast Facts section of each chapter.

Hot Lines The tourist assistance hot line is 065.

Internet Access In large cities and resort areas, a growing number of top hotels offer business centers with Internet access. You'll also find cybercafes in destinations that are popular with expats and business travelers. Even in remote spots, Internet access is common, although that's less true in Baja than on the mainland.

Language English is widely spoken throughout Baja, and most of all in the border towns and Los Cabos. In situations where communication doesn't flow as smoothly, consult the Spanish glossary on p. 203.

Laundromats You will find Laundromats, or *lavanderías,* speckling the downtown area of most towns in Baja. If you'd like to leave something to be dry-cleaned, be sure to specify that the item needs the *tintorería* so it doesn't get washed in water and ironed, like everything else.

Liquor & Drug Laws To be blunt, don't use or possess illegal drugs in Mexico. Mexican officials have no tolerance for drug users, and jail is their solution, with little hope of getting out until the sentence (usually a long one) is completed or heavy fines or bribes are paid. Remember, in Mexico the legal system assumes you are guilty until proven innocent. *Important note:* It isn't uncommon to be befriended by a fellow user, only to be turned in by that "friend," who's collected a bounty. Bring prescription drugs in their original containers. If possible, pack a copy of the original prescription with the generic name of the drug.

U.S. Customs officials are also on the lookout for diet drugs sold in Mexico but illegal in the U.S., possession of which could land you in a U.S. jail. If you buy antibiotics over the counter (which you can do in Mexico) and still have some left, you probably won't be hassled by U.S. Customs.

The legal drinking age in Mexico is 18; however, asking for ID or denying purchase is extremely rare. Grocery stores sell everything from beer and wine to national and imported liquors. You can buy liquor 24 hours a day, but during major elections, dry laws are enacted for as much as 72 hours in advance of the election—and they apply to tourists as well as local residents, so plan ahead if needed. Mexico does not have laws that apply to transporting liquor in cars, but authorities are beginning to target drunk drivers more aggressively. It's a good idea to drive defensively and never after you've been drinking.

Although it is not legal to drink in the street, many tourists do so. Use your judgment—if you are getting drunk, you shouldn't drink in the street, because you are more likely to get stopped by the police. As is the custom in Mexico, it is not so much what you do, but how you do it.

Lost & Found To replace a **lost passport,** contact your embassy or nearest consular agent. You must establish a record of your citizenship and fill out a form requesting another FMT (tourist permit) if it, too, was lost. If your documents are stolen, get a police report from local authorities; having one *might* lessen the hassle of exiting the country without all your identification. Without the FMT, you can't leave the country, and without an affidavit affirming your passport request and citizenship, you may have problems at U.S. Customs when you get home. It's important to clear everything up *before* trying to leave. Mexican Customs may, however, accept the police report of the loss of the FMT and allow you to leave.

If you lose your **wallet** anywhere outside of Mexico City, before panicking, retrace your steps—you'll be surprised at how honest people are, and you'll likely find someone trying to find you to return your wallet.

Be sure to tell all of your credit card companies the minute you discover your wallet has been lost or stolen and file a report at the nearest police precinct. Your credit card company or insurer may require a police report number or record of the loss. Most credit card companies have an emergency toll-free number to call if your card is lost or stolen; they may be able to wire you a cash advance immediately or deliver an emergency credit card in a day or two. **Visa** cardholders who lose their card traveling in Mexico and wish to cancel may call Mexico's toll-free number, ⓒ **001-800-847-2911; American Express** customers may call collect at ⓒ **336/393-1111;** and **MasterCard** customers may call the toll-free number in Mexico, ⓒ **001-800-307-7309,** to report a missing or stolen card.

If you need emergency cash over the weekend when all banks and American Express offices are closed, you can have money wired to you via **Western Union** (ⓒ **800/325-6000;** www.westernunion.com).

Mail The Mexican postal service is not the most reliable, especially when sending something important, so it's usually best to send mail through DHL, FedEx, or the UPS Store. A postcard through the *Correo* (Mexico mail) costs about 10¢, or $2 through the UPS store. Packages vary depending on the destination, weight, and service you select.

Newspapers & Magazines In southern Baja, a number of local English-language papers are available at newsstands in all the places tourists frequent, including *Los Cabos Guide* (www.loscabosguide.com), *Los Cabos News, Destino Los Cabos,* and the irreverent, entertaining *Gringo Gazette* (www.gringo gazette.com), which has Southern Baja and Northern Baja editions. *The Baja Real Estate Guide* (www.tregintl.com) is the ultimate literature for the traveler who's fallen in love with Southern Baja and wants to own a piece of it. There's also a magazine of the same name in northern Baja.

Passports Allow plenty of time before your trip to apply for a passport; processing now takes 8 to 10 weeks but can take longer during busy periods (especially spring). And keep in mind that if you need a passport in a hurry, you'll pay a higher processing fee.

For Residents of Australia: You can pick up an application from your local post office or any branch of Passports Australia, but you must schedule an interview at the passport office to present your application materials. Call the **Australian Passport Information Service** at ⓒ **131-232,** or visit the government website at **www.passports.gov.au.**

For Residents of Canada: Passport applications are available at travel agencies throughout Canada or from the central **Passport Office,** Department of Foreign Affairs and International Trade, Ottawa, ON K1A 0G3 (ⓒ **800/567-6868;** www.ppt.gc.ca).

For Residents of Ireland: You can apply for a 10-year passport at the **Passport Office,** Setanta Centre, Molesworth Street, Dublin 2 (ⓒ **01/671-1633;** www.irl gov.ie/iveagh). Those under age 18 and over 65 must apply for a 3-year passport. You can also apply at 1A South Mall, Cork (ⓒ **021/272-525**) or at most main post offices.

For Residents of New Zealand: You can pick up a passport application at any New Zealand Passports Office or download it from their website. Contact the **Passports Office** at ⓒ **0800/225-050** in New Zealand or 04/474-8100, or log on to **www.passports.govt.nz.**

For Residents of the United Kingdom: To pick up an application for a standard 10-year passport (5-yr. passport for children under 16), visit your nearest passport office, major post office, or travel agency or contact the **United Kingdom Passport Service** at ⓒ **0870/521-0410** (www.ukpa.gov.uk).

For Residents of the United States: Whether you're applying in person or by mail, you can download passport applications from the U.S. Department of

State website at **http://travel.state.gov**. To find your regional passport office, either check the U.S. Department of State website or call the **National Passport Information Center** toll-free number (© **877/487-2778**) for automated information.

Police The emergency telephone number throughout Mexico is © 066.

Restrooms Public toilets are not common in Mexico, but an increasing number are available, especially at fast-food restaurants and Pemex gas stations. These facilities and restaurant and club restrooms commonly have attendants who expect a small tip (about 50¢). Although some bathrooms allow the disposal of paper in the basin, most of Baja's plumbing is not up to the task of processing toilet paper, so if you see a basket or trash can inside the stall, it is meant for the disposal of used paper. A good source is **www.thebathroomdiaries.com**, which surveys the globe's restrooms. At press time, only Tijuana had reviews in Baja, but check back as more may be forthcoming.

Smoking Most of Mexico is a free-for-all for smokers. Smoking is permitted and generally accepted in most public places, including restaurants, bars, and hotel lobbies. Nonsmoking areas and hotel rooms for nonsmokers are becoming more common in higher-end establishments, but they tend to be the exception rather than the rule.

Taxes There's a 15% IVA (*Impuesto al Valor Agregado*, or value-added tax, pronounced "ee-bah") on goods and services in most of Mexico, and it's supposed to be included in the posted price. This tax is 10% in Los Cabos; as a port of entry, the towns receive a break on taxes. There is a 5% tax on food and drinks consumed in restaurants that sell alcoholic beverages with an alcohol content of more than 10%; this tax applies whether you drink alcohol or not. Tequila is subject to a 25% tax. Hotels charge the usual 15% IVA, plus a locally administered bed tax of 2% (in many but not all areas), for a total of 17%. In Los Cabos, hotels charge the 10% IVA plus 2% room tax. Prices quoted by hotels and restaurants will not necessarily include IVA. You may find that upper-end properties quote prices without IVA included, while lower-priced hotels include IVA. Always ask to see a printed price sheet, and always ask if the tax is included. Mexico imposes an exit tax of around $18, which usually is applied to your ticket at purchase, on every foreigner leaving the country.

Time Zone The state of Baja California Norte—from Tijuana to Guerrero Negro—is on Pacific standard time, and Baja California Sur—from south of Guerrero Negro to Los Cabos—is on mountain standard time. Mexico observes daylight savings time. The rest of Mexico observes central standard time.

Tipping Most service employees in Mexico count on tips to make up the majority of their income—especially bellboys and waiters. Bellboys receive the equivalent of $1 per bag; waiters generally receive 15% to 20% of the bill, depending on the level of service. In Mexico, it is not customary to tip taxi drivers, unless they are hired by the hour or provide touring or other special services.

Water Most hotels have decanters or bottles of purified water in the rooms; the better hotels have either purified water from regular taps, or special taps marked *agua purificada*. Some hotels will charge for in-room bottled water. Virtually any hotel, restaurant, or bar will bring you purified water if you specifically request it, but you'll usually be charged for it. In Los Cabos, it's generally safe to drink resort tap water, but bottled is always safer. Bottled purified water is sold at drugstores and grocery stores (popular brands include Santa María, Ciel, and Bonafont). Evian and other imported brands are also widely available. For more information on drinking water in Baja, see "Health" and "Safety" earlier in the chapter.

3

Suggested Los Cabos & Baja Itineraries

The vast majority of travelers to Baja either park themselves in lively Los Cabos or experiences a brief border visit to the temptations of Tijuana. However, the peninsula offers much more, and it's easy to combine several of its attractive destinations into a single visit. Most of the suggested itineraries described below combine some resort-style relaxation with explorations of the natural treasures of Baja, sampling some small-town Mexican life along the way. Note that it is now possible to enter through one airport and leave through another without having to pay extra in many cases. For explorations in northern Baja, you may choose to fly directly into Tijuana or to San Diego, crossing the border via one of the regular shuttle buses or in a car.

Unlike the rest of Mexico, Baja does not have regular bus service between the major towns. You'll either need to drive—rental cars are widely available—or participate in an organized tour with a chartered bus, though I personally wouldn't choose this option, as there's less flexibility to linger in places you're enjoying. In many areas, a four-wheel-drive vehicle, or one that sits higher up, such as an SUV, are the best bets—it's still a rugged landscape here.

None of the following itineraries can be called exhaustive explorations of Baja, but neither are they exhausting. Consider them as a sampler of the best of Baja, so that upon a return visit you'll know more about where you'd like to concentrate your time.

1 Northern Baja in 6 Days

This trip takes you to Mexico's most infamous town, Tijuana, and then down the coast to sample more authentic Baja. The early part of this journey takes in a few kitschy sites—consider it a sampling of the singular Mexican vision of magic realism—then on to some lovely places that will give you an appreciation of the natural beauty and range of experiences available here. The area that this itinerary covers is relatively compact, not requiring a lot of travel time, but you should cater the trip to suit your needs, spending more time in the places you like best. For example, not listed below is the magical **San Felipe** (p. 181), which is a 6-hour drive from San Diego. Depending on your mission, the laid-back nature of this town may inspire you to speed through the rest of Northern Baja in lieu of spending a long weekend drenched in sun and sand, peace and quiet, and fish tacos and cerveza. The choice is yours.

Day ❶: Arrive in Tijuana

Although most people equate Tijuana with **Avenida Revolución,** there is truly a wealth of places to visit here, which you can choose between depending upon your preferences—the Centro Cultural Tijuana, watching a bullfight, and shopping are a few of the favored activities. If you're traveling with children, a visit to the **Mundo Divertido La Mesa** amusement center (p. 154) will be highly appreciated. I recommend a stop at the **Museo de Cera** (Wax Museum; p. 153) or a generous sampling of Baja's wines at the **Cava de Vinos L.A. Cetto** (L.A. Cetto Winery; p. 154). Your evening here should be dedicated to taking in the color and revelry of **Avenida Revolución** (p. 153) so you can truly say you've been to Tijuana.

Day ❷: Rosarito Beach

Drive just 20 minutes (29km/18 miles) south of Tijuana and you'll find a complete departure in ambience as you start to relax into the beauty of this area. The drive itself on a wide, modern coastal highway is lovely. Stop for a break at the **Rosarito Beach Hotel** (p. 165), which attracted scores of celebrities and other notables during the later days of Prohibition. Then continue on a few miles south of Rosarito proper to Fox Studios' **Fox-ploration!** (p. 163), a cinema-themed museum and entertainment center. You can lose yourself for hours in the interactive exhibits, but the main event remains the Titanic Expo. When you're finished, head back to Rosarito Beach for the evening, where enjoying a sunset cerveza at **Papas & Beer** (p. 166) on the beach is de rigueur.

Days ❸ & ❹: Exploring Ensenada

Driving south from Rosarito, choose the toll road for efficiency or the local-access road that parallels it for more local color as you head south toward Ensenada. Don't miss a stop in **Puerto Nuevo** for a sampling of the local lobster. After passing the La Fonda resort, be sure to get back on the toll road, because the old road veers inland. Eighteen kilometers (11 miles) from here, stop off at **El Mirador** to admire the dramatic coastal views, and if you dare to look straight down, take a gander at the collection of cars that lie on the rocks at the bottom. A few miles beyond the lookout point is Salsipuedes Bay, and 24km (15 miles) beyond this you'll arrive in Ensenada. If you arrive early enough, spend the afternoon exploring this classic town so the next day can be free for fishing, kayaking, surfing, or a visit to either of the two national parks, the **Parque Nacional Constitución de 1857** (p. 170) or the **Parque Nacional Sierra San Pedro Mártir** (p. 170). At some point, you'll want to be sure to visit the **La Bufadora** sea spout (p. 168). For an unforgettable meal in Ensenada, dine at **La Embotelladora Vieja** (p. 174) at the Bodegas de Santo Tomás Winery—it will prepare you for what's on the agenda for the next day. For a more casual good time, you have your choice of **Hussong's Cantina** (p. 176) or the Ensenada location of **Papas & Beer** (p. 176), both institutions of the partying crowd.

Day ❺: Valle de Guadalupe (Mexico's Wine Country)

With 1 day to spend here, you'll only get a small (but sufficient) survey of Mexico's wine country. I'd start with a visit to the **Museo Comunitario del Valle de Guadalupe** (p. 178) and the **Museo Histórico Comunitario** (p. 178), just across the street, to gain an appreciation of the odd history of this region. They're both quite small, so this won't take much time. Then choose two to three vineyards to visit to partake in wine tastings. My preferred wineries are the boutique **Monte Xanic** (p. 179), **Chateau Camou** (p. 179), and **Mogor Badan** (p. 179), but you may enjoy visiting one of the larger establishments at **L.A. Cetto** (p. 179) or **Domecq** (p. 179). Highly recommended

Suggested Los Cabos & Baja Itineraries

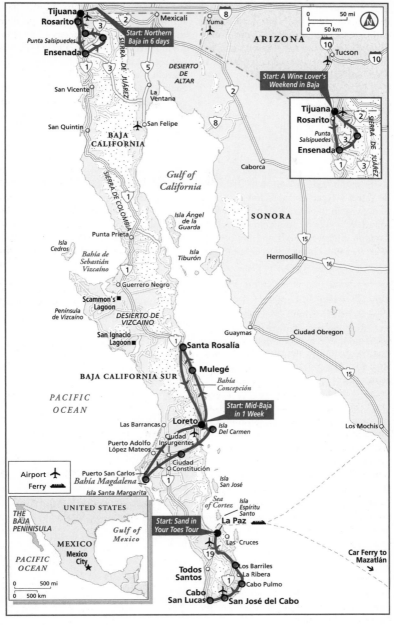

is a stop for lunch (reservations recommended) at **Laja** (p. 180). Just driving through this exquisite and easily navigable valley is a pleasure. I would also recommend staying the evening here, at **La Villa del Valle** (p. 180).

Day ❻: Bajamar & Return to Tijuana

On your way back up the coast, stop in at either **Bajamar** (32km/20 miles north of Ensenada) or **Real del Mar** (16km/10 miles south of Tijuana; p. 160) to play a round of golf or relax with a spa treatment. You may choose to spend your last night at either of these places, which offer "Americanized" accommodations. Alternatively, head back to Tijuana for one final evening of its seductive charms. And, if you bypassed the Puerto Nuevo lobsters on the way down the coast, don't miss them on the return trip.

2 Mid-Baja in 1 Week

This trip is especially appealing for those who prefer their travels with a generous dose of activity in the mix. Tour of the peninsula's oldest and most impressive missions followed by a visit to the painted caves of La Trinidad. Then commune with nature at Loreto's offshore islands and the Sea of Cortez. Finally, catch a glimpse of the Wild West in a quick road trip to Mulegé and Santa Rosalía. Great food and awe-inspiring views are around every corner.

Day ❶: Arrive in Loreto

Upon arrival in Loreto, you'll want to take the afternoon to explore this small, lovely town and stop in the **Misión Nuestra Señora de Loreto** (p. 125), the first mission established in Baja, dating back to 1699, and in the **Museo de las Misiones,** which is next door. The town is remarkably easy to navigate, with one main road that runs parallel to the waterfront boardwalk. Most attractions are near the central square and old mission, but take the time to walk the short pedestrian-only length of Salvatierra to look at the wood homes that date back to the 1800s. For your first evening in town, I'd recommend dinner at **Pachamama,** an Argentinean restaurant on Zapata (p. 131).

Day ❷: Isla del Carmen

You'll need to arrange this trip through one of Loreto's tour companies, but plan on an enchanting day of kayaking, snorkeling, or hiking at Isla del Carmen, the largest of Loreto's offshore islands. Even if your preference is for water-bound activities, it would be a shame to miss a walk or nap on the white-sand beaches of this or Coronado Island. See p. 123.

Day ❸: San Javier

Explore a bit of Baja's interior by visiting the **Misión San Francisco Javier** (p. 126), about 2 hours from Loreto along the old Camino Real dirt road. From here, if you're traveling with an authorized guide, you can stop to view some of the **indigenous cave paintings** (p. 126), or you may choose to combine your trip with a visit to **Primer Agua** for a picnic, swimming in the natural spring, or hiking the area. See p. 127.

Day ❹: Whale-Watching in Magdalena Bay (or Alternate Exploration)

Although **Magdalena Bay** is on the opposite side of the peninsula (on the Pacific Coast), it's an easy trip and, once there, you can board a skiff and spend a few hours watching the gray whales that migrate to this area in large numbers. It's a remarkable sight (p. 146). If you're traveling in months other than December to May, however, the whales won't be there, so you'll need to plan an alternate activity, perhaps a round of tennis or golf. For the truly adventurous, I'd pick the challenging 12-hour trip offered by C&C Tours to the foothills of the Guadalupe Mountains, where you'll hike over mountain, stream, and valley to view the mystical cave paintings (p. 125).

Day ❺: Kayaking, Fishing, or More Island Explorations

Use this day to explore more of what Loreto has to offer, whether it is offshore fishing, kayaking, snorkeling, diving, hiking, or horseback riding. Loreto also is the ideal place to relax with your favorite beverage and get a feel for the intriguing expatriate culture.

Day ❻: Mulegé & Santa Rosalía

Although Mulegé is closer to Loreto, I'd recommend driving to Santa Rosalía first and stopping in Mulegé on your return trip. Santa Rosalía is 61km (38 miles) north of Loreto. The main reason to visit Santa Rosalía is to view its historical sites of interest, including the Gustave Eiffel–designed **Iglesia de Santa Barbara** (p. 143) and the **Museo Histórico Minero de Santa Rosalía** (p. 143). However, I would argue that the number-one attraction is the **El Boleo** bakery (p. 142). If you prefer activities to sightseeing and the South Beach Diet to a carb wonderland, you may want to forego Santa Rosalía and concentrate your time in Mulegé instead, where you can visit, with a guide, the series of caves in **La Trinidad,** a remote ranch 29km (18 miles) west of Mulegé (p. 137), or at **San Borjitas** (p. 137). Literally an oasis in the desert, Mulegé is a small, slightly rundown town with a large English-speaking community, but beyond the **Misión Santa Rosalía de Mulegé** and the **Museo Regional de Historía** (p. 138 and 139 respectively), the town itself doesn't offer much in the way of sightseeing. Time spent here generally revolves around visiting its lovely surrounding beaches or indulging in the famed Mulegé pig roast. The return trip from Mulegé to Loreto is 137km (85 miles), taking about an 1½ hours.

Day ❼: Departing Loreto

Use your final day to relax, or, if it's your pleasure, play a round of golf at the **Campo de Golf Loreto** (p. 122) or tennis at the **Centro Tenístico Loreto** (p. 122). The **Inn at Loreto Bay** (p. 129) also has a full-service spa, so a body treatment may be just the thing to cap your stay.

3 Southern Baja in 1 Week: A Sand-in-Your-Toes Tour

Baja's most popular areas are, of course, the twin towns at its tip, San José del Cabo and Cabo San Lucas—but if the only sound you want to hear is waves rolling in, this is the trip for you. Pacific-side beaches can be a little rough, so unless you're a surfer, stick to the Sea of Cortez (which resembles a Corona commercial). Outside of Médano Beach in Cabo, it's a good idea to pack a cooler because you won't find food vendors elsewhere. And feel free to take that unmarked dirt road that squiggles toward the shoreline and beckons you from the highway; just make sure you have four-wheel drive before even thinking about exploring.

Day ❶: La Paz

No B.C.S. beaches are more pristine than those in La Paz. Even better are the Caribbean-like coves of Isla Espíritu Santo. Book a kayaking, scuba, or freediving tour to the island's surrounding waters, rest a spell on the sugary sand, and take plenty of time to enjoy the colors above and below the water's surface. See p. 103.

Spring Break Revisited: 3 Days in Cabo San Lucas

For those who missed out on Spring Breaks of old, Cabo San Lucas is an eager hostess for partiers of any age. Book a long weekend at the **ME Cabo** resort (p. 86) on Médano Beach and the rest of your stay will unfold before you. The spring break schedule is simple: Sleep as late as you want, lounge by the **Nikki Beach** pool in the morning, lunch in the sun, sip fruity cocktails in the afternoon, then shower and get glam for the main event. Evenings start with a late dinner in San Lucas, drinks at a marina-front bar till 11pm, and dancing in a club till your stiletto-clad tootsies can't bear another step (flip-flops are welcome, too). Then back to the resort for low-key partying until first light or straight to bed to rest up for the next day.

Day ❷: Los Barriles

Drive south through the towns of San Bartolo and El Triunfo toward Los Barriles, where the beaches are breathtaking and fishing is life. A fishing excursion followed by an overnight here is a must, so book a night at **Palmas de Cortez** (p. 94) and they'll take care of the rest—be it a day of fishing, windsurfing, or diving.

Days ❸ & ❹: Cabo Pulmo

One day is not enough in this out-of-the-way paradise. Grab a mask and snorkel and swim out from the shore to explore the coral reef. Just before dusk, pull into Playa Los Arbolitos and take the cliff-side coastal hike to Playa La Iguana, where the setting sun adds a warm glow to one of the most beautiful—and private—coves in all of Baja. Sleep tight in one of **Cabo Pulmo Beach Resort**'s (p. 92) bungalows and rise early to hike, bike, or jog the desert trails before spending a day on—or in—the water of this protected marine park.

Days ❺ to ❼: Los Cabos

Follow Highway 1 to Los Cabos along a beautiful, hilly highway. No matter whether you stay in San José, the Corridor, or San Lucas, you'll no doubt explore all three areas. Devote a day to golf, if you're a golfer (p. 80). If not, indulge in one of the area's sumptuous spas or take a surf lesson on Playa Acapulquito with **Costa Azul Surf Shop** (p. 63). Be sure to spend an evening reveling in Cabo's nightlife, starting on the Cabo San Lucas Marina at sunset. A daytime cruise to **El Arco,** where you can see the famed rock formation and a sea-lion colony, and on to **Playa de Amor** is a singular Cabo experience. And, of course, don't forget just relaxing at the beach. **Médano Beach** is tops for eating, drinking, and watersports. See chapter 4.

4 A Wine Lover's Long Weekend in Baja

Admittedly, Mexico is not the first country to come to mind when thinking of wine, but the emerging wine country in Baja does make for a memorable exploration and a unique and easy trip from Southern California. You can also stay in Ensenada, but it's a winding 29km (18-mile) drive between Ensenada and the Valle de Guadalupe along Highway 3.

Day ❶: Tijuana to Ensenada

Cross the border into Mexico and make a stop in Tijuana for a generous sampling of Baja's wines at the **Cava de Vinos L.A. Cetto** (L.A. Cetto Winery; p. 154). Cava is big and commercial, but it will give you an introduction to what Mexican wines have traditionally been known for. The cork-covered building is certainly a sight to see in and of itself. When you're finished (making sure you're sober enough to drive), head down the coast to Ensenada, but not before enjoying a truly wonderful meal at **La Embotelladora Vieja** (p. 174) at the Bodegas de Santo Tomás winery, which crafts its menu to complement wines. Be sure to book a room in advance at **La Villa del Valle** (p. 180) if you want to truly immerse yourself in the majesty of the Valle de Guadalupe. You also can stay in Ensenada, but it's a winding 29km (18-mile) drive between Cabo San Lucas and San José del Cabo along Highway 3.

Days ❷ & ❸: Valle de Guadalupe

To orient yourself and ensure that you start your explorations with some knowledge of the area's unusual history, pay a visit to the **Museo Comunitario del Valle de Guadalupe** (p. 178) and the **Museo Histórico Comunitario** (p. 178). Fill the rest of your days with visits to the various wineries where you can view bottling processes and partake in tastings. My preference is to visit the smaller, boutique wineries, such as **Adobe Guadalupe, Monte Xanic, Chateau Camou,** or **Mogor Badan,** but you may also enjoy visiting one of the larger establishments at **L.A. Cetto** or **Domecq.** Be certain to plan a meal (reservations are recommended) at **Laja** before heading back. Get more information on all of the above in "Valle de Guadalupe: Mexico's Wine Country" on p. 176.

4

Los Cabos

Nearly two million visitors and growing are lured to Los Cabos ("the capes"), the twin towns at the peninsula's southern-most tip, each year. **Cabo San Lucas** holds court on the Western cape and **San José del Cabo** rounds out the Eastern cape. Connected only by the **Tourist Corridor,** 33km (21 miles) of coastline studded with golf courses, luxury resorts, dramatic beaches, and master-planned communities, the two capes could not be more different.

Cabo San Lucas, also known as Land's End, is the rowdy younger sister who shoots cheap tequila while dancing on the table chanting, "what happens in Cabo stays in Cabo." The other side of San Lucas is a bling-flashing second cousin who frequents swanky clubs, ends the night in his oceanfront Jacuzzi, and cruises the coast in his luxury yacht. Somewhere in between are the fun-loving aunts and uncles who've come to fish for marlin and/or for a peep at Sammy Hagar.

On the other hand, San José del Cabo, on the eastern side of Baja's tip, is a decid-edly more "Mexican" experience. Colorful 18th-century homes-turned-artisan shops, vibrant flowering trees, world-class waves, and exquisite restaurants draw well-tanned surf gypsies; jolly snowbirds in search of sun and margaritas, celebrities and execu-tives looking for respite from the rat race, and couples and families who wake up early to enjoy a full day of outdoor fun. The tree-lined streets of the downtown area are particularly enchanting, and the melodies of Ranchera or Banda music float from century-old homes still inhabited after generations.

The golden days of Los Cabos began when silver-screen greats such as Bing Crosby, John Wayne, and Ava Gardner ventured south in the 1950s. Sportfishing was the first draw, but the transfixing landscape, rich waters, and nearly flawless climate quickly gained the favor of other explorers. The only way to get to the soon-to-be "marlin capital of the world" was by boat or private airplane. As such, Los Cabos was born of exclusivity and extravagance. Fishing remains a lure today, although surfing, hiking, diving, whale-watching, sea kayaking, and even spa-going are right up there. To be sure, golf may have overtaken it as the princi-pal attraction. By the early 1980s, the Mexican government realized the growth potential of Los Cabos and invested in new highways, airport facilities, golf courses, and modern marine facilities. The increase in air access and the opening of Transpeninsular Highway 1 (in 1973) paved the way for spectacular growth.

The Los Cabos area is more expensive than other Mexican resorts because lux-ury is the norm among local hotels, and real-estate prices make the San Diego market seem tame. However, a new boom in all-inclusive resorts and off-season travel deals is making Los Cabos vaca-tions more affordable.

You should consider renting a car, even if only for a day or two, because there's too much to see to spend an hour waiting at the bus stop or hundreds of dollars on expensive taxis. And to best understand Los Cabos, both capes need your attention.

Because of the distinctive character and attractions of each of the Cabos, they are treated separately here. It is common to stay in one—or in the Corridor between—and make day trips to the other.

1 San José del Cabo ★★★

180km (112 miles) SE of La Paz; 33km (20 miles) NE of Cabo San Lucas; 1,760km (1,091 miles) SE of Tijuana

San José del Cabo, with its pastel cottages and flowering trees lining the narrow streets, retains the air of a provincial Mexican town. Originally founded in 1730 by Jesuit missionaries, it remains the seat of the Los Cabos government and the center of its business community. The main square, adorned with a wrought-iron bandstand and shaded benches, faces the cathedral, which was built on the site of an early mission.

San José is becoming increasingly sophisticated, with a collection of noteworthy cafes, art galleries, and intriguing small inns adding a newly refined flavor to the central downtown area. This is the best choice for those who want to enjoy the paradoxical landscape but still be aware that they're in Mexico.

ESSENTIALS
GETTING THERE & DEPARTING

By Plane   **Aeroméxico** (© 800/237-6639 in the U.S., 01-800/021-4000 in Mexico, or 624/146-5098 or 624/146-5097; www.aeromexico.com), flies nonstop from San Diego and Ontario, and has connecting flights from other cities; **American Airlines** (© 800/223-5436 in the U.S., or 624/146-5300 or 624/146-5309; www.aa. com) flies from Dallas/Ft. Worth, Los Angeles, Chicago, and New York; **US Airways/ America West** (© 800/235-9292 in the U.S., or 624/146-5380; www.usairways. com) operates nonstop flights from Phoenix, Las Vegas, Oakland, and San Diego; **Alaska Airlines** (© 800/252-7522 in the U.S., or 624/146-5100 or 624/146-5101; www.alaskaair.com) flies from Los Angeles, Portland, San Diego, Seattle, and San Francisco; **Continental** (© 800/537-9222 in the U.S., or 624/146-5040 or 624/ 146-5080; www.continental.com) flies nonstop from Houston and Newark; **Delta** (© 800/241-4141 in the U.S. or 624/146-5003; www.delta.com) has flights from Atlanta, Cincinnati, New York, and Salt Lake City; **Frontier** (© 800/432-1359 in the U.S. or 624/146-5421; www.frontierairlines.com) has nonstop service from Denver, Kansas City, Los Angeles, Sacramento, and San José; **Mexicana** (© 800/531-7921 in the U.S., or 624/146-5001 or 624/143-5352; www.mexicana.com), has direct or connecting flights from Guadalajara, Las Vegas, Los Angeles, Sacramento, and Mexico City; **United Airlines** (© 800/538-2929 in the U.S., or 624/146-5433; www. united.com) flies nonstop from Chicago, San Francisco, and Denver; **Aereo Calafia** (© 624/143-4302; www.aereocalafia.com) is a small regional airline that offers regularly scheduled service and charters on Cessna Grand Caravans throughout Baja and between Los Cabos and Mazatlán, Puerto Vallarta, Culiacán, and Los Mochis.

By Car   From San Diego, drive south on Highway 1 all the way to the tip—as night driving is not recommended, the drive takes about 2½ days. From La Paz, take Highway 1 south; the drive takes 3 to 4 hours. Or take Highway 1 south just past the village of San Pedro, and then take Highway 19 south (a less winding road) through

Todos Santos to Cabo San Lucas, where you pick up Highway 1 east to San José del Cabo. From Cabo San Lucas, it's a half-hour drive to San José.

By Bus   The **Terminal de Autobuses (bus station),** on Valerio Gonzalez, a block east of Highway 1 (© **624/142-1100**), is open daily from 5:30am to 8pm. Buses between Cabo San Lucas and La Paz run almost hourly during the day. For points farther north, you usually change buses in La Paz. The trip to Cabo San Lucas takes 40 minutes; to La Paz, 3 hours. Buses also go to Todos Santos; the trip takes around 3 hours.

ORIENTATION

ARRIVING   Los Cabos International **Airport** (© **624/146-5111**) serves both Cabos and the Corridor in between. San José is 13km (8 miles) from the airport and Cabo San Lucas is a 48km drive (30 miles). As Los Cabos grows in popularity, the number of flights coming into the destination has increased steadily each year—from 18,963 flights in 2005 to 20,898 in 2006—justifying continuous construction and two separate terminals. Be sure to request the correct terminal when you head home. Upon arriving in Los Cabos, pass Customs and baggage claim, and turn right once you exit the sliding doors. Ask for the shuttle desk while breezing past the timeshare booths that hawk free amenities in exchange for attending their sales-pitch presentation. You'll have plenty of encounters with timeshare salespeople—especially in Cabo San Lucas—so feel free to head straight for a taxi or shuttle if you want to get to the beach in a hurry. At about $10 to $17 per person, depending on the location of your hotel, shuttles are the most economic transportation option, and **Josefinos** (© **624/ 146-5354**) is located in the airport. A private van for up to five passengers is $70 and may be able to whisk away your large group more quickly than a regular shuttle. Taxis charge about $20 to San José and upwards of $35 to San Lucas.

For those who like their freedom, it's helpful to have a car in Los Cabos, and rental is very affordable when booked online in advance. However, the major car-rental agencies all have counters at the airport, open during flight arrivals: **Avis** (© **800/331-1212** from the U.S., or 624/146-0201; avissjd@avis.com.mx; Mon–Sat 7am–9pm, Sun 6am–9pm); **Budget** (© **800/527-0700** from the U.S., 624/146-5333 at the airport, or 624/143-4190 in Cabo San Lucas; daily 8am–6pm); **Hertz** (© **800/654-3131** from the U.S., 624/146-5088 or 624/142-0375 in San José del Cabo; daily 8am–8pm); and **National** (© **800/328-4567** from the U.S., 624/146-5022 at the airport, or 624/142-2424 in San José; daily 8am–8pm). Advance reservations are not always necessary.

If you arrive at the bus station, it's too far from the hotels to walk with luggage. A taxi from the bus station to downtown or the hotel zone costs $2 to $5.

VISITOR INFORMATION   San José's city tourist information office (©/fax **624/ 142-3310,** or 624/142-9628) is in the old post-office building on Zaragoza at Mijares. It offers maps, free local publications, and other basic information about the area. It's open Monday through Friday from 8:30am to 3pm. Prior to arrival, contact the **Los Cabos Tourism Board** (© **866/567-2226** in the U.S., or 624/143-4777; www.visitloscabos.org).

CITY LAYOUT   San José del Cabo sprawls from the airport half way to San Lucas, but two main areas are most enticing to visitors: *el centro,* or downtown, has restaurants, shopping, sophisticated inns, and traditional budget hotels, while the **hotel zone** is lined with all-inclusive resorts along the beach.

San José del Cabo

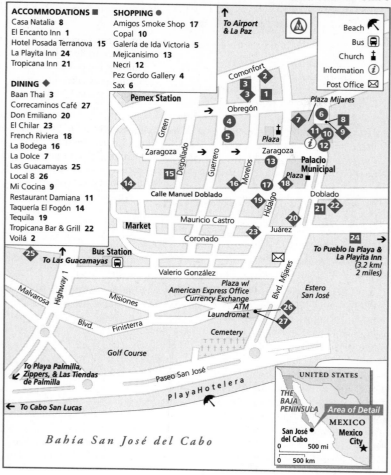

Zaragoza is the main street leading from the highway into town; **Paseo San José** runs parallel to the beach and is the principal boulevard of the hotel zone. The mile-long **Bulevar Mijares** connects the two areas and is the center of most tourist activity in San José.

GETTING AROUND

There is no local bus service between downtown and the beach, but it's about a 30-minute walk from the center of downtown to the sand, and **taxis** (© 624/142-0580) connect the two for about $5 each way. For day trips to **Cabo San Lucas,** ask your concierge if your hotel has a daily shuttle, or just catch a **bus** (see "Getting There & Departing," above) or a cab.

FAST FACTS: **San José del Cabo**

Area Code The local telephone area code is **624**.

Banks Banks exchange currency during business hours, which are generally Monday through Friday from 8:30am to 6pm, and Saturday from 10am to 2pm. There are several major banks with ATMs on Zaragoza between Morelos and Degollado and in the downtown. There's also a plaza with a bank, ATM, American Express office, and currency exchange at the south end of Bulevar Mijares.

Emergencies Dial *©* **066,** or the local police number at City Hall: *©* **624/142-0361.**

Hospital **Hospital General** is at Retorno Atunero s/n, Col. Chamizal ((*©* **624/142-0013).**

Internet Access **Trazzo Internet,** on the corner of Zaragoza and Morelos, across from the cathedral downtown ((*©* **624/142-0303;** fax 624/142-1220; www.trazzo digital.com) is open Monday through Friday 8am to 9pm, and Saturday from 9am to 7pm. They charge $2.50 for 30 minutes or less of high-speed access. They also have printing, copy, and fax services available.

Pharmacy **Farmacia ISSSTE,** Carretera Transpeninsular Km 34, Plaza California Local 7 (*©* **624/142-2645),** is open daily from 8am to 8pm.

Post Office The *correo,* Bulevar Mijares 1924, at Valerio Gonzalez (*©* **624/142-0911),** is open Monday through Friday from 8am to 6pm, Saturday from 9am to noon. For more substantial mailings, Mail Boxes Etc., Plaza Las Palmas Km 31 (*©* **624/142-4355),** is open Monday through Friday from 8:30am to 5:30pm and Saturday from 9am to noon.

BEACHES & OUTDOOR ACTIVITIES

The relaxed pace of San José del Cabo makes it an ideal place to unwind and absorb authentic Mexican flavor. Beach aficionados who want to explore the beautiful coves and beaches along the 35km (22-mile) coast between the two Cabos should consider renting a car for a day or so (from $50 per day). Frequent bus service between San José del Cabo and Cabo San Lucas also makes it possible to visit both towns (see "Getting There & Departing," above).

BEACHES

The best beach safe for swimming is **Palmilla Beach,** which fronts the glitzy One&Only Palmilla resort 8km (5 miles) west of San José. With its rocky coves, soft sand, and visible sea life, this beach has been home to fishermen for centuries and it is the preeminent picnic destination for Mexican families on Sunday afternoons. Past the rock formations, the beach curves east and the culminating swim is well worth the pebble-strewn stroll. Locals agree there's just something about the water on the other side of the rocks. Perfect for swimming, the water in Palmilla Bay has a sort of magic unlike anywhere else and, when you emerge, you'll feel it for yourself. To reach Playa Palmilla, enter the lush Palmilla community at Km 27.5 on the highway, take the road toward the beach, then take the fork to the left (without entering the hotel grounds), and park in the lot.

Estero San José, a natural freshwater estuary on which the ancient Pericúe Indians built their civilization centuries ago, has at least 270 species of birds and is on the east end of the hotel zone. The estuary is a protected ecological reserve and merits a sunset beach walk from the Hotel Presidente InterContinental to the river mouth where the spring-fed estuary meets the Sea of Cortez.

For a list of other nearby beaches worth exploring if you have a rental car, see "Beaches & Outdoor Activities" under "Cabo San Lucas," later in this chapter.

CRUISES

Boats depart from Cabo San Lucas; prices and offerings vary, but cruises generally include music, open bar, and snacks for $40 to $50 per person. Daytime and sunset cruises are available. Arrange cruises through a travel agency or through **BookCabo.com** (© 624/142-9200), or call **Xplora Adventours** (© 624/142-9135 or 624/142-9000, ext. 8050; www.xploraloscabos.com). Both companies work with several tour providers in the area and can give unbiased information.

LAND SPORTS

ADVENTURE TOURS   **Tío Sports** (© 624/143-3399) arranges a variety of land- and water-based adventure and nature tours, including popular ATV tours to La Candelaria; parasailing; and kayak, catamaran, snorkeling, and diving trips. The website gives current prices. **Baja Wild** (© 624/172-6300; www.bajawild.com) is ideal for a wide range of adventure, as they offer every excursion imaginable in Los Cabos from rock climbing to kayaking, hiking to rappelling, and more. **Baja Outback** (© 624/142-9215; www.bajaoutback.com) provides single- and multiday adventure tours throughout Southern Baja. Armed with a naturalist guide and an expedition guide, who provide information and offer driving instruction over the two-way radios that connect each Hummer in the caravan, you take the wheel of your own H2 Hummer and discover mountain, desert, and sea.

GOLF   Los Cabos has become Latin America's leading golf destination, with a collection of top signature courses and others under construction. The lowest greens fees in the area are at the 9-hole **Mayan Palace Golf Los Cabos** (© 624/142-0900 or 624/142-0901), Paseo Finisterra 1, which is the first right turn east of the yellow Fonatur statue in the highway roundabout. The 7th hole offers a wonderful view of the ocean on your left and mountains facing you as you approach the green. The 9th is a good finishing hole, with a wide, sloping fairway with sand traps to the top, right, and bottom of the green. Early-morning greens fees (6am–2pm) are just $69 for 9 holes and $99 for 18 holes with equipment; rates drop to $80 for 18 holes after 3pm. All greens fees include use of cart. For more information about playing golf in Los Cabos, see "The Lowdown on Golf in Cabo" on p. 80.

(Moments Festivals & Special Events in Los Cabos

San José del Cabo celebrates the feast of its patron saint on March 19. June 19 is the festival of the patron saint of San Bartolo, a village 100km (62 miles) north. July 25 is the festival of the patron saint of Santiago, a village 55km (34 miles) north. These festivals usually feature fairs, music, dancing, feasting, horse races, and cockfights.

⌒ *Tips* **Swimming Safety**

Although this area is ideal for watersports, occasional strong currents and undertows can make swimming dangerous at most beaches in **San José**, the **Tourist Corridor,** and **Cabo San Lucas.** Check conditions before entering the surf. Swimming is generally safe at **Palmilla Beach** (see "Beaches," above), though it, too, can be rough. The safest area beach for swimming is **Médano Beach** in Cabo San Lucas.

HORSEBACK RIDING   Horses can be rented near the Presidente InterContinental, Fiesta Inn, and in the Costa Azul canyon for $15 to $20 per hour. Most people choose to ride on the beach, but a trip up the arroyo offers a different beauty. For a more organized riding experience—English or Western—there's **Cuadra San Francisco Equestrian Center,** Km 19.5 along the Corridor, in front of the Casa del Mar resort (© **624/144-0160;** www.loscaboshorses.com). Master horseman Francisco Barrena has more than 30 years of experience in training horses and operating equestrian schools, and will assist any level rider in selecting and fitting a horse to their skill level. Your choice of English or Western saddles is available on exceptional, well-trained horses. A 2-hour canyon ride in and around Arroyo San Carlos or Venado Blanco costs $85; a 1-hour ride to the beach or desert is $40. Private tours go for $55 per hour and equestrian aficionados may schedule a dressage class for $80.

TENNIS   You can play tennis at most resorts throughout Los Cabos, but if you're staying somewhere tennis isn't available, the two courts at the **Mayan Palace Resort Golf Los Cabos** (© **624/142-0905**), Paseo Finisterra 1, rent for $14 an hour during the day, $28 an hour at night. Call the club to reserve.

WATERSPORTS

FISHING   The least expensive way to enjoy deep-sea fishing is to pair up with another angler and charter a *panga,* a 7m (23-ft.) skiff used by local fishermen, from Pueblo la Playa, the beach near the new Puerto Los Cabos Marina. Several *panga* fleets offer 6-hour sportfishing trips, usually from 6am to noon, for $200 to $500. Two or three people can split the cost. For information, visit the fishermen's cooperative in Pueblo la Playa (no phone) or contact **Gordo Banks Pangas** (© **624/142-1147;** www.gordobanks.com). For larger charter boats, you'll depart from the marina in Cabo San Lucas (later in this chapter).

SEA KAYAKING   Fully guided, ecologically oriented **ocean kayak tours** are available through **Ramon's Ecotours** (© **624/122-3696;** www.ramonsecotours.com) and **Cabo Acuadeportes** (© **624/143-0117;** www.baja-cabo.com/cabosanlucaswatersports. html). Most ocean-kayaking tours depart from Cabo San Lucas, curve around the bay toward the Arch, and break for snorkeling at Lover's Beach.

SNORKELING/DIVING   **Manta** (© **624/144-3871;** www.caboscuba.com) and **Amigos del Mar** in Cabo San Lucas (© **800/344-3349** in the U.S., or 624/143-0505; www.amigosdelmar.com) are two of the most reputable dive operations in Los Cabos. Manta offers everything from advanced dive trips to PADI open-water diver certification. Prices start at $50 for a one-tank dive and $150 for 2 days of diving. Night dives are $65 per person. The 4-day PADI certification course, which certifies you to scuba dive anywhere in the world, costs $430. Among the area's best dive sites are **Gordo Banks** and **Cabo Pulmo.** Gordo Banks is an advanced dive site where you can see whale sharks and hammerhead sharks. It's a deep dive—27 to 30m (90–98 ft.)—with limited visibility (9–12m/30–40 ft.). Most dives are drift dives, and wetsuits are highly recommended. Cabo Pulmo, a protected marine park 72km (45 miles) northeast of San José, has seven sites geared for divers of all experience levels, plus some of the most beautiful stretches of Baja beach, so it never feels crowded.

SURFING   Surfing is becoming one of the hottest trends in the entire destination, drawing landlocked Midwesterners and SoCal surf aficionados alike to the wide range of waves at Baja's tip. **Playa Costa Azul,** at Km 29 on Highway 1 just south of San José, has the most popular surfing beaches in the area. The **Costa Azul Surf Shop,** Km 28, Playa Costa Azul (© 624/142-2771; www.costa-azul.com.mx), offers surfing lessons, surfboard and snorkeling equipment rentals, and specialized surf excursions to any of the 15 local breaks. Excursions include transportation and a DVD video of the day, and owner Alejandro Olea handcrafts all rental boards in his San José workshop. Just $20 per day will get you a board, leash, shade umbrella, beach chair, and rack for your rental car. One-hour lessons are $55, and other special packages are available. **Cabo Surf Hotel** (© 624/172-6188; www.cabosurfhotel.com) also offers surf lessons and daily board rentals for $35.

The surf switches sides with the seasons, so the waves break on the eastern side of the peninsula in the spring and summer (Mar–Oct) and the Pacific plays host to surfers in the fall and winter (Nov–Mar). The most popular summer breaks start at Acapulquito and extend up the East Cape, while the hot spot for winter waves is Los Cerritos Beach, south of Todos Santos. As every break has its secret—from rocks covered in sea urchins to territorial locals—your best bet is to hook up with a reputable surf shop or guide to take you to the break that's right for you.

WHALE-WATCHING   From January through March, migrating gray and humpback whales visit Los Cabos to breed and bear their calves, creating one of Baja's most impressive spectacles. Practically every local tour company advertises whale-watching tours that range from an hour to a half-day. Options include Zodiac-style rafts, sportfishing boats, glass-bottom boats, and cruise catamarans, all of which depart from the Cabo San Lucas Marina and cost $35 to $50, depending on the type of boat and whether the price includes snacks and beverages. The ultimate whale excursion is a trip to **Magdalena Bay. BookCabo.com** (© 624/142-9200; www.bookcabo.com) offers luxury bus tours from San José to San Carlos, where lobster dinners, charming accommodations, daytime whale-watching, and lunch on Margarita Island await. The cost is $227 per person double occupancy and $126 for kids 3 to 10 years old. Tours on Baja-based airline **Aereo Calafia** (© 624/143-4302; www.aereocalafia.com) fly 75 minutes from San Lucas to Magdalena, where you board a *panga* and spend 3 hours watching gray whales and humpbacks loll around the coastal lagoons before returning the same day. This tour is $420, including air transportation, the tour, and lunch. You also can spot whales from the shore in Los Cabos; good spots include the beach by the Westin Resort & Spa, at Esperanza Resort in the Punta Ballena community, and along the beaches and cliffs of the Corridor. For more information, see "Whale-Watching in Baja: A Primer," in chapter 6.

SHOPPING

San José is the two capes' seat of artisan finery, design boutiques, and hip art galleries. They cluster around **Bulevar Mijares** and **Zaragoza.** Start in the main plaza and head northwest toward the historic gallery district, around Guerrero and Obregón streets, for a peek at the paintings and sculptures of Pez Gordo Gallery, the Fine Art Annex, Old Towne Gallery, and Galería de Ida Victoria. Head any other direction from the main plaza for boutiques specializing in handcrafts. The following businesses accept credit cards (American Express, MasterCard, and Visa).

Amigos Smokeshop and Cigar Bar For fine Cuban cigars and cigarettes, a visit here is a must. They sell not only high-quality cigars, but also a range of smoking accessories, including humidors and cutters. Also available is a bar with an excellent selection of single-malts and California wines. Open Monday through Wednesday 9am to 8pm; Thursday through Saturday 9am to 1pm. Doblado and Morelos, across from the French Riviera bakery. ⓒ 624/142-1138.

Las Tiendas de Palmilla The ultimate in luxury, style, and home design can be found in San José's opulent shopping center. Among other shops, Casa Vieja sells fine linen dresses and Pineda Covalín silk scarves, Cabana sells chic women's clothing and resort wear, Tiki Lounge is the local Tommy Bahama outpost, Q Boutique houses Diamonds International's connoisseur collection, and the Guadalajara-headquartered Antigua de México sells furniture from the state of Jalisco. Store hours vary. ⓒ 624/144-6999. www.lastiendasdepalmilla.com.

Mejicanisimo This shop sells everything from locally made soaps and Damiana tea to embroidered linens and exquisite Emilia Castillo sterling silver–embedded porcelain. The luminous owner, Magdalena del Río, supplies most of the area's luxury resorts with their fine Oaxacan embroidery, often used for tablecloths and throw pillows. Open Monday through Saturday from 9am to 10pm and from 9am to 9pm Sunday. Zaragoza, across from the cathedral. ⓒ 624/142-3090.

Necri 🅐 This shop sells the finest in Talavera ceramics and pewter accessories. Shipping is available. Open Monday through Saturday from 9am to 9pm. Zaragoza at Hidalgo, fronting the giant fig tree in the plaza. ⓒ 624/142-2777.

SAX For original and well-priced jewelry, visit this small shop where two local designers (who also happen to be sisters) create one-of-a-kind pieces using silver and semiprecious stones. They'll even create a special-request design for you and have it ready in 24 hours. Open Monday through Saturday from 10am to 9pm, closed Sundays. On Mijares next to Casa Natalia. ⓒ 624/142-0704.

WHERE TO STAY

There's more demand than supply in Baja Sur—especially during the idyllic winter months—so prices tend to be higher than those for equivalent accommodations in other parts of Mexico. It's best to call ahead for reservations. Properties in the beachside hotel zone often offer package deals that bring room rates down to the moderate range, especially during summer months. Check with your travel agent. High season generally denotes December through April and low season is May through November. Rates listed below do not include tax, which is 12%, and most resorts in Los Cabos offer free parking, although that, too, is changing.

EXPENSIVE

Casa Natalia 🅐🅐🅐 (Finds) This acclaimed boutique hotel is exquisite. Owners Nathalie and Loic have transformed a former residence into a beautiful amalgam of palms, waterfalls, and flowers. The inn is a completely renovated historic home that combines modern architecture with traditional Mexican touches. All have sliding glass doors that open onto small private terraces or balconies with hammocks and chairs, shaded by bougainvillea and bamboo. The two spa suites each have a private terrace with a whirlpool and hammock. Tall California palms surround a small courtyard pool, and the terraces face onto it. Casa Natalia offers its guests privacy, style, and romance. It's in the heart of downtown San José, just off the central plaza, and the restaurant, Mi Cocina, is often visitors' favorite dining experience of an entire trip.

Bulevar Mijares 4, 23400 San José del Cabo, B.C.S. (C) 888/277-3814 in the U.S., 866/826-1170 in Canada, or 624/142-5100. Fax 624/142-5110. www.casanatalia.com. 20 units. High season $295 double, $475 spa suite; low season $220 double, $350 spa suite. AE, MC, V. Children under 14 not accepted. **Amenities:** Gourmet restaurant (see Mi Cocina in "Where to Dine," below); bar; heated outdoor pool w/waterfall and swim-up bar; access and transportation to private beach club; concierge; room service; in-room spa services; laundry service. *In room:* A/C, fan, TV/DVD, high-speed Internet, hair dryer, safe, bathrobes, CD player, DVD library.

MODERATE

El Encanto Inn *(Value)*   On a quiet street in the historic downtown district, this charming inn surrounds a grassy courtyard with a fountain, small pool, and a tasteful mission-style chapel for weddings. It offers a relaxing, elegant alternative to busy hotels, as well as excellent value. Rooms are decorated with rustic wood and contemporary iron furniture. Nice-size bathrooms have colorful tile accents. Rooms have two double beds, while suites have king-size beds and a sitting room. A pool area with *palapa* bar, and 14 impeccable poolside suites were added in 2003. These newer suites have minibars and other extras, while all rooms offer satellite DirecTV. The owners, Cliff and Blanca (a lifelong resident of San José), can help arrange fishing packages and golf and diving outings. The inn is a half-block from the church.

Morelos 133 (between Obregón and Comonfort), 23400 San José del Cabo, B.C.S. (C) 210/858-6649 or 624/142-0388. www.elencantoinn.com. 26 units. $75 double; $105–$175 suite. MC, V. Limited street parking available. **Amenities:** Restaurant; *palapa* bar; small outdoor pool; spa. *In room:* A/C, fan, TV, coffeemaker.

La Playita Inn   Removed from even the slow pace of San José, this courtyard hotel is older yet impeccably clean and friendly, and it's ideal for fishermen and those looking for something different from a traditional resort vacation. As it's smack in the middle of the Puerto Los Cabos master-planned community, it's not the quiet getaway it once was. However, it's the only hotel on the only beach in San José that's considered safe for swimming. Just steps from the water and the lineup of fishing *pangas,* the two stories of sunlit rooms frame a patio with a pool just large enough to allow you to swim laps. Each room is spacious, with high-quality basic furnishings, screened windows, a nicely tiled bathroom, and cable TV. Two large suites on the second floor have full kitchens. Next door, the hotel's new La Playita Grill serves breakfast and bloody marys from 7am to noon, and Tommy's Barefoot Bar (daily noon–9pm) offers a great mix of seafood and standard favorites, plus occasional live jazz or tropical music.

Pueblo la Playa, Apdo. Postal 437, 23400 San José del Cabo, B.C.S. (C)/fax 624/142-4166. www.laplayitahotel.com. 26 units. $69 double; $99–$159 suite. MC, V. Free parking. From Bulevar Mijares, follow sign pointing to Pueblo la Playa (dirt road) for about 3km (2 miles); hotel is on the left. **Amenities:** Restaurant; bar; outdoor pool; kayak rental. *In room:* A/C, TV.

Tropicana Inn *(*   This hacienda-style hotel, a longstanding favorite in San José, welcomes many repeat visitors. Just behind the Tropicana Bar and Grill, it frames a plant-filled courtyard with a graceful arcade bordering the rooms and inviting swimming pool. Each nicely furnished, medium-size room in the L-shaped building (which has a two- and three-story wing) has tile floors, two double beds, a window looking out on the courtyard, and a brightly tiled bathroom with shower. Each morning, freshly brewed coffee, delicious sweet rolls, and fresh fruit are set out for hotel guests. There's room service until 11pm from the adjacent Tropicana Bar and Grill (owned by the hotel).

Bulevar Mijares 30 (1 block south of the town square), 23400 San José del Cabo, B.C.S. ⓒ **624/142-0907** or 624/ 142-1580. Fax 624/142-1590. 38 units. High season $79 double; low season 10% less. Rates include continental breakfast. AE, MC, V. Free limited parking. **Amenities:** Restaurant; bar; small outdoor pool; tour desk; room service; laundry service. *In room:* A/C, TV, minibar, coffeemaker.

INEXPENSIVE
Hotel Posada Terranova   This small, family-owned hotel is so famous for its traditional Mexican breakfasts and charming outdoor dining terrace that locals often forget it's even a hotel. However, while local Mexicans and expats love it for weekend brunch, the budget traveler will love it for its spare decor, clean rooms, soft sheets, ideal location in the center of downtown San José and, yes, for its Huevos Rancheros and fresh-squeezed O.J. in the morning.

Degollado between Doblado and Zaragoza, 23400 San José del Cabo, B.C.S. ⓒ **624/142-0534.** Fax 624/142-0902. www.hterranova.com.mx. 25 units. $60 single and double. Seasonal rates available. Rates include continental breakfast. MC, V. **Amenities:** Restaurant; bar; room service. *In room:* A/C, fan, satellite TV.

WHERE TO DINE
The dining in this once-provincial town is anything but humble. On pace with the area's magnificent resort growth are the evolving culinary pursuits in downtown San José. There's not enough room to go into detail about every restaurant that's worth your attention—like the new and ingenious **La Bodega Steak & Wine House** (ⓒ **624/142-6619;** www.labodegadesanjose.com); the longtime Mexican-food classic **Damiana Restaurant Bar & Patio** (ⓒ **624/142-0499**); the ever-reliable locals-and-expats coffee shop, **Correcaminos Café** (no phone); the pastry-laden **French Riviera** (ⓒ **624/104-3125**); the dirt-cheap-and-delicious **Taquería El Fogón** (ⓒ **624/132-8485**), which is wildly popular with local teens; the resounding Italian favorite, **La Dolce** (ⓒ **624/142-6621**); the delectably experimental **Local 8** (ⓒ **624/142-6655**); and the luscious precision of **Voilá** (ⓒ **624/130-7569**)—but below is a cross-section of what's available. Don't stop here; San José is in the midst of a culinary renaissance and new places are opening on a regular basis. So be bold and let your senses lead you—in this town, it's hard to pick a bad place to eat.

EXPENSIVE
Baan Thai ⓐ *Finds* PAN-ASIAN   Asian food is hard to come by in Los Cabos, and Baan Thai—set in one of San José's lovely historic buildings—does an impressive job of innovating these flavors to incorporate a hint of Mexico in this exceptional restaurant, under the direction of chef/owner Carl Marts. Move beyond such traditional starters as spring rolls or satay to one of Baan Thai's more unique offerings, such as blue crab stir-fried with chile, garlic, and tomatoes, or mild chilies stuffed with smoked marlin and served with a soy-ginger dipping sauce. From there, move on to entrees such as wok-tossed salmon; steamed Baja mussels in a coconut-herb broth; or seared steak tossed with mangos, green apples, and chiles. An impressive wine list and full bar service are available to complement your meal. Air-conditioned indoor dining, as well as outdoor dining, in an exotic garden patio, is available.

Morelos s/n, 1 block behind the church and plaza. ⓒ **624/142-3344.** Main courses $8–$21. MC, V. Mon–Sat noon–10:30pm.

Don Emiliano ★★★ *(finds)* MEXICAN   If years of queso dip and fried chimichangas have framed your vision of Mexican food, be prepared for your world to come crashing delightfully down. Sparkling seasonal menus rooted in such Mexican traditions as Day of the Dead and Independence Day bring rare mole sauces and stuffed chiles drenched in walnut-cream sauce and pomegranate seeds *(chile en nogada)*, while traditional staples such as flavored tamales and grilled farm cheese atop roasted tomatillo salsa grace the menu on a regular basis. A uniquely extensive Mexican and imported wine list and ample supply of fresh-mint mojitos paired with the warmth of the staff and perfect portions ensure a festive evening that will change the way you view Mexican food. For nearly a decade, Chef Margarita C. de Salinas has been the official gala chef for the Mexican government, which means she travels the world preparing gourmet Mexican fare for heads of state, while her son, Angel, holds down the fort with such graciousness and culinary perfection, it must be a secret family recipe. Try the tasting menu or create your own, but whatever you do, don't miss the *queso corazón* (local farm cheese grilled atop smoky salsa) to start.

Bulevar Mijares 27 in downtown San José. (C) **624/142-0266**. www.donemiliano.com.mx. Main courses $18–$25. AE, MC, V. Daily 6–10pm.

El Chilar ★★ MEXICAN   El Chilar traditionalists beware: This is not the place you fell in love with. Rest assured, one visit to the renovated El Chilar will inspire you to take your relationship to the next level. Chef Armando Montano has transformed this once casual jewel into a vibrant restaurant and wine bar so packed that reservations are a must. His passion for playful Mexican cuisine is evident, as he blends the traditional flavors of this country into imaginative and heavenly offerings. Among the most popular dinner options are the duck enchiladas or the cascabel chile–marinated flank steak. These choices may not be offered when you arrive, however, as Chef Armando is known to frequently change his menu. At night, candlelight adds a sparkle of romance to the setting. El Chilar also offers a full bar, an ample selection of wines, and a sleek wine bar area in which to enjoy them. Air-conditioned indoor dining is available.

Benito Juárez 1497, at Morelos near the Telmex tower. (C) **624/142-2544** or 624/146-9798. Main courses $5–$29. No credit cards. Mon–Sat 3–10pm.

Mi Cocina ★★★ NOUVELLE MEXICAN/EURO   Widely appreciated as one of Los Cabos' finest restaurants, Mi Cocina doesn't rely solely on the romance of its setting—the food is superb, creative, and consistently flavorful. Notable starters include steamed baby clams topped with a creamy cilantro sauce and served with garlic croutons, or a healthy slice of Camembert cheese, fried and served with homemade toast and grapes. Among the favorite main courses are the baked baby rack of lamb served with grilled vegetables, and the Provençal-style shrimp served with risotto, roasted tomato, basil, and cilantro-fish consommé. Save room for dessert; choices include their famous chocolate-chocolate cake and a perfect crème brûlée. The full-service *palapa* bar offers an excellent selection of wines, premium tequilas, and single-malt scotches. Be adventurous and try one of their special martinis—like the Flor de México, an adaptation of the Cosmo, using Jamaica (hibiscus-flower infusion) rather than cranberry juice.

In the Casa Natalia hotel, Bulevar Mijares. (C) **624/142-5100**. www.casanatalia.com/dining.cfm. Main courses $15–$32. AE, MC, V. Daily 6:30–10pm (hotel guests only 6:30am–6pm).

Tequila ★ MEDITERRANEAN/ASIAN   Contemporary fusion cuisine with a light and flavorful touch is the star attraction here, although the garden setting is lovely, with rustic *equipal* furniture and lanterns scattered among palms and mango trees. Organic produce and nice, dark greens are hard to find in these parts, so Tequila's homegrown produce, harvested from owner Enrique Silva's ranch, is a welcome dose of light-and-fresh fare that accompanies almost every entree. Try the shrimp risotto or beef tenderloin in rosemary-cabernet sauce. Other enjoyable options include perfectly seared tuna with cilantro and ginger, and rack of lamb topped with tamarind sauce. The accompanying whole-grain bread arrives fresh and hot with a pesto-infused olive oil, and attentive service complements the fine meal. Cuban cigars and an excellent selection of tequilas are available, as is an extensive wine list emphasizing California vintages.

Manuel Doblado s/n, near Hidalgo. © **624/142-1155** or 624/142-3753. www.tequilarestaurant.com. Lunch $9–$22; dinner main courses $10–$45. AE. Daily 5:30–10:30pm.

MODERATE

Tropicana Bar and Grill SEAFOOD/MEAT   The Tropicana remains a popular mainstay, especially for tourists. The lively restaurant and bar retains its steady clientele day and night, as well as its offerings of live nightly mariachi music and special sporting events on satellite TV. The dining area, renovated in 2003, is in a courtyard pavilion with a tiled mural at one end. Cafe-style sidewalk dining is also available, complete with cool-water misters for the summer months. The menu is too extensive to lay claim to any specialty; it aims to please everyone, but the appetizer sampler for two offers a good selection of traditional Mexican *botanas* that are sure to please the table.

Bulevar Mijares 30, 1 block south of the Plaza Mijares. © **624/142-1580** or 624/142-0907. Breakfast $4–$6; main courses $10–$25. AE, MC, V. Daily 8am–midnight.

Zipper's ★★ MEXICAN/BEACHFRONT GRILL   If a cheeseburger in paradise is your mission, Zipper's is the real deal. Located along the Corridor near San José del Cabo, surfers downing icy Pacíficos and fresh shrimp ceviche merge with fishermen bolting Sauza and fried-fish tacos. However, the not-so-humble cheeseburger is the star of Zipper's gringo-fabulous menu. Service is slow, so pass the time watching pelicans swoop the swells, catching rays in board shorts and bikinis, and blissing out to the Jimmy Buffet–laced Radio Margaritaville, which is Zipper's 24/7 soundtrack. You won't find dance contests and jet-ski vendors here; located beneath a beachfront *palapa* that faces a surf break of the same name, Zipper's is a stripped-down sensory experience that rivals even the swankiest Los Cabos restaurant—at a slightly lesser price tag.

Km 28.5 on Transpeninsular Hwy., in Playa Costa Azul, just south of San José. © **624/172-6162.** Cheeseburgers and sandwiches $8–$10; main courses $13–$18. No credit cards. Daily 11am–10:30pm.

INEXPENSIVE

Las Guacamayas ★★★ *(Moments* TACOS   This off-the-beaten-path dive is home to the most delectable tacos in all of Los Cabos. If you can get over the plastic chairs, occasional wandering roosters, and low-hanging fruit trees in this packed-nightly courtyard, you'll be mesmerized by this meticulously operated gringo and Mexican hot spot. Traditionalists wisely go for the *tacos al pastor*—shaved pork tacos with onion, cilantro, and pineapple in a corn or flour tortilla, but the *quesadillas chilangas*—crispy fried tortillas stuffed with an assortment of fillings—are a blissful indulgence. Pace yourself. The addicting flavors and rock-bottom prices may inspire you to stay all night.

Driving east on Transpeninsular Hwy., turn left at the Pescador street sign. The street winds into the Chamizal neighborhood. Take your second left and look for the neon sign. Guacamayas is on the right side. © 624/172-6162. Tacos,
stuffed potatoes, and more $1.50–$7. No credit cards. Mon, Wed, Thurs 6pm–midnight; Fri–Sat 6pm–4am. Closed Tues.

SAN JOSE AFTER DARK

The nightlife in San José may seem a bit more understated than its wild-nights coun-
terpart in San Lucas, yet a new crop of swanky clubs, wine bars, and neighborhood
hangouts, all pumped with varying kinds of music till 2 or 3am on the weekends, is
offering a nighttime release for the local hospitality industry jet set and San José visitors alike. Those intent on American music and bump-and-grind dance clubs will
have better luck in San Lucas.

El Moro   Located in San José's gallery district in the old brick building formerly
known as Rawhide, Pez Gordo Gallery owner Dana Lieb has opened this rustic bar for
locals looking for a place to kick back and, well, drink. Obregón and Zaragoza,. No phone.

La Santa Wine Bar ⭑   This posh cavern of fine wine and comfortable lounge decor
serves light food, desserts, and electronic music in San José's gallery district. Hidalgo and
Obregón. © **624/172-6767.**

O2 Restaurant, Dance Club, and Oxygen Bar   This is one place to dance to
American hip-hop in San José and, located right on the beach on the north side of the
hotel zone, it's also the area's only public beach club. Take in a hit of pure oxygen
before heading home. On the beach in Plaza Los Soles, behind Mega supermarket. No phone.

Red ⭑⭑   A sleek martini bar facing the hotel zone, this San Lucas spin-off also
offers light meals, awesome wood-fired pizza, and DJ music. Paseo San José, adjacent to
the roundabout behind Mega supermarket. No phone.

Tropicana   This bar, featuring American sports events and live mariachi music
nightly from 6 to 9pm and live Mexican and Cuban dance music from 9:30pm until
about 1am on weekends, stays open Tuesday through Sunday from 7am to 2am. Bulevar Mijares. © **624/142-1580.**

2 The Corridor: Between the Two Cabos ⭑⭑

The 29-kilometer (18-mile) Corridor between the towns of San José del Cabo and
Cabo San Lucas contains some of Mexico's most lavish resorts. Most growth at the tip
of the peninsula is occurring along the Corridor, which already has become center
stage for championship golf. The five major resort areas are **Palmilla, Querencia,
Cabo Real, Cabo del Sol,** and **Punta Ballena,** and each is an enclosed master-
planned community sprinkled with multimillion-dollar homes (or the promise of
them). All but Punta Ballena have championship golf, and all but Querencia, which
is a private residential community, have ultra-luxury resorts within their gates. If you
plan to explore the region while staying at a Corridor hotel, you'll need a rental car
(available at the hotels) for at least 1 or 2 days. Even if you're not staying here, the
beaches and dining options are worth investigating. All hotels listed here qualify as
very expensive. Most resorts offer golf and fishing packages, as well as free parking.
Rates listed below do not include tax.

WHERE TO STAY

Casa del Mar ⭑ *Finds*   A little-known treasure, this intimate resort is one of the best
values along the Corridor, and its 2006 renovation makes it even better. The hacienda-
style building offers luxury accommodations in an intimate setting, as well as an on-site

The Two Cabos & the Corridor

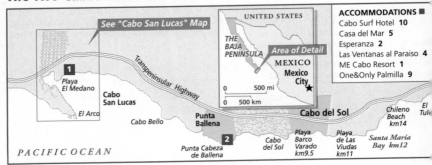

spa and nearby golf facilities. It's convenient to the 18-hole championship Cabo Real, a Robert Trent Jones, Jr., golf course. Guest rooms have a bright feel, with white marble floors, light wicker furnishings, a separate sitting area, and a large whirlpool tub plus separate shower. Balconies have oversize chairs with a view of the ocean beyond the pool. It's a romantic hotel for couples and honeymooners; it's known for welcoming, personalized service.

Km 19.5 on Hwy. 1, Cabo San Lucas, B.C.S. (C) **888/227-9621** in the U.S., or 624/144-0030 or 624/145-7700. Fax 624/144-0034. www.casadelmarmexico.com. 56 units. High season $470 double, $500 suite; low season $290 double, $340 suite. AE, MC, V. **Amenities:** Restaurant; lobby bar; beach club (adults only) w/open-air restaurant, pool bar, outdoor pool, and hot tub; 6 other outdoor pools (2 w/whirlpools and swim-up bars); privileges at Cabo Real golf club; 2 lighted tennis courts; small workout room; full-service spa; tour desk; room service; babysitting; laundry service; dry cleaning. *In room:* A/C, TV, minibar, hair dryer, safe, bathrobes, Jacuzzi.

Esperanza ✦✦✦ Although this luxury resort along Cabo's over-the-top Corridor sits on a bluff overlooking two small, rocky coves, the absence of a sandy beach doesn't seem to matter much to its guests—the hotel more than makes up for it in terms of pampering services and stylish details. Created by the famed Auberge Resorts group, the architecture of this hotel is dramatic, elegant, and comfortable. The casitas and villas are spread across 7 hectares (17 acres), designed to resemble a Mexican village, and are connected to the resort facilities by stone footpaths. The top-floor suites have handmade *palapa* ceilings and a private outdoor whirlpool spa. All rooms are exceptionally spacious, with woven wicker and tropical wood furnishings, original art, rugs and fabrics in muted colors with jewel-tone color accents, and Frette linens gracing the extra-comfortable feather beds. Terraces are large, extending the living area to the outdoors, and all have hammocks and views of the Sea of Cortez. The oversize bathrooms have separate tubs and showers with dual showerheads. The Spa is not to be missed, and the new yoga studio offers complimentary classes daily.

Carretera Transpeninsular Km 7 on Hwy. 1, at Punta Ballena, Cabo San Lucas, B.C.S. (C) **866/311-2226** in the U.S., or 624/145-6400. Fax 624/145-6403. www.esperanzaresort.com. 50 suites, 6 villas. High season $875–$1,225 oceanview casita, $1,075–$1,325 beachfront casita, $4,000–$5,500 oceanfront suite; low season $675–$1,025 oceanview casita, $675–$1,025 beachfront casita, $2,500–$3,500 oceanfront suite. AE, MC, V. Free valet parking. **Amenities:** Oceanfront restaurant; sushi and ceviche bar; pool; golf privileges; fitness center; full-service luxury spa; yoga studio with complimentary daily classes; concierge; room service; babysitting; laundry service; dry cleaning; art gallery; gourmet market; private beach w/club. *In room:* A/C, plasma TV w/DVD, Wi-Fi, hair dryer, safe, bathrobes, stereo, in-suite bar.

Las Ventanas al Paraíso ✦✦✦ Las Ventanas is known for its luxury accommodations and attention to detail. The architecture, with adobe structures and rough-hewn

Westin Resort & Spa,
   Los Cabos **6**

DINING ◆
C Restaurant **9**
Nick San **8**
Zippers **13**

ATTRACTIONS ●
Playa Acapulquito surfing beach **11**
Costa Azul Surf Shop **14**
Cuadra San Francisco Equestrian Center **3**
Las Tiendas de Palmilla shopping center **7**
MEGA-Comercial Mexicana supermarket **15**
Zipper's surf break **12**

wood accents, provides a soothing complement to the desert landscape. The only color comes from the dazzling *ventanas* (windows) of pebbled rainbow glass hand-made by regional artisans. Richly furnished, Mediterranean-style rooms are large (starting at 292 sq. m/960 sq. ft.) and appointed with every conceivable amenity, from wood-burning fireplaces to computerized telescopes for star- or whale-gazing. Sizable whirlpool tubs overlook the room and may be closed off for privacy. Larger suites offer extras such as rooftop terraces, sunken whirlpools on a private patio, or a personal pool. Note that Las Ventanas is also booking the surrounding Las Ventanas condo-miniums as part of its room inventory, so be certain to verify where you'll be placed, if this is not your preference. Although spacious and boasting a full kitchen, the con-dominiums do lack the views of the resort rooms and suites. The spa, based in Ayurveda, is considered among the best in Mexico, and the resort's three new Spa Suites offer a suite-contained resort spa experience tailored to the guest's goals and needs ranging from health and beauty to fitness and weight loss. With a staff that out-numbers guests by four to one and a focus on holistic healing, this is the place for those who want (and can afford) to be seriously spoiled. They even have Porsche Boxsters for guest rental and special packages for pampered pets. The 15% service charge is not included in the prices below, which do include taxes.

Km 19.5 on Hwy. 1, 23410 San José del Cabo, B.C.S. ✆ 888/525-0483 or 888/767-3966 in the U.S., or 624/144-2800. Fax 624/144-2801. www.lasventanas.com. 61 suites. High season $700 gardenview double, $950 oceanview double, $1,150 split-level oceanview suite with rooftop terrace, $1,325 split-level oceanfront suite with rooftop ter-race, $2,800–$5,500 luxury suites (1–3 bedrooms); low season $500 gardenview double, $700 oceanview double, $850 split-level oceanview suite with rooftop terrace, $975 split-level oceanfront suite with rooftop terrace, $2,000–$4,300 luxury suites. Spa Suites packages start at $13,425 for a 4-night program for 2. Spa and golf pack-ages and inclusive meal plans available. AE, DC, MC, V. Free valet parking. Pets accepted. **Amenities:** Oceanview restaurant; terrace bar w/live music; seaside grill; fresh-juice bar; infinity swimming pool; access to adjoining cham-pionship Cabo Real golf course; deluxe European spa w/complete treatment and exercise facilities; watersports; sportfishing and luxury yachts; tour services; Porsche Boxster rental; shuttle services; room service; laundry service; pet packages, including treats and massages. *In room:* A/C, TV/DVD, Wi-Fi, minibar, hair dryer, iron, safe, aromather-apy turn-down service, bathrobes CD player, iPods.

One&Only Palmilla *(Overrated*   One of the most luxurious hotels in Mexico, the One&Only Palmilla completed a thorough renovation in late 2003, making it among the most spectacular resort hotels anywhere. The new decor features muted desert col-ors and luxury fabrics, with special extras such as flatscreen TVs with DVD/CD play-ers, and Bose surround-sound systems. Guests may receive a personal butler and an aromatherapy menu—but they may not. Service is hit-and-miss, and unless you're a

Fortune 500 CEO or a Hollywood A-lister, the royal treatment is hard to come by. Although there are welcome exceptions, staff runs the gamut from indifferent to defiant. Nonetheless, Charlie Trotter's C restaurant offers impeccable 24-hour in-room dining and the *palapa*-topped Agua restaurant, with "Mexiterranean" cuisine, is a high point of the destination. The guest-only spa and its 13 private treatment villas offer a spectacular bit of pampering and may be reason enough to put up with the resort's too-cool attitude. Across the highway, the resort's own championship golf course, designed by Jack Nicklaus, is available for guests. The lush tropical resort also has two lighted tennis courts, a 600-sq.-m (6,458-sq.-ft.) fitness center, and yoga garden.

Carretera Transpeninsular Km 7.5, 23400 San José del Cabo, B.C.S. ℂ 800/637-2226 in the U.S., or 624/146-7000. Fax 624/144-5100. www.oneandonlypalmilla.com. 172 units. High season $600 double, $1,025–$2,600 suite; low season $450 double, $825–$2,050 suite. AE, MC, V. **Amenities:** 2 restaurants; 2 bars; pool bar; 2 infinity swimming pools; championship Palmilla golf course; deluxe European spa w/complete treatment and exercise facilities; watersports; sportfishing; tour services; car rental; shuttle services; room service; laundry service; dry cleaning, yoga garden. *In room:* A/C, TV/DVD, minibar, hair dryer, iron, safe, bathrobes, CD player.

Westin Resort & Spa, Los Cabos ★★ (Kids)   The architecturally dramatic Westin sits at the end of a long, paved road atop a seaside cliff. Vivid terra-cotta, yellow, and pink walls rise against a landscape of sandstone, cacti, and palms, with fountains and gardens lining the long pathways from the lobby to the rooms. The rooms, all of which are ocean view, are sleek and spacious, with fluffy Heavenly Beds and walk-in showers separate from the bathtubs. The seaside 18-hole putting green, first-rate fitness facility, and freshly renovated La Cascada restaurant set this property apart from other Corridor resorts. Plus, it's one of the best among our selections for families vacationing along the corridor; it is smoke-free and offers a wealth of activities for children—not to mention Heavenly Dog Beds for beloveds of the canine persuasion.

Hwy. 1 Km 22.5, 23400 San José del Cabo, B.C.S. ℂ 800/228-3000 in the U.S., or 624/142-9000. Fax 624/142-9010. www.westin.com/loscabos. 243 units. High season $529 oceanview double; $835 suite; low season $239 oceanview double, $535 suite. AE, DC, MC, V. Pets accepted. **Amenities:** 6 restaurants; 2 bars; 3 outdoor pools; nearby Palmilla and Cabo Real golf courses; 18-hole putting course; 2 tennis courts; full fitness center and spa; children's activities; concierge; Xplora Adventours services; car-rental desk; business services; salon; room service; babysitting; laundry service. *In room:* A/C, TV, minibar, hair dryer, safe.

WHERE TO DINE

C ★★★ GOURMET   Under the direction of renowned Chicago chef Charlie Trotter (this is his first restaurant outside the U.S.), a table for dinner at C is the ultimate special-occasion reservation in Cabo. Baja's influence on Trotter's culinary innovation is obvious in the menu selections, which change daily, but emphasize seafood and indigenous ingredients, although there are also selections of meat and game. To experience the best, order the signature *degustation* (tasting) menu, offering a variety of small courses, each paired with individual wine selection. The 110-seat dining room is L.A.-chic and gives no hint that you're in Mexico, despite the prevalent water theme and the series of blue cylindrical aquariums that separate the dining room from the exhibition kitchen. There are also two glass-enclosed wine rooms in the main dining area, and the overall atmosphere is bright and a bit loud. C also offers a 10-seat private dining room, and an invitation-only Chef's Kitchen Table, seating eight. Many consider a meal at C worth the trip to Cabo, and although the setting is visually stunning, and the flavors superb, I found the service pretentious and the prices excessive—even for Cabo, which is saying a lot. Formal resort attire is requested, and reservations are an absolute must during high season.

Los Cabos: Your Home Away from Home?

If you spend any time eavesdropping at local coffee shops and gringo bars, you'll find the Baja Peninsula is full of Americans, Canadians, and Europeans who came for a visit and never left. Owning property in Mexico is no longer as simple as plunking an RV on the beach, a la 30 years ago, but if you fall in love with Los Cabos—or Baja in general—you never have to leave, either.

Mexico has made it easy for foreigners to own their dream home on its shores. Through a *fideicomiso*, which is essentially a renewable trust, your home, condo, fractional ownership, or land by the sea is within reach. If you want to learn more about what's available in Los Cabos, check out the **Baja Real Estate Guide** (www.tregintl.com), a Los Cabos listings magazine that's not sponsored by any one particular real estate company and therefore showcases an unbiased range of options. Second, choose a reputable real-estate brokerage, such as **Snell Real Estate** (© **866/650-5845** in the U.S., or 624/105-8100; www.snellrealestate.com). A good agent will walk you through the process and help you find the ownership option that's right for you.

Another great resource for investors thinking about buying in Mexico is Mitch Creekmore and Tom Kelly's book, *Cashing in on a Second Home in Mexico: How to Buy, Rent, and Profit from Real Estate South of the Border* (Partners Pub Group Inc., 2005).

In the One&Only Palmilla, Hwy. 1 Km 7.5. © **624/146-7000**. www.oneandonlyresorts.com. Reservations required during high season. Main courses $45–$200. AE, MC, V. Daily 5–11pm.

Nick San ✦✦✦ JAPANESE/SUSHI   If you eat one meal out in Los Cabos, do it at Nick San. No matter your fancy—raw, cooked, veggies, meats, traditional, or out there—this dining experience is so superb it may shift your world view. Owned by Masayuki Niikura, Angel Carbajal, and his sister, Carmen Carbajal, who started their sushi dynasty 12 years ago at the original Nick San in downtown Cabo San Lucas, the newer and swankier outpost at Las Tiendas de Palmilla ensures a taste of Teppanyaki nirvana on both ends of the Corridor. The fire of Mexico meets traditional Japanese ingredients in such delicacies as tuna tostada, locally caught sea bass sashimi, and lobster with curried cream sauce. The low-lit atmosphere suits an intimate occasion or a night out with friends, and the meticulous service is always warm and personal. Because the entire menu is too delectable to pick one thing, let someone else make the decision for you: Ask for the chef's tasting plate and, whatever you do, do not miss the lobster tempura roll or the crab-stuffed salmon yuzu. Just be sure to let your server know when you've had enough, or the plates will keep on coming. By the time the check rolls around, you'll be so enamored it won't even faze you.

Tiendas de Palmilla, Hwy. 1 Km 27.5. © **624/144-6262** or 624/142-6263. www.nicksan.com. Reservations required unless you sit at the bar. Sashimi, rolls, and main courses $15–$50. AE, MC, V. Tues–Sun 12:30–10:30pm.

3 Cabo San Lucas ★ ★

176km (109 miles) S of La Paz; 35km (22 miles) W of San José del Cabo; 1,803km (1,118 miles) SE of Tijuana

The hundreds of luxury hotel rooms along the corridor north of Cabo San Lucas have transformed the very essence of this formerly rustic and rowdy outpost. Although it retains boisterous nightlife, Cabo San Lucas is no longer the simple town Steinbeck wrote about and enjoyed. Once legendary for the big-game fish that lurk offshore and for the beachside festivities that ensued after reeling them in, Cabo San Lucas now draws more people for its nearby fairways and greens—and the world-class golf being played on them. Cabo San Lucas has become Mexico's most elite resort destination, catering to travelers getting away for long weekends or indulging in sports and relaxation.

Travelers here can enjoy a growing roster of adventure-oriented activities, and play-time doesn't end when the sun goes down. The nightlife here is as hot as the desert in July, and oddly casual, having grown up away from the Corridor's glitzy resorts and rebelling against the well-groomed style of mainland Mexico. It remains the raucous, playful party scene that helped put Cabo on the map. A collection of popular restaurants and bars along Cabo's main street stay open and active until the morning's first fishing charters head out to sea. Despite the growth in diversions, Cabo remains more or less a one-stoplight town, with almost everything within easy walking distance along the main strip.

ESSENTIALS
GETTING THERE & DEPARTING

BY PLANE   For information, see "Getting There & Departing," earlier, under San José del Cabo. Local airline numbers are as follows: **Alaska Airlines** (© **624/146-5100** or 624/146-5101) and **Mexicana** (© **624/143-5352,** 624/143-5353, or 624/146-5001).

BY CAR   From La Paz, the best route is Highway 1 south past the village of San Pedro, and then Highway 19 south through Todos Santos to Cabo San Lucas, a 2-hour drive.

BY BUS   The bus terminal (© **624/143-5020**) is on Héroes at Morelos; it is open daily from 7am to 10pm. Buses go to La Paz every 2 hours starting at 7:15am, with the last departure at 8:15pm. To and from San José, the more convenient and economical **Suburcabos** public bus service runs every 15 minutes and costs $2.50.

ORIENTATION

ARRIVING   At the airport, either buy a ticket for a *colectivo* (shuttle) from **Josefinos** (© **624/146-5354**), the authorized transportation booth inside the building (about $13), or arrange for a rental car, the most economical way to explore the area. Up to four people can share a private taxi, which costs about $60.

The walk from the bus station to most of the budget hotels is manageable with light luggage or backpacks, and taxis are readily available.

VISITOR INFORMATION   The **Los Cabos Tourism Office** (© **624/146-9628**) is in San José, in the Plaza San José, Locales 3 and 4, and is open daily from 8am to 3pm. The English-language *Los Cabos Guide, Los Cabos News, Destino Los Cabos,* and the irreverent and extremely entertaining *Gringo Gazette* are distributed free at most hotels and shops, and have up-to-date information on new restaurants and clubs. If you fall so deeply in love with Los Cabos as to want to own a piece of it, *The Baja*

Cabo San Lucas

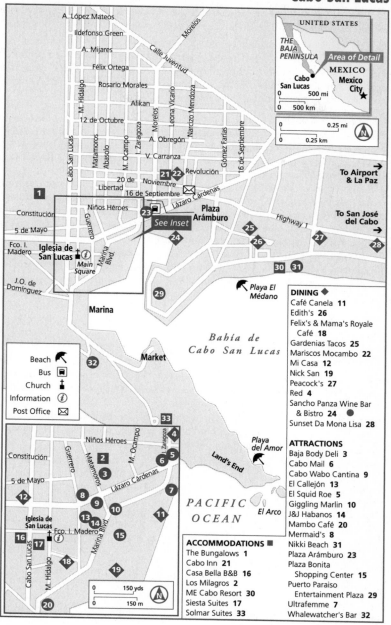

Beach 🏖️
Bus 🚌
Church ✝
Information ⓘ
Post Office ✉

DINING ◆
Café Canela **11**
Edith's **26**
Felix's & Mama's Royale Café **18**
Gardenias Tacos **25**
Mariscos Mocambo **22**
Mi Casa **12**
Nick San **19**
Peacock's **27**
Red **4**
Sancho Panza Wine Bar & Bistro **24** ●
Sunset Da Mona Lisa **28**

ATTRACTIONS
Baja Body Deli **3**
Cabo Mail **6**
Cabo Wabo Cantina **9**
El Callejón **13**
El Squid Roe **5**
Giggling Marlin **10**
J&J Habanos **14**
Mambo Café **20**
Mermaid's **8**
Nikki Beach **31**
Plaza Arámburo **23**
Plaza Bonita Shopping Center **15**
Puerto Paraiso Entertainment Plaza **29**
Ultrafemme **7**
Whalewatcher's Bar **32**

ACCOMMODATIONS ■
The Bungalows **1**
Cabo Inn **21**
Casa Bella B&B **16**
Los Milagros **2**
ME Cabo Resort **30**
Siesta Suites **17**
Solmar Suites **33**

Real Estate Guide (www.tregintl.com) is a great place to start, as it's a comprehensive listings magazine not affiliated with any particular real-estate brokerage or agent.

CITY LAYOUT   The small town spreads out north and west of the harbor of Cabo San Lucas Bay, edged by foothills and desert mountains to the west and south. The main street leading into town from the airport and San José del Cabo is Lázaro Cárdenas; as it nears the harbor, Marina Boulevard branches off from it and becomes the main artery that curves around the waterfront.

GETTING AROUND

Plan to walk everywhere within San Lucas proper. The town is fairly concentrated and provides a wealth of people-watching opportunities. Taxis are easy to find but are expensive within Cabo, in keeping with the high cost of everything else. Expect to pay about $15 to $25 for a taxi between Cabo and the Corridor hotels.

For day trips to San José del Cabo, catch a bus (see "Getting There & Departing" under "San José del Cabo," earlier) or a cab. You'll see car-rental specials advertised in town, but before signing on, be sure you understand the total price, including insurance and taxes. Rates can run between $50 and $75 per day, with insurance an extra $10 per day. One of the best and most economical agencies is **Advantage Rent-A-Car** (© 624/143-0909 or ©/fax 624/143-0466), on Lázaro Cárdenas between Leona Vicario and Morelos. VW sedans rent for $80 per day, and weekly renters receive 1 free day. A collision damage waiver will add $22 per day to the price. If you pick up the car downtown, you can return it to the airport at no extra charge.

FAST FACTS: Cabo San Lucas

Area Code   The telephone area code is **624**.

Beach Safety   Before swimming in the open water, *check if conditions are safe.* Undertows and large waves are common. **Médano Beach,** close to the marina and town, is the principal beach that's safe for swimming. The ME Cabo resort on Médano Beach has a roped-off swimming area to protect swimmers from personal watercraft and boats. Colored flags to signal swimming safety aren't generally found in Cabo, and neither are lifeguards, so be aware.

Currency Exchange   Banks exchange currency during normal business hours, generally Monday through Friday from 9am to 6pm and Saturday from 9am to 2pm. Currency-exchange booths, found throughout Cabo's main tourist areas, aren't as competitive but are more convenient. ATMs are widely available and even more convenient, dispensing pesos—and in some cases dollars—at bank exchange rates.

Emergencies & Hospital   In Cabo, **Amerimed** (© 624/143-9671) is a 24-hour, American-standards clinic with bilingual physicians and emergency air-evacuation services, and it accepts major credit cards. Most of the larger hotels have a doctor on call.

Internet Access   **Cabo Mail** (© 624/143-7796), Plaza Aramburo on Lázaro Cárdenas, charges $1 for 1 to 10 minutes, and 10¢ for each additional minute. They also offer long-distance VoIP access, fax, copies, memory stick photo downloads, color printing, and CD/DVD recording. It's open Monday through Friday from 9am to 9pm, Saturday from 9:30am to 6pm, and Sunday from noon to 6pm.

Pharmacy A drugstore with a wide selection of toiletries as well as medicine is **Farmacia Aramburo,** in Plaza Aramburo, on Lázaro Cárdenas at Zaragoza (© **624/143-1489**). It's open daily from 8am to 10pm and accepts MasterCard and Visa.

Post Office The *correo* (© **624/143-0048**) is at Lázaro Cárdenas and Francisco Villa, on the highway to San José del Cabo, east of the bar El Squid Roe. It's open Monday through Friday from 9am to 5pm, and Saturday from 9am to 3pm.

BEACHES & OUTDOOR ACTIVITIES

Although superb sportfishing put Cabo San Lucas on the map, there's more to do here than drop your line and wait for the Big One. For most fishing cruises and excursions, try to make reservations at least a day in advance; keep in mind that some trips require a minimum number of people. Most sports and outings can be arranged through your hotel concierge or a travel agency; fishing also can be arranged directly at one of the fishing-fleet offices at the marina, which is on the south side of the harbor.

Besides fishing, there are kayaking ($65 for a sunset trip around the Arch rock formation; $40 for morning trips) and boat trips to Los Arcos or uninhabited beaches. All-inclusive daytime or sunset cruises are available on a variety of boats, including a pirate ship replica. Many of these trips include snorkeling; and serious divers have great underwater venues to explore with the dive operator of their choice. Horseback riding on both Sea of Cortez and Pacific beaches (very popular at sunset) costs about $35 an hour. Whale-watching, between January and March, has become one of the most popular local activities. Guided ATV (all-terrain vehicle) tours take you down dirt roads and through a desert landscape to an ancient Indian village. And then, of course, there's the challenge of world-class golf, a major attraction of Los Cabos.

For a complete rundown of what's available, look to **Book Cabo** (© **624/142-9200;** www.bookcabo.com). It offers tours from the best local companies and you can book ahead online. Most businesses in this section are open from 10am to 2pm and 4 to 7pm.

ATV TRIPS   Expeditions on ATVs to visit La Candelaria, an Indian pueblo in the mountains, are available through concierge and travel agencies. A 200 kilogram (440 lb.) weight limit per two-person vehicle applies.

Tío Sports (© **624/143-3399**) offers day trips to La Candelaria, an isolated Indian village in the mountains 40km (25 miles) north of Cabo San Lucas. Described in *National Geographic,* the old pueblo is known for the practice of white and black witchcraft, but the locals chuckle at the mention of *brujería,* as if to tolerate a rumor that's brought tourism to their town. Lush with palms, mango trees, and bamboo, the settlement gets its water from an underground river that emerges at the pueblo. The return trip of the tour travels down a steep canyon, along a beach (giving you time to swim), and through town. Departing at 9am, Tío's 5-hour La Candelaria tour costs around $80 per person or $100 for two on the same ATV.

DRIVING TOURS   A uniquely "Cabo" experience is offered by **Baja Outback** (© **624/142-9215;** fax 624/142-3166; www.bajaoutback.com) via their caravan-style Hummer Adventures. You drive these luxury H2 Hummers, going off-road to cruise desert and beachfront terrain in style, while learning about the surrounding area

⌒Moments Festivals & Events in Cabo San Lucas

October 18 is the feast of the patron saint of Cabo San Lucas, celebrated with a fair, feasting, music, dancing, and other special events. However, the biggest event of the year for more than 25 years, also in late October, has been Bisbee's Black & Blue Tournament, which draws thousands of party-ready anglers in search of the multimillion-dollar purse that comes with catching the biggest marlin.

through expert guides who are in one of the Hummers. Communication devices link up to 10 vehicles in the caravan, allowing you to listen to the narrations of the guide. There's a choice of four routes, which include treks to Todos Santos, the East Cape, Santiago and Cañon de la Zorra, and Rancho la Verdad. Tours depart at 9am and return at 3pm, with prices ranging from $165 to $220, depending upon the route, and include lunch. Inquire about multiday tours that focus on the Jesuit missions, migrating whales, and Baja cuisine. Visa, MasterCard, and American Express are accepted, and you must have your valid driver's license. Special group rates are also available.

If this sounds too tame, **Wide Open Baja Racing Experience** (© **888/788-2252** or 949/340-1155 in the U.S., or 624/143-4170; office in Plaza Náutica; www.wide opencabo.com) gives you the chance to drive actual Chenowth Magnum racecars at their 600-hectare (1,500-acre) racing ranch on the Pacific Coast. There's a varied terrain to drive, with twists, turns, sand washes, and plenty of bumps for thrill-seekers. Session times for the **test drive** are at 10am and 1:30pm. The $250 price includes shuttle transportation from downtown Cabo to the ranch, driver orientation, and safety equipment. Private group rates are also available. Wide Open Baja also offers multiday tours driving race vehicles through Cabo, Ensenada, and the entire Baja peninsula.

BEACHES

All along the curving sweep of sand known as **Playa El Médano (Médano Beach),** on the northeast side of the bay, you can rent snorkeling gear, boats, WaveRunners ($70 per hr.), kayaks, pedal boats, and windsurf boards. (You can also take windsurfing lessons.) This is the town's main beach; it's a great place for safe swimming, happy-hour-imbibing, and people-watching from one of the many outdoor restaurants, such as **The Office** (© **624/143-3464;** www.theofficeonthebeach.com) or **Baja Cantina** (© **624/143-9773**), the less-expensive option, which is just as good and has a better atmosphere for all-day lounging along its shore.

Beach aficionados may want to rent a car (see "Getting Around," above) and explore the five more-remote beaches and coves between the two Cabos: **playas Palmilla, Chileno, Santa María, Barco Varado,** and **Lovers Beach.** Palmilla, Chileno, Santa María, and Lovers Beach are generally safe for swimming—but always be careful, especially if the waves look rough or if you know a storm is offshore. Even the "safe" beaches can be treacherous in the wrong conditions. Most visitors should be honest about their comfort level in the water and enter accordingly; the aforementioned beaches are fine for experienced snorkelers and swimmers. Always check at a hotel or travel agency for directions and swimming conditions. Although a few travel agencies run snorkeling tours to some of these beaches, there's no public transportation. Your options for beach exploring are to rent a car or have a cab drop you off at the beach of your choice.

CRUISES

Glass-bottom boats leave from the town marina daily every 45 minutes between 9am and 4pm. They cost $14 for a 1-hour tour, which passes sea lions and pelicans on its way to the famous "El Arco" (Rock Arch) at Land's End, where the Pacific and the Sea of Cortez meet. Boats can drop you off at Playa del Amor if you wish to snorkel or sun; make sure you understand which boat will pick you up—it's usually a smaller one run by the same company that ferries people back at regular intervals. Check the timing to make sure you have the correct boat, or expect an additional $10 charge for boarding a competitor's boat.

A number of **daylong** and **sunset cruises** come in a variety of boats and catamarans. They cost $30 to $50 per person, depending on the boat, duration of cruise, and amenities. A sunset cruise on the 13m (43-ft.) catamaran *Pez Gato* (© **624/143-3797**; www.pezgatocabo.com) departs from the Tesoro Resort dock (Dock no. 4, 50m/164 ft. from the main dock) between 4:30 and 5:30pm, depending on the season. A 2-hour cruise costs $35 and includes an open bar and appetizers. The seasonal (winter) whale-watching tour leaves at 10:30am and returns at 1:30pm. It costs $35 and includes open bar and snacks. Similar boats, such as the **Tropicat** (© **624/143-3797**; www.tropicatcabo.com), leave from the marina and the Tesoro Resort. Check with travel agencies or hotel tour desks.

LAND SPORTS

Aside from the obvious—golf, ATV tours, and horseback riding—Cabo is hot on mountain biking, rock climbing, and hiking as well.

GOLF   Los Cabos has become the golf capital of Mexico, and though most courses are along the Corridor, people look to Cabo San Lucas for information about this sport in Baja Sur. The master plan for Los Cabos golf calls for a future total of 207 holes. Fees listed below are for 18 holes, including golf cart, water, club service, and tax. Summer rates are about 25% lower, and many hotels offer golf packages. (For specifics on the various courses, see "The Lowdown on Golf in Cabo," below.)

Several specialty tour operators offer golf packages to Los Cabos, which include accommodations, greens fees, and other amenities. These include **Golf Adventures** (© **800/841-6570** from the U.S.; www.golfadventures.com) and **Sportours** (© **888/465-3639** from the U.S.; www.sportours.com).

The 27-hole course at the **Palmilla Golf Club** (© **800/386-2465** in the U.S., or 624/144-5250; www.oneandonlyresorts.com; daily 7am–7pm) was the first Jack Nicklaus Signature layout in Mexico, on 360 hectares (900 acres) of dramatic oceanfront desert. The course offers your choice of two back-9 options, with high-season greens fees of $255 (lower after 1pm), and low-season greens fees running between $190 and $210. Guests at some hotels pay discounted rates.

Just a few kilometers away is another Jack Nicklaus Signature course, the 18-hole Ocean Course at **Cabo del Sol,** the posh resort development in the Corridor (© **866/231-4677** in the U.S.:, or 624/145-8200; www.cabodelsol.com). The 7,100-yard Ocean Course is known for its challenging 3 finishing holes and greens fees start at $250 in the low season and range to $350 for the high season. Tom Weiskopf designed the new 18-hole Desert Course, for which greens fees are $220 in the high season,

The Lowdown on Golf in Cabo

Los Cabos, one of the world's finest golf destinations, offers an ample and intriguing variety of courses to challenge golfers of all levels.

The reason so many choose to play here is not just the selection, quality, and beauty of the courses, but the reliable weather. The courses highlighted below compare to the great ones in Palm Springs and Scottsdale, with the added beauty of ocean views and a wider variety of desert cacti and flowering plants.

Course fees are high in Cabo—generally more than $200 per round. But these are world-class courses, worth the world-class price. Courses generally offer 20% to 30% off rates if you play after 2 or 2:30pm. This can be a great time because play is generally faster.

The golf offerings in Los Cabos will only continue to expand; an untold number of courses are in various phases of construction. At **Puerto Los Cabos,** a new mega-development northeast of San José del Cabo, construction has started on two 18-hole courses, the public course designed by Jack Nicklaus and a private course by Greg Norman. The East Cape's **Hotel Palmas de Cortez** opened a 9-hole par-3 course last year. **Club Campestre,** in the heart of San José, will have an 18-hole Jack Nicklaus course. The **Chileno Bay Project,** in the center of the Corridor, has set aside 2½ miles of coastline for luxury-home sites and two championship courses by Tom Fazio. At the other end of the peninsula, near Cabo San Lucas on the Pacific side, the **Cabo Pacifica** development will soon be launching two more championship courses.

The area's premier open-to-the-public courses are listed below in order of location, from north to south.

Palmilla Golf Club   The original Cabo course is now a 27-hole layout. The original 18 holes are known as the Arroyo; the new holes are the Ocean 9. It's a bit of a misnomer—although the newer holes lie closer to the water, only one has a true ocean view, with spectacular play directly down to the beach. You must play the Arroyo for your first 9 holes and then choose between Mountain and Ocean for your back 9. If you play this course only once, choose the Mountain, which offers better ocean views. The signature

$185 in the low season. Desert Course twilight play ranges from $140 to $165 in low and high seasons, respectively.

The 18-hole, 6,945-yard course at **Cabo Real,** by the Meliá Cabo Real Hotel in the Corridor (© **877/795-8727** in the U.S., or 624/173-9400; www.caboreal.com; daily 6:30am–6pm), was designed by Robert Trent Jones, Jr., and features holes that sit high on mesas overlooking the Sea of Cortez. Fees run $260 for 18 holes. After 3pm, rates drop to $132 in the low season and $480 in the high season. Kids 16 and under play for $92 year round.

An 18-hole course designed by Roy Dye is at the **Raven Club,** formerly the Cabo San Lucas Country Club (© **888/328-8501** in the U.S., or 624/143-4653; fax 624/143-5809). The entire Dye-designed course overlooks the juncture of the Pacific hole is the Mountain 5; you hit over a canyon, and then down to the green below over a forced carry. The 14th hole here is considered one of the world's most beautiful golf holes, a forced carry from the hillside tee boxes to an island. From there, players line up on a green set on the side of a steep arroyo. The hole opens up to spectacular vistas and seems a lot longer than it plays. This is target golf, on a Jack Nicklaus course that was constructed with strategy in mind. A mountaintop clubhouse provides spectacular views. Although it is currently a semiprivate club, most Corridor hotels have membership benefits.

Cabo Del Sol   The Ocean Course at Cabo de Sol was the second Jack Nicklaus course constructed in Los Cabos. It is much more difficult than the Palmilla course, with less room for error.

Don't be fooled by the wide, welcoming 1st hole. This is challenging target golf, with numerous forced carries—even from the red tees. Seven holes are along the water. At the par-3 signature 17th hole, the golfer is faced with a 178-yard shot over sandy beach and rocky outcroppings to a tiny green framed by bunkers on one side and a drop to the ocean on the other. The finishing hole, guarded by desert and cactus on the right and rock cliffs leading to the sea on the left, is modeled after the 18th at Pebble Beach.

Cabo del Sol offers another option, the Desert Course, which is Tom Weiskopf's first course design in Mexico. It is spread out over 56 hectares (140 acres) of gently rolling desert terrain and provides sweeping ocean views.

Cabo Real   This Robert Trent Jones, Jr., design is known for its holes along the Sea of Cortez; exceptional among these is the frequently photographed 12th hole, which sits high on a mesa facing the sea. Jones designed the course to test low handicappers, but multiple tees make it enjoyable for average players as well. While the first 6 holes are in mountainous terrain, others skirt the shore. Rolling greens and strategically placed bunkers on narrow terrain work their way up to the 6th tee, 138m (460 ft.) above sea level. The most celebrated hole, the 15th, sits right on the beach between the Meliá Cabo Real Golf & Beach Resort and Las Ventanas al Paraíso.

Ocean and Sea of Cortez, including the famous rocks of Land's End. It includes a 607-yard, par-5 7th hole. High-season greens fees are $186 for 18 holes, $149 for the noon rate, and $105 after 2:30pm. In the summer months, greens fees drop to $109 for 18 holes and to $79 after 10:30am.

The lowest greens fees in the area are at the public 9-hole **Mayan Palace Golf Los Cabos** (© **624/142-0900** or 624/142-0901) in San José del Cabo (see earlier in this chapter). Early-morning greens fees are just $69 for 9 holes, and $99 for 18 holes with equipment, from 6am to 2pm; rates drop to $80 for 18 holes after 3pm. All greens fees include use of cart.

The consensus among avid golfers is that two of the area's best courses are the Fazio-designed Querencia and the soon-to-be reopened El Dorado, a Jack Nicklaus design.

However, both courses are private and open only to Querencia and El Dorado members and homeowners. As Los Cabos becomes increasingly exclusive, and as more luxury travelers look to own a piece of it, expect to see more private members-only golf clubs within opulent master-planned residential communities. In fact, the trend already is well under way within the new communities of Chileno Bay, Puerto Los Cabos, Cabo Pacífica, and El Dorado.

HORSEBACK RIDING   For horseback riding, I highly recommend **Cuadra San Francisco Equestrian Center** (see p. 62 for more information). You can rent **horses** through **Rancho Colín** (© **624/143-3652**) for $25 per hour. Tours for sunset riding on Sea of Cortez beaches cost $35 per hour, the 2-hour desert-and-beach trail ride is $60, and the 3½-hour tour through the mountains is $80. The ranch is open daily from 8am to noon and 2 to 5pm, and is across from the Hotel Club Las Cascadas.

ECOTOURS   There's an increasing array of adventure tours and extreme sports available in the Los Cabos area. **Ramon's EcoTours** (© **624/122-3696;** www.ramons ecotours.com) is a good place to start, namely for kayaking and hiking adventures. Another of the best is **Baja Wild** (© **624/142-5300;** www.bajawild.com), which offers kayaking, mountain biking, rock climbing, and guided hiking excursions in the Sierra de la Laguna mountains 2 hours north of Los Cabos. The range runs north to south in the Baja peninsula and reaches elevations of more than 2,100m (7,000 ft.), accommodating a unique biosphere where oak and pine trees flourish. Although you sense you are in Baja's desert landscape, you'll be awed by the amount of wildlife you'll see: frogs, doves, Monarch butterflies, deer, giant golden eagles, lizards, and much more. There are also cool, spring-fed mountain pools ready to soothe your muscles after the 5-mile round-trip hike. Group sizes are limited to about eight, and transportation to the hiking area is by air-conditioned minivan. This tour costs $95 per person and includes morning coffee and baked goods, snacks on the hike, and lunch upon return.

WATERSPORTS

SNORKELING/DIVING   Several companies offer snorkeling; a 2-hour cruise to sites around El Arco costs $30, and a 4-hour trip to Santa María costs $55, including gear rental. Among the beaches visited on different trips are Playa del Amor, Santa María, Chileno, and Barco Varado. Snorkeling gear rents for $10 to $15. Contact **Book Cabo** (© **624/142-9200;** www.bookcabo.com). For scuba diving, contact **Manta divers** (© **624/144-3871;** www.caboscuba.com) and **Amigos del Mar** in Cabo San Lucas (© **800/344-3349** in the U.S., or 624/143-0505; www.amigosdel mar.com). Dives are along the wall of a canyon in San Lucas Bay, where you can see the cascading sand falls by Anegada Rock. There are also scuba trips to Santa María Beach and more distant places, including Gordo Banks and Cabo Pulmo. Prices start at $50 for a one-tank dive and from $150 for 2 days of diving. Night dives are $65 per person. Trips to the coral outcropping at Cabo Pulmo start at $130. You'll need a wetsuit for winter dives. A 5-hour resort course is available for $100, and open-water certification costs $430.

SPORTFISHING   You can call on a concierge or a travel agent, but it's more fun to make your own arrangements for a fishing trip. Just go to the marina on the south side of the harbor, where you'll find several fleet operators with offices near the docks. The *panga* fleets east of San José in La Playita offer the best deals; 5 hours of fishing for two or three people costs $200 to $450, plus a 20% tip (see **Gordo Banks Pangas;**

> **Tips Don't Sweat the One That Got Away**
>
> "Catch and release" is strongly encouraged in Los Cabos. Anglers reel in their fish, which are then tagged and released unharmed. The angler gets a certificate and the knowledge that there will still be fish in the sea when he returns.

© 624/142-1147; www.gordobanks.com). In Cabo, try **Pisces Fleet,** located in the Cabo Maritime Center, behind Tesoro Resort and next to Captain Tony's on the marina (© **624/143-1288;** www.piscessportfishing.com; daily 10am–4pm; Visa and MasterCard accepted), or **Minerva's** (© **624/143-1282;** www.minervas.com; daily 6am–8pm; American Express, MasterCard, and Visa accepted). It doesn't get any better than these two companies. A day on a fully equipped cruiser with captain and guide starts at around $800 for up to six people. For deluxe trips with everything included aboard a 12m (40-ft.) boat, you'll have to budget around $1,500 and up. If you're traveling in your own vessel, you'll need a fishing permit, which you can get at **Minerva's Baja Tackle,** on the corner of Bulevar Marina and Madero. Depending on the size of the boat, it will cost $15 to $45 per month. Daily permits ($4–$10) and annual permits are also available.

The fishing here lives up to its reputation: Bringing in a 100-pound marlin is routine, although decades of pressure on Sea of Cortez fisheries should inspire you to release your prized catch. Angling is good all year, though the catch varies with the season. Sailfish and wahoo are best from June through November; yellowfin tuna, May through December; yellowtail, January through April; black and blue marlin, July through December. Striped marlin, dorado, and mahimahi are prevalent year-round.

SURFING   Stellar surfing can be found from November through April all along the Pacific beaches north and west of town, and the East Cape is the ultimate North American surfing destination from May through October. (Also see "Surfing" in "San José del Cabo," earlier in this chapter, for details on Costa Azul and East Cape breaks.)

The areas to the east and west of Los Cabos, known as the East Cape and the Pacific side, respectively, have yet to face the onslaught of development that's so rapidly changed the tip. An hour-long drive up the western coast to the little towns of Pescadero and Todos Santos can be a great surf journey, as can a summer trek up the Sea of Cortez coastline toward Cabo Pulmo. Your best bet is to visit **www.costa-azul.com.mx/areas_maps.htm** for a detailed look at the different breaks, excursions, rental equipment, and lessons available for the time of year you're planning to visit.

Many beach breaks are ride-worthy at different times, depending on the wave conditions, but a vicious shore break and strong undertow characterize much of the beach around Todos Santos. While the unruliness of the ocean has helped keep industrial tourism at bay, it also means you have to hunt a little harder to find playful waves.

WHALE-WATCHING   Whale-watching cruises are the best way to get up close and personal with nature's most majestic seafaring mammals. For information about the excursions, which operate between January and March, see "Whale-Watching" under "San José del Cabo," earlier in this chapter, and "Whale-Watching in Baja: A Primer," in chapter 6.

Surf & Sleep

If you can't get enough of the surf, stay where this is the specialty, and not just an activity. The Los Cabos area has two outposts that cater to surfers, one along Los Cabos Corridor, and the other on the Pacific coast, near Todos Santos.

The **Cabo Surf Hotel** (© 858/964-5146 from the U.S., or 624/142-2666; www. cabosurfhotel.com) has 16 beachfront rooms in a secluded, gated boutique resort. It's 13km (8 miles) west of San José del Cabo, across from the Querencia golf course, on Playa Acapulquito, which is the most popular surfing beach in Los Cabos. Along with a choice of rooms and suites, it's equipped with an oceanfront terrace restaurant, surf shop, and the Mike Doyle Surf School, which offers day lessons and more intensive instruction. Rates range from $260 to $325 for a double, and $275 to $780 for suites and villas. Promotional rates are available during summer months, which is optimum for surfers who seek the Sea of Cortez's summertime swells.

The **Pescadero Surf Camp** (© 612/130-3022 or 612/134-0480; www.pescadero surf.com) is a sparse Pacific getaway on Highway 1 toward Todos Santos at Km 64. Eight pool-front casitas, each equipped with a minifridge, start at $25, and the two-story suite rents for $60 per night. Although it's 1km from the beach, this surf camp is a comfortable step up from the beach camping that's a way of life for most surf mongers. And, in the winter, when the waves—and sometimes winds—are at their strongest, it's nice to have a roof overhead. The property's brand-new pool has a B.Y.O.B. swim-up bar that's ideal for cooling off between surf excursions, and a large outdoor kitchen provides a space to prepare your own meals. Owner Jaime Dobies also offers 1½-hour lessons for $50, board rental for $15 a day, boogie and skim board rental for $10 a day, and daylong guided surf safaris starting at $100 per person. He also repairs boards, should your baby get dinged in action. Of course, if you're coming to Baja strictly for the surf, you may join the other hardcore wave-riders and camp along the sugary beaches of the East Cape in the summer and the Pacific in the winter. Most beaches—especially the ones fronting secluded surf breaks—are safe and accommodating for overnight stays.

EXPLORING CABO SAN LUCAS

HISTORIC CABO SAN LUCAS

Watersports and partying are Cabo's main attractions, but there are also a few cultural and historical points of interest. The Spanish missionary Nicolás Tamaral established the stone **Iglesia de San Lucas** (Church of San Lucas) on Calle Cabo San Lucas near the main plaza in 1730; a large bell in a stone archway commemorates the completion of the church in 1746. The Pericúe Indians, who reportedly resisted Tamaral's demands that they practice monogamy, eventually killed him. Buildings on the streets facing the main plaza are gradually being renovated to house restaurants and shops, and the picturesque neighborhood promises to have the strongest Mexican ambience in town.

NEARBY DAY TRIPS

Most local hotels and travel agencies can book day trips to the city of La Paz for around $60, including beverages and a tour of the countryside along the way. Usually there's a stop at the weaving shop of Fortunato Silva, who spins his own cotton and weaves it into wonderfully textured rugs and textiles. For more information, see chapter 5, "La Paz: Peaceful Port Town." Day trips are also available to Todos Santos ($60), with a guided walking tour of the Cathedral Mission, museum, Hotel California, and various artists' homes. For more on Todos Santos, see "Todos Santos: A Creative Oasis," later in this chapter.

SHOPPING

San José has the better shopping of the two towns when it comes to quality and uniqueness, but if you're after a beer-themed T-shirt, Cabo San Lucas can't be topped. Nevertheless, the **Puerto Paraíso Entertainment Plaza** (© 624/144-3000; www. puertoparaiso.com) does have a selection of designer clothing stores, knickknack shops, and swimwear boutiques. Opened in 2002, this is now the focal point for locals' entertainment and tourists' exploration. It's a truly world-class mall, complete with free parking, movie theaters, a video arcade, a food court, and various restaurants, not the least of which is **Ruth's Chris Steak House,** adjacent to the marina (© 624/144-3232; www.ruthschris.com.mx; daily 1–11:30pm). With more than 50,000 sq. m (538,195 sq. ft.) of air-conditioned space on three levels, it's a shame so much of the mall is still empty. Rumor has it the developers are taking their time to complete construction and to rent the spaces to the right tenants, so don't expect the equivalent of a U.S. shopping mall experience for a few years. The plaza is located marina-side between the Plaza Bonita Mall and Marina Fiesta Resort—you can't miss it if you try. Most other shops in Cabo are on or within a block or two of Boulevard Marina and the plaza.

In addition to the mall, I recommend the following specialty stores:

Baja Body Deli 😺😺   This is a true gem of a spa boutique. Fragrant candles, Baja-grown loose teas and dried herbs, handmade cut-to-order soaps, luxury bathrobes, and other pampering products make this a stylish oasis in a sea of commercial shops. They specialize in custom-scented body lotion, hair care, massage oil, sprays, and scrubs. Open Monday through Saturday 10am to 7:30pm. Matamoros, near corner of Lázaro Cardenas. © 624/143-3272.

El Callejón   This has San Lucas' best selection of fine Mexican furniture and decor items, plus gifts, accessories, tableware, fabrics, and lamps. Open Monday through Saturday 9:30am to 7pm. Guerrero between Madero and Bulevar Marina (across from the main plaza). © 624/143-3188.

J & J Habanos   This is Cabo's go-to cigar shop, selling premium Cuban and fine Mexican cigars; it even has a walk-in humidor. They also sell fine tequila and espresso. Open Monday through Saturday 9am to 10pm, Sunday 9am to 9pm. Madero between Bulevar Marina and Guerrero. © 624/143-6160 or 624/143-3839.

UltraFemme   Mexico's largest duty-free shop has an excellent selection of fine jewelry and watches, including Rolex, Cartier, Omega, TAG Heuer, Tiffany, and Tissot; perfumes, including Lancôme, Chanel, Armani, and Carolina Herrera; and other gift items, all at duty-free prices. Open daily 10am to 9:30pm. Plaza UltraFemme, Bulevar Marina. © 624/145-6090. www.ultrafemme.com.mx.

WHERE TO STAY

High-season prices are in effect from December to Easter. Several hotels offer package deals that significantly lower the nightly rate, so ask your travel agent for information.

Budget accommodations are scarce, but the number of small inns and B&Bs is growing; several notable ones have opened in recent years. Also the all-inclusive market is growing at a brisk pace, offering travelers more options for economical accommodations with food and drink included in the price. Because most of the larger hotels are well maintained and offer packages through travel agents and online hospitality search engines, I will focus on smaller, unique accommodations, all of which include free parking. The 12% tax is not included in the rate.

VERY EXPENSIVE

ME Cabo ✸✸   If you've come to Cabo to party, this is your place. Formerly the Meliá San Lucas, the newly renovated ME Cabo is Sol Meliá's foray into hip, making it Cabo's hottest hot spot. Upgraded rooms, a new adult-focused floor called "The Level," and the presence of the swank Nikki Beach stake a glam claim on this beachfront property, which is geared toward those looking for a party in addition to relaxation. Its location on Médano Beach is central to any other action you may want to seek, but with Nikki Beach and Passion, you'll find plenty right here. Rooms are awash in fiery red and white, with sleek, contemporary decor. All suites have ocean views, and private terraces look across to the famed El Arco. Master suites have separate living-room areas. Guests gather by the beachfront pool where oversized daybeds perfectly accommodate this lounge atmosphere. There are also VIP teepees, and the live DJ music keeps the party here going day and night.

Playa El Médano s/n; 23410 Cabo San Lucas, B.C.S. ✆ **624/145-7800.** Fax 624/143-0420. www.mebymelia.com. 150 units. High season $356–$540 double, $1,100 chic suite, $2,100 loft suite; low season $311–$441 double, $756 chic suite, $1,100 loft suite. AE, MC, V. **Amenities:** Restaurant; bar/dance club; 3 outdoor pools; beach club; Jacuzzi; concierge; boutique; tour desk; car-rental desk; room service; laundry service; dry cleaning. *In room:* A/C, TV, Wi-Fi, minibar, coffeemaker, hair dryer, safe, iPods.

MODERATE

The Bungalows ✸ *(Finds)*   This is one of the most special places to stay in Los Cabos. Each "bungalow" is a charming retreat decorated with authentic Mexican furnishings. Terra-cotta tiles, hand-painted sinks, wooden chests, blown glass, and other creative touches make you feel as if you're a guest at a friend's home rather than a hotel. Each room has a kitchenette, purified water, VCR, and comfortable bedding. Rooms surround a lovely heated pool with cushioned lounges and tropical gardens. A brick-paved breakfast nook serves a gourmet breakfast with fresh-ground coffee and fresh juices. Under the owner's warm and welcoming management, this is Cabo's most spacious, comfortable, full-service inn. A 100% smoke-free environment, it is 5 blocks from downtown Cabo.

Miguel A. Herrera s/n, in front of Lienzo Charro, 23410 Cabo San Lucas, B.C.S. ✆/fax **624/143-5035** or 624/143-0585. www.cabobungalows.com. 16 units. High season $115–$165 suite; low season $105–$115 suite. Extra person $20. Rates include full breakfast. AE, V. Street parking available. **Amenities:** Breakfast room; outdoor pool; concierge; tour desk. *In room:* A/C, TV/VCR, kitchenette, fridge, coffeemaker.

Casa Bella B&B ✸✸✸ *(Finds)*   This hacienda-style boutique hotel is right on the main plaza in Cabo San Lucas yet retains a sense of privacy and tranquillity, even though you're close to everything in downtown Cabo. This is made possible thanks to a wall with windows and arches that surrounds the series of white stucco buildings comprising this lovely place. The seven guest rooms and one suite surround a central courtyard and pool, landscaped paths, and terraces. The common living area has the only TV on the property, and a small, lovely terraced dining area serves the complimentary continental breakfast as well as other meals. Each of the rooms is individually decorated with antiques and handcrafted furnishings. The large tiled bathrooms have open showers, and some have small gardens. The hotel is open from October 15 to July 31.

Hidalgo 10, Col. Centro, 23410 Cabo San Lucas, B.C.S. ℂ/fax **624/143-6400**. Fax 624/143-6401. www.loscabosguide. com/hotels/casa-bella-hotel.htm. 12 units. High season $145–$185; low-season specials available upon request. Rates include continental breakfast. AE, MC, V. Street parking available. **Amenities:** Restaurant; pool; concierge; Internet connection; room service; laundry facilities; TV. *In room:* A/C.

Los Milagros

The elegant, whitewashed, two-level buildings containing the 12 suites and rooms of Los Milagros (The Miracles) border either a grassy garden area or the small tile pool. Rooms contain contemporary iron beds with straw headboards, buff-colored tile floors, and artistic details. Some units have kitchenettes, the master suite has a sunken tub, and there's coffee service in the mornings on the patio. Evenings are romantic: Candles light the garden, and classical music plays. Request a room in one of the back buildings, where pomegranate trees buffer others' conversations. It's just 1½ blocks from Cabo Wabo Cantina (p. 90).

Matamoros 116, 23410 Cabo San Lucas, B.C.S. ℂ/fax **718/928-6647** in the U.S., or 624/143-4566. www.losmilagros. com.mx. 11 units. $75 double; $90 kitchenette suite; $115 master suite. Ask about summer discounts, group rates, and long-term discounts. No credit cards, but payable through PayPal. Limited street parking. **Amenities:** Small outdoor pool; cactus garden; rooftop terrace; fax; business services. *In room:* A/C, cable TV, Wi-Fi.

INEXPENSIVE

Cabo Inn ★★ *Finds*

This three-story hotel on a quiet street is a real find, and it keeps getting better. It offers a rare combination of low rates, extra-friendly management, and great, funky style. Rooms are basic and very small, with either two twin beds or one queen; although this was a bordello in a prior incarnation, everything is kept new and updated, from the mattresses to the minifridges. Muted desert colors add a spark of personality. The rooms surround a courtyard where you can enjoy satellite TV, a barbecue grill, and free coffee. The third floor has a rooftop terrace with *palapa* and a small swimming pool. Also on this floor is a suite equipped with a king-size bed and Jacuzzi. It's a colorful, *palapa*-topped, open-air room with hanging *tapetes* (woven palm mats) for additional privacy. A large fish freezer is available, and most rooms have kitchenettes. The hotel's just 2 blocks from downtown and the marina. A lively restaurant next door will even deliver pitchers of margaritas and dinner to your room.

20 de Noviembre and Leona Vicario, 23410 Cabo San Lucas, B.C.S. ℂ/fax **619/819-2727** in the U.S., or 624/143-0819. www.caboinnhotel.com. 23 units. $39 single; $58 double; $79 triple; $120 up to 6 people; $120 suite with Jacuzzi. No credit cards. Street parking. **Amenities:** Small rooftop pool and sunning area; communal TV and barbecue. *In room:* A/C, minifridge.

Siesta Suites

Reservations are a must at this immaculate, small inn popular with return visitors. (It's especially popular with fishermen.) The very basic rooms have white-tile floors and white walls, kitchenettes with seating areas, refrigerators, and sinks. The mattresses are firm, and the bathrooms are large and sparkling clean. Rooms on the fourth floor have two queen-size beds each. The accommodating proprietors offer free movies and VCRs, a barbecue pit and outdoor patio table on the second floor, and a comfortable lobby with TV. They also arrange fishing trips. Weekly and monthly rates are available. The hotel is 1½ blocks from the marina, where parking is available.

Calle Emiliano Zapata between Guerrero and Hidalgo, 23410 Cabo San Lucas, B.C.S. ℂ **866/271-0952** in the U.S., or 624/143-2773. www.cabosiestasuites.com. 20 suites (15 w/kitchenette). $55–$69 double; $340–$460 weekly rates. AE, MC, V. **Amenities:** Outdoor pool; TV in common area; barbecue pit. *In room:* A/C, fan, TV/VCR, fridges.

WHERE TO DINE

It's not uncommon to pay a lot for mediocre food in Cabo, so try to get a couple of unbiased recommendations. If people are only drinking and not dining, take that as a clue—many seemingly popular places are long on party atmosphere but short on food. Prices may decrease the farther you walk inland. The absolute local favorite is **Gardenia's Tacos,** a bare-bones eatery on Paseo Pescadores (same street as McDonald's) that serves Cabo San Lucas' best tacos. Streets to explore for other good restaurants include Hidalgo and Lázaro Cárdenas, plus the marina at the Plaza Bonita. Note that many restaurants automatically add the tip (15%) to the bill.

VERY EXPENSIVE

Edith's Restaurant ★★★ SEAFOOD/STEAKS/MEXICAN   Prices may seem over-the-top and reservations hard to come by, but once you sit down at one of Edith Jiménez's cheerful tables, you will see you're not only paying for an exquisite meal, but also for the time of your life. Lanterns light the open-air way for highly trained waiters, and bouquets of fresh lilies always perfume the entrance and washrooms. No detail is overlooked and, without exception, everyone in the house is in full celebration mode. You will be, too, after a celestial pitcher of margaritas or a bottle from Edith's carefully stocked cellar. While the lobster, shrimp, seafood, and steak combinations are worth every last peso, the grilled tuna is beyond compare when it comes to quality and value. And if Mexican food is what you crave, both the Tampiqueña and the Pancho Villa offer a magnanimous sampling of some of Mexico's most prized traditional dishes, which are abundant enough for two, especially when kicked off with the squash-blossom quesadillas or a Caesar salad.

Camino a Playa Médano. © 624/143-0801. www.edithscabo.com. Reservations strongly recommended. Main courses $20–$84. MC, V. Daily 5–11pm.

EXPENSIVE

Nick-San ★★ JAPANESE/SUSHI   This is the original branch of exceptional Japanese cuisine and sushi in Los Cabos. Now joined by a second location in the Corridor near San José, Nick-San's innovative flavors have two splendid homes. (See the San José del Cabo "Where to Dine" section for menu details.)

Bulevar Marina, Plaza de la Danza, Local 2. © 624/143-7342. Reservations recommended. Main courses $15–$50. MC, V. Tues–Sun 11:30am–10:30pm.

Peacocks ★★ INTERNATIONAL   One of Cabo's most exclusive patio-dining establishments, Peacocks emphasizes fresh seafood creatively prepared. Start with the house pâté or a salad of feta cheese with cucumber, tomato, and onion. For a main course, try one of the pastas—linguini with grilled chicken and sun-dried tomatoes is a good choice. More filling entrees include steaks, shrimp, and lamb, all prepared several ways.

Paseo del Pescador s/n, near Hotel Meliá Cabo San Lucas. © 624/143-1858. Reservations recommended. Main courses $15–$35. AE, MC, V. Daily 6–10:30pm.

MODERATE

Mi Casa ★ MEXICAN   The building's vivid cobalt-blue facade is your first clue that this place celebrates Mexico, and the menu confirms that impression. This is one of Cabo's most renowned Mexican restaurants. Traditional specialties such as *manchamanteles* (literally, "tablecloth stainers"), *cochinita pibil,* and *chiles en nogada* are menu staples. Fresh fish is prepared with delicious seasonings from throughout Mexico. Especially pleasant at night, the restaurant's tables, scattered around a large patio, are set with colorful cloths, traditional pottery, and glassware. It's across from the main plaza.

Calle Cabo San Lucas (at Madero). ✆ 624/143-1933. www.micasarestaurant.com. Reservations recommended. Main courses $13–$40. MC, V. Daily 1–10pm.

INEXPENSIVE

Cafe Canela ★ COFFEE/PASTRY/LIGHT MEALS   This cozy, tasty cafe and bistro is a welcome addition to the Cabo Marina boardwalk. Espresso drinks or fruit smoothies and muffins are good eye-openers for early risers. Enjoy a light meal or a tropical drink either inside or on the bustling waterfront terrace. The appealing menu also offers breakfast egg wraps, salads (for example, curried chicken salad with fresh fruit), sandwiches (such as blue-cheese quesadillas with smoked tuna and mango), and pastas—all reasonably priced. Full bar service is also available.

Marina boardwalk, below Tesoro Resort. ✆ 624/143-3435. Reservations not accepted. Main courses $5–$35; coffee $1.75–$4.20. AE, MC, V. Daily 6am–8pm.

Felix's ★ MEXICAN   This colorful, friendly, family-run place has grown up since opening in 1958, going from just serving tacos to offering a full array of tasty Mexican and seafood dishes. Everything's fresh and homemade, including corn tortillas and the numerous and varied salsas—more than 30! Fish tacos made with fresh dorado are superb, as are the shrimp dishes—the coconut-mango version, served with homemade mango chutney, is especially tasty. Don't leave without sampling the original Mexican bouillabaisse, a rich stew of shrimp, crab, sea bass, scallops, Italian sausage, and savory seasonings. Mexican specialties include chimichangas and *carne asada* (grilled marinated beef) with chile verde sauce. There is full bar service; the specialties are fresh-fruit margaritas and daiquiris. At breakfast time, this is Mama's Royale Café (see below).

Hidalgo and Zapata s/n. ✆ 624/143-4290. Reservations not accepted. Main courses $8–$15. MC, V. Mon–Sat 3–10pm.

Mama's Royale Café ★★ BREAKFAST   This is a great place to start the day. The shady patio decked with cloth-covered tables and the bright, inviting dining room are both comfortable places to settle in, and the food's just as appetizing. Efraín and Pedro preside over this dining hot spot with well-prepared breakfast selections that include grilled sausage; French toast stuffed with cream cheese and topped with pecans, strawberries, and orange liqueur; several variations of eggs Benedict; home fries; fruit crepes; and, of course, traditional breakfasts, plus free coffee refills. The orange juice is fresh squeezed, and there usually is live marimba or mariachi music to get your morning off to a lively start.

Hidalgo at Zapata. ✆ 624/143-4290. Reservations not accepted. Breakfast special $2.50; breakfast a la carte $2.50–$10. MC, V. Daily 7:30am–1pm.

Mariscos Mocambo ★ SEAFOOD   The location of this longstanding Cabo favorite is not inspiring—it's basically a large cement building—but the food obviously is. The place is always packed, generally with locals tired of high prices and small portions. Ocean-fresh seafood is the order of the day, and the specialty platter can easily serve four people. The restaurant is 1½ blocks inland from Lázaro Cárdenas.

Av. Leona Vicario and 20 de Noviembre. ✆ 624/143-6070. Reservations not accepted. Main courses $5–$30. MC, V. Daily noon–10pm.

CABO SAN LUCAS AFTER DARK

Cabo San Lucas is the nightlife capital of Baja. After-dark fun starts with the casual bars and restaurants on Marina Boulevard or facing the marina, and transforms into a tequila-fueled dance-club scene after midnight. You can easily find a happy hour with live music and a place to dance, or a Mexican fiesta with mariachis.

MEXICAN FIESTAS & THEME NIGHTS　　Some larger hotels have weekly fiesta nights and other buffet-plus-entertainment theme nights that can be fun as well as a good buy. Check travel agencies and the **Solmar** (© 624/143-3535) and **Finisterra** (© 624/143-3333) hotels. Prices range from $25 (not including drinks, tax, and tips) to $50 (which covers everything, including an open bar with national drinks). Otherwise, **Mi Casa** (© 624/143-1933; see the "Where to Dine" section) is a veritable Mexican theme night every night.

SUNSET WATCHING　　At twilight, check out Land's End, where the two seas meet. **Restaurant Sunset Da Mona Lisa** (© 624/145-8160), located on the eastern side of Cabo San Lucas Bay, is Los Cabos' premier place for sunset watching. Spectacular Arch views, dramatic terraces, and a specialty in Italian and seafood make this the ultimate place for watching the sun dive past the horizon. It's open from 8am to 11pm daily. Another option is the **Whale Watcher's Bar,** in the Hotel Finisterra (© 624/143-3333). Its location at Land's End offers a world-class view of the sun sinking into the Pacific. Mariachis play on Friday from 6:30 to 9pm. The bar is open daily from 10am to 11pm. "Whale margaritas" cost $4, beer $3. There are two-for-one drinks during happy hour from 4 to 6pm.

HAPPY HOURS & HANGOUTS

If you shop around, you can usually find an *hora feliz* (happy hour) somewhere in town between 10am and 7pm. The most popular places to drink and carouse until all hours are longstanding favorites like El Squid Roe, and the Cabo Wabo Cantina.

Two places to enjoy a more refined setting are the **Sancho Panza Wine Bar and Bistro** (see below) and **Red** (© 624/143-5645), a food, wine, and martini bar on Zaragoza around the corner from Squid Roe. While Sancho Panza offers live classic jazz, Red brings smooth electronica, both of which set the stage for rich conversation.

Cabo Wabo Cantina　　Owned by Sammy Hagar (formerly of Van Halen) and his Mexican and American partners, this "cantina" packs in youthful crowds, especially when rumors (frequent, and frequently false, just to draw a crowd) fly that a surprise appearance by a vacationing musician is imminent. One of Cabo's few air-conditioned dance venues, it's especially popular in the summer months. When there isn't a live band, a very loud dance club–type sound system plays mostly rock and some alternative and techno. Overstuffed furniture frames the dance floor. Beer goes for $3, margaritas for $5. For snacks, the Taco Wabo, just outside the club's entrance, stays up late, too. The cantina is open daily from 11am to 4am. Vicente Guerrero at Lázaro Cárdenas. © 624/143-1188. www.cabowabo.com.

El Squid Roe *Moments*　　El Squid Roe is one of the late Carlos Anderson's inspirations, and it still attracts wild, fun-loving crowds of all ages with its two stories of nostalgic decor. The eclectic food is far better than you'd expect from such a party place and, as fashionable as blue jeans, you can't come to Cabo without a visit here. Skin-to-win is the theme as the dancing on tables moves into high gear around 9pm. The scene is mostly tourists jerking to American hip-hop from early evening to around midnight, and at 1am, the local Mexican crowd—just getting their night started—flow in and the hips don't stop shaking until first light. Open daily from noon to 4am. Bulevar Marina, opposite Plaza Bonita. © **624/143-0655.** www.elsquidroe.com.

Nikki Beach   This haven of the hip hails from South Beach, Miami, and brought its ultracool vibe to the beach of the ME Cabo resort in March 2005. White-draped lounge beds scatter the outdoor area, under a canopy of umbrellas, surrounding a pool, and overlooking Cabo's best swimming beach. A teak deck offers covered dining. The music is the latest in electronic, house, and chill, with visiting DJs often playing on weekend nights. Sundays feature the signature beach brunch. It's a great choice for catching rays during the day while sipping tropical drinks, but its real appeal is the nocturnal action. Open Sunday to Wednesday from 11am to 1am (food service stops at 11pm), and Thursday to Saturday from 11am to 3am (food service stops at 1am). On the beach at the ME Cabo resort, on Médano Beach. © **624/145-7800.** www.nikkibeach.com.

Sancho Panza Wine Bar and Bistro   Sancho Panza combines a gourmet food market with a wine bar that features live jazz music plus an intriguing menu of Nuevo Latino cuisine (Mediterranean food with Latin flair). The place has a cozy neighborhood feeling, with tourists and locals sampling the selection of more than 150 wines, plus espresso drinks. During high season, make reservations. It's open daily from 4pm to midnight. Plaza Tesoro boardwalk, next to the Lighthouse. © **624/143-3212.** www.sanchopanza.com.

DANCING

Mambo Café   Make no mistake: You go to Mambo Café to dance. Part of a chain of bars around Mexico, it features a Caribbean concept with a marine tropical ambience, playing contemporary Latin music. Tiered levels of seating lead to the expansive dance floor, where high-energy live music sets the tone. It's open Wednesday through Sunday from 9pm. Thursday is ladies' night, which means women drink free from 9 to 11pm. Bulevar Marina Local 9–10, next to the Tesoro Resort. © **624/143-1484.** www.mambocafe. com.mx. Cover varies by night.

Passion   ME Cabo's most recent contribution to Cabo's growing high-end nightlife scene is Passion, arguably the most aphrodisiacal club in San Lucas. Champagne cocktails, the house music of resident and guest DJs, and a low-lit atmosphere prime Los Cabos' jet set for dancing and partying as long as they want. Open Sunday to Wednesday from 10am to 2am, and Thursday to Saturday from 10am to 4am. In the ME Cabo resort, on Médano Beach. © **624/145-7800.**

MENS' CLUBS

If you don't see enough skin on spring breakers swerving at El Squid Roe, Cabo's strip clubs are your answer. One place to start if you want to make plans ahead of time is **www.cabobabes.com.** There's a changing—and growing—selection of strip clubs from which to choose, but the mainstays include **Mermaid's** (corner of Lázaro Cárdenas and Vicente Guerrero; © **624/143-5370**), which offers its patrons their choice of topless stage shows or private dances. Admission is $5 for the general show, or $20 for the private dances. It's open nightly from 7pm to 3am. Another popular option is **Twenty/20 Showgirls** (Lázaro Cárdenas at Francisco Villa; © **624/143-5380**). It's the largest of these clubs in Cabo. In addition to a topless cabaret show, it offers topless lap dances, as well as televised sports, pool tables, and food service. It's open from 8:30pm to 3am; closed Tuesdays.

4 East of San José: The East Cape

The coastline of the Sea of Cortez northeast of San José has long been a favored destination of wave-hungry surfers, diehard anglers, and motivated escape artists who either challenge the dusty dirt roads by car, cruise by in sailboats or yachts, or fly their private planes to airstrips at out-of-the-way lodges. Little by little, this magnificent region—so close yet so far from the pulse of Los Cabos—is getting discovered and developed.

Technically, the East Cape region starts just east of downtown San José and continues about 89km (55 miles) up the coast to Buenavista. The drive can take up to 4 hours if you take the coastal road instead of the more efficient Highway 1, which winds through the mountains, but you'll get a first-rate view of everything the area has to offer: secret surf spots, desolate beaches, a coral-reef marine park, road runners, majestic cliffs, empty coves, lone burros, cactus forests, palm groves, craggy mountains, and more. And if you need proof of the East Cape's magic, take note of the size and opulence of the off-the-grid homes you'll find en route. If you're mesmerized by the natural beauty of the region, but can't decide where to lay your head, here's a quick guide to East Cape villages and resorts and a bit of what they have to offer. This is by no means comprehensive, as many of the surf spots and coves are home to small inns, private home rentals, and soft plots of tent-ready beach. The areas with more established resorts are listed below in the order you'd find them if you took the coastal road northeast of San José.

BEACHES & RESORT TOWNS

Just east of San José, on the outskirts of the Puerto Los Cabos development, is **Laguna Hills,** an area once loved for its empty beaches and pristine beachfront wilderness. Today, solar-powered homes and El Encanto de La Laguna, a new fractional ownership development, speckle the landscape beneath three mountain peaks, but Laguna Hills still retains its out-of-the-way charm, and it's a great jumping-off point for summer surf seekers. The only restaurant is the kitschy **Buzzard's Bar & Grill (✆ 951/ 303-9384** in the U.S.; www.vivacabo.com), which fronts **La Fonda del Mar,** three *palapa*-topped casitas that make up this beachfront bed-and-breakfast.

Slightly northeast, the stretch of **Zacatitos beach** is heaven. Although only surfers and a community of homes are there now, it's rumored to be the site of an expansive Mayan Resorts golf course, resort, and real-estate development.

The beautiful bay of **Los Frailes** is just outside of the Cabo Pulmo Marine Park, and it's an angler's dream come true. The exclusive eight-cabana resort, **Hotel Bahía Los Frailes** (www.losfrailes.com) is closed for renovations indefinitely.

Cabo Pulmo ★★★ is the tiny beach town 72km (45 miles) northeast of San José, and here the Sea of Cortez breaks on a coral reef, allowing only the finest bits of sand and smooth pebbles to pad the spectacular coastline. The coral itself is a sight to behold, but the real attraction is the flourishing fish life in this protected marine park. More than seven dive sites, desert hiking trails, secret coves, and some of the most beautiful stretches of beach in Baja make this my favorite place in the world to get away from it all. Pack a cooler of food and stay in a *palapa*-topped bungalow—they all have kitchens—at the **Cabo Pulmo Beach Resort (✆ 562/366-0398** in the U.S., or 624/141-0885; www.cabopulmo.com).

In **Punta Colorada** ★, just past Punta Arena, the renowned gathering point for migrating warm-water game fish, the **Hotel Punta Colorada (✆ 877/777-8862** in

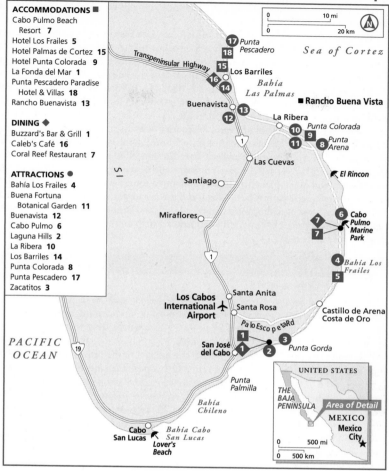

the U.S.; www.vanwormerresorts.com) brings charming accommodations to this breathtaking landscape. This area is ideal for bird-watching, hiking, fly-fishing, and catching roosterfish.

There's not much in the way of resorts in **La Ribera,** but this slow-paced fishing village is tops for relaxing by the sea. It's also home to the impressive **Buena Fortuna Botanical Garden** (no phone; siempresemillas@yahoo.com), which is open to visitors every day but Saturday.

In **Buenavista** ⭐⭐, a fishing resort with no pretensions, **Rancho Buena Vista** (© 800/258-8200 in the U.S.; www.ranchobuenavista.com) has several one-story bungalows spread about the grounds. The simple rooms have red-tiled floors, good showers, double beds, and small patios. Hammocks hang under palms and by the swimming pool, and the bar/restaurant is the center of the action. The hotel has an excellent deep-sea-fishing fleet with its own dock and a private airstrip. Note that the info on the website is outdated.

The hills give way to sandy flats as you roll into **Los Barriles** ✮✮✮ off Highway 1. Colorful buildings accented by bright green palms may either be the inspiration for or the result of the thriving community of artists who live here. And the exquisite beaches, gentle breezes, excellent fishing, and subdued vibe draw expats in droves. Stay at the popular **Hotel Palmas de Cortez** (✆ 888/241-1543 in the U.S.; www.palmas-decortez.com) and visit **Caleb's Café** (✆ 624/141-0531) for breakfast, lunch, and the best Sunday-morning sticky buns of your life.

The remote coastal retreat of **Punta Pescadero** ✮✮✮ is simple in its finery, located on a point named for the top-notch fishing offshore, about 14km (8.7 miles) from Los Barriles. The 24-unit **Punta Pescadero Paradise Hotel & Villas** (✆ 800/332-4442 in the U.S., or 624/141-0101; www.puntapescaderoparadise.com) celebrates the luxury of peace and quiet. Delightfully well-appointed rooms and bathrooms are the best of any off-the-beaten-path resort in Baja, and the restaurant, which serves a full breakfast menu and two entree options daily for lunch and dinner, surprises and delights. Take into account the 1,050m (3,500-ft.) landing strip on the property and you've got rustic luxury at its best.

5 Todos Santos: A Creative Oasis ✮✮✮

68km (42 miles) N of Cabo San Lucas

Although Todos Santos is well past its off-the-beaten-path days, it's still a favorite among Bohemian types looking either for regional up-and-coming artists or simply a piece of art that makes them feel good—and it's a prime destination among those weary of the L.A.-ization of Cabo San Lucas.

The art and artistry created here—from the kitchen to the canvas—is of an evolved type that seems to care less about commercial appeal than quality. In doing so, it becomes more of a draw. Not to be overlooked are the arts of agriculture, masonry, and weaving created by some of the town's original residents. From superb meals at **Café Santa Fe** to an afternoon browsing at **El Tecolote Libros,** Todos Santos is intriguing to its core. In fact, the Mexican government dubbed it a "Pueblo Mágico" (Magical Village) in 2006, bringing official recognition, not to mention various infrastructure updates, to the town.

Not only is the town a cultural oasis in Baja, it's an oasis in the true sense of the word—in this desert landscape, Todos Santos enjoys an almost continuous water supply from the peaks of the Sierra de la Laguna mountains. It's just over an hour's drive up the Pacific coast from Cabo San Lucas; you'll know you've arrived when the arid coastal scenery suddenly gives way to verdant groves of palms, mangos, avocados, and papayas.

During the Mission Period of Baja, this oasis valley was deemed the only area south and west of La Paz worth settling—it had the only reliable water supply. In 1723, an outpost mission was established, followed by the full-fledged Misión Santa Rosa de Las Palmas in 1733. At the time, the town was known as Santa Rosa de Todos Santos; eventually shortened to its current name, it translates as "All Saints."

Over the next 200 years, the town alternated between prosperity and difficulty. Its most recent boom lasted from the mid-19th century until the 1950s, when the town flourished as a sugar-cane production center and began to develop a strong cultural core. Local history museum **La Casa de La Cultura** (no phone), on Av. Juárez, charts

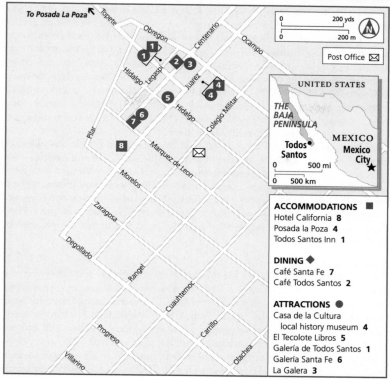

ACCOMMODATIONS ■
Hotel California **8**
Posada la Poza **4**
Todos Santos Inn **1**

DINING ◆
Café Santa Fe **7**
Café Todos Santos **2**

ATTRACTIONS ●
Casa de la Cultura
    local history museum **4**
El Tecolote Libros **5**
Galería de Todos Santos **1**
Galería Santa Fe **6**
La Galera **3**

much of the history of Todos Santos and exhibits artwork from local artists, past and present. Many of the buildings now being restored and converted into galleries, studios, shops, and restaurants were built during this era. It wasn't until the 1980s that a paved road connected Todos Santos with La Paz, and tourism began to draw new attention to this tranquil town.

The demand for the town's older colonial-style structures by artists, entrepreneurs, and foreign residents has resulted in a real-estate boom, and new shops, galleries, and cafes crop up continuously. The coastal strip south of Todos Santos, which once was the exclusive hideaway of impassioned surfers, has plans for development; so visit soon, before this perfect stretch of beach and desert changes. For the casual visitor, Todos Santos is easy to explore in a day, but a few tranquil inns welcome guests who want to stay a little longer. For additional information and current events, visit **www. todossantos-baja.com**.

WHAT TO DO IN TODOS SANTOS

During the **Festival Fundador** (Oct 10–14), which celebrates the founding of the town in 1723, streets around the main plaza fill with food, games, and wandering troubadours. Many of the shops and the Café Santa Fe close from the end of September through the festival. The Arts Festival, held in February, seems to be gaining importance, with film festivals, dance and music performances, and more.

Todos Santos is a good stopover for those traveling between Cabo and La Paz; a day's visit can be arranged through tour companies in Los Cabos or done on your own with a rental car. Todos Santos has at least a dozen galleries, including the noted **Galería de Todos Santos,** corner of Topete and Legaspi (ⓒ **612/145-0500**), which features a changing collection of works by regional artists. It's open daily from 11am to 4pm (closed Sun May–Nov) and doesn't accept credit cards. The new **La Galera** 𝒢, on Obregón (ⓒ **612/145-0215**), houses a striking collection of local and regional Mexican artists, plus some handcrafts and jewelry from mainland Mexico. Keep an eye out for the brooding paintings of local Sebastián Díaz Duarte, La Galera's featured artist. It's open Monday through Saturday from 10am to 5pm.

El Tecolote Libros 𝒢𝒢𝒢 (ⓒ **612/145-0295**), though tiny, gets our vote for the best bookstore in Mexico. It carries an exceptional selection of Latin American literature, poetry, children's books, and reference books centering on Mexico. Both English and Spanish editions, new and used, are in stock, along with maps, magazines, cards, used VHS tapes and books, and art supplies. Information on upcoming writing workshops and local reading groups also is posted here. The shop is at the corner of Hidalgo and Juárez. It's open Monday through Saturday from 9am to 5pm, and Sunday from 10am to 3pm.

WHERE TO STAY

Hotel California   This place has been the stuff of legends—and the verdict is still out as to whether it's the source of inspiration for the Eagles' song of the same name. A few years back it was a dilapidated guesthouse; however, after an extensive renovation, it's now the hippest place to stay in the area. Think Philippe Stark in the desert—the decor here is a fusion of jewel-tone colors with eclectic Mexican and Moroccan accents. Each room features a different decor, but all of it is high style, with rich hues and captivating details. Most rooms also offer an outdoor terrace or seating area. On the ground floor, you'll find the lobby, the low-lit library—with deep blue walls, a profusion of candles, and tin stars—and a small outdoor pool with sun chairs. Also at ground level is the Emporio Hotel California boutique and the La Coronela Restaurant and Bar, the area's current nocturnal hot spot with live guitar, jazz, and blues music on Saturday evenings. On Sundays, the restaurant serves a mixed grill of steak, fish, chicken breast, and sausage for $13 per person. The recently added **Tequila Bar** is a small, decadently decorated spot, with red and black settees, and an extensive selection of tequilas, including their own Hotel California label.

Calle Juárez, corner of Morelos, 23305 Todos Santos, B.C.S. ⓒ 612/145-0525 or 612/145-0522. 11 units. $125–$250 double; off season $100–$200 double. MC, V. **Amenities:** Restaurant/bar; tequila bar; pool; boutique; library.

Posada La Poza 𝒢𝒢   On a lagoon and bird sanctuary, the Posada La Poza (Inn at the Spring) opened its doors in 2002 and has been earning rave reviews for its artistic and serene atmosphere. In fact, *In Style* magazine did a fashion shoot there with Sandra Bullock in the winter of 2005. Each of the seven boutique suites features a private terrace or patio, comfortable sitting areas, colorful walk-in showers, and large windows overlooking the garden, lagoon, and ocean. Two junior suites and the honeymoon suite also offer a spa or hot tub. Guest beds are fitted with fine Swiss linens. The original artwork is by Libusche, who together with her Swiss-born husband, Juerg Wiesendanger, created this unique inn. The honeymoon suite has an oversized bathroom, fireplace, and expansive terrace. Rates include a full breakfast served in the El Gusto! gourmet Mexican restaurant, which is part of the inn and serves simple creations in which exquisite individual flavors shine for lunch and dinner. Guests may enjoy the saltwater swimming pool with a small waterfall, and the exercise facility (on a lovely garden patio). Hiking and walking paths surround the hotel, and bikes are available for guest use. The inn is part of a bird sanctuary that is home to more than 70 species and is also located along the migratory route of the gray whales (Nov–Mar). For more information on whale-watching, see "Whale-Watching" under "San José del Cabo," earlier in this chapter, and "Whale-Watching in Baja: A Primer," in chapter 6.

Apdo. Postal 10, Col. La Poza, 23305 Todos Santos, B.C.S. © 612/145-0400. 7 units. www.lapoza.com. $145–$190 double; $245–$285 junior suite; $380–$480 honeymoon suite. Rates include full breakfast. MC, V. **Amenities:** Saltwater swimming pool; exercise facility; hiking paths.

Todos Santos Inn ⊙   An intimate place to stay, the inn is in a historic house that has served as a general store, cantina, school, and private residence. Now under new ownership, it retains its air of casual elegance, with luxurious white bed linens, netting draped romantically over the beds, Talavera tile bathrooms, antique furniture, and high, wood-beamed ceilings. Rooms and suites border a courtyard terrace, pool, and garden. The suites are air-conditioned but have neither television nor telephone. The hotel's wine bar, **La Copa,** is open to the public, serves libations Tuesdays through Saturdays from 5 to 9pm, and has an excellent selection of California and other imported wines. Currently, no credit cards are accepted. Seasonal discounts are available, but the inn closes for the month of September.

Calle Legaspi 33, between Topete and Obregón, 23305 Todos Santos, B.C.S. © 612/145-0040. 6 units. $125 double; $325 suite, depending on season. No credit cards. Closed Sept. **Amenities:** Pool. *In room:* A/C in suites.

WHERE TO DINE

Café Santa Fe ⊙⊙ CAFE   For myself—and I would suspect many others—a meal here is reason enough to visit Todos Santos. Much of the attention the town has received in recent years can be directly attributed to this outstanding cafe, and it continues to live up to its lofty reputation. Owners Ezio and Paula Colombo refurbished a large stucco house across from the plaza, creating an exhibition kitchen, several dining rooms, and a lovely courtyard adjacent to a garden of hibiscus, bougainvillea, papaya trees, and herbs. The excellent Northern Italian cuisine emphasizes local produce and seafood; try ravioli stuffed with spinach and ricotta in a Gorgonzola sauce, or ravioli with lobster and shrimp accompanied by an organic salad. In high season, the wait for a table can be long since everything is prepared to order.

Centenario 4. © 612/145-0340. Reservations recommended. Main courses $10–$20. MC, V. Wed–Mon noon–9pm. Closed Sept–early Nov.

Café Todos Santos CAFE ⊙   The garden setting here is a more casual option and is a magical place to start the day. Among the espresso drinks is the bowl-size caffe latte, which is accompanied by a freshly baked croissant or one of the signature cinnamon buns. Lunch or a light meal may include a frittata, a filling sandwich on home-baked bread, or a fish filet wrapped in banana leaves with coconut milk.

Centenario 33, across from the Todos Santos Inn. © 612/145-0300. Reservations not accepted. Main courses $3–$6. No credit cards. Tues–Sun 7am–9pm.

5

La Paz: Peaceful Port Town

La Paz means "peace," and the feeling seems to float on the ocean breezes of this provincial town. Despite being an important port, home to almost 200,000 inhabitants, and the capital of the state of Baja California Sur, it remains slow-paced and relaxed. Beautiful deserted beaches just minutes away complement the lively beach and palm-fringed *malecón* (seaside boulevard) that front the town center. The easygoing city is the guardian of "old Baja" atmosphere, and it has an unmistakable air of outdoor adventure, thanks to the ubiquity of skilled anglers, competitive freedivers, Baja 1000 racers, recreational (as in, noncommercial) spearfishermen, a marina full of large yachts, and kayak-rental agencies.

Adventurous travelers enjoy countless options, including hiking, rock climbing, diving, fishing, and sea kayaking. Islands and islets sit just offshore, once hiding places for looting pirates but now magnets for kayakers and beachcombers. At Espíritu Santo and Los Islotes, it's possible to camp overnight, posh safari-style, at **Baja Camp** (www.bajacamp.com), and swim with sea lions, respectively.

The University of Southern Baja California adds a unique cultural presence

that includes museums and a theater and arts center. The surrounding tropical desert diversity and endemic wildlife are also compelling reasons to visit. Despite its name, La Paz has historically been a place of conflict between explorers and indigenous populations. Beginning in 1535, Spanish conquistadors and Jesuit missionaries arrived and exerted their influence on the town's architecture and traditions. From the time conquistadors saw local Indians wearing pearl ornaments, mass pearl harvesting lasted through the late 1930s, when all the pearls eventually were wiped out. John Steinbeck immortalized a local legend in his novella *The Pearl.*

La Paz is ideal for anyone nostalgic for Los Cabos the way it used to be—and it has the breathtaking sunsets not always visible at Baja's tip. From accommodations to taxis, it's also one of Mexico's most outstanding beach vacation values and a great place for family travelers. However, as is the case throughout Mexico, development activity in the areas immediately surrounding La Paz may change this in the coming years, so plan a visit now to experience the pearl of La Paz in its natural state.

1 Essentials

177km (110 miles) N of Cabo San Lucas; 196km (122 miles) NW of San José del Cabo; 1,578km (978 miles) SE of Tijuana

GETTING THERE & DEPARTING

BY PLANE Both **Alaska Airlines** (© **800/252-7522**) and **Delta** (© **800/241-4141**) have nonstop flights from Los Angeles. **Aeroméxico** (© **800/237-6639** in the U.S., or 612/122-0091, 612/122-0093, or 612/122-1636) connects through Tucson

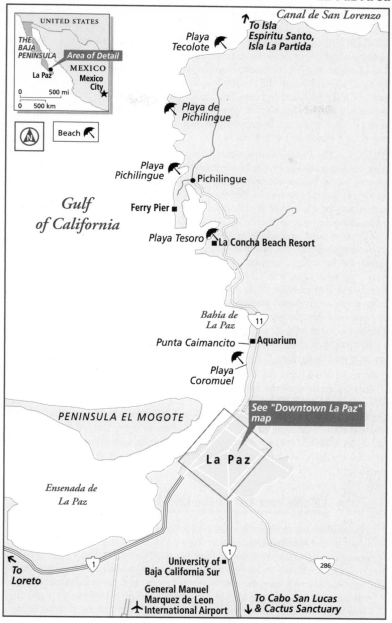

and Los Angeles in the United States, and flies from Mexico City and other points within Mexico.

BY CAR   From San José del Cabo, Highway 1 north is the more scenic route and it passes through a mountain town called San Bartolo, where heavenly homemade macaroons made of thick, fresh-cut coconut and pralines made from *cajeta* (goat's-milk caramel) are well worth the slightly longer drive. An arguably faster route is heading east of Cabo San Lucas and then north to Highway 19 through Todos Santos. A little before San Pedro, Highway 19 rejoins Highway 1 and runs north into La Paz; both trips take 2½ to 3 hours. From northern Baja, Highway 1 south is the only choice; the trip from Loreto takes 4 to 5 hours.

BY BUS   The Central Camionera (main bus station) is at Jalisco and Héroes de la Independencia, about 25 blocks southwest of the center of town; it's open daily from 6am to 10pm. Bus service operates from the south (Los Cabos, 2½–3½ hr.) and north (as far as Tijuana). It's best to buy your ticket in person the day before, though reservations can be made over the phone at the bus station in your point of origin. Taxis are available in front of the station.

All routes north and south, as well as buses to Pichilingue, the ferry pier, and close to outlying beaches, are available through the Transportes Aguila station, sometimes called the beach bus terminal, on the *malecón* at Alvaro Obregón and Cinco de Mayo (© **612/122-7898**). The station is open daily from 6am to 10pm. Buses to Pichilingue depart seven times a day from 8am to 5pm and cost $2 one way. Local buses arrive at the **beach station,** along the *malecón.* Taxis line up out front of both.

More local destinations are handled from the beach bus station, where the main bus station has more long-distance trips to major points in Baja. Buses from the Central Camionera tend to be more modern and have better facilities.

BY FERRY   Baja Ferries serves La Paz from Topolobampo (the port for Los Mochis) daily at 11:30pm, and the return trip to Topolobampo leaves La Paz at 3pm daily. Tickets are available at the Baja Ferries office in La Paz, on the corner of Allende and Marcelo Rubio (© **612/123-6600** or 612/123-1313), or at any Banamex bank throughout Mexico (make payable to Baja Ferries, SA de CV, account #7145468 sucursal 001). The local office is open daily 8am to 6pm. For toll-free information, call © **01-800/122-1414** within Mexico. Several tour agencies in town book reservations on the ferry, but it is best to buy your ticket in person at the ferry office.

(*Tips*   **Taking Your Car to the Mainland**

Those planning to take their cars on the ferry to the Mexican mainland must meet all the requirements listed in "Getting There" in chapter 2. Additionally, every traveler going to the mainland needs a Mexican Tourist Permit (FMT).

Tourism officials in La Paz say that FMTs are available only in Mexicali, Tecate, Tijuana, Ensenada, and Guerrero Negro, and not in La Paz, although car permits to cross over into the mainland can be issued there. If you do happen to make it as far as La Paz, or anywhere outside the frontier zone, and are found not to have an FMT, you will be subject to a $40 fine.

Moments Festivals & Events in La Paz

February features the biggest and best *carnaval,* or Mardi Gras, in Baja, as well as a month-long Festival of the Gray Whale (starting in Feb or Mar). On May 3, La Fiesta de La Paz celebrates the city's founding by Cortez in 1535 and features *artesanía* exhibitions from throughout southern Baja. The annual marlin-fishing tournament is in August, with other fishing tournaments in September and November. And on November 1 and 2, the Days of the Dead, altars are on display at the Anthropology Museum.

The ferry departs for Topolobampo daily at 11:30pm and arrives in La Paz 6 hours later. The ferries can carry 1,000 passengers as well as accommodate vehicles. Passengers pay one fee for themselves ($68 for a seat, $34 for children ages 3–11, or $144 for a cabin with four beds and one bathroom) and another for their vehicles ($100). The ferries offer restaurant and bar service, as well as a coffee shop and live music, and a hot meal is included in the cost of the ticket. Access for those with disabilities is offered as well. Passengers are requested to arrive 3 hours prior to departure time. Information and updated schedules are available at **www.bajaferries.com**.

Reserve your space on the ferry as early as possible and confirm your reservation 24 hours before departure; you can pick up tickets at the port terminal ticket office as late as the morning of the day you are leaving. The dock is at Pichilingue, 18km (11 miles) north of La Paz.

Buses to Pichilingue depart from the beach bus terminal of **Transportes Aguila** (© **612/122-7898**) on the *malecón* at Independencia on the hour, from 7am to 8pm, and cost $2 each way.

ORIENTATION
ARRIVING

BY PLANE   The airport is 18km (11 miles) northwest of town along the highway to Ciudad Constitución and Tijuana. Airport *colectivos* (around $12 per person) run only from the airport to town, not vice versa, and a group shuttle is a flat charge of $25. **Taxi** service (around $27) is available as well. Most major rental-car agencies have booths inside the airport. **Budget**'s local number is © **612/124-6433** or 612/122-7655; you can contact **Avis** at © **612/122-2651**, or **Alamo** at © **612/122-6262**.

BY BUS   Buses arrive at the Central Camionera, about 25 blocks southwest of downtown, or at the beach station along the *malecón.* Taxis line up in front of both.

BY FERRY   Buses line up in front of the ferry dock at Pichilingue to meet every arriving ferry. They stop at the beach bus station on the *malecón* at Independencia; it's within walking distance of many downtown hotels if you're not encumbered with luggage. Taxis also meet each ferry and cost about $8 to downtown La Paz.

VISITOR INFORMATION

The most accessible visitor information office is on the corner of Alvaro Obregón and Nicolas Bravo (© **612/122-5939** or 612/124-0100; turismo@gbcs.gob.mx or turismo@lapaz.cromwell.com.mx). It's open daily from 8am to 8pm. The extremely helpful staff speaks English and can supply information on La Paz, Los Cabos, and the rest of the region. The official website of the La Paz Tourism Board is **www.viva lapaz.com**.

CITY LAYOUT

Although La Paz sprawls well inland from the *malecón* (the seaside boulevard, Alvaro Obregón), you'll probably spend most of your time in the older, more congenial downtown section within a few blocks of the waterfront. The main plaza, Plaza Pública (or Jardín Velasco), is bounded by Madero, Independencia, Revolución, and Cinco de Mayo. The plaza centers on an iron bandstand where public concerts frequently take place in the evening and the *malecón* is dotted with the bronze sculptures of Guadalajara artist Alejandro Colunga.

GETTING AROUND

Because most of what you'll need and want in town is on the *malecón* between the tourist information office and the Hotel Los Arcos, or a few blocks inland from the waterfront, it's easy to get around La Paz on foot. Public buses go to some of the beaches north of town (see "Beaches & Outdoor Activities," below), but to explore the many beaches within 81km (50 miles) of La Paz, your best bet is to rent a car or hire a taxi. Several car-rental agencies have offices on the *malecón*.

FAST FACTS: La Paz

Area Code The telephone area code is **612**.

Banks Banks generally exchange currency during normal business hours: Monday through Friday from 9am to 6pm and Saturday from 10am to 2pm. ATMs are readily available and offer bank exchange rates on withdrawals.

Emergencies Dial © **066** for general emergency assistance, or © **060** for police. Both calls are free.

Hospitals The two hospitals in the area are **Hospital Especialidades Médicas,** at Km 4.5 on the highway toward the airport (© **612/124-0400**), and **Hospital Juan María de Salvatierra** (© **612/122-1497**), Nicolás Bravo 1010, Col. Centro. Both are open 24 hours and the former offers access to emergency air evacuation.

Internet Access In the fleeting world of Internet cafes, your best bet is to scan the *malecón* or ask your hotel concierge for their recommendations. However, **Omni Services,** which doubles as an Internet center and a real-estate agency, offers Internet, Wi-Fi, fax, and long-distance VoIP phone service to the U.S. and Canada for 30¢ per minute on the *malecón*, Alvaro Obregón 460-C, close to Burger King (© **612/123-4888**; www.osmx.com). It also offers hookups for laptops, color printers, and copiers.

Marinas La Paz has a growing number of marinas: **Marina de La Paz,** at the west end of the *malecón* at Legaspi (© **612/125-2112**; marinalapaz@prodigy. net.mx); **Marina Palmira,** south of town at Carretera a Pichilingue Km 2.5, Edificio la Plaza (© **877/217-1513** in the U.S., 612/121-7000; eloisa@marinapalmira. com); and **Marina Costa Baja,** Carretera a Pichilingue Km 7.5 (© **866/899-7567** in the U.S.; www.costabajaresort.com). The large ships arrive at the commercial port of **Pichilingue,** Carretera a Pichilingue Km 2.5, Puerto Pichilingue (© **612/ 122-7010**), 17km (11 miles) from La Paz.

Municipal Market The public market is 3 blocks inland, at Degollado and Revolución. It mainly sells produce, meats, and utilitarian wares. Hours are Monday through Saturday 6am to 6pm and Sunday 6am to 1pm.

Parking In high season, street parking may be hard to find in the downtown area, but there are several guarded lots, which cost from $2 to $5, and side streets are less crowded. Most hotels and resorts have parking.

Pharmacy One of the largest pharmacies is **Farmacia Baja California**, Independencia and Madero (© **612/122-0240** or 612/123-4408). Open 7am to 9:30pm Monday to Saturday and Sunday from 8am to 9:30pm.

Post Office The *correo* is 3 blocks inland, at Constitución and Revolución (© **612/122-0388**); it's open Monday through Friday 8am to 5pm, Saturday 8am to 1pm.

Tourism Office Located at Carretera al Norte Km 5.5, Edificio Fidepaz (© **612/124-0199**), it's open daily from 8am to 3pm. A tourist information module/booth is also on the *malecón,* open daily from 8am to 8pm.

2 Beaches & Outdoor Activities

La Paz combines the unselfconscious bustle of a small capital port city with beautiful, isolated beaches not far from town. Well on its way to becoming the undisputed adventure-tourism capital of Baja, it's the starting point for whale-watching, diving, sea kayaking, climbing, freediving, and hiking tours throughout the peninsula. Those interested in day adventures can usually arrange any of those activities, plus beach tours, sunset cruises, and visits to the sea-lion colony, through travel agencies in major hotels or along the *malecón.* You can also arrange activities through agencies in the United States that specialize in Baja's natural history. (See "Special-Interest Trips," in chapter 2.)

BEACHES

Within a 10- to 45-minute drive from La Paz lie some of the loveliest beaches in Baja. Many rival those of the Caribbean with their clear, turquoise water.

The beaches that line the ***malecón*** are the most convenient in town. Although the sand lining the Bay of La Paz is soft and white, and the water appears turquoise and gentle, locals don't generally swim there. Because La Paz is a commercial port, the water is not considered as clean as that in the very accessible outlying beaches. With its colorful playgrounds dotting the central beachfront, as well as numerous open-air restaurants that front the water, the *malecón* is best for a casual afternoon of post-sightseeing lunch and playtime.

The best beach in the area is immediately north of town at **La Concha Beach Resort;** nonguests may use the hotel restaurant/bar and rent equipment for snorkeling, diving, skiing, and sailing. It's 10km (6¼ miles) north of town on the Pichilingue Highway, at Km 5.5. The other beaches are farther north of town, but midweek you may have these far-distant beaches to yourself.

At least 10 public buses from the beach bus station at Independencia on the *malecón* depart from 8am to 5:30pm for beaches to the north. The buses stop at the

La Paz's Top Dive Spots

La Paz is among the world's great dive destinations: More than 25 dive sites surround the islands outside La Paz's bay, such as Espíritu Santo, San José, and Cerralvo. What sets La Paz diving apart is the opportunity to view giant mantas, sea lions, and impressive numbers of sharks, including whale sharks and hammerheads. Here are the area's most notable dive sites:

- **El Bajo:** Advanced divers revel in the underwater mountain rising to 18m (60 ft.) below the surface, with a relatively flat top. It's especially notable for its schooling hammerhead sharks; groups of several to hundreds travel clockwise around the seamount for unknown reasons. You're also likely to see Panamic green morays; over 50 live in a small canyon on the mountain. Additional sea mounts nearby have peaks at between 18 and 45m (60–150 ft.) from the surface; visibility is good year-round.
- **El Bajito:** Just next to the Los Islotes sea lion colony is this beautiful dive site where crevices in the sea floor are covered in soft corals.
- **Los Islotes:** Divers here can view the underwater rock caves and frolic with the friendly colony of sea lions. The two large rock islands, one of which is a natural arch whose center you can dive through, are a 1½-hour boat ride from La Paz, north of Espíritu Santo, and offer depths of 4.5 to 30m (15–100 ft.).
- **La Reina and La Reinita:** Enjoy a wreck dive and wall diving to 45m (150-ft.) depths at these islets in front of Cerralvo Island, 1½ hours from La Paz.

small **Playa Caimancito** (5km/3 miles), **Playa Coromuel** (8km/5 miles), **Playa Tesoro** (14km/8¾ miles), and **Pichilingue** (17km/11 miles); from where the bus lets you off at the ferry stop, walk north on the highway to the beach. Ask when the last bus will make the return trip. Pichilingue, Coromuel, and Tesoro beaches have *palapa*-shaded bars or restaurants, which may not be open midweek. You can pack a lunch and rent a shade umbrella for $1 per group, with tables and chairs available for a minimal additional charge.

The most beautiful of these outlying beaches is **Playa Tecolote** ⟨⟩⟨⟩, approximately 29km (18 miles) from La Paz at the end of a paved road. The water is a heavenly cerulean blue, the beach looks out upon Isla Espíritu Santo, and there are several restaurants. To get to Playa Tecolote on your own, take a bus to Pichilingue; from there, take a taxi the remaining 13km (8 miles). When the taxi drops you off, make arrangements for it to return. The road is paved as far as Playa Tecolote and Playa Balandra (29km/18 miles; good but with no services), and turnoffs to these and other beaches are well marked.

For more information about beaches and maps, check at the tourist information office on the *malecón*. If you want to take a general tour of all the beaches before deciding where to spend your precious vacation days, **Viajes Lybs** (© **612/122-4680**) offers a 4-hour beach tour for $25 per person, with stops at Pichilingue, Balandra, and El Tecolote beaches.

You'll see brain coral, tropical fish, rays, and several types of morays here. During the summer you can see giant seahorses. Whale encounters are common in the channel during season while heading toward this site.

- *Salvatierra* **Wreck:** In 1976, this 75m (250-ft.) ferryboat sank after colliding with a nearby reef. It now lies on a sandbar at a depth of 18m (60 ft.) in the San Lorenzo Channel and the southern end of Espíritu Santo. Filled with sea life, it makes for a fascinating dive site and is good for novice divers.
- **San Francisquito:** Similar to El Bajo, this popular site for advanced divers, with varied depths, has an abundance of sea life.
- **Whale Island:** This small, whale-shaped island has dive-through caves, crevices, rocky reefs, and a coral forest at depths from 6 to 18m (20–60 ft.). Between the caves is a sand shelf containing a large "garden" of conger eels, which extend their bodies vertically from the sea floor and sway in the currents while feeding on passing morsels. This area is tranquil and protected from wind; its mild current makes it a good choice for beginning divers, or for a second dive of the day.
- Two rusting Chinese long liner boats, the *Lapas 03* and the *Fang Ming,* were sunk in 1999 to promote **artificial reef** development for sport diving. They're at a depth of 21m (70 ft.) and offer full penetration diving over numerous levels.

CRUISES

A popular and very worthwhile cruise is to **Isla Espíritu Santo** and **Los Islotes.** You visit the largest sea-lion colony in Baja, stunning rock formations, and remote beaches, with stops for snorkeling, swimming, and lunch. If conditions permit, you may even be able to snorkel beside the sea lions at Los Islotes. (*Note:* Remember sea lions are wild animals. Blowing bubbles in your face is their sign of warning, not of play, so steer clear of the giant bulls—who can be quite protective of their females—and let the curious babies come to you.) Both boat and bus tours are available to **Puerto Balandra,** where bold rock formations rising up like humpback whales frame pristine coves of crystal-blue water and ivory sand. **Viajes Lybs** (see above) and other travel agencies can arrange these all-day trips, weather permitting. Price is $80 per person.

WATERSPORTS

SCUBA DIVING Scuba-diving trips are best from June through September. You can arrange them through Fernando Aguilar's **Baja Diving and Services,** Obregón 1665-2 (© **612/122-1826;** fax 612/122-8644; www.clubcantamar.com). Diving sites include the sea-lion colony at Los Islotes, distant Cerralvo Island, the sunken ship *Salvatierra,* an 18m (59-ft. wall dive, and several sea mounts (underwater mountains) and reefs. Also available is a trip to see hammerhead sharks and manta rays. Rates start at $102 per person for an all-day outing and two-tank dive. Baja Diving also has a 40-unit sports lodge and beach resort, **Club Hotel Cantamar** (© **612/122-7010**). Rates

Snorkeling with Baja's Sea Lions

Among the many treasures of Baja, prime among them are the colonies of sea lions that live in the Sea of Cortez. These playful, curious sea creatures prove a powerful lure for many travelers to this area. One of the largest colonies is found at Los Islotes, a cluster of tiny rock islands north of La Paz, the desert capital of Baja, Mexico. The islands' claim to fame is that they're the year-round home to a colony or "rookery" of some 250 California brown sea lions.

Many tour operators in La Paz offer trips to Los Islotes, generally in *pangas*— the trip, by boat, takes about 2½ hours from La Paz. Here, the sea lions lay in the sun along the jagged rock shelves, bark out greetings to visitors, and occasionally belly-flop into the water.

Trip participants don wet suits or skins, lifejackets, and snorkels to join the sea lions, which will occasionally instigate play by mimicking your movements in the water.

California sea lions are considered to be the smartest of the pinnipeds, the class of mammals with flippers. However, they're also kind of like seafaring guard dogs. While they are adorable, don't let their big brown eyes fool you: They are wild animals and should be treated as such. No feeding, no touching, and don't get too close to their rocky home. The chocolate-brown "bulls" can weigh up to 1,000 pounds and can occasionally become aggressive, so keeping your distance from the males and the females and pups they're protecting is a good idea. For example, if a sea lion blows bubbles in your face, consider it a warning that you're too close.

Among the operators offering sea-lion snorkeling trips is **Cortez Club**, at the La Concha Beach Resort (© 612/121-6120; www.cortezclub.com). The full-day excursion departs at 8:30am and costs $77 per person, which includes wet suit, snorkel gear, and a box lunch, which you'll eat on the beach at Isla Partida. Dive trips are also available, with depths at Los Islotes averaging 7½ to 15m (25–49 ft.).

---

for a double room run about $65. Another excellent dive operator is **Baja Quest** (© 612/123-5320; www.bajaquest.com.mx), at Rangel 10, between Sonora and Sinaloa. Day boat trips run approximately $110 for two tanks, $125 for three-tank dives. They also offer other outdoor adventures, including kayaking and various wildlife watching, not to mention service in English, Spanish, and Japanese.

Also of note is **DeSea Baja Adventures,** Marina Palmira L3, Carretera a Pichilingue Km 2.5 (© 612/121-5100; www.deseabaja.com), a complete tour company with expertise in diving and sportfishing. Prices are $145 for three-tank dives, including equipment, or $170 including a resort dive course. DeSea also has private boats with guides for underwater photo or video diving, and private dive masters or instructors for yachts or charters. DeSea also offers **freediving,** including instruction from internationally experienced freedive instructors Aharon and María Teresa Solomon. Courses include yoga-based breathing exercises, mental control, and the physiology of breath hold. Beginning through advanced instruction is available, as are live-aboard charters and **spearfishing** instruction.

Another excellent dive operator is **Grupo Fun Baja,** Reforma 395, on the corner of Guillermo Prieto (© 612/121-5884 or 612/125-2366; www.funbaja.com; daily

8am–8pm), which offers one- or two-tank dive trips to all the top area dive sites, as well as scuba camping trips. These trips combine diving and camping on the island of Espíritu Santo. All equipment for camping is provided, with comfortable twin-size beds. A chef prepares the meals, providing a changing menu that may include fresh fish, clams, chicken, or vegetarian fare upon request. The Mini Safari scuba-camping trip lasts 2 days and 1 night, while the Big Safari trip is 4 days and 3 nights. Safari packages include all camping gear, meals, and drinks (mineral water, soft drinks, beer, tequila), as well as basic bathroom facilities (toilet and shower with fresh water). The Mini Safari costs $440 per person with dives, or $289 without dives; the Big Safari costs $999 with dives, or $599 without dives.

Baja Expeditions, Sonora 586 (© 800/843-6967 in the U.S., or 612/123-4900; fax 858/581-6542 in the U.S.; www.bajaex.com; daily 9am–4pm PST), runs live-aboard and single-day dive trips to the above-mentioned locations and other areas in the Sea of Cortez. The cost is $125 for a two-tank dive. See p. 35 for contact information in the U.S. and Canada.

SEA KAYAKING   Kayaking in the many bays and coves near La Paz is a paddler's dream, and because some of the area's special sites for swimming and snorkeling are accessible only by kayak, daylong or multiday trips can't be beat. In the waters near La Paz, the water clarity gives the sensation of being suspended in the air. Bring your own equipment, or let the local companies take care of you. Several companies in the United States (see "Special-Interest Trips," in chapter 2) can book trips in advance. Locally, Baja Quest (see above; day trips start at $90 and multiday trips also are available) and Mar y Aventuras (© 612/123-0559; fax 612/122-3559; www.kayakbaja.com) arrange extended kayak adventures.

SPORTFISHING   La Paz, justly famous for its sportfishing, attracts anglers from all over the world. Its waters are home to more than 850 species of fish. The most economical approach is to rent a *panga* boat with a captain and equipment. It costs $125 for 3 hours, but you don't go very far out. Super *pangas,* which have a shade cover and comfortable seats, start at around $180 for two persons. Larger cruisers with bathrooms start at $240. Local hotels and tour agencies arrange sportfishing trips.

You can arrange sportfishing trips locally through hotels and tour agencies. DeSea Baja's (© 310/691-8040; www.lapazsportfishing.com) rates start at $220 per day for two people. David Jones of The Fishermen's Fleet (© 612/122-1313; fax 612/125-7334; www.fishermensfleet.com) uses the locally popular *panga*-style fishing boat. David is superprofessional, speaks English, and truly understands area fishing. Average price is $225 for the boat, but double-check what the price includes—you may need to bring your own food and drinks.

WHALE-WATCHING   Between January and March (and sometimes as early as Dec), 3,000 to 5,000 gray whales migrate from the Bering Strait to the Pacific coast of Baja. The main whale-watching spots are Laguna San Ignacio (on the Pacific, near San Ignacio), Bahía Magdalena (on the Pacific, near Puerto López Mateos—about a 2-hr. drive from La Paz), and Scammon's Lagoon (near Guerrero Negro).

Although it is across the peninsula on the Sea of Cortez, La Paz has the only major international airport in the area and thus has become a center of Baja's whale-watching excursions. Most tours originating in La Paz go to Bahía Magdalena, where the whales give birth in calm waters. Several companies arrange whale-watching tours originating in La Paz or other Baja towns or in the United States; 12-hour tours from La Paz start at around $115 per person, including breakfast, lunch, transportation, and an English-speaking guide. Make reservations at **Viajes Lybs,** 16 de Septiembre 408, between Revolución and Serdán (© **612/122-4680;** fax 612/125-9600).

Most tours from the United States offer birding, sea kayaking, and other close-to-nature experiences during the same trip. See "Special-Interest Trips," in chapter 2, for details.

You can go whale-watching without joining a tour by taking a bus from La Paz to Puerto López Mateos or Puerto San Carlos at Magdalena Bay (a 3-hr. ride) and hiring a boat there. It's a long trip to do in a day, but there are a few modest hotels in San Carlos. Check at the La Paz tourist office for information.

For a more in-depth discussion, see "Whale-Watching in Baja: A Primer" on p. 144.

ECOTOURS

A wide selection of ecotours and adventure activities are available through **Baja Quest** and **Grupo Fun Baja** (© **612/121-5884** or 612/125-2366; www.funbaja.com). In addition to diving excursions (the company's specialty), they also offer ATV tours and kite surfing. **DeSea Baja** (see above) offers driving tours in rental vehicles equipped for off-road adventures.

---

3 A Break from the Beaches: Exploring La Paz

Most tour agencies offer city tours of all of La Paz's major sights. Tours last 2 to 3 hours, include time for shopping, and cost around $15 per person.

HISTORIC LA PAZ

When Cortez landed here on May 3, 1535, he named it Bahía Santa Cruz. The name didn't stick. In April 1683, Eusebio Kino, a Spanish Jesuit priest, arrived and dubbed the place Nuestra Señora de la Paz (Our Lady of Peace). It wasn't until November 1, 1720, however, that Jaime Bravo, another Jesuit priest, set up a permanent mission. He used the same name as his immediate predecessor, calling it the Misión de Nuestra Señora de la Paz. The mission church stands on La Paz's main square on Revolución between Cinco de Mayo and Independencia, and today the city is called simply La Paz.

Biblioteca de las Californias   The small collection of historical documents and books at the Library of the Californias is the most comprehensive in Baja. The library sometimes shows free international films in the evening.

In the Casa de Gobierno, across the plaza from the mission church on Madero, between Cinco de Mayo and Independencia. For information, call the tourism office at © **612/122-2640.** Free admission. Mon–Fri 9am–4pm.

El Teatro de la Ciudad   The city theater is La Paz's cultural center, with performances by visiting and local artists. There's no extended calendar available, but bookings include small ballet companies, experimental and popular theater, popular music, and an occasional classical concert or symphony. Contact the box office for details and ticket prices.

Av. Navarro 700, corner of Independencia. © **612/125-0486.**

Museo de Antropología (Anthropology Museum) ✦   This museum features large, though faded, color photos of Baja's prehistoric cave paintings. There are also exhibits on various topics, including the geological history of the peninsula, fossils, missions, colonial history, and daily life. All information is in Spanish.

Corner of Altamirano and Cinco de Mayo. © **612/122-0162** or 612/125-6424. Free admission (donations encouraged). Daily 9am–6pm.

To Airport & Marina de La Paz
Bahia de La Paz
To Ferry Terminal, La Concha Beach Resort, Aquarium & Marina Palmira →

Alvaro Obregón
Francisco Madero
Revolución de 1910
Aquiles Serdán
16 de Septiembre
Independencia
Cathedral
Manuel Pineda
Ignacio Allende
Antonio Rosales
Degollado
Ignacio Altamirano
Valentín Gómez Farías
5 de Mayo
Miguel Hidalgo y Costilla
Constitución
Josefa Ortíz de Domínguez
Lic. Primo Verdad
Marcelo Rubio R.

Church †
Information (i)
Post Office ⊠

ACCOMMODATIONS ■
Grand Plaza La Paz 2
Hacienda del Cortez 1
Hotel Los Arcos 5
Hotel Mediterrane 14
Posada de las Flores 12

DINING ◆
Bismark II 17
Buffalo BBQ 11
Caffe Expresso 7
El Quinto Sol 22
Trattoria La Pazta 15

ATTRACTIONS ●
Antigua California 10
Artesanías Cuauhtémoc
  (The Weaver) 4
Biblioteca de las Californias 13
Chinatown 8
Dorian's 6
El Teatro de la Ciudad 20

Ibarra's Pottery 19
La Pazlapa & Casa de Villa 9
Las Varitas 21
Municipal Market 16
Serpentarium 3
The Anthropology Museum 18

NATURE MUSEUMS OF LA PAZ

Increasingly, La Paz is drawing a number of travelers enchanted with the beauty of the area's diverse natural environment. Several new centers have emerged, combining entertainment with environmental education. You may see information about an open-water **Dolphinarium** in La Paz, but it was closed after hurricanes damaged the facilities in 2003 and put the dolphins at risk (they were transferred to Dolphin Adventures in Puerto Vallarta, where they are now thriving). However, there is talk of repairing and reopening the facility at some point.

Aquarium ⚚   The newest of La Paz's natural museums opened in late 2003 and recently underwent a major renovation to improve visitors' introduction to marine life in the Sea of Cortez. They're reopening as we go to print in summer 2007; new attractions include a shark tank, a turtle exhibit, and an audiovisual center that further enables education to students and groups. Guided tours are now available.

Pichilingue Km 5.5, next to the Hotel La Concha. ✆ **612/121-5872.** Admission $5 adults. Tues–Sun 10am–6pm.

Cactus Sanctuary ⚚   This 50-hectare (124-acre) natural reserve features 1,000m (over a half-mile) of marked pathways and self-guided tours with information about the plants and animals of La Paz's desert region. Fifty unique areas have been identified, which you can explore in consecutive order or any progression of your choosing.

Route maps and guided tours are available, as are descriptive signs for many of the plants. There's a surprising amount of wildlife to see here, from the myriad types of cacti, many of which are endemic to Baja California, to the numerous plants and animals that support this unique ecosystem. The sanctuary is in the Ejido El Rosario (an *ejido* is a village that is a community-owned piece of land). Go to the *ejido*'s *delegación* (main office), and they will provide you with a key to enter the reserve.

Ejido El Rosario. (C) 612/124-0245 (Dr. Hector Nolasco). hnolasco@cibnor.mx. Admission $2 donation. No fixed hours. 45 min. south of La Paz; take Hwy. 1 toward the town of El Triunfo; drive 10 min. inland along a dirt road.

Serpentarium 😿   This mostly open-air natural museum offers plenty of opportunities to observe various species of reptiles that inhabit the region's ecosystem, including snakes, turtles, iguanas, lizards, and crocodiles. It's on the corner of Calle Brecha California and Calle La Posada. To get there, go to the southernmost point of the *malecón* at Abasolo Street, where the last streetlights are, and just before the beach you'll see an unpaved street—that's Brecha California. If you're going with a group, e-mail cobra293@hotmail.com to make a reservation.

Calles Brecha California and La Posada. (C) 612/123-5731. cobra293@hotmail.com. Admission $8 adults, $5 children. Daily 10am–4pm.

4 Shopping

La Paz has little in the way of folk art or other treasures from mainland Mexico. But the dense cluster of streets behind the **Hotel Perla,** between 16 de Septiembre and Degollado, abounds with small shops—some tacky, others quite upscale. This area also holds a very small but authentic **Chinatown** dating to the time when Chinese laborers were brought to settle in Baja. Serdán Street, from Degollado south, offers dozens of sellers of dried spices, piñatas, and candy. Stores selling crafts, folk art, clothing, and handmade furniture and accessories lie mostly along the *malecón* (Alvaro Obregón) or a block or two in. The **municipal market,** at Revolución and Degollado, has little of interest to visitors. Something you're sure to notice if you explore around the central plaza is the abundance of stores selling electronic equipment, including stereos, cameras, and televisions. This is because La Paz is a principal port for electronic imports to Mexico from the Far East and therefore offers some of the best prices in Baja and mainland Mexico.

Antigua California   This shop manages to stay in business as others come and go. It carries a good selection of folk art from throughout Mexico. It's open Monday to Saturday from 9:30am to 8:30pm, Sunday from 10:30am to 2:30pm. Paseo Alvaro Obregón 220, at Arreola. (C) 612/125-5230.

Artesanías Cuauhtémoc (The Weaver)   If you like beautiful handwoven tablecloths, placemats, rugs, and other textiles, it's worth the long walk or taxi ride to this unique shop. Fortunato Silva, an elderly gentleman, weaves wonderfully textured cotton textiles from yarn he spins and dyes himself. He charges far less than what you'd pay for equivalent artistry in the United States. Open Monday through Saturday from 10am to 3:30pm and 6 to 7pm. On the corner of Abasolo and Oaxaca, between Jalisco and Nayarit. (C) 612/122-4575.

Dorian's   If you've forgotten essentials or want to stock up on duty-free perfume or cosmetics, head for Dorian's, La Paz's major department store. La Paz is a duty-free port city, so prices are excellent. Dorian's carries a wide selection of stylish clothing, shoes, lingerie, jewelry, and accessories as well. Open daily from 10am to 9pm. 16 de Septiembre, between Esquerro and 21 de Agosto. ℭ 612/122-8014.

Ibarra's Pottery   Here, you not only shop for tableware, hand-painted tiles, and decorative pottery, you can watch it being made. Each piece is individually hand-painted or glazed, and then fired. Open Monday to Saturday from 9am to 3pm. You can call ahead to schedule a tour. Guillermo Prieto 625, between Torre Iglesias and República. ℭ 612/122-0404.

5 Where to Stay

EXPENSIVE

Grand Plaza La Paz ☆   Among La Paz's newest options in places to stay, this all-suite resort offers travelers a comfortable sense of U.S. standards and modern conveniences. It's considered the best option for business travelers to the area, one of the few in town with a full business center, Internet access, secretarial assistance, and meeting space. Vacationers also will enjoy the hotel's location on the marina, as well as its range of helpful tour services and pleasant pool area. The clean, modern, and well-equipped rooms on three floors offer either views to the bay or overlooking the courtyard pool, with a choice of king or two double beds. Five different kinds of suites have a private balcony, and all have ocean views. The hotel is at the northern end of town, 5.6km (3½ miles) from downtown, at the Marina Fidepaz.

Lote A Marina Fidepaz, P.O. Box 482, 23090 La Paz, B.C.S. ℭ 800/227-6963 in the U.S., or 612/124-0830 or 612/124-0833. Fax 612/124-0837. www.grandplazalapaz.com. 54 suites. High season $186 double; 30% discount during low season. AE, DC, MC, V. Free guarded parking. **Amenities:** Restaurant; 2 bars; outdoor pool; squash court; fitness center; whirlpool; sauna; concierge; tour desk; business center; gift shop; room service; babysitting; Wi-Fi in lobby; laundry service; safe. *In room:* A/C, TV, coffeemaker, hair dryer, safe, iron, microwaves (in some suites).

Posada de las Flores ☆   New owner Giuseppe Marceletti has continued the tradition of hospitality in this elegant B&B (formerly Posada Santa Fe), the best bet for travelers looking for a more refined place to stay in La Paz. Each room is individually decorated with high-quality Mexican furniture and antiques, hand-loomed fabrics, and exquisite artisan details. Bathrooms are especially welcoming, with marble tubs and thick towels. Breakfast is served from 8 to 11am daily. Telephone, fax, and Internet service are available through the office. It's at the northern end of the *malecón*.

Av. Alvaro Obregón 440, 23000 La Paz, B.C.S. ℭ 877/245-2860 in the U.S., or 612/125-5871. www.posadadelas flores.com. 8 units. High season $180 double, $290 suite; low season $150 double, $250 suite. Rates include full breakfast. No children under 12 accepted. MC, V. Street parking. **Amenities:** Small outdoor pool; Internet access; hospitality desk; teatime. *In room:* A/C, TV, minibar, hair dryer, bathrobes, complimentary wake-up coffee service on request.

MODERATE

Hotel Los Arcos (Value   This three-story, neocolonial-style hotel at the west end of the *malecón* is the best place for downtown accommodations with a touch of tranquility. Although the hotel is a bit dated, Los Arcos has functional furnishings and amenities, and the hotel is filled with fountains, plants, and even rocking chairs. Most of the rooms and suites come with two double beds. Each has a balcony overlooking the pool in the inner courtyard or the waterfront, plus a whirlpool tub. I prefer the South Pacific–style bungalows with thatched roofs and fireplaces in the back part of the property. Satellite TVs carry U.S. channels.

Av. Alvaro Obregón 498, between Rosales and Allende (Apdo. Postal 112), 23000 La Paz, B.C.S. ℂ **800/347-2252** in the U.S., 714/450-9000, or 612/122-2744. Fax 612/125-4313. www.losarcos.com. 130 units (52 bungalows). $100 double; $80–$100 bungalow; $115 suite. AE, MC, V. Free guarded parking. **Amenities:** Cafeteria; restaurant; bar w/live music; 2 outdoor pools (1 heated); sauna; travel agency; fishing information desk; room service; laundry service; Ping-Pong. *In room:* A/C, TV, minibar.

La Concha Beach Resort 🔒🔒   Ten kilometers (6 miles) north of downtown La Paz, this resort's setting is perfect: on a curved beach ideal for swimming and water-sports. All rooms face the water and have double beds, balconies or patios, and small tables and chairs. Condos with full kitchens and one or three bedrooms are available on a nightly basis in the high-rise complex next door. If available, they're worth the extra price for a perfect family-vacation stay. The hotel offers scuba, fishing, and whale-watching packages. No children under 14 are allowed in the condos.

Carretera Pichilingue Km 5, 23000 La Paz, B.C.S. ℂ **612/121-6161**. www.laconcha.com. 113 units. $95 double; $125 junior suite; $137–$259 condo. AE, DC, MC, V. Free guarded parking. **Amenities:** Restaurant (w/theme nights); 2 bars; beachside pool; Jacuzzi; complete watersports center w/Wave Runners, kayaks, and paddleboats; tour desk; business center; free twice-daily shuttle to town; room service; laundry service; babysitting; beach club w/scuba program. *In room:* A/C, TV, dataport, minibar.

INEXPENSIVE

Hotel Mediterrane 🔒🔒   Simple yet stylish, this unique inn mixes Mediterranean with Mexican, making a cozy place for couples or friends to share. All rooms face an interior courtyard and have white-tile floors and *equipal* furniture (a common type of Mexican furniture made from tanned leather and woven branches, rustic in style, and though inexpensive, durable and attractive), with colorful Mexican serapes draped over the beds. The location is great—just a block from the *malecón*. The adjacent Trattoria La Pazta restaurant (see "Where to Dine," below) is one of La Paz's best. Rates include the use of kayaks and bicycles for exploring the town and wireless Internet access. Those not traveling with their laptop can use the computer center, included with the rates. This is a gay-friendly hotel.

Allende 36, 23000 La Paz, B.C.S. ℂ/fax **612/125-1195**. www.hotelmed.com. 9 units. $66 double; $83 suite. Extra person $10. Weekly discounts available. Street parking. AE, MC, V. **Amenities:** Sports equipment; Wi-Fi; computer center. *In room:* A/C, TV/VCR, minifridge (in some).

6 Where to Dine

Although La Paz is not known for culinary achievements, it has a growing assortment of small, pleasant restaurants that are good and reasonably priced. In addition to the usual seafood and Mexican dishes, you can find Italian, French, Spanish, Chinese, and even vegetarian offerings in town. Restaurants along the seaside *malecón* tend to be more expensive than those a few blocks inland. Generally, restaurant reservations are unnecessary, except perhaps during Easter and Christmas weeks.

MODERATE

Bismark II 🔒 SEAFOOD/MEXICAN   Bismark excels at seafood; you can order fish tacos, chiles rellenos stuffed with lobster salad, marlin "meatballs" and paella, breaded oysters, or a sundae glass filled with ceviche or shrimp. The kitchen prepares extremely fresh dorado, halibut, snapper, or whatever else is in season in a number of ways. Chips and creamy dip are served while you wait. It's a good place to linger over a late lunch. The decor of pine walls and dark wood chairs is reminiscent of a country cafe.

Degollado and Altamirano. ✆ **612/122-4854.** Breakfast $2–$5; main courses $4–$17. Daily 10am–10pm. Walk 7 blocks inland on Degollado to Altamirano.

Buffalo BBQ ✦✦ ARGENTINEAN/GRILLED HAMBURGERS   This is the ulti-mate sendoff meal before a fishing, diving, or cruising trip, where dinner no doubt will be the daily catch. Indoor seating plays second fiddle to the interior outdoor courtyard, which fronts a fiery grill on which prime cuts are turned into delicacies. The hamburgers are big, flavorful, and come in so many delectable styles—from the special-sauced New Mexico burger to the standard cheeseburger—that a carnivore may just call this heaven. Otherwise, Buffalo BBQ's steaks, ribs, and wine list are a worthy tribute to the chef's Argentinean roots.

Madero 1240 (corner of 5 de Mayo and Madero). ✆ **612/128-8755.** www.buffalo-bbq.com. Hamburgers and main courses $8–$15. AE, MC, V. Wed–Mon 2pm–midnight.

Trattoria La Pazta ✦✦ ITALIAN/SWISS   The trendiest restaurant in town, La Pazta gleams with black lacquered tables and white tile as the aromas of garlic and espresso float in the air. The menu features local fresh seafood such as pasta with squid in wine-and-cream sauce and crispy fried calamari. The lasagna is homemade, baked in a wood-fired oven. An extensive wine list complements the menu. La Pazta's day-time cafe is also appealing for breakfast, or you can simply opt for an espresso and croissant. The restaurant is in front of the Hotel Mediterrane.

Allende 36. ✆ **612/125-1195.** www.hotelmed.com. Breakfast $2–$4; main courses $8–$15. AE, MC, V. Thurs–Tues 7am–11pm cafe only, 3–11pm cafe and restaurant.

INEXPENSIVE

Caffé Expresso FRENCH/CAFE   You'll feel as if you've suddenly been transported across the Atlantic in this incongruous but welcoming spot. Indulge in any number of espresso coffee drinks, plus French and Austrian pastries, while sitting at marble-topped bistro tables. Jazz music plays in the background.

Av. Obregón and 16 de Septiembre. ✆ **612/123-4373.** Coffees and pastries $1–$3. No credit cards. Tues–Sun 6pm–4am.

El Quinto Sol ✦ *(Finds* VEGETARIAN   Not only is this La Paz's principal health-food market, it's a cheerful, excellent cafe for fresh-fruit *licuados* (smoothies), *tortas* (sandwiches), and vegetarian dishes. Tables sit beside oversized wood-framed win-dows, with flowering planters in the sills. Sandwiches are served on whole-grain bread—also available for sale—and the potato tacos are an excellent way for vegetari-ans to indulge in a Mexican staple. Owner Marta Alonso also offers free nightly med-itation classes to clients.

Av. Independencia and B. Domínguez. ✆ **612/122-1692.** Main courses $1.50–$7. No credit cards. Mon–Sat 8am–4pm; store hours 8am–9pm.

7 La Paz After Dark

A night in La Paz logically begins in a cafe along the *malecón* as the sun sinks into the sea—have your camera ready.

A favorite ringside seat at dusk is a table at **La Terraza,** next to the Hotel Perla (✆ **612/122-0777**). La Terraza makes good, schooner-size margaritas. **Pelícanos Bar,** on the second story of the Hotel Los Arcos (✆ **612/122-2744**), has a good view of the waterfront and a clubby, cozy feel. Later in the night, **Carlos 'n' Charlie's La**

Paz–Lapa (© **612/122-9290**) has live music on the weekends. **La Cabaña** nightclub (© **612/122-0777**) in the Hotel Perla features Latin rhythms. It opens at 9pm daily, and there's a $4 cover on weekends.

For dancing, a few of the hottest clubs are **Casa de Villa** (no phone), where current pop music commingles with young *Paceños* (La Paz locals) till late on the second-floor terrace above La Paz–Lapa on the *malecón*. **Las Varitas** (© **612/125-2025**), Independencia and Dominguez, plays Latin rock, ranchero, and salsa. Both are open from 9pm to 3 or 4am Thursday through Saturday (occasionally open earlier in the week as well), with cover charges around $5 (the charge may be waived or increased, depending on the crowd).

6

Mid-Baja: Loreto, Mulegé & Santa Rosalía

Halfway between the resort sophistication of Los Cabos and the frontier exuberance of Tijuana lies Baja's midsection, an area rich in history and culture. The indigenous cave paintings here are a UNESCO World Heritage Site, and the area was home to numerous Jesuit missions in the 1700s. These days, mid-Baja is known for its sea-kayaking, freediving, sportfishing, off-road racing, hiking, and simply as a place to take in breathtaking quantities of natural beauty.

Overlooked by many travelers (except avid sportfishermen and the off-road racers who pass through several times a year), **Loreto** is a rare gem that sparkles under the desert sky. The purple hues of the Giganta Mountains meet the indigo waters of the Sea of Cortez, providing a spectacular backdrop of natural contrasts for the historic town. **Mulegé** is, literally, an oasis in the Baja desert. The only freshwater river (Río Mulegé) in the peninsula flows through town. And the port town of **Santa Rosalía,** while a century or so past its prime, makes a worthy detour, with its pastel clapboard houses

and unusual steel-and-stained-glass church, designed by Gustave Eiffel (of Eiffel Tower fame).

Far enough away from the polished tourism gem of Los Cabos, the people's smiles are more sincere and you rarely hear the entrée to a timeshare sales pitch, "Hola, amiga. You wanna go fishing?" as you walk the streets of mid-Baja. Nonetheless, plans may be in the works to change that. North-of-the-border developers have snapped up Ensenada Blanca Bay, Loreto Bay, and more. Although mid-Baja is still a decade or more from being a hot spot for anyone besides adventurers, racing teams, and RV caravans, the plans are there, so if you want a glimpse of the Wild West, now is the time to visit Loreto, Mulegé, Santa Rosalía, and San Ignacio.

The region is also a popular jumping-off point for many whale-watching tours; to find out when, where, and how to view these gentle giants, consult "Whale-Watching in Baja: A Primer," at the end of this chapter.

1 Loreto & the Offshore Islands ★★

389km (241 miles) NW of La Paz; 533km (330 miles) N of Cabo San Lucas; 1,125km (698 miles) SE of Tijuana

The unpretentious feel of the town of Loreto belies its historical importance. Loreto was the center of the Spanish mission effort during colonial times, the first capital of the Californias, and the first European settlement in the peninsula. Founded on October 25, 1697, it was Father Juan María Salvatierra's choice as the site of the first mission in the Californias. (California, at the time, extended from Cabo San Lucas in the south to the Oregon border in the north.) He held Mass beneath a figure of the

Virgin of Loreto, brought from a town in Italy bearing the same name. For 132 years, Loreto served as the state capital, until an 1829 hurricane destroyed most of the town. The state capital moved to La Paz (see chapter 5) the following year.

During the late 1970s and early 1980s, the Mexican government saw in Loreto the possibility for another megadevelopment along the lines of Cancún, Ixtapa, or Los Cabos. It invested in a golf course and championship tennis facility, modernized the town's infrastructure, and built an international airport and full marina facilities at Nopoló, 26km (16 miles) south of town. The economics, however, didn't make sense at the time, and few hotel investors and even fewer tourists came. In the past 4 years, however, this effort has been revitalized, and the area is seeing a welcome influx of flights, as well as the addition of its first new hotel in years, a sprawling Inn at Loreto Bay (formerly the Camino Real). The Loreto Bay residential development has been a major part of renewed interest in the area and is bringing homes, condos, and other facilities to the area, with a rental program in place for vacation stays (© **877/865-6738** toll-free from the U.S. for rental information).

Soon, Loreto may become the next "new" place to go, but for now, downtown Loreto remains the heart rate–relaxing fishing village and gringo hideaway it's been for decades. The celebration of the town's 300th anniversary in 1997 had the added benefit of updating the streets, plaza, and mission: Old Town Loreto is now a quaint showplace.

The *Loretanos,* or Loreto locals, are friendly and helpful; unlike the swarms of proprietary tourists that dominate the peninsula's northern and southern reaches, the mid-Baja region attracts a more unassuming set of visitors, and locals play the part of gracious hosts. Canadian and American expatriates who've settled in Loreto may be a bit more aloof with passing tourists, and who can blame them? They settled here when there was nothing, and they can't help but want it to stay that way for as long as possible.

The main reasons to come to Loreto center on the Sea of Cortez and the five islands just offshore, but the Sierra de La Giganta Mountains offer a wealth of opportunities for exploration as well. The reefs around Isla Coronado are home to schools of giant grouper, and beachgoers won't find a bay more beautiful than the one on Isla del Carmen or on Coronado's north side. The natural port of Puerto Escondido shelters a growing yachting community; and the area is so lovely that most of the sailboats stay put year round. Kayakers launch here for trips to Isla del Carmen and Isla Danzante, or down the remote mountain coast to La Paz, and history buffs head for the mountains to visit some of the oldest Jesuit missions.

ESSENTIALS

GETTING THERE & DEPARTING

BY PLANE   The **Loreto International Airport** (airport code: LTO; © **613/135-0499** or 613/135-0498) is 6km (3¾ miles) southwest of Loreto. **Aeroméxico** (© **800/237-6639** in the U.S., or 613/135-1837; fax 613/135-1838; www.aeromexico.com), **Alaska Airlines** (© **800/252-7522;** www.alaskaair.com), and **Delta** (© **800/241-4141** in the U.S.; www.delta.com) all have nonstop flights from Los Angeles. **Aereo Calafia** (© **613/135-2503;** www.aereocalafia.com) has nonstop flights from Cabo San Lucas and Ciudad Obregón. Be aware that Aereo Calafia flights rarely take off as scheduled, so be patient and just plan to arrive in your final destination at least 30 to 45 minutes later than expected.

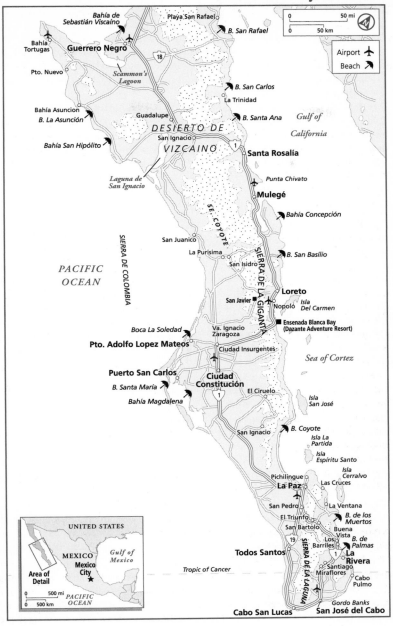

The Lower Baja Peninsula

Bahía de
Sebastián Viscaíno
Playa San Rafael
B. San Rafael

Bahía
Tortugas
Guerrero Negro

Pto. Nuevo

*Scammon's
Lagoon*

B. San Carlos
La Trinidad

Bahía Asuncion
B. La Asunción
Guadalupe
B. Santa Ana
*Gulf of
California*

DESIERTO DE
San Ignacio

Bahía San Hipólito
VIZCAINO
Santa Rosalía

*Laguna de
San Ignacio*
Punta Chivato

Mulegé

Bahía Concepción

San Juanico
SIERRA DE COLOMBIA
B. San Basílio

La Purisima
San Isidro

*PACIFIC
OCEAN*
Loreto

San Javier
*Isla
Del Carmen*
Nopoló

Boca La Soledad
Va. Ignacio
Zaragoza
Ensenada Blanca Bay
(Dazante Adventure Resort)

Pto. Adolfo Lopez Mateos
Ciudad Insurgentes

Sea of Cortez

Puerto San Carlos
**Ciudad
Constitución**
El Ciruelo

B. Santa María
*Isla
San José*

Bahía Magdalena

San Ignacio
B. Coyote
*Isla La
Partida*

*Isla
Espíritu Santo*

*Isla
Cerralvo*
Pichilingue
La Paz
Las Cruces

San Pedro
La Ventana
El Triunfo
B. de los
Muertos
San Bartolo
Buena
Vista
Los
Barriles
B. de
Palmas

Todos Santos
19
**La
Rivera**

Santiago
Miraflores

Tropic of Cancer
*Cabo
Pulmo*

Gordo Banks

Cabo San Lucas
San José del Cabo

Airport ✈
Beach ↗

0   50 mi
0   50 km

SE. COYOTE

SIERRA DE LA GIGANTA

SIERRA DE LA LAGUNA

Area of Detail

UNITED STATES

MEXICO
*Gulf of
Mexico*
Mexico
City ★

Area of
Detail

0   500 mi
0   500 km
*PACIFIC
OCEAN*

117

BY CAR   From La Paz (a 4½–5 hr. drive), take Carretera Transpeninsular (Hwy. 1) northwest to Ciudad Constitución; from there, continue northeast on Carretera Transpeninsular to Loreto. This route takes you twice over the mountain range that stretches down the Baja peninsula, through mountain and desert landscapes, and into the heart of the old mission country. From Tijuana, travel south on Carretera Transpeninsular. The drive takes 17 to 20 hours straight into Loreto, and driving after dark is strongly discouraged.

BY BUS   The bus station, or Terminal de Autobuses (℡ **613/135-0767**), is on Salvatierra and Paseo Tamaral, a 10-minute walk from downtown. It's open 24 hours. Buses stop in Loreto en route to Santa Rosalía, Tijuana, Mexicali, Guerrero Negro, and La Paz. The trip to La Paz takes 5 hours and costs $25. You can usually get a ticket for any bus, except during Easter, summer, and Christmas holidays, when buses tend to be more crowded. The bus terminal is a simple building and the staff there is very friendly and helpful.

ORIENTATION

ARRIVING   At the airport, taxis (℡ **613/135-1255**) line up on the street to receive incoming passengers. They charge about $16 to Loreto, and the ride takes approximately 10 minutes.

If you plan to rent a car, it's best to do so in advance because the airport is so small that car-rental desks aren't always staffed on your arrival. **Budget Baja** has a counter at the airport (℡ **613/135-0937**) and a branch office in town. The branch is on Hidalgo between Pípila and López Mateos (℡ **613/135-1149;** daily 8am–8pm). Advance reservations are not always necessary, but it will save you time. Be sure to confirm the reservation and your arrival time before you start your trip.

If you arrive at the bus station, it's about a 10-minute walk to the downtown area and a little farther to the hotels by the water. A taxi from the bus station to the hotels costs $2 to $5.

VISITOR INFORMATION   The city **tourist information office** (℡ **613/135-0036** or 613/135-0411) is in the southeast corner of the Palacio de Gobierno building, across from the town square. It offers maps, local free publications, and other basic information about the area. It's open Monday through Friday from 8am to 3pm. Information, which may be outdated, is also available at **www.gotoloreto.com** and **www.loreto.com**.

CITY LAYOUT   Salvatierra is the main street that runs northeast, merging into Paseo Hidalgo, which runs toward the beach. Bulevar López Mateos, also known as the *malecón,* parallels the water; along this road you'll find many hotels, seafood restaurants, fishing charters, bars, and the marina. Most of the town's social life revolves around the central square, the old mission, and the *malecón.* There's an old section of town along Salvatierra, between Madera and Playa, with mahogany and teak homes that date back to the 1800s.

GETTING AROUND   Most addresses in Loreto don't have a street number; the references are usually the perpendicular streets or the main square and the mission. There is no local bus service around town. Taxis or walking are your only options and, luckily, the town is quite small and manageable for walking. Taxis are inexpensive, with average fares in town ranging from $1.50 to $2.50. The main taxi stand is on Salvatierra, in front of the El Pescador supermarket.

The Loreto Area

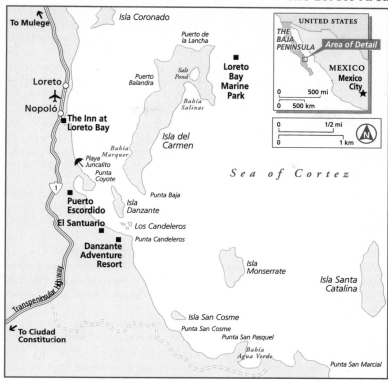

FAST FACTS: Loreto

Area Code The telephone area code is **613**.

Banks There is only one bank in Loreto. Come here to exchange currency. **Bancomer** (© **613/135-0315** or 613/135-0014) is on Francisco I. Madero, across the street from the Palacio Municipal (City Hall). Bank hours are Monday through Friday from 8:30am to 4pm. This is also the location of the only ATM in town. There is a *casa de cambio* (money-exchange house) on Salvatierra, near the main square.

Beach Safety The beaches are generally safe for swimming, with the main beach along the *malecón* (sea wall).

Emergencies Dial 060 for emergency assistance; **city police** can be reached at © **613/135-0035**, or 613/135-2270 (Paseo Tamaral, next to University of La Paz, Loreto Campus); the **Red Cross** at © **613/135-1111**; and the fire department at © **613/135-1566**.

General Store **Super El Pescador,** on Salvatierra and Independencia (© **613/ 135-0060),** is the best place to get toiletries, film, bottled water, and other basic staples as well as newspapers and telephone calling cards.

Internet Access Loreto is paradise for budget travelers looking to stay connected. Practically every restaurant, hotel, and RV park in Loreto offers free wireless Internet access to patrons. One of the more popular places to hook up is **Augie's Bar and Bait Shop** (© **613/135-1224)** on the *malecón.*

Marinas Loreto's marina for *pangas* (small fishing boats) is along the *malecón.* Cruise ships and other large boats anchor at Puerto Loreto, also known as Puerto Escondido, 26km (16 miles) south of Loreto. For details about the marina and docking fees, contact the Capitanía de Puerto in Loreto (© **613/ 133-0992** or 613/135-0465).

Medical Care Medical services are offered at the **Centro de Salud** hospital (© **613/135-0039),** Salvatierra 68, near the corner with Allende. The center is open 24 hours for emergencies (a standard visit costs $10), and from 8 to 10am and 3 to 5pm for general consultations, which cost $5.

Parking Street parking is generally easy to find in the downtown area.

Pharmacy The **Farmacia del Rosario** (© **613/135-0670)** is at Independencia and Zapata, and is open daily from 8am to 10pm. The **Farmacia de los Americas** (© **613/135-0670)** is on the west corner of Independencia and Juárez, open 8am to 10pm daily.

Post Office The *correo* (© **613/135-0647)** is at Deportiva between Salvatierra and Benito Juárez, and is open Monday through Friday from 8am to 4pm.

Taxis Taxis can generally be found parked on the north side of Loreto's main street, just east of the El Pescador market, and near large hotels. There are two taxi companies in Loreto, **Sitio Loreto** (© **613/135-0424)** and **Sitio Juárez** (© **613/135-0915).**

BEACHES & CRUISES

BEACHES Beautiful beaches front Loreto and the hotels that surround it. The beaches are safe for swimming, with the main beaches holding court at either end of the *malecón.* The beach is a popular place for Loretanos, especially on Sundays. Most visitors go to Loreto for the excellent sportfishing and other outdoor activities, so relaxing at the beach is one of the optional pleasures offered by this naturalist's paradise. For those seeking more pristine, secluded beaches, the options are unlimited in the several islands offshore. **Isla Coronado** and **Isla del Carmen** offer several top-tier beaches, with the best anchorage on the western shores of both islands. You can either take one of the cruises mentioned below or hire a *lancha* (small wooden fishing boats available along the *malecón*) to take you there; the price depends on what you want and how sharp your bargaining skills are (the *lancheros,* or captains, take cash only).

CRUISES More than cruises, Loreto offers island exploration tours that take in one, or a combination, of the five islands located just offshore. They usually offer the opportunity to visit sea-lion colonies and do some snorkeling and beachcombing for around $40. Arrange cruises through a travel agency or your hotel, or call **Arturo's Sport** (© **613/135-0766;** www.arturosport.com). Their most popular cruise visits the

— I don't speak sign language.

A hotel can close for all kinds of reasons.
Our Guarantee ensures that if your hotel's undergoing construction, we'll let you know in advance. In fact, we cover your entire travel experience. See www.travelocity.com/guarantee for details.

You'll never roam alone.

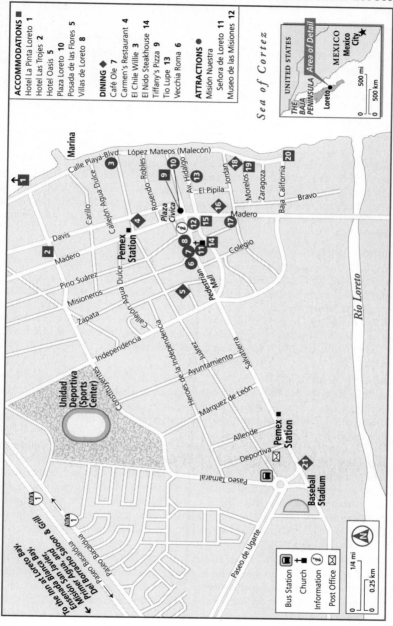

ACCOMMODATIONS ■
Hotel La Pinta Loreto **1**
Hotel Las Trojes **2**
Hotel Oasis **5**
Plaza Loreto **10**
Posada de las Flores **5**
Villas de Loreto **8**

DINING ◆
Café Ole **7**
Carmen's Restaurant **4**
El Chile Willie **3**
El Nido Steakhouse **14**
Tiffany's Pizza **9**
Tio Lupe **13**
Vecchia Roma **6**

ATTRACTIONS ●
Misión Nuestra
Señora de Loreto **11**
Museo de las Misiones **12**

Sea of Cortez

(Moments   Festivals in Loreto

The feast of the patron saint of Loreto is celebrated September 5 to September 8, with a fair, music, dancing, and other cultural events, closing with the procession of the miraculous figure of the Virgin of Loreto. During the month of October, Loreto celebrates the anniversary of its founding with a series of cultural events that include music and dance. There is also a reenactment of the landing of the Spanish missionaries that is part of a popular festival held from October 19 to October 25.

---

four offshore islands, Coronado, Carmen, Danzante, and Montserrat. The 8-hour cruise from island to island incorporates snorkeling and sunning at one paradise after another for $125. Prices include snacks, beverages, and lunch. Each island is unique and offers a spectrum of activities such as sea kayaking, snorkeling, diving, hiking, or simply exploring the local desert flora and fauna (see "A Visit to Isla del Carmen," below).

LAND SPORTS

GOLF   The 18-hole **Campo de Golf Loreto,** Bulevar Misión San Ignacio, Fraccionamiento Nopoló (© **613/133-0554** or 613/133-0788), is in the process of an eco-focused renovation, at the helm of which is David Duval, 2001 British Open champion. When the 18-hole course renovation is complete, it will mirror the natural environment: The front 9 holes will be a links-style course with gently sloping fairways, and the back 9 will incorporate mangroves and water features. Until the course is complete in mid-2008, play is free, a deal that can't be beat, and golf-club rentals go for $30.

HIKING & MOUNTAIN BIKING   Since 1983 Trudi Angell and Douglas Knapp of **Tour Baja** (© **800/398-6200;** www.tourbaja.com) have been offering a range of adventure tours, including hiking, mountain biking, kayaking, sailing, and horseback riding, and they were adventurers in this rugged territory long before they decided to become guides.

As hiking goes, there are virtually no formal trails in the Sierra de la Giganta, so a locals' perspective is invaluable and will land you in many magical spots in these towering mountains. Tour Baja's **Pedaling South** tour offers vehicle-supported guided mountain-bike treks for all skill levels. Choose from tours into the mountains, along the coast, and to the San Javier Mission, and combine your favorite with snorkeling or kayaking. Call Tour Baja for information on backpacking and day-hike trips into the mountains. A 3-day guided backpacking trip costs $95 per hiker per day, and a mountain-biking excursion costs $125 per day or $95 if you bring your own bike.

HORSEBACK RIDING   Tour Baja's (© **800/398-6200;** www.tourbaja.com) **Saddling South** offers pack trips on horseback into the Sierra de La Giganta range and through historic ranches along the way. If you're looking to experience life on the California frontier, this is for you. The cost is $125 per day for a minimum 3-day and maximum 8-day tour.

TENNIS   You can play tennis at the Nopoló Sports Center's **Loreto Bay Tennis Center** (© **613/133-0788**), which was dedicated by John McEnroe. There are eight courts, a pool, a sun deck, a stadium that holds 250 people, a racquetball court, and

(Kids) A Visit to Isla del Carmen

Isla del Carmen is the largest of Loreto's offshore islands. It is mostly inaccessible and privately owned, so you'll need permission to go ashore. Access to Isla del Carmen is available through one of a number of tour companies in Loreto. Chose your company based on your preferred activity and mode of exploration (usually kayaking or snorkeling, sometimes hiking).

The island was once the site of an impressive salt-mining operation, but increased competition—not to mention the opportunity to earn a dollar from granting landing permissions to tourism purveyors—encouraged the company to shut down and refocus its economic endeavors. You can see the remains of the salt-mining town, completely abandoned in 1983, at the northeastern tip of the island.

Volcanic in origin, Isla del Carmen also has deposits of *coquina*, a limestonelike rock of cemented shell material that was quarried by the Jesuit missionaries for use in constructing the church and other buildings in Loreto. One favorite cove on Isla del Carmen is Puerto Balandra, where bold rock formations rising up like humpback whales frame crystal-blue water and ivory sand.

The craggy desert terrain offers a cornucopia of plant life, including elephant trees, desert asparagus (pickleweed), mesquite trees, jojoba, agave, cardón cacti, and passionflower vines. Be careful of the cholla cacti, whose spines enter your skin in a crisscross pattern. To remove them, cut the spines from the plant and then pull them out one at a time.

The topography on the island alternates between salt-crusted ground, spongy surfaces—a sure sign that snakes, iguanas, and burrowing animals are nearby—and the rocky remains of former riverbeds. There is a variety of fauna as well, including a population of goats that were introduced to the island to provide a meat supply for its inhabitants. You'll spot feral cats, blacktailed hares, and birds ranging from osprey to gila woodpeckers, among other wildlife.

a pro shop. As with golf, court fees are free until further notice; adult racquet rentals are $6 and racquets are $3 for kids. The center is open Sunday through Saturday from 7am to 8pm.

WATERSPORTS & ACTIVITIES

The Sea of Cortez is the star in Loreto and the five islands just offshore make for some of the best kayaking, sailing, diving, and fishing in North America. Freediving, or breath-hold diving as opposed to diving with tanks, is becoming more popular as well. Loreto is the nearest major airport and city to Bahía de Magdalena (Magdalena Bay), the southernmost of the major gray whale calving lagoons on the Pacific coast of Baja, and Loreto was their stage in winter 2007 while a documentary called *Whales* was being filmed on them.

SEA KAYAKING   Kayaking season is October through December and April through May, and although Loreto attracts mostly avid kayakers, there are options for novice recreational paddlers as well. **Arturo's Sport** operates the tour desk at **Inn at Loreto Bay,** which is situated on a stellar bay for sea kayaking, and offers kayaking day trips and by-the-hour options for $10 an hour. **Tour Baja** (© **800/398-6200;** www.tourbaja.com) offers **Paddling South** multiday trips ($595–$1,295) in one- or two-person fiberglass sea kayaks. Puerto Escondido is also an ideal starting point for experienced kayakers who want to reach Isla Montserrat; call Tour Baja for details.

SNORKELING/DIVING   Several companies offer snorkeling; most island explo- ration trips include snorkeling, and trips to Isla del Carmen, Isla Coronado, Isla Mon- serrate, and Isla Catalina all include snorkeling opportunities. Some fishing trips carry snorkeling gear on board to give anglers a chance to check out the underwater world. For scuba diving, contact **Dolphin Dive Center** (© **613/135-1914;** www.dolphin divebaja.com); it offers several diving sites where you can admire the underwater bounty of the Sea of Cortez. The two-tank trips cost $89 to $110 per diver, and a PADI dive master guides all tours. Snacks, Loreto Bay Marine Park fees, weights, two tanks, and a boat are included, but any equipment needed comes at an extra charge (air costs $5/tank, wetsuit $10, BC [buoyancy compensator] $10, regulator with dive computer $12, mask/fins/snorkel $10). If you're new to scuba and would like to get certified, or if you want an advanced certification, Dolphin Dive Center also offers several PADI resort courses, which range from $150 for a daylong resort course to $650 for dive-master certification.

For something more unusual and boldly adventurous, take advantage of the run of giant Humboldt squid that pass inshore to spawn between Isla del Carmen and Isla Danzante from May through October. Encounters with these ink-squirting apex pred- ators, which can grow up to 200 pounds and travel in packs called "shoals," can be arranged, at depths of 12m (40 ft.), through **Sea Wolves Unlimited** (© **562/221-1274** in the U.S.; www.squiddiving.com or www.sea-wolves.com). Scott Cassell, Sea Wolves owner, guide, and the world's leading expert on Humboldt squid—he's all over *National Geographic* and the Discovery Channel—outfits divers in special shark-repel- lent wetsuits and tethers them to the boat to ensure the total safety of his clients. For $2,200, not only do you get to experience how it feels to be at the bottom of the food chain, you get 3 nights of all-inclusive luxury accommodations at the Inn at Loreto Bay, a daily informational squid school, and 3 days of diving with these fascinating animals with three hearts, blue blood, pinniped brains, and the habit of swimming from arctic depths of 300m (1,000 ft.) to the tropical Sea of Cortez surface every 2 hours.

SPORTFISHING   The fishing near Loreto is exceptional, with a different game fish for every season. Winter and spring months are great for yellowtail, sea bass, rooster- fish, and grouper; and summer is the time for big marlin, sailfish, tuna, and dorado.

There are several different sportfishing operations in town, most of which are no- frills excursions. This is not Cabo, and if you came here to fish, that's just what you'll get. The least expensive way to enjoy deep-sea fishing is to pair up with another angler and charter a *panga* from the **Loreto Sportfishing Cooperative** at the main pier in Loreto. Prices range from $150 to $180 per boat, depending on the size and availabil- ity of shade. You can also arrange your trip in advance through most resorts and tour operators or contact the fleets directly. One of Loreto's best tour companies for fish- ing, spearfishing, and freediving is **Pelagic Tours,** owned and operated by three local expats, Brenda, Shane, and John (© **613/113-8678** or 613/113-8677 to inquire about pricing and details). Decades of first-hand expertise and a passion for sport set the stage for a host of tourist services, including freediving adventures, fishing and spearfishing charters, marriages at sea, sunset cruises, land tours, and bungalow rentals. Shane also runs the **Loreto Smokehouse & Fish Factory** (loretosmokehouse fishfactory@yahoo.com), which means you can have your fish and smoke it, too. For $2 to $4 per pound, don't miss his awesome candied dorado. People with their own boats can launch at the ramp just north of the *malecón* in town or at Puerto Loreto, 26km (16 miles) south of town. If you plan on running out to Isla del Carmen, it's better to launch from Puerto Loreto, which cuts 10km (6 miles) off the crossing. For tackle, head to **Deportes Blazer** (© 613/135-0766) on Hidalgo, the catchall sporting-goods store in town.

WHALE-WATCHING ✹✹✹   Loreto is the nearest major airport and city to Bahía Magdalena (Magdalena Bay), the southernmost of the major gray-whale-calving lagoons on the Pacific coast of Baja. For more information on popular whale-watching spots and tour operators, see the "Whale-Watching in Baja: A Primer" section later in this chapter. **Arturo's Sport** (© 613/135-0766; www.arturosport.com) conducts whale-watching trips within the Loreto Marine Park, where you'll see the giant blue whale, and to Magdalena Bay on the Pacific Coast to see gray whales. The cost is $125 for the 8-hour trip, which includes an average of 2 hours in a skiff watching the whales, transportation, snacks, beverages, and a seafood lunch.

HISTORIC LORETO & OTHER INTERESTING SITES

For cultural explorations in the area other than those listed below, contact **C&C Tours** (© 310/227-6522 in the U.S., or 613/133-0151; candclto@prodigy.net.mx). Among the guided excursions this quality company offers are the Historic Loreto City Tour (morning and evening options available), hiking in Tabor Canyon, Mulegé (see later for more on Mulegé), whale-watching tours, Wine & Cheese and Tortillas & Ceviche parties, and folkloric dance classes. They also offer a hike to the mission in San Javier and grilled-seafood picnics on Isla Coronado.

MISION NUESTRA SEÑORA DE LORETO   The first mission in the Californias was started here in 1699. The catechization of California by Jesuit missionaries was based from this mission and lasted through the 18th century. The inscription above the entrance reads CABEZA Y MADRE DE LAS MISIONES DE BAJA Y ALTA CALIFORNIA (Head and Mother of the Missions of Lower and Upper California). The current church, a simple building in the shape of a Greek cross, was finished in 1752 and restored in 1976. The original Virgen de Loreto, brought to shore by Padre Kino in 1667, is on display in the church's 18th-century gilded altar. The mission is on Salvatierra, across from the central square.

MUSEO DE LAS MISIONES   Even better than the mission itself, this museum is next to the Misión Nuestra Señora de Loreto church (see above). It has a small but complete collection of historical and anthropological exhibits. On display are interesting facts about the indigenous Guaycura, Pericúe, and Cochimí populations, along with accomplishments of the Jesuit missionaries—including their zoological studies, scientific writings, architectural sketches, and details of the role they played in the demise of indigenous cultures. Also on display are several religious paintings, original wooden beams and tools, and sculptures dating to the 18th century. The museum, located at Salvatierra 16 (© 613/135-0441), has a small shop where the INAH (Instituto Nacional de Antropología e Historia) sells books about the history of Mexico and

(*Finds* **Baja's Cave Paintings: An Exploration of the Mysterious**

One fascinating excursion that demands good physical condition is a visit to the **aboriginal cave paintings of Baja**. The origin of these cave paintings is still unknown, with some researchers placing them as far back as 10,000 years (during the Prehistoric Age), with a general consensus that they are at least 1,500 years old. They are so impressive that UNESCO has designated them a part of the historical patrimony of mankind.

The cave paintings are concentrated in the San Francisco de la Sierra and Santa Martha mountain ranges. It is believed that thousands of years ago, the shallow pools and oases that existed in this region allowed groups of people to survive here. The primitive rock paintings they left behind are the only examples of this kind of art on the North American continent. The cave paintings are spectacular murals done on rocks, with representations of larger-than-life humanlike and animal forms, in scenes that could be ritual ceremonies, pilgrimages, hunting, or battle. The colors used are ochre, red, white, yellow, and black, with the faceless humanlike figures painted in red and black, standing with their arms extended and often depicted with unusual headpieces above their heads, possibly a symbol of an experience of a hallucinatory state. There is a strong magical-spiritual content to the paintings. Other figures appear to be jaguars, reptiles, deer-headed snakes, and human hands. Often the figures appear overlain on one another, meaning they were likely painted by various artists at different periods of time.

The first mention of the paintings was by the Jesuit missionary Francisco Javier Clavijero in 1789. Since then, scholars around the world have attempted to date and interpret these mystical scenes. Mexico's National Institute of Anthropology (INAH) oversees these sites now and makes only selected sites open for public viewing, and even then, entry is allowed only with authorized guides.

Baja California. The museum is open Tuesday through Sunday from 9am to 1pm and 1:45 to 6pm. Admission is $3.

MISION SAN FRANCISCO JAVIER (*★* About 2 hours of dirt-road driving from Loreto and in a section of the old Camino Real used by Spanish missionaries and explorers, this mission is one of the best-preserved, most spectacularly set missions in Baja—high in a mountain valley beneath volcanic walls. Founded in 1699 by the Jesuit priest Francisco María Píccolo, it was completed in 1758 and was the second mission established in California. The church was built with blocks of volcanic stone from the Sierra de la Giganta Mountains. It is very well preserved, with its original walls, floors, gilded altar, and religious artifacts, and the surrounding ranches—filled with onion fields and olive-tree orchards—make for a pastoral setting and a nice stroll. Day tours from Loreto, organized by several local tour operators, visit the mission, with stops to view aboriginal cave paintings along the way and an oasis settlement with a small chapel. The trips cost $40 to $65, and some offer mule riding and hiking options. If

Due to the summer rains and heat, it is recommended that you visit between October and May. Guides can be found in the town of San Ignacio to take you to the cave known as La Pintada, distinguished due to the diversity and size of its paintings. However, La Pintada is a long and difficult trek. A more accessible option in the San Francisco de la Sierra is the cave known as El Raton, about 37km (23 miles) away on the Carretera Transpeninsular. From this cave, it's a short distance to another location, Las Flechas. Near Mulegé, your visit could include La Trinidad (an aboveground site), Piedras Pintas (a group of rocks with petroglyphs), and San Borjita cave.

The entire region where these paintings are located covers almost 19,000 sq. km (7,500 square miles) in the central part of the Baja peninsula. In the San Francisco de la Sierra, a grouping of over 300 sites is known as the Great Wall; it is the largest and most mysterious concentration of ancient rock paintings in the world.

C&C Tours (© **310/227-6522 in the U.S.**, or 613/133-0151; candclto@ prodigy.net.mx) in Loreto offers tours of local cave paintings, and Salvador Castro of **Mulegé Tours** (© **615/153-0232**; at the Las Casitas Hotel in downtown Mulegé) guides tours to the La Trinidad cave paintings.

Castro's tour lasts approximately 12 hours and takes you to the foothills of the Guadalupe Mountains, between Loreto and Bahía de los Angeles, where you hike through the desert and then swim in a couple of canyons before you reach the site. There is also an INAH museum in the area, which has displays and additional information about the cave paintings and the research that has been done on them.

you are driving a high-clearance four-wheel-drive vehicle and are an experienced off-road driver, you can get there yourself by traveling south on Carretera Transpeninsular and taking the detour marked "San Javier" on Km 118, 3.2km (2 miles) south of Loreto. The 40km (25-mile) drive takes about 2 hours on a rocky, graded road.

PRIMER AGUA   A palm oasis in a fenced-off section of the Arroyo de San Javier, this serves as a prime picnic spot, complete with natural spring and swimming pool. The area had been closed for renovations after a hurricane tore through in 2006 and then reopened to the public in summer 2007. Call or stop by the **Nopoló Fonatur** offices, Carretera Transpeninsular Km 111 (© **613/133-0245** or 613/133-0301), 1 or 2 days prior to your visit to make sure the oasis will be open to visitors on the day you plan your visit and to pay the entrance fee. Access is $10 per person, and it's open Thursday to Tuesday from 9am until 6pm. The oasis is closed on Wednesdays for pool cleaning. The road to Primer Agua is unpaved and graded, affording fairly easy access during the dry season. The entrance is 6km (3¾ miles) off Carretera Transpeninsular on the Km 114 detour.

SHOPPING

Quite frankly, you won't be coming to Loreto to shop, and if you do, you're going to be disappointed. Loreto has little in the way of shopping, either for basics or for folk art and other collectibles from mainland Mexico. There are a handful of the requisite shops selling souvenirs and some *artesanía*, all within a block of the mission. Some, such as the following, are better than others.

Conchita's Curios   This shop carries a fine selection of arts and crafts from throughout Mexico. Open daily from 9am to 8pm. Corner of Misioneros and Fernando Jordan. ℭ 613/135-1054.

El Alacrán   This shop has a quality selection of arts and crafts, as well as interesting books about Baja, fine silver jewelry, and handmade and cotton clothing. Open Monday through Saturday from 9:30am to 1pm and 3 to 7pm. The gallery next door showcases fine art by Carlos Díaz Uroz in acrylics on handmade paper and canvas. Salvatierra and Misioneros. ℭ 613/135-0029.

La Casa de la Abuela   "Grandma's House" offers better-than-average knickknacks with an emphasis on indigenous crafts. In the oldest house in Loreto, it also serves coffee, pastries, and light meals. Open Wednesday through Monday from 9am to 10pm. No credit cards. Salvatierra and Misioneros, across from the Mission. No phone.

Silver Desert   Exquisite—and original—silver jewelry is the order of the day here. Open daily from 9am to 2pm and 3 to 9pm. Salvatierra 36, next to the bank. ℭ 613/135-0684.

WHERE TO STAY

In general, accommodations in Loreto are the kind travelers to Mexico used to find all over: inexpensive and unique, with genuine and friendly owner-operators. And, as mid-Baja is a mecca of sorts for RV explorers, **Rivera del Mar RV Park & Camping** (ℭ 613/135-0718; www.riveradelmar.com) has the deluxe hook-ups just 2 blocks from the beach. Also of note, as people fall in love with Loreto and build their dream homes there, vacation-rental properties are on the rise, and Kathy and Hector at **Rentals Loreto** (ℭ 613/135-2505; www.rentalsloreto.com) have the best selection in town. Gorgeous beachfront homes that sleep up to eight can go for a max of $170 a night and most also rent by the week.

EXPENSIVE

Danzante Adventure Resort 🌟🌟 *(Finds)*   This all-inclusive eco-resort offers guests everything that's wonderful about this area—sandy beaches, tranquillity, easy access to eco- and adventure activities—all in a lovely place to stay. It's 40km (25 miles) south of Loreto on serene Ensenada Blanca bay, home also to a tiny fishing village. The resort itself covers 4 hectares (10 acres) and is composed of nine suites perched in a rocky hill facing the sea. Each king or queen room has a large Mexican-tile bath, beamed ceilings, handmade furnishings, large windows, and French doors that open onto a private thatched palm-covered terrace with hammocks. Lying in them soaking in the view seems to be the favored activity of guests, yet there's much more you can do here—all activities are included in the room rate and include hiking, kayaking, snorkeling, and swimming at their secluded beach. Horseback riding is also available in the surrounding canyons, and diving, fishing, massage services, whale- and dolphin-watching, mission and cave painting tours, and "safari at sea" excursions can be arranged for an additional charge. For meals, included in the room rate, they serve a delicious selection of seafood, local fruits and vegetables, and organic produce from the on-site garden. The resort itself is 100% solar powered and is owned by a couple who counts among their many accomplishments published books on Mexico travel and diving, underwater documentaries, explorations for sunken treasure, and guiding adventure tours worldwide. This may be their best achievement yet.

Hwy. 1 at Ligui, Ensenada Blanca, Loreto, B.C.S. ✆ 408/354-0042. www.danzante.com. 9 units. High season $199/person queen suite, $225/person king suite; low season $180/person queen suite, $205/person king suite. All meals and activities included in rates. MC, V. **Amenities:** Restaurant; bar; hilltop freshwater swimming pool; watersports; tour services; land and marine excursions; cell phone at front desk; horses; kayaks; lending library; telescope for stargazing. In room: Fan, hammock.

Inn at Loreto Bay ✹ Kids
Loreto's newest place to stay, the Inn at Loreto Bay (formerly the Camino Real) is on its own private cove a few miles outside of town, on a lovely beach, with calm waters perfect for swimming or kayaking. The hotel's brightly colored architecture compliments sleek stone-floored guest rooms and warm-toned woven comforters. Master suites and presidential suites have large terraces and private Jacuzzis that overlook the bay. The ample space and recreational programs make this a great choice for families. Adjacent to Loreto's golf course, it's also ideal for anyone with a passion for the links. The upper-level Lobby Bar is a spectacular spot for a sunset cocktail, but the best place to take in the Sea of Cortez moonglow is from the terrace whirlpool tub of a master suite.

Paseo de la Mission s/n, Nopoló, Loreto, B.C.S. ✆ 877/865-6738 in the U.S., or 613/133-0010. reservations@ loretobay.com. 156 units. High season $165–$190 standard double, $230 junior suite, $290 master suite; low season $125–$150 standard double, $210 junior suite, $270 master suite. Meal plans available. AE, MC, V. **Amenities:** 2 restaurants; 2 bars; outdoor pool; golf course; fitness center; concierge; tour desk; car-rental desk; gift shop; room service; babysitting; laundry service; Internet access. In room: A/C, fan, satellite TV, minibar, hair dryer, safe.

La Posada de las Flores ✹✹✹
The most luxurious place to stay in Loreto conveniently sits adjacent to the main square, in the heart of historic Loreto. Every room is beautifully decorated with fine Mexican arts and crafts, including heavy wood doors, Talavera pottery, painted tiles, candles, and Mexican scenic paintings. The colors and decor of the hotel are nouveau-colonial Mexico, with wood and tin accents. Large bathrooms have thick white towels and bamboo doors, with Frette bathrobes hanging in the closet. Every detail has been carefully selected, including the down comforters and numerous antiques tucked into corners. This hotel exudes class and refinement, from the general ambience to the warm polish of its employees. Italian-owned and operated, the sophisticated service has a European style to it. Only children over 12 are welcome.

Salvatierra and Francisco I. Madera, Centro, 23880 Loreto, B.C.S. ✆ 877/245-2860 in the U.S., or 613/135-1162. Fax 613/135-1099. www.posadadelasflores.com. 15 units. High season $180 double, $290 suite; low season $150 double, $250 suite. Rates include continental breakfast. MC, V. Street parking. **Amenities:** Breakfast restaurant; rooftop glass-bottom swimming pool; hospitality desk. In room: A/C, TV, Wi-Fi, minibar.

MODERATE

El Santuario de Baja ✹✹✹
In all of Baja, no place compares to El Santuario. This healing eco-retreat nestled in the silent sand dunes of Ensenada Blanca Bay, about 48km (30 miles) south of Loreto, is guaranteed to free your mind, relax your body, and renew your spirit. The ever gracious owners, Bill and Denise, foster an environment of simple, sustainable living and overall healing, which can take place through outdoor adventure, contact with nature, acupuncture and massage therapies, or yoga and meditation; a session with Bill, a talented psychotherapist whose philosophy

incorporates, among other things, the mind-body connection for healing, may also prove helpful. Perhaps the most unique aspect of a stay at El Santuario is the way guests are able to truly immerse themselves in their natural environment. Spring-fed drinking water, composting toilets, minimal electricity, natural spa products, solar-heated showers, and a diet of local seafood and produce only add to El Santuario's all-natural experience of desert, mountain, and sea. The resort can play host to up to 16 people in six *palapa*-topped casitas, which are spaced throughout the property for maximum privacy. Groups of all kinds are welcome, and a local Mexican cook pre-pares the organic and mostly vegetarian meals in an open-air kitchen. Denise, an equine veterinarian, also runs **Animalandia,** Loreto's nonprofit spay-and-neuter pro-gram. For more information, visit **www.animalandia.org**.

Ensenada Blanca Bay, 48km (30 miles) south of Loreto off Hwy. 1, Ensenada Blanca, B.C.S. © **805/541-7921** in the U.S., or 613/104-4254. 6 units. $1,000 per week includes meals and use of all facilities. AE, MC, V. **Amenities:** Kitchen; yoga room; massage/facial room; kayaks; large yurt for yoga, counseling, or events; fire pit area for music and dancing; chimenea sitting area; . *In room:* No phone.

Hotel Oasis Fishermen who regularly visit this area seem to prefer this beachfront hotel, which caters to their needs with specialized services, excursions, and its own fleet of boats and equipment. In operation since 1960, Hotel Oasis has a friendly and knowledgeable staff. The simple but spacious rooms have two double beds and a pri-vate balcony or terrace, with either pool or ocean views. Summer rates with manda-tory meal service are more expensive. It's on the beach at the south end of the *malecón,* close to restaurants, shops, and the historic downtown. Their restaurant gets high marks from guests, and it even serves a 5am fisherman's breakfast.

Apdo. Postal 17, 23880 Loreto, B.C.S. © **800/497-3923** from the U.S., or 613/135-0211. Fax 613/135-0795. www.hoteloasis.com. 40 units. $115–$130 double; $144 suite. Bed and breakfast, as well as full meal plans avail-able. MC, V. Private parking. **Amenities:** Restaurant; bar; heated outdoor pool; travel desk; fishing services including boat and gear rentals. *In room:* A/C, coffeemaker; TVs and phones on request.

INEXPENSIVE

Desert Inn ✦✦ Formerly the Hotel La Pinta Loreto, the newly named Desert Inn is on the beach and close to downtown. Its spacious rooms have stone accents, heavy wood furnishings, and views of the offshore islands from individual terraces and pri-vate balconies. Accommodations are in two-story buildings that border a central pool and grassy courtyard. Twenty units have fireplaces. Pets are welcome.

Francisco I. Madero s/n, Playas de Loreto, 23880 Loreto, B.C.S. © **800/800-9632** in the U.S., or 613/135-0025 or 612/135-0690. 50 units. $110 double w/fireplace; $79 double. Extra person $15. MC, V. Pets accepted. **Amenities:** Restaurant; 2 bars; swimming pool; tour desk; private fishing fleet. *In room:* A/C, satellite TV.

La Damiana Inn ✦✦ *Value* The location of the new La Damiana Inn—in the heart of town on Madero Street—is reason enough to book a reservation, but the warmth of color, style, and ownership make it the best accommodations value in Loreto. Deb-ora Simmons lovingly operates this former family home, built in 1917. Today, its five rooms, all equipped with air-conditioning and ceiling fans, offer a blend of twin, queen, and king beds that provide cozy resting places when you're not exploring the area. Wireless Internet throughout the hotel, laundry facilities, a shared living room, use of the kitchen and free cuddles from two friendly house dogs are the extras that make La Damiana Inn seem more like a gracious friend's home than anything else.

Madero, between Hidalgo and Jordan, Centro, 23880 Loreto, B.C.S. ⓒ 613/135-0356. www.ladamianainn.com. 5 units. $50 double; $55 suite. No credit cards (American checks accepted). Pets accepted upon prior approval. **Amenities:** Complimentary use of bikes; Wi-Fi; laundry service; library; phone for local calls; TV in common area. *In room:* A/C, fan, no phone.

SuKasa ⭐⭐ *Finds*   This is the place for travelers who want to have their own homey space right on the *malecón*. The name doesn't mislead—SuKasa feels like *su casa* and comes with friendly owners, swaying hammocks, and well-appointed Mexican decor. Two fully furnished bungalows, which contain kitchens, master bedrooms, and charming living areas; one pristine casita; a sprawling two-story main house that's available for rent by the week; and one modern and spacious yurt make for a charming resort retreat that feels like it was created just for you and your vacation. The property is shrouded in towering palms and desert blooms that foster an oasislike environment. Just steps away from the sea, SuKasa's yurt, in particular, is without a doubt downtown Loreto's most unique and charming accommodations. Ask about their weekly and monthly rates. Smoking is prohibited on the property.

Malecón. 23880 Loreto, B.C.S. ⓒ 613/135-0490. www.loreto.com/sukasa. 5 units. $75 bungalow; $85 casita; $55 yurt; $1,050 weekly main house. MC, V. **Amenities:** Kayaks; bicycles; Wi-Fi throughout property; barbecue grill. *In room:* A/C, ceiling fan, TV/VCR, kitchens, no phone.

WHERE TO DINE

Dining in Loreto affords surprising variety, given the small size and laid-back nature of the town. However, don't expect anything fancy, even at the nicest restaurant. Big flavors come in humble packages in Loreto. In addition to the below hubs, a vegetarian wood-fired pizza at **Pachamama** on Zapata and fried shrimp tacos at **Tacos el Rey** on Benito Juárez will keep you coming back for more.

MODERATE

Augie's Bar & Bait Shop ⭐ PIZZA/BAR   Located on the *malecón,* this is the pre-eminent happy-hour hotspot for the gringo community. Augie, who hales from the California video arcade business and does fun for a living, offers dancing lessons to patrons after they've had six drinks—and he makes good on his promise. With TV sports of all kinds, ocean views, fabulous margaritas, tortilla pizzas, and an upstairs terrace that showcases Loreto's big-sky sunsets, this is the place to be after 4pm any day of the week. From 4 to 7pm daily, all drinks are half price. Happy hour in Loreto doesn't get any better than Augie's.

On the *malecón* at the corner of Zaragoza. ⓒ 613/135-1224. Tortilla pizzas $7–$10. MC, V. Daily 8am–10pm.

Del Borracho ⭐ BURGERS/SANDWICHES   If you're a *Three Amigos* fan from way back, Mike and Andrea Patterson's tribute to the obscure bar in the classic comedy will not disappoint. The movie sometimes plays on loop in the background of this wooden saloon outside of town while chilidogs, milkshakes, sandwiches, and burgers make the rounds among a happy-bellied crowd chugging draft beer. The only place in town to serve Modelo Light and Modelo Negro on draft, Del Borracho's real claim to fame is the $3.50 bowl of blow-your-mind clam chowder that comes with a side of Andrea's homemade bread every Friday. Ask about the smoked fish for sale from the **Loreto Smokehouse and Fish Factory;** and, of note for sports fans, Del Borracho has the NFL Sunday Ticket.

.5km (⅓ mile) down the road to San Javier, 2 miles south of Loreto. ⓒ 613/137-0112. Main courses $3–$5. No credit cards. Daily sunrise–sunset.

El Nido Steakhouse ✦ STEAK/SEAFOOD   The main link in a Baja chain of steak restaurants, El Nido satisfies hearty appetites. Its specialty is a thick cut of prime, tender beef served with the obligatory salad and baked potato. Seafood options are also available, but discerning locals say El Nido's porterhouse is the very best in the world. It's on the main boulevard as you enter Loreto from Carretera Transpeninsular.

Salvatierra 154. ✆ 613/135-0027 or 613/135-0284. Main courses $6–$20. No credit cards. Daily 2–10:30pm.

La Tarea/Sushi Time ✦ SUSHI/SEAFOOD   Likely inspired by the flashy and chile-spiced creations at Nick San in Los Cabos, whence the chef/owner hails, La Tarea's uniquely Mexican sushi rolls—sans the typical cream cheese overload—comprise the can't-miss meal of the destination. Wednesday are two-for-one sushi nights and, if you have any kind of appetite, it's worth it to brave the crowds of locals for one of the best meals in town.

Malecón. No phone. Main courses $3–$10. No credit cards. Daily 4–10pm.

INEXPENSIVE

Café Olé LIGHT FARE   Although an espresso machine is hard to come by in this town, the breezy Café Olé is the best option for breakfast. Try eggs with *nopal* cactus, hotcakes, or a not-so-light lunch of a burger and fries. Tacos and some Mexican standards are also on the menu, as are fresh-fruit smoothies, or *licuados.*

Madero 14. ✆ 613/135-0496. Breakfast $2–$5; sandwiches $2–$3.50. No credit cards. Mon–Sat 7am–10pm; Sun 7am–2pm.

LORETO AFTER DARK

Although selection is limited, Loreto after dark seems to offer a place for almost every nightlife preference. Happy hour starts in the late afternoon and ends shortly after sundown at bars like **Augie's, Del Borracho,** and **Mike's Bar.** Cocktails, music, and tapas flow into the wee hours at **Antigua Casa del Negro Meza** on Salvatierra and Madero; and, if dancing is your game, the *malecón's* **Black&White** club gets going around 10pm Friday and Saturday nights. In addition, as is the tradition throughout Mexico, Loreto's central plaza offers a **free concert** in the bandstand most Sundays. However, Loretanos and their families are so hospitable that the best party may be the one to which you're unexpectedly invited. In Loreto, magic is bound to happen.

2 Mulegé: Oasis in the Desert ✦✦

998km (619 miles) SE of Tijuana; 137km (85 miles) N of Loreto; 496km (308 miles) NW of La Paz; 710km (440 miles) NW of Cabo San Lucas

Verdant Mulegé offers shady cool in an otherwise scorching part of the world. Founded in 1705, it is home to one of the most well-preserved and beautifully situated Jesuit missions in Baja. Mulegé lies between two hills, in a valley where a creek runs down to the ocean. The landscape consists of immense palms, orchards, and tangles of bougainvillea. Unfortunately, much of the area is littered with trash, a sign that the beauty of this land is taken for granted by some.

Besides the respite inherent in the views, Mulegé (pronounced moo-leh-*hay*), at the mouth of beautiful Bahía Concepción, has great diving, kayaking, and fishing—and the RV following to prove it. The origin of the name comes from the Cochimies (indigenous inhabitants of the area) and means "big ravine of the white mouth."

Mulegé & Santa Rosalía Areas

There are also several well-preserved Indian caves with stunning paintings, which can be reached by guided hikes into the mountains. Accommodations are limited and basic, and trailer parks are nearby. Good beach camping is also available just south of town along the Bahía Concepción, as is a landing strip for small planes.

ESSENTIALS

GETTING THERE & DEPARTING

BY PLANE   The closest international airport is in Loreto, 137km (85 miles) south. From Loreto, you'll need to rent a car or hire a taxi for the 1½-hour trip; taxis average $75 each way. Three airlines fly into Loreto: **Aeroméxico** (© 800/237-6639 in the U.S., or 613/135-1837; fax 613/135-1838; www.aeromexico.com), **Alaska Airlines** (© 800/252-7522; www.alaskaair.com), and **Delta** (© 800/241-4141 in the U.S.; www.delta.com) all have nonstop flights from Los Angeles.

Small regional or private charter planes can get you all the way to town: **El Gallito,** a well-maintained, graded, 1,200m (4,000-ft.) airstrip, adjoins the Hotel Serenidad, Carretera Transpeninsular Km 30 (no phone, use radio frequency UNICOM 122.8). For additional information, contact the Comandancia del Aeropuerto in Loreto (© 613/135-0565), from 7am to 7pm daily.

BY CAR   From Tijuana, take Carretera Transpeninsular (Hwy. 1) direct to the Mulegé turnoff, 998km (619 miles) south (approximately 16 hr.). From La Paz, take Carretera Transpeninsular north, a scenic route that winds through foothills and then skirts the eastern coastline. The trip takes about 6 hours; it's roughly 496km (308 miles).

BY BUS   Mulegé's new **bus station** (© 615/153-0409), located on the highway just north of the entrance to town by La Noria restaurant, can accommodate travelers in regular and luxury buses up and down the Baja. A ticket to/from Loreto ranges from $12 to $20 and a ride to Santa Rosalía ranges from $6 to $10, depending on whether you select the regular or luxury option. Schedules are highly variable, but buses stay for about 20 minutes while dropping off and picking up passengers. Tickets to Tijuana average $30; the one-way fare to La Paz is about $15.

ORIENTATION

ARRIVING   If you arrive by bus, you will be dropped off at the entrance to town. From there, you can walk the few blocks downhill and east into town, or take a taxi. Taxis also line up around the plaza and usually charge around $2.50 to $6 for a trip anywhere in town.

VISITOR INFORMATION   There is no official office, but tourist information is available at the office of the centrally located **Hotel Las Casitas,** Calle Francisco Madero 50 (© 615/153-0019). Several maps that list key attractions, as well as a local biweekly English-language newspaper, the *Mulegé Post,* are available throughout town. Also of interest to serious travelers to Mulegé is Kerry Otterstrom's self-published book *Mulegé: The Complete Tourism, Souvenir, and Historical Guide,* available at shops and hotels in town.

The **State Tourism Office of Baja California Sur** can be reached by calling © 612/124-0199, or you may contact the City of Mulegé (© 615/152-0148).

CITY LAYOUT   Mulegé has an essentially east-west orientation, running from the Carretera Transpeninsular in the west to the Sea of Cortez. The Mulegé River (also known as Río Santa Rosalía) borders the town to the south, with a few hotels and RV parks along its southern shore. It's easy to find the principal sights downtown, where two main streets will take you either east or west; both border the town's central plaza. The main church is several blocks east of the plaza, breaking with the traditional layout of most Mexican towns. The Bahía Concepción is 11km (6¾ miles) south of town.

GETTING AROUND   There is no local bus service in town or to the beach, but you can easily walk or take a taxi. Taxis line up around the central plaza, or you can call the taxi dispatch at © 615/153-0420.

Bicycles are available for rent from **Cortez Explorers,** Moctezuma 75-A (© 615/153-0500; www.cortez-explorers.com). Prices start at $15 for the first day, then drop to $10 per day for the first week, and are $8 per day after that. It also has full dive- and snorkel-equipment rentals. It's open Monday through Saturday from 10am to 1pm and 4 to 7pm.

Mulegé is so small that it's easy to find anything you're looking for, even though most buildings don't have numbered addresses.

Downtown Mulegé

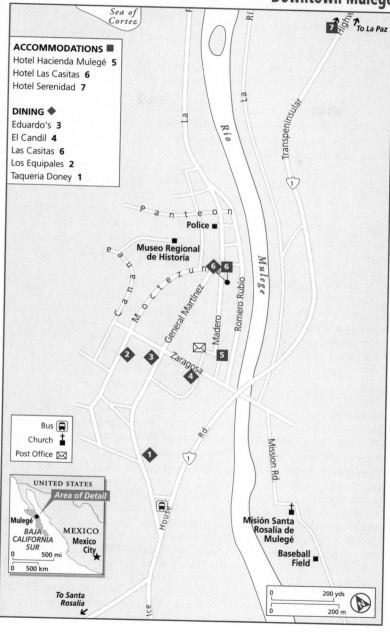

ACCOMMODATIONS ■
Hotel Hacienda Mulegé **5**
Hotel Las Casitas **6**
Hotel Serenidad **7**

DINING ◆
Eduardo's **3**
El Candil **4**
Las Casitas **6**
Los Equipales **2**
Taqueria Doney **1**

To La Paz

Sea of Cortez

Río

La

Transpeninsular

Panteon

Police ■

Museo Regional de Historía

Montezuma

General Martinez

Madero

Romero Rubio

Zaragosa

Río Mulegé

Bus 🚌
Church ✝
Post Office ✉

House Rd.

UNITED STATES
Area of Detail
Mulegé
BAJA CALIFORNIA SUR
MEXICO
Mexico City ★
0   500 mi
0   500 km

Mission Rd.

Misión Santa Rosalía de Mulegé ✝

Baseball Field ■

To Santa Rosalía

0   200 yds
0   200 m

FAST FACTS: Mulegé

Area Code The telephone area code is **615**.

Banks ***Important note:*** There are no banks in Mulegé. Plan ahead or you'll need to drive to the bank in Loreto, about 1½ hours away.

Beach Safety Beaches in the area are generally tranquil and safe for swimming. The more protected waters of Bahía Concepción are especially calm. Avoid swimming at the mouth of the Mulegé River, which is said to be polluted.

Internet Access Most of the hotels in town offer Internet access and wireless connections for hotel guests and visitors.

Medical Care Emergency medical services are offered by the **Mexican Red Cross** (© **615/153-0110**) and the **Health Center ISSSTE** (© **615/153-0298**).

Parking Street parking is generally easy to find in the downtown area. Note, however, that Mulegé's streets are very narrow and difficult for RVs and other large vehicles to navigate. Also, many streets are one-way.

Pharmacy **Farmacia Ruben,** Calle Francisco Madero s/n, at the northwest corner of the central plaza (no phone), is a small drugstore with a sampling of basic necessities and medicines. The owner speaks some English. Across the plaza, **Supermercado Alba** (no phone) has a somewhat wider selection of other goods and toiletries. Both are open Monday through Saturday from 9am to 7pm.

Post Office The *correo* is at the intersection of calles Francisco Madero and General Martínez, on the north side of the street, opposite the downtown Pemex station (© **615/153-0205**). It is open Monday through Friday from 8am to 3pm, and Saturday from 8 to 11am.

BEACHES & OUTDOOR ACTIVITIES

Mulegé has long been a favorite destination for adventurous travelers looking for a place to relax and enjoy the diversity of nature. Divers, sportfishermen, kayakers, history buffs, and admirers of beautiful beaches all find reasons to stay in this oasis just a little longer.

BEACHES   To the north and east of Mulegé lies the Sea of Cortez, known for its abundance and variety of species of fish, marine birds, and sea mammals. To the north are the mostly secluded beaches of **Bahía Santa Inez** and **Punta Chivato,** both known for their beauty and tranquillity. Santa Inez is reachable by way of a long dirt road that turns off from Carretera Transpeninsular at Km 151. Twenty-five kilometers (16 miles) south is the majestic **Bahía Concepción,** a 48km-long (30-mile) body of water protected on three sides by more than 80km (50 miles) of beaches, and dotted with islands. The mountainous peninsula borders its crystal-clear turquoise waters to the east. Along with fantastic landscapes, the bay has numerous soft, white-sand beaches such as **Santispác, Concepción, Los Cocos, El Burro, El Coyote, Buenaventura, El Requesón,** and **Armenta.** Swimming, diving, windsurfing, kayaking, and other watersports are easily enjoyed, with equipment rentals locally available. Here's a rundown on some of the area beaches with restaurant service:

Punta Arena is accessible off Carretera Transpeninsular, at Km 119. A very good *palapa* restaurant is there, along with camping facilities and primitive beach *palapas*.

Playa Santispác, at Km 114, has a nice beachfront, lots of RVs in the winter, and two good restaurants (Ana's is the more popular).

Playa El Coyote is the most popular and crowded of the Bahía Concepción beaches. The restaurant El Coyote is on the west side of Carretera Transpeninsular at the entrance to this beach, .8km (½ mile) from the water; Restaurant Bertha's serves simple meals on the beachfront.

Playa Buenaventura, at Km 94, is the most developed of the beaches, with a large RV park, motel, convenience store, boat ramp, and public restrooms, along with George's Olé restaurant and bar.

FISHING   All of the hotels in town can arrange guided fishing trips to Punta Chivato, Isla San Marcos, or Punta de Concepción, the outermost tip of Bahía Concepción.

The best fishing in the area is for yellowtail, which run in the winter, and summer catches of dorado, tuna, and billfish like marlin and sailfish. Prices run $120 per day for up to three people in a *panga,* $180 for four in a small cruiser, or $200 and up for larger boats. **Mulegé Sportfishing** (© **615/153-0244** or 615/153-0482) organizes fishing trips in the area.

HIKING & PAINTED CAVE EXPLORATIONS 🌟🌟🌟   One of the big attractions of this region are the large cave paintings in the Sierra de Guadalupe. UNESCO declared the cave paintings a World Heritage Site, and the locals take great pride in protecting them. Unlike many cave paintings, these are huge, complex murals. You are legally allowed to visit the caves only with a licensed guide.

The most popular series of caves is in **La Trinidad,** a remote rancho 29km (18 miles) west of Mulegé. After your guide drives you there, the hiking begins (count on hiking about 6km/3¾ miles and getting wet). To reach the caves, several river crossings are necessary in spots deep enough to swim. Indeed, at one point, rock walls fringe a tight canyon, and there is no way through except by swimming. This river in Cañón La Trinidad allegedly is the source of the river that flows through Mulegé, although it disappears underground for many miles in between.

Among the representations of the cave murals are large deer silhouettes and a human figure called the "cardón man" because of his resemblance to a cardoon cactus.

Another favorite cave-art site is **San Borjitas.** To get there, you travel down a bad four-wheel-drive road to Rancho Las Tinajas, where your guide will take you on foot or by mule to the caves.

For about $35 per person (6 hours, minimum five people, lunch included), you can arrange for a guide in Mulegé to take you to La Trinidad; San Borjitas will cost around $50 per person (7 hours, two meals included). Check at **Hotel Las Casitas** for guide recommendations. One recommended guide is **Salvador Castro** (© **615/153-0232**) and his Mulegé tours, and Hotel Las Casitas owner Javier Aguiar Zuniga also guides tours locally.

SCUBA DIVING & SNORKELING   Although diving in the area is very popular, be aware that visibility right in Mulegé is marred by the fresh and not-so-fresh water that seems to flow into the sea from the numerous septic tanks in this area (do not swim or snorkel close to town). But as you head south into Bahía Concepción, there is excellent snorkeling at the numerous shallow coves and tiny offshore islands. Work the middle of the sandy coves looking for oysters and scallops. For bigger fish and colorful sea life, you'll have to swim out to deeper waters along the edges of each cove.

Boat diving around Mulegé tends to be around Punta de Concepción or north of town at Punta Chivato and the small offshore islands of Santa Inez and San Marcos.

Numerous sites are perfect for both snorkeling and scuba. The marine life here is colorful—you're likely to see green moray eels, angelfish, parrotfish, and a variety of lobster. In addition, dolphins and other sea mammals are common sights. The best diving is between August and November, when the visibility averages 30m (98 ft.) and water temperatures are warmer (mid-80s Fahrenheit/high 20s Celsius).

Bea and Andy Sidler's **Cortez Explorers,** Moctezuma 75-A (©/fax **615/153-0500;** www.cortez-explorer.com), bought out and took over the operations of the well-known Mulegé Divers, and maintains its reputation as one of the best-run dive operations in the state. If Mulegé has become known as a prime dive site in Baja, credit goes to this shop for its excellent prices and exceptional services. It has a great environmental consciousness, too. Cortez Explorers runs trips from a large, custom dive boat and uses only well-maintained, current equipment.

Two-tank dive trips generally involve a 45-minute boat ride offshore and cost $70 to $135 per person, depending on the equipment needed. Snorkeling trips go for $21 to $95 (again, based on the need to rent equipment and how far you're going). Wetsuits, jackets, and Farmer Johns are available, and they're necessary during winter months. Resort courses are also available at a cost of $90.

SEA KAYAKING Kayaks are the most popular and practical way to explore the pristine coves that dot this shoreline, and Bahía Concepción is a kayaker's dream—clear, calm water, fascinating shorelines, and lots of tempting coves to pull into, with white, sandy beaches.

If you just want to paddle around a bit, rent a kayak at El Candil restaurant for $29 per day and explore on your own.

Serious kayakers may want to book ahead with a kayak-specific tour group such as the Montana-based **Sea & Adventures** (© **800/355-7140** in the U.S., or 612/123-0559 in Mexico; www.kayakbaja.com) to book the adventure that's right for them. Their Mexico branch is known as **Mar Y Aventuras** and is located in La Paz (© **612/123-0559**), but they offer kayaking expeditions throughout the peninsula.

WINDSURFING Bahía Concepción, south of Mulegé, gets quite windy in the afternoon and has numerous coves for beginners to practice in. It has yet to develop the cachet with the hardcore kite-boarding crowd that such places as Buenavista and La Ventana have, but it's a worthy place to stop and rig up nevertheless.

EXPLORING MULEGE

MISION SANTA ROSALIA DE MULEGE Founded in 1706 by Father Juan de Ugarte and Juan María Basaldúa, this site is just upstream from the bridge where the Carretera Transpeninsular crosses the Mulegé River. The original mission building was completed in 1766 to serve a local Indian population of about 2,000. In 1770, a flood destroyed nearly all the common buildings, and the mission was rebuilt on the site it occupies today, on a bluff overlooking the river. Built of stone, it is notable for its "L" formation. Its tower is several meters behind the main building. Although not the most architecturally interesting of Baja's missions, it remains in excellent condition and still functions as a Catholic church, although mission operations halted in 1828. Inside, there is a perfectly preserved statue of Santa Rosalía and a bell, both from the 18th century.

The mission is also a popular tour site. A lookout point 30m (98 ft.) behind the mission provides a spectacular vantage point for taking in the view of a grove of palm trees backed by the Sea of Cortez.

To reach the mission from town, take Calle Zaragoza (the longest north-south street in Mulegé) south, and then cross the river using the small footbridge beneath the elevated highway bridge. Turn back sharply to the right and follow the dirt road through palm groves and up a graded path to the mission. The towers of the church will be visible.

MUSEO REGIONAL DE HISTORIA (REGIONAL MUSEUM OF HISTORY)

In 1907, a state penitentiary was built on a hill overlooking the town of Mulegé. About 20 years ago, a local historian and citizen's group established this small museum inside. The institution was known as the "prison without doors" because it operated on an honor system—inmates were allowed to leave every morning to work in town, on the condition that they return when the afternoon horn sounded. Escape attempts were rare, and when they occurred, the other prisoners pursued the escapees to bring them back. It functioned that way until the mid-1970s.

The museum (no phone) details the prison's operations and houses an eclectic collection of local historical artifacts. Admission is by donation, and hours are supposed to be Monday through Friday from 9am to 1pm, but have been known to vary. The museum is at the end of Calle Cananea.

WHERE TO STAY

Accommodations in Mulegé are basic but generally clean and comfortable. The biggest hotel in town, the Hotel Serenidad, has a recent history of closings due to ownership disputes with the local *ejido* (indigenous) community. It is open now and claims to have resolved all questions of proprietorship.

EXPENSIVE

Posada de las Flores Resort at Punta Chivato ★★★ *Finds*   Not exactly in Mulegé, but near enough, is the elegant and tranquil Resort at Punta Chivato. Owned by the Posada de las Flores group, it's one of their three boutique hotels in Baja. Punta Chivato is 42km (26 miles) north of Mulegé, on Santa Ines bay. The hotel is on 3 hectares (7½ acres) fronting the Sea of Cortez, in one of the most beautiful settings you can imagine, a combination of desert landscape and aquamarine waters. The large and beautifully decorated guest rooms blend Mexican and colonial tastes. The 10 standard rooms have garden views and a terrace with swing chairs. An additional 10 junior suites are situated on the beach, with ocean views and porches with sun beds. Meals are included—there really are no other options nearby—and are served at scheduled times in the either the Hacienda Chivato air-conditioned restaurant or at the outside *palapa* dining area. Resort activities, included in the price, are tennis, mountain biking, kayaking, snorkeling, and hiking; fishing or boat rentals as well as excursions can be arranged by the tour desk. The hotel has its own private airstrip (frequency 122.80) and offers fuel service. If you're coming from Loreto, the trip will take about 2½ hours and cost about $200 by taxi. ***Note:*** Children under 12 are not allowed here, and all rooms are nonsmoking.

Domocilio conocido, Punta Chivato, B.C.S. (© 615/153-0188. Fax 615/155-5600. www.posadadelasflores.com. 18 units. High season $280 double, $380 junior suite; low season $250 double, $350 junior suite. Rates include all meals. MC, V. Free parking; private airstrip available. Children under 12 not admitted. **Amenities:** 2 restaurants; bar; daily tea time; swimming pool; tennis court; tour desk; video library; Internet satellite desk, satellite TV in public areas. *In room:* A/C, TV/VCR; minibar.

MODERATE

Hotel Serenidad ★★   Simplicity, seclusion, and casual comfort are the hallmarks of the Serenidad, just south of town between the airstrip and a long stretch of beach.

Low-rise, Mediterranean-style buildings border either Mulegé's largest pool (with *palapa* bar) or a courtyard. Most rooms have working fireplaces, and all have ceiling fans plus a large bathroom with a skylight. Decor is spare, but stylish for the area, and all rooms have a king-size bed, tile floors, and a small seating area with a glass-topped table and chairs. The larger casitas (bungalows) have two bedrooms and two baths, a small living area, and a terrace, making them ideal for families or friends traveling together.

The locally popular restaurant/bar has satellite TV, and on Saturdays the place fills up for the weekly pig roast and fiesta with mariachis, a regional specialty ($15 per person). The Serenidad has an adjacent RV park with 10 available spaces. It's on the south side of the mouth of the river, 4km (2½ miles) south of the town center, off the Carretera Transpeninsular. The hotel stays open year-round, but the restaurant closes for the month of September.

Carretera Transpeninsular Sur, P.O. Box 9, CP 23900 Mulegé, B.C.S. ℂ 615/153-0530. Fax 615/153-0311. www.serenidad.com. 48 units. $79 double. MC, V. Free parking; private airstrip available. **Amenities:** Restaurant/bar; swimming pool w/bar; Wi-Fi; telephone and fax service available through the front desk. *In room:* A/C, some have fireplaces, no phone.

INEXPENSIVE

Hotel Hacienda Mulegé ★ ⓥalue   A former 18th-century hacienda with double courtyards and a small, shaded swimming pool makes for a comfortable and value-priced place to stay. You couldn't be more centrally located in Mulegé, and the Hacienda is known for its popular bar, which also has satellite TV featuring sporting events. The bar closes for the night between 10 and 11pm, so it shouldn't keep you awake. The cozy restaurant with stone walls and a fireplace also has a pleasant patio. Rooms surround the courtyard and have beds with foam mattresses and brightly colored Mexican accents. Bathrooms are simple but large, with showers.

Calle Francisco Madero 3, Mulegé, B.C.S., a half-block east of the central plaza. ℂ 615/153-0021. Fax 615/153-0046. 24 units. $35 per room. No credit cards. Free parking. **Amenities:** Bar; small swimming pool; tourist guide services; fax available at front desk. *In room:* A/C, TV.

Hotel Las Casitas ★ ⓥalue   This longstanding favorite welcomes many repeat visitors, along with the local literati—it is the birthplace of Mexican poet Alan Gorosave. Rooms are in a courtyard just behind (and adjacent to) the Las Casitas restaurant, one of Mulegé's most popular. The basic accommodations have high ceilings, tile bathrooms, and rustic decor. Plants fill a small central patio for guests' use, but the more socially inclined gravitate to the restaurant and bar, which is open daily from 7am to 10pm. The place is especially lively on weekends—on Friday evenings there's a Mexican fiesta. The inn and restaurant are on the main east-west street in Mulegé, 1 block from the central plaza.

Calle Francisco Madero 50, Col. Centro, 23900 Mulegé, B.C.S. ℂ 615/153-0019. Fax 615/153-0190. 8 units. $40 double; $49 triple. MC, V. **Amenities:** Restaurant; bar; tour desk. *In room:* A/C, TV, Wi-Fi.

WHERE TO DINE

The must-have meal in Mulegé is the traditional pig roast. It's an event, with the pig roasted Polynesian-style in a palm-lined open pit for hours, generally while guests enjoy a few beers or other beverages. Homemade tortillas, salsas, an assortment of toppings, and the ubiquitous rice and beans accompany the succulent cooked pork. Remember—it's more than a pig, it's a party. The perennially popular pig roasts happen each Saturday night at both the **Las Casitas** restaurant (see below) and the **Hotel Serenidad** (see "Where to Stay," above). The meal costs $15.

Another Mulegé—and Mexican—dining staple is the taco. The best are reportedly found at the taco stand adjoining Las Casitas or at the popular **Taqueria Doney,** at Madero and Romero Rubio, just as you enter town, past the *depósito* (warehouse) on the right.

MODERATE

Las Casitas ⭐⭐ SEAFOOD/MEXICAN   Las Casitas remains a popular mainstay with both locals and visitors to Mulegé. The bar has a steady clientele day and night and often features special sporting events on satellite TV. Dine either in the interior stone-walled dining area or on its adjoining, plant-filled patio. After 6pm Friday, mariachi music sets the mood for a Mexican fiesta and buffet. If you're dining off the menu, how can you resist fresh lobster for $12 on Tuesdays? Menu offerings are standard fare with an emphasis on fresh seafood, but the quality is good and you can see the extra-clean exhibition kitchen as you enter.

Calle Francisco Madero 50. ℂ **615/153-0019.** Breakfast $2–$4.50; main courses $3.50–$11. MC, V. Daily 7am–10pm.

Los Equipales ⭐ MEXICAN/SEAFOOD   First off, you won't find any *equipales* (rustic palm-and-leather bucket chairs) here. In their place, the restaurant has white faux-wicker chairs that are comfy but hardly authentic. This is one of Mulegé's ever-popular hangouts, with home-style cooking matched by family-friendly service. Its second-story location offers diners the only lofty view in town, and this is the only place in Mulegé that serves complimentary chips and salsa with the meal. The specialties are traditional Mexican fare and Sonoran beef, especially barbecued ribs. Tropical drinks, such as mango margaritas, are also popular.

Calle Moctezuma, 2nd floor. ℂ **615/153-0330.** Main courses $3–$10. MC, V. Daily 8am–10pm.

INEXPENSIVE

Eduardo's MEAT/CHINESE   Eduardo's is known for its grilled meats—tender ribs, traditional *carne asada* (grilled marinated beef), and thick steaks, but it also serves an extensive buffet of Chinese food. White plastic chairs somewhat diminish the attractiveness of the stone-walled dining area, but the graciously friendly service compensates. Full bar service is also available. Across the street from the downtown Pemex station, the restaurant is currently only open for dinner on Saturdays and Sundays, but they serve hot dogs and hamburgers daily from 5 to 11pm.

General Martínez. ℂ **615/153-0258.** Main courses $3–$17. No credit cards. Sun 1–11pm.

El Candil MEXICAN   Filling platters of traditional Mexican fare at reasonable prices are the specialty of this casual restaurant, which has been run by the same family for more than 3 decades. Tacos are always popular, but the best of the house is the heaping Mexican combination plate.

Zaragoza 8, near the central plaza. No phone. Main courses $2–$8. No credit cards. Mon–Sat 11am–11pm; Sun 1–8pm.

MULEGE AFTER DARK

Mulegé's nightlife pretty much centers on the **bars** of the **Hacienda Hotel** and **Las Casitas,** in town. In addition, **La Jungla Bambú,** corner of General Martínez and Zaragoza (no phone), is an American-style sports bar gone tropical. After Hurricane John in 2006, the **Plaza Jose San Antonio** disco (directly behind Las Casitas) began a remodeling project and will be up and running with their signature dance music within the year. Also of note is the bar at the **Hotel Serenidad.**

3 A Side Trip from Mulegé: Santa Rosalía

61km (38 miles) N of Mulegé

Located in an *arroyo* (dry riverbed) north of Mulegé, Santa Rosalía looks more like an old Colorado mining town than a Mexican port city, and in fact this unique mining town dates to 1855. Founded by the French, Santa Rosalía has a decidedly European architectural ambience, though a distinctly Mexican culture inhabits it. Pastel clapboard houses surrounded by picket fences line the streets, giving the town its nickname, *ciudad de madera* (city of wood). Its large harbor and the rusted ghost of its copper-smelting facility dominate the central part of town bordering the waterfront, and the highlight of downtown Santa Rosalía is, without a doubt, the old **El Boleo bakery** (see below).

The town served as the center for copper mining in Mexico for years; a French company, Compañía de Boleo (part of the Rothschild family holdings), obtained a 99-year lease in the 1800s. Mexican President Porfirio Díaz originally granted the lease to the German shipping company Casa Moeller, which sold the mining operation rights to the Rothschild family but retained exclusive rights to transport ore from the mine. The agreement was that in exchange for access to the rich deposits of copper the company would build a town, the harbor, and public buildings, and establish a maritime route between Santa Rosalía and Guaymas, creating employment for Mexican workers. Operations began in 1885 and continued until 1954, when the Mexicans regained the use of the land through legislation. During the French operation, more than 644km (399 miles) of tunnels were built underground and in the surrounding hills, primarily by Indian and Chinese laborers. Following the reversion of the mining operations to the Mexican government, the facility was plagued with problems, including the alleged leakage of arsenic into the local water supply, so the plant was permanently closed in 1985.

The French influence is apparent everywhere in Santa Rosalía—especially in the colonial-style wooden houses. The French also brought over thousands of Asian workers who have since integrated into the local population (Chinese cuisine is still popular here) along with the German and French residents. The French administrators built their homes on the northern Mesa Francia, the part of town where you'll find the museum and historic buildings, while the Mexican residents settled on the southern Mesa Mexico. The town still has a somewhat segregated feel.

Today, Santa Rosalía, with a population of 14,000, is notable for its manmade harbor—the recently constructed Marina Santa Rosalía, complete with concrete piers, floating docks, and full docking accommodations for a dozen ocean cruisers. Santa Rosalía is the main seaport of northern Baja, directly across from Guaymas. A ferry link established during the mining days still operates between the two ports. Because this is the prime entry point of manufactured goods into Baja, the town abounds with autoparts and electronic appliance stores, along with shops selling Nikes and sunglasses.

The town has no real beach to speak of, and fewer recreational attractions. The rusted, dilapidated smelting foundry, railroad, and pier all border the docks and give the waterfront an abandoned, neglected atmosphere.

EXPLORING SANTA ROSALÍA

Here, in this bustling ghost town, you won't find hacienda-style architecture or red-tile roofs, but you will find the best bakery in Baja. **El Boleo,** on Avenida Obregón at Calle 4 (© **615/152-0310**), has been baking French baguettes since the late 1800s,

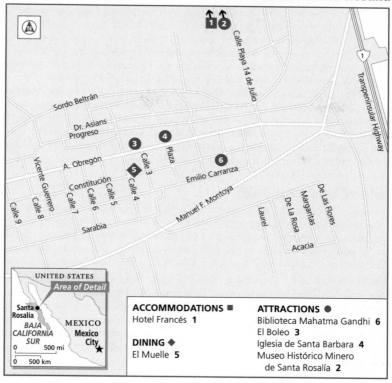

ACCOMMODATIONS ■
Hotel Francés **1**

DINING ◆
El Muelle **5**

ATTRACTIONS ●
Biblioteca Mahatma Gandhi **6**
El Boleo **3**
Iglesia de Santa Barbara **4**
Museo Histórico Minero
  de Santa Rosalía **2**

but I recommend the pitahaya, a dense sweetbread stuffed with a kind of almond paste. It's 3 blocks west of the church and is open from 8am to 9pm Monday to Saturday, and Sunday 8am to 2pm.

Second only to the bakery, the principal attraction in Santa Rosalía is the **Iglesia de Santa Barbara,** a structure of galvanized steel designed by Gustave Eiffel (of Eiffel Tower fame) in 1884. It was originally created for the 1889 Paris World Expo, where it was displayed as a prototype for what Eiffel envisioned as a sort of prefab mission. The concept never took off, and the structure was left in a warehouse in Brussels, where it was later discovered and sent to Baja by officials of the mining company. Section by section, the church was transported then reassembled in Santa Rosalía in 1897. The somber gray exterior belies the beauty of the intricate stained-glass windows viewed from inside.

Along with the church, the other site to see is the **ex-Fundación del Pacífico** (former Foundry of the Pacific), or **Museo Histórico Minero de Santa Rosalía.** In a landmark wooden building, it houses a permanent display of artifacts from the days of Santa Rosalía's mining operations. There are miniature models of the town and its buildings, old accounting ledgers and office equipment, and samples of the minerals extracted from local mines. It's open Monday through Saturday from 8:30am to 2pm and 5 to 7pm. Admission is $1.50.

However, the city itself is the macro attraction. Wooden saloons, wraparound verandas, and mountainous terrain make for a paradoxical contrast to the Mexicans milling in the streets. Bordering the museum are the most attractive of the clapboard houses, painted in a rainbow of colors—mango, lemon, blueberry, and cherry. The wood used to construct these houses was the return cargo on ships that transported copper to refineries in Oregon and British Columbia during the 1800s.

Other sites of note are the Plaza Benito Juárez, or central *zócalo* (square) that fronts the Palacio Municipal, or City Hall, an intriguing structure of French colonial design. The streets of Constitución, Carranza, Plaza, and Altamirano border the square. Just down Constitución is the **Biblioteca Mahatma Gandhi,** more notable for the uniqueness of its name in Mexico than for the library itself, which is the only one in operation between Ensenada and La Paz. The library has a permanent exhibition of historic photos on display.

WHERE TO STAY & DINE

Dining is limited in the small town of Santa Rosalía, but lunch at **El Muelle** restaurant, on Obregón (no phone), right across from the central plaza, is superb. The tacos, enchiladas in spicy, fresh tomato sauce, and breaded fish bathed in peppers and cheese are all good reasons to visit, but the main draw is the creamy, chipotle smoked tuna dip that comes with chips before the meal. Follow it up with dessert bread from El Boleo.

Hotel Francés ★★   Founded in 1886, the Hotel Francés once set the standard of hospitality in Baja Sur, welcoming European dignitaries and hosting the French administrators and businessmen of the mining operations. Today it has a worn air of elegance but retains its position as the most welcoming accommodation in Santa Rosalía. Rooms are in the back, with wooden porches and balconies overlooking a small courtyard pool. Each room has individually controlled air-conditioning, plus windows that open for ventilation. Floors are wood-planked, and the small bathrooms are beautifully tiled. You have a choice of two double beds or one king. Telephone service is available in the lobby. The popular restaurant serves breakfast until noon.

Calle Jean Michel Cousteau s/n, 23920 Santa Rosalía B.C.S. ℂ/fax 615/152-2052. 16 units. High season $71 double (includes breakfast); low season $65 single or double. No credit cards. Free parking. **Amenities:** Restaurant (7am–noon); small courtyard pool. *In room:* A/C, TV, free Wi-Fi, no phones.

4 Whale-Watching in Baja: A Primer

Few sights inspire as much reverence as close contact with a whale in its natural habitat. The thrill of seeing one of these giant inhabitants of the sea up close is a life-changing event for many people, and few places in the world can offer as complete an experience as Mexico's Baja peninsula. The various protected bays and lagoons on the Pacific coast are the preferred winter waters for migrating gray whales as they journey south to mate and give birth to their calves.

While the entire Pacific coast of the Baja peninsula offers opportunities for whale sightings, the experience is particularly rewarding in the protected areas of the El Vizcaíno Biosphere Reserve, where a large number of whales can be seen easily. This area encompasses the famous Laguna Ojo de Liebre—also known as Scammon's Lagoon—close to Guerrero Negro, Laguna San Ignacio, and Bahía Magdalena.

Because these protected waters offer ideal conditions for gray whales during the winter, the neighboring towns have developed the necessary infrastructure and services to accommodate whale-watchers. Avid eco- and adventure-lovers seem to follow

> **Tips Should I Take a Tour or Hire a Boat?**
>
> You'll often get a better deal if you head down to the local pier to hire a local *panga* operator. Expect to pay anywhere from $30 to $45 per person for a day trip with a local guide (plus a tip for good service). An organized tour can run almost double that price, but the services and respect for the whales that come at a higher price tag are worth it in most cases. It's always a good idea to check for licensed, experienced operators (they must have photo-ID credentials showing they are licensed tour guides) who know how to approach the whales with calm, caution, and respect for the environment. The most important thing about whale-watching is to enjoy it while practicing guidelines that ensure both your safety and the safety of the whales. (We've recommended several tour operators and organizations below.)

their own migratory patterns and arrive at these shores between January and March to gaze in awe at the gentle cetaceans.

WHAT YOU'LL SEE

Gray whales are the favorite species for whale-watchers because they tend to swim and feed mostly in coastal shallows, occasionally resting with their abdomens on the bottom, while their close relatives prefer to frequent the deeper realms of the ocean. Whale-watching in one of Baja's lagoons can be truly exciting—at times, gray whales appear to be on all sides, displaying the full spectrum of typical whale behavior.

Watchers might be showered with a cloud of water from a whale spouting (clearing its blowhole) or might witness an enormous male spyhopping—lifting its head vertically out of the water, just above eye level, to pivot around before slipping back into the water. Perhaps the most breathtaking spectacle of all is a breach, when a whale propels itself out of the water and arches through the air to land on its back with a splash. These gray whales are known to be so friendly and curious that they frequently come up to the whale-watching boats and stay close by, sometimes allowing people to pet them.

To be close to these magnificent creatures is a privilege. Above all, respect their environment and their integrity as inhabitants of the marine world.

WHICH TOWN? WHICH TOUR?

Regardless of where you decide to stay in Baja, you most likely will find tours to the whale-watching areas of Bahía Magdalena and the lagoons of Ojo de Liebre and San Ignacio. (For whale-watching tours that depart from La Paz, see chapter 5.) If you want to center your visit on whale-watching, the best places to visit are Guerrero Negro, San Ignacio, Ciudad Constitución, Puerto San Carlos, and Puerto López Mateos.

While the above-mentioned towns have basic facilities, Loreto may actually be the wisest base to choose; it has a well-developed tourist infrastructure and a number of lovely hotels and restaurants. From here, whale-watching cruises along the Pacific coast are easily accessible. The trips take you by road to Bahía Magdalena, where you board a skiff to get up close to the gentle giants. En route you get a chance to view the spectacular desert landscape; guides offer a wealth of natural and historical information. Locally based **Arturo's Sport** (© **613/135-0766;** www.arturosport.com) offers excellent daylong excursions for $125. Another is the U.S.-based **Baja Expeditions** (© **800/843-6967** in the U.S., or 612/125-3828 in La Paz; www.bajaex.com), which

The Bay of La Paz Project: Saving the Sea of Cortez

Although the best whale-watching is in the Pacific, it's the Sea of Cortez that once inspired Jacques Cousteau to call it the "world's aquarium." Apart from gray and humpback whales—plus remarkable pelagic and reef life—divers have spotted blue whales and even orcas in this extraordinary body of water, also known as the Gulf of California. Sadly, marine populations have declined between 70% and 90% since the 1960s and, until now, nothing has been done to ensure future generations will have fish in the sea.

SeaWatch, a La Paz-based organization dedicated to exposing and stopping destructive fishing practices in the Sea of Cortez for the past 15 years, has launched a public awareness campaign in Southern Baja to stop commercial fishermen from wiping out reefs and snaring hammerhead schools in nets. The **Bay of La Paz Project,** under the auspices of SeaWatch and three NGOs (Niparajá, The Billfish Foundation, and Pronatura), will be reaching out to kids, adults, and government officials throughout the state of Baja California Sur. Ultimately, the Bay of La Paz Project hopes to limit commercial fishing in various high-pressure areas over time, thereby allowing fish populations the chance to reproduce. If you would like to know more or find out how you can help, visit **www.seawatch.org** or call ©️ **503/616-4421.**

runs multiday cruising and camping excursions in Magdalena Bay starting at $1,000 per person.

Guerrero Negro sits on the dividing line between southern and northern Baja. It has a modest but well-developed tourism infrastructure in an otherwise industrial town (it's the site of the world's largest evaporative saltworks). Despite the industrial nature of the town, the lagoon where gray whales calve and spend the winter has remained safe and has witnessed a remarkable comeback of this almost-extinct species. This is partly because the salt produced in Guerrero Negro is shipped from an offshore artificial island, built away from the whale area, and also because of the designation of the area as part of the El Vizcaíno Biosphere Reserve in 1988.

San Ignacio is a small town built by the Spaniards in the middle of a palm oasis and is full of Jesuit history. It is the ideal point of departure for **Laguna San Ignacio** 🐋🐋, 74km (46 miles) southwest of the town. The San Ignacio lagoon is an excellent spot for whale-watching because it is common for whales in this area to approach the small whale-watching boats, occasionally coming close enough to allow you to touch them.

Bahía Magdalena is another spot preferred by wintering gray whales. Two towns on the bay's shore offer whale-watching tours. **Puerto López Mateos,** on the northern shore, is the closest town to the whales' calving areas. Accommodations are limited to a few modest hotels and restaurants, but several boat operators offer tours. Flying tours on Baja-based airline **Aereo Calafia** (©️ **624/143-4302;** www.aereo calafia.com),fly from Cabo San Lucas—a 75-minute flight—to Magdalena, where you board a *panga* and spend 3 hours watching gray whales and humpbacks loll around the coastal lagoons before returning the same day. This tour is $420, including air transportation, the tour, and lunch.

Puerto San Carlos offers a more developed tourism infrastructure, with well-appointed hotels and restaurants, trailer parks, travel agencies, a bus station, and other services. To arrange a tour, try **Viajes Mar y Arena,** Puerto La Paz s/n (📞 **613/136-0076,** 613/136-0599, 613/136-0676, or 613/137-8093). From Los Cabos, the ultimate whale excursion to Puerto San Carlos can be found on **BookCabo.com** (📞 **624/142-9200;** www.bookcabo.com). Operated by renowned destination-management company Terramar Destinations, this tour offers luxury bus transportation from San José del Cabo to San Carlos, where lobster dinners await in your 2-night stay at the quaint Alcatraz Hotel. The next morning entails cruising around the bay observing the whales and, hours later, lunching on Margarita Island. The cost is $227/person double occupancy and $126 for kids 3 to 10 years old.

Ciudad Constitución, the largest of the three towns, is 61km (38 miles) inland. It has a well-developed tourism infrastructure, with tour organizers that offer daily whale-watching tours during the season.

GETTING THERE   To get to Puerto López Mateos, take the only road going west from Loreto for about 121km (75 miles). When you arrive in the town of Insurgentes, turn right and continue 2.4km (1½ miles) to the Puerto López Mateos exit. Turn left and continue 34km (21 miles) to Puerto López Mateos. To get to Puerto San Carlos, take the same road west to Insurgentes, and then drive south about 24km (15 miles) until you reach Ciudad Constitución. From Ciudad Constitución, take the exit marked PUERTO SAN CARLOS, and continue the remaining 63km (39 miles) to town. Both routes are well paved and maintained.

7

Northern Baja: Tijuana, Rosarito Beach, Ensenada & San Felipe

The region that holds Mexico's most infamous border crossing also claims to be the birthplace of the original Caesar salad and the margarita. Who could resist that? This trip into northern Baja California combines the boisterous (Tijuana), the beachy (Rosarito Beach and San Felipe), and the beautiful (Ensenada and the Valle de Guadalupe), towns that comprise some of the most important introductions to Mexico.

Long notorious as a party-hard border town, 10-block Tijuana has cleaned up its act a bit on its way to becoming a full-scale city with explosive population growth. The town's traditional lures—the legendary nightlife and hardcore souvenir shopping—are now augmented by a number of family-friendly sports and cultural attractions.

For a slightly more tranquil experience—provided you steer clear of Spring Break—the resort town of Rosarito Beach remains a laidback beach destination despite spending time in Hollywood's spotlight as the location where much of the movie *Titanic* was filmed.

Continue south past surf breaks, golf courses, and fish-taco stands, and the lovely town of Ensenada emerges, a favored port of call with plenty of appeal for travelers active and low-key alike. Take time to travel inland from Ensenada to explore Mexico's emerging wine country. And from there, nothing beats the flat-lining pulse of San Felipe's beaches. Although the town is experiencing a boom in resort and real estate development, the center of town is unchanged and it makes for a good glimpse of old Baja.

EXPLORING NORTHERN BAJA

If you have a car, it's easy to venture into Baja Norte from Southern California for a few days' getaway. Since 1991, American car-rental companies have allowed customers to drive their cars into Baja. Whether you drive your own car or a rented one, you'll need Mexican auto insurance in addition to your own; it's available at the border in San Ysidro or through the car-rental companies (see "Getting Around" in chapter 2).

It takes relatively little time to cross the international border in Tijuana, especially considering about 300,000 people cross the border daily, but be prepared for a delay of an hour or more on your return to the United States through San Diego—with increased security measures for entering the U.S., this is an especially diligent point of entry. Even the crossing at less popular Tecate can take an hour or more, and evenings and weekends make for a longer wait anywhere you cross. If you take local buses down the Baja coast (which is possible), the delays come en route rather than at the border.

1 Tijuana: Bawdy Border Town

26km (16 miles) S of San Diego

Don't expect to find the Mexico of your fantasies—charming, sun-dappled town squares and churches blanketed in bougainvillea; women in colorful embroidered skirts and blouses—in infamous Tijuana, Mexico's first point of entry from the West Coast of the U.S. Although quaint plazas filled with families do exist, you're more likely to encounter a dynamic city with a decidedly urban culture, a profusion of U.S.–inspired goods and services, and relentless hawkers playing to the thousands of tourists who come for a taste of Mexico.

Like many burgeoning cities in developing nations, Tijuana is a mixture of new and old, rich and poor, modern and traditional. But Tijuana is increasingly an important city in Mexico; the population has swelled to nearly two million, making it the second-largest city on the Pacific coast of North America (after Los Angeles). Despite obvious signs of widespread poverty, the town claims one of the lowest unemployment rates in the country, thanks to the rise in *maquiladoras,* the foreign-owned manufacturing operations that continue to proliferate under NAFTA (the North American Free Trade Agreement). High-rise office buildings testify to increased prosperity, as does the emergence of a white-collar middle class that shops at modern shopping centers away from the tourist zone. And the availability of imported goods and the lure of a big-city experience draw visitors.

Tijuana has long been renowned for its hustling, carnival-like atmosphere and easily accessible decadence, a reputation stemming from its early notoriety as a playground of illicit pleasures during the U.S. Prohibition, when scores of visitors flocked here to the site of the world's largest saloon bar, The Whale. Not long after, the $10 million Hotel Casino de Agua Caliente—the first "megaresort" in Mexico—attracted Hollywood stars and other celebrities with its casino, greyhound racing, and hot-springs spa.

But Tijuana's "sin city" image is gradually morphing as the city develops into a more culturally diverse destination. Vineyards associated with the growing wine industry are nearby, and an increasing number of museums and other cultural offerings are joining the traditional sporting attractions of greyhound racing and bullfights. Perhaps one of the more overt signs of a Tijuana transformation is the construction of the **Trump Ocean Resort** (www.trump-baja.com), where guests and owners will be able to enjoy Trump-style luxury as early as 2008.

GETTING THERE & DEPARTING

A visit to Tijuana requires little in the way of formalities—people who stay less than 72 hours in the border zone do not need a tourist card. If you plan to stay longer, a tourist card is required and, beginning in January 2008, a passport will be required as well, no matter how long you're staying. If you're staying 7 days or less, tourist cards are available free of charge from the border-crossing station or from any immigration office and will cost a small fee for any time over 7 days.

BY PLANE   There are no nonstop flights from the U.S. to Tijuana; however, **Aeroméxico** (© 800/237-6639 in the U.S., 664/683-2700, or 664/638-8444; www.aeromexico.com) has nonstop flights from Culiacán, Guadalajara, Hermosillo, and Mexico City. **Mexicana** (© 800/531-7921 in the U.S., or 664/634-6566; www.mexicana.com) has nonstop flights from Guadalajara and Mexico City; all Mexicana flights originating in the U.S. connect in Mexico City before going to Tijuana. **Alma**

de Mexico (© 888/811-2562 in the U.S., or 333/836-0770; www.alma.com.mx) has nonstop flights from Ciudad Juárez, Ciudad Obregón, La Paz, and Los Mochis. **Volaris** (© 866/988-3527 in the U.S., or 551/102-8000; www.volaris.com.mx) flies nonstop from Culiacán, Guadalajara, León, Los Cabos, Morelia, and Toluca.

BY CAR   If you plan to visit only Tijuana and are arriving from Southern California, you should consider leaving your car behind, since traffic can be challenging. One alternative is to walk across the border; you can either park your car in one of the safe, long-term parking lots on the San Diego side for about $12 a day, or take the San Diego Trolley (see below for more information) to the border. If you don't want to walk across the border, hop a bus (© 664/621-2982), which is right next to the trolley station. Once you're in Tijuana, it's easier to get around by taxi than to take on the local drivers. Cab fares from the border to downtown Tijuana run about $5. You can also charter a taxi to Rosarito for about $20 (one-way) or to Ensenada for $100 (one-way).

To reach Tijuana from the U.S., take I-5 south to the Mexican border at San Ysidro. The 18-mile (29km) drive from downtown San Diego takes about half an hour.

From the south, take the Carretera Transpeninsular north to Tijuana. It's a long and sometimes difficult drive, but once you reach Guerrero Negro from the south, the roads are more manageable.

BY TROLLEY   From the San Diego border, you also have the option of taking the bright-red trolley in San Ysidro at the Plaza Las Americas and getting off in Tijuana at Revolución and Calle 2 (it's nicknamed the Tijuana Trolley for good reason). It's simple, quick, and inexpensive; the one-way trolley fare is $2. The last trolley leaving for San Ysidro departs downtown around midnight; the last returning trolley from San Ysidro is at 1am. On Saturday, the trolley runs 24 hours. Departures leave about every 30 minutes.

BY BUS   **Five Star Tours,** in San Diego at the intersection of Broadway and Kettner (© 619/232-5049; fax 619/575-3075; www.fivestartours.com), offers specialized trips across the border. For $35 per person, the company will take you on a tour of Tijuana, teach you how to make traditional tacos, and return to San Diego at a preestablished time.

Also from San Diego, **Contact Tours** (© 619/477-8687) offers a tour to Tijuana for $29, including stops at the must-see tourist sights, including Avenida Revolución, and stops for shopping and lunch. It's not a regularly scheduled tour, so call ahead to check departure dates and times.

Mexicoach (© 664/428-9517 or 664/685-1470; www.mexicoach.com) specializes in cross-border transportation at a cost of just $5 each way. It's open daily with departures every 30 minutes from 8am to 9pm, 365 days per year. Board the bus at the Border Station Parking (next to the San Diego Factory Outlet Center, a huge outlet mall right near the border crossing—you can't miss it) or from the trolley's (see above) last stop at the border, and it will take you to the **Tijuana Tourist Terminal** (© 664/685-1470) on Avenida Revolución, between calles 6 and 7. Returns to the border leave from the same terminal. These buses also travel to Rosarito Beach ($14 each way). Note that the special bus lanes through the border are also, on average, much faster than the car lanes.

VISITOR INFORMATION

Prior to your visit, you can write for information, brochures, and maps from the **Tijuana Convention & Visitors Bureau,** P.O. Box 434523, San Diego, CA 92143-4523. You

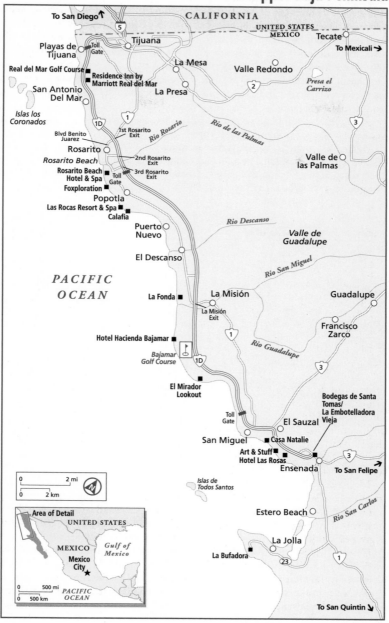

The Upper Baja Peninsula

CALIFORNIA

UNITED STATES
MEXICO

To San Diego
Tijuana
Tecate
To Mexicali →
Playas de Tijuana
Toll Gate
La Mesa
Valle Redondo
Real del Mar Golf Course
Residence Inn by Marriott Real del Mar
La Presa
Presa el Carrizo
San Antonio Del Mar
Islas los Coronados
1st Rosarito Exit
Rio Rosario
Rio de las Palmas
Valle de las Palmas
Blvd Benito Juarez
Rosarito
2nd Rosarito Exit
Rosarito Beach
Rosarito Beach Hotel & Spa
3rd Rosarito Exit
Toll Gate
Foxploration
Popotla
Las Rocas Resort & Spa
Calafia
Puerto Nuevo
Rio Descanso
Valle de Guadalupe
El Descanso
Rio San Miguel
PACIFIC OCEAN
La Fonda
La Misión
Guadalupe
La Misión Exit
Francisco Zarco
Hotel Hacienda Bajamar
Rio Guadalupe
Bajamar Golf Course
El Mirador Lookout
Toll Gate
Bodegas de Santa Tomas/ La Embotelladora Vieja
El Sauzal
San Miguel
Casa Natalie
Art & Stuff
Hotel Las Rosas
Ensenada
To San Felipe →
Islas de Todos Santos
Estero Beach
Rio San Carlos
La Jolla
La Bufadora
To San Quintin ↘

0   2 mi
0   2 km

Area of Detail
UNITED STATES
MEXICO
Gulf of Mexico
Mexico City
PACIFIC OCEAN
0   500 mi
0   500 km

can also get a preview of events, restaurants, and more online at **www.seetijuana.com**. Once in Tijuana, pick up visitor information at the **Tijuana Tourism Board,** Paseo de los Héroes 9365, Zona Río (© **888/775-2417** toll-free in the U.S., or 664/687-9600; www.seetijuana.com). You can also try the **National Chamber of Commerce** (© **664/ 685-8472;** Mon–Fri 9am–2pm and 4–7pm). Its offices are at the corner of Avenida Revolución and Calle 1, and its staff are extremely helpful with maps and orientation, local events of interest, and accommodations; in addition, the Tijuana Tourism Board provides legal assistance for visitors who encounter problems while in Tijuana.

For additional information online, visit www.tijuanaonline.org, www.seetijuana. com, and www.baja.gob.mx.

Tijuana has a special **tourist assist number** (© **078;** this is a free call) to help visitors with special needs. The following countries have **consulate offices** in Tijuana: the **United States** (© **664/622-7400**), **Canada** (© **664/684-0461**), and the **United Kingdom** (© **664/681-7323** or 664/686-5320).

FAST FACTS: Tijuana

Area Code The local telephone area code is **664**.

Banks Banks exchange currency during business hours, generally Monday through Friday from 8:30am to 6pm and Saturday from 9am to 2pm. Major banks with ATMs and *casas de cambio* (money-exchange houses) are easy to find in all the heavily trafficked areas discussed in this book. The currency of Mexico is the peso, but you can easily visit Tijuana (or Rosarito and Ensenada, for that matter) without changing money since dollars are accepted virtually everywhere.

Climate & Weather Tijuana's climate is similar to Southern California's: Don't expect sweltering heat just because you're south of the border, and remember that the Pacific waters won't be much warmer than off San Diego. The first beaches you'll find are about 24km (15 miles) south of Tijuana.

Emergencies Dial © **078** to reach **Tourist Assist;** © **066** to reach the **Police** or **Red Cross.** Both are free calls. To reach the **Green Angels** (a government service that travels the roadways of Mexico looking for cars with problems, equipped to make minor repairs and only charging for parts used or gas consumed) servicing the Tijuana area, call © **664/624-3479.**

Internet Changes come fast in Tijuana, so the Internet cafe that was there the last time you visited is probably not there anymore. Most hotels offer a high-speed connection or Wi-Fi for a nominal charge and, if you're just passing through and need to get connected, scan Avenida Revolución for the occasional "Internet" or "Cafe Internet" sign. You won't have to go far to get online.

Pharmacy **Sanborn's** (© **664/688-1462**) is a 24-hour megastore with a 24-hour pharmacy. It has several locations in Tijuana; one is at the corner of Avenida Revolución and Calle 8. Numerous discount pharmacies are also found along avenidas Constitución and Revolución.

Taxes & Tipping A value-added tax of 10%, called **IVA** *(Impuesto al Valor Agregado),* is added to most bills, including those in restaurants. This does not represent the tip; the bill will read "IVA incluído," but you should add about 15% for the tip if the service warrants.

Taxis **Yellow Cabs (Taxis Amarillos)** can be reached by calling © **664/682-9892.** You might also want to try catching a "local" *combi* taxi (VW vans that drive along a particular route; similar to a bus but traveling on more routes and transporting multiple passengers).

EXPLORING TIJUANA

One of the first major tourist attractions below the border is also one of the strangest—the **Museo de Cera (Wax Museum),** Calle 1 no. 8281 (downtown), at the corner of Madero (© **664/688-2478**). Featured statues include the eclectic mix of Whoopi Goldberg, Frida Kahlo, Laurel and Hardy, and Bill Clinton arranged in an exhibit otherwise dominated by figures from Mexican history. If you aren't spooked by the not-so-lifelike figures of Aztec warriors, brown-robed friars, Spanish princes, and 20th-century military leaders (all posed in period dioramas), step into the Chamber of Horrors, where wax werewolves and sinister sadists lurk in the shadows. When the museum is mostly empty, which is most of the time, the dramatically lit Chamber of Horrors can be a little creepy. This side-street freak show is open daily from 10am to 6pm, and admission is $1.50.

For many visitors, Tijuana's "main event" is the bustling **Avenida Revolución,** the street whose reputation precedes it. Since its construction in 1889, Avenida Revolución has been a mecca for tourists visiting Tijuana. In the 1920s, American college students, servicemen, and hedonistic tourists discovered "La Revo" as a bawdy center for illicit fun. Since then, however, some of the original attractions have fallen by the wayside: Gambling was outlawed in the 1930s, back-alley cockfights are also illegal, and the same civic improvements that gave Revolución trees, benches, and wider sidewalks also vanquished the girlie shows whose barkers once accosted passersby. Don't expect staid and sedentary, however: Drinking and shopping are the main order of business these days; while revelers from across the border knock back tequila shooters and dangle precariously from the upstairs railings of glaring bars, bargain hunters peruse the never-ending array of goods (and not-so-goods) for sale. You'll find the action between calles 1 and 9; the information centers (mentioned above) are at the north end, and the landmark jai alai palace anchors the southern portion. To help make sense of all the tchotchkes sold here, see "Shopping," below.

Although the lightning-paced indoor ballgame jai alai (pronounced "*high* ah-*lye*") is no longer played here, it's still worth a visit to the **Jai Alai Frontón Palacio,** Avenida Revolución at Calle 8 (© **664/685-3687,** 664/688-0125, or 619/231-1910 in San Diego), for its exquisite neoclassical architecture. Built in 1925, the building, for years, was the site of jai alai matches, an ancient Basque tradition incorporating elements of tennis, hockey, and basketball. Now the arena is used just for cultural events or occasional boxing matches.

Another building of architectural interest on Avenida Revolución (at Calle 2) is the **HSBC Bank Building.** One of Tijuana's oldest private buildings, the structure was built in 1929 to resemble the French Nouveau style popular in the early 1900s.

Visitors can be easily seduced—then quickly repulsed—by tourist-trap areas like Avenida Revolución, but it's important to remember that there's more to Tijuana than

American tourism. If you're looking to see a different side of Tijuana, the best place to start is the **Centro Cultural Tijuana (Tijuana Cultural Center),** Paseo de los Héroes at Mina (© **664/687-9600;** www.cecut.gob.mx). You can easily spot the ultramodern complex, designed by irrepressible modern architect Pedro Ramírez Vásquez, by its centerpiece gigantic sand-colored dome housing an OMNIMAX theater, which screens various 45-minute films (subjects range from science to space travel). The center also houses the **Museo de las Identidades Mexicanas (Museum of Mexican Identities)** permanent collection of artifacts from pre-Hispanic times through the modern political era, plus a gallery for visiting exhibits that has included everything from the works of artist Diego Rivera to a well-curated yet disturbing exhibit chronicling torture and human-rights violations through the ages. Music, theater, and dance performances take place in the center's concert hall and courtyard, and there's also a cafe and an excellent museum bookshop. Call to check the concert schedule during your visit. The center also holds the new **Museo de las Californias (Museum of the Californias),** with exhibits that trace the history of the Californias, dating back to prehistoric times. The center is open daily from 10am to 7pm. Admission to the museum's permanent exhibits is free; there's a $2 charge for the special-event gallery, and tickets for OMNIMAX films are $4 for adults and $2.50 for children. The OMNIMAX theater is open Monday through Friday 1 to 9pm, and Saturdays and Sundays 10am to 9pm.

The Cultural Center may sound like a field trip for schoolchildren, but it's a must-see, if only to drag you away from tourist kitsch and into the more sophisticated **Zona Río (river area)** of Tijuana. While there, stop to admire the wide, European-style **Paseo de los Héroes.** The boulevard's intersections are gigantic *glorietas* (traffic circles), at the center of which stand statuesque monuments to leaders ranging from Aztec Emperor Cuauhtémoc to Abraham Lincoln. Navigating the congested *glorietas* will require your undivided attention, however, so it's best to pull over to admire the monuments. The Zona Río also has some classier shopping options, a colorful local marketplace, and the **Baja California Cultural Institute,** which has exhibits showcasing the culture of the region. It's at 10151 Av. Centenario.

The ultimate kid destination in Tijuana is **Mundo Divertido La Mesa,** 15035 Vía Rápida Poniente, Fracc. San José (© **664/701-7133** or 664/701-7134). Literally translated, it means "fun world," and one parent described it as the Mexican equivalent of "a Chuck E. Cheese's restaurant built inside a Malibu Grand Prix." You get the idea—noisy and frenetic, it's the kind of place kids dream about. Let them choose from miniature golf, batting cages, a roller coaster, a kid-size train, a video-game parlor, a bowling alley, movie theaters, and go-karts. There's a food court with tacos and hamburgers; if you're in luck, the picnic area will be festooned with streamers and piñatas for some fortunate child's birthday party. The park is open weekdays noon to 9pm, Saturday and Sunday 11am until 10pm. Admission is free, and several booths inside sell tickets for the various rides, which cost from $1 to $11.

The fertile valleys of northern Baja produce most of Mexico's finest wines; many high-quality vintages are exported to Europe but most are not available in the U.S. For an introduction to Mexican wines, stop into **Cava de Vinos L.A. Cetto (L.A. Cetto Winery),** Av. Cañón Johnson 2108, at Avenida Constitución Sur (© **664/685-3031** or 664/685-1644; www.lacetto.com) or make an appointment for a tasting. Shaped like a wine barrel, this building's striking facade was fashioned from old oak aging barrels in an inspired bit of recycling. The entrance has a couple of wine presses

Tijuana

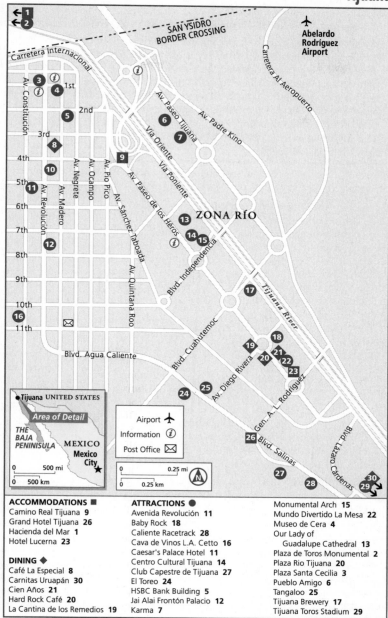

ACCOMMODATIONS ■
Camino Real Tijuana **9**
Grand Hotel Tijuana **26**
Hacienda del Mar **1**
Hotel Lucerna **23**

DINING ◆
Café La Especial **8**
Carnitas Uruapán **30**
Cien Años **21**
Hard Rock Café **20**
La Cantina de los Remedios **19**

ATTRACTIONS ●
Avenida Revolución **11**
Baby Rock **18**
Caliente Racetrack **28**
Cava de Vinos L.A. Cetto **16**
Caesar's Palace Hotel **11**
Centro Cultural Tijuana **14**
Club Capestre de Tijuana **27**
El Toreo **24**
HSBC Bank Building **5**
Jai Alai Frontón Palacio **12**
Karma **7**

Monumental Arch **15**
Mundo Divertido La Mesa **22**
Museo de Cera **4**
Our Lady of
    Guadalupe Cathedral **13**
Plaza de Toros Monumental **2**
Plaza Rio Tijuana **20**
Plaza Santa Cecilia **3**
Pueblo Amigo **6**
Tangaloo **25**
Tijuana Brewery **17**
Tijuana Toros Stadium **29**

Moments **First Crush: The Annual Harvest Festival**

If you enjoyed a visit to **L.A. Cetto,** Tijuana's winery (p. 154) or Ensenada's **Bodegas de Santo Tomás** (p. 168), then you might want to return during the **Fiesta de la Vendimia (Harvest Festival),** held each year in late August or early September. Set among the endless vineyards of the fertile Valle de Guadalupe, the day's events include the traditional blessing of the grapes, wine tastings, live music and dancing, riding exhibitions, and a country-style Mexican meal. L.A. Cetto offers a group excursion from Tijuana (about an hour's drive); San Diego's **Baja California Tours** (℘ 800/336-5454 or 858/454-7166) also organizes a day-long trip from San Diego.

(ca. 1928) that Don Angel Cetto used back in the early days of production. His family still runs the winery, which opened the impressive visitor center in 1993. L.A. Cetto bottles both red and white wines, some of them award winners, including Petite Sirah, Nebbiolo, chardonnay, and cabernet sauvignon. Most bottles cost about $5; the special reserves are a little more than $15. The company also produces tequila and olive oil, for sale here. Admission is $3 for a tour and generous tasting (for those 18 and older only; those under 18 are admitted free with an adult but cannot taste the wines), $5 with souvenir wine glass. L.A. Cetto is open Monday through Friday 10am to 5:30pm, and Saturday 10am to 4:30pm. Tours and tastings run Monday through Friday 10am to noon and 2 to 5pm.

If your tastes run more toward cerveza than wine, plan to visit the **Cerveza Tijuana brewery,** Fundadores 2951, Col. Juárez (℘ 664/684-2406 or 664/638-8662; www.tj beer.com). Here, guided tours (by prior appointment) demonstrate the beer-making process at the brewery, where all beers are made from a select group of hops and malt. The family that owns the company has a long tradition of master brewers who worked in breweries in the Czech Republic and brought their knowledge back home to Tijuana. Cerveza Tijuana was founded in January 2000, and now has select distribution in the U.S. Its lager, dark, and light beers are all available to sample in the adjoining European-style pub, which features karaoke on Monday and Tuesday nights and live music Wednesday through Saturday. A menu of appetizers and entrees is also available. It's open Monday to Saturday 1pm to 2am.

SITES OF INTEREST Tijuana's long and varied history has given rise to a number of intriguing sites of interest. Here are a few of my favorites:

Although the original **Caesar's Palace Hotel,** Av. Revolución 1059, at Calle 5 (℘ 664/685-1666), is one of Tijuana's oldest hotels, its real claim to fame is as the probable birthplace of the Caesar salad (tossed by Caesar Cardini in 1924).

The oldest church in Tijuana is the **Catedral de Nuestra Señora de Guadalupe (Our Lady of Guadalupe Cathedral),** in front of City Hall, at Paseo Centenario 10150 and Josefa Ortiz de Domínguez, in Zona Río (℘ 664/607-3775). First inaugurated in 1902 as a parish church, it was appointed cathedral status in 1964, at which time an expanded construction began, which was completed in the mid-1970s. A more recent expansion began in 2001 and is still underway. You can watch the progress at **www.nuevacatedraldetijuana.org**. When finished, the renovated cathedral will seat 3,000, with standing room for 14,000. Its hallmark will be a brilliant white obelisk bell tower 25 stories high in front of a large statue of the Virgin of

Guadalupe, Mexico's patron saint. Mass is celebrated Monday through Friday at 8am and 7pm, Saturdays at 7pm, and Sundays at 9am, noon, and 6pm.

A modern symbol of Tijuana, the **Monumental Arch** (also referred to as the Tijuana or Millennium Arch, or Monumental Clock) was constructed to celebrate the millennium and has become a source of local debate as to whether it's loved or hated (its modern architecture leaves some with a bad taste in their mouth, as it sits in a historical district). It's at the mouth of Plaza Santa Cecilia, where Calle 1 meets Avenida Revolución.

Plaza Santa Cecilia, also known as Arguello Square, is Tijuana's oldest plaza; at Calle 1 and Avenida Revolución, near the Tourist Assistance kiosk, it is the only plaza in the city that is on a transverse street from the original city-planning grid. Today it's home to a variety of colorfully painted restaurants and shops, and you'll almost always find a mariachi band playing for tips. At the center of the plaza is a monument to Santa Cecilia, the patron saint of musicians.

SPECTATOR SPORTS

BASEBALL   Enjoy the all-American pastime Mexico-style, at the grand new **Calimax** stadium (© 664/660-9863), Río Eufrates s/n, in the Col. Capistrano neighborhood. For a schedule, visit **www.potrosdetijuana.com**. Tickets range in price from $1 to $2—season packages also are offered—and are available for purchase at the stadium.

BULLFIGHTING   While some insist this spectacle promotes a cruel disregard for animal rights, others esteem it as a richly symbolic drama involving the courage Ernest Hemingway called "grace under pressure." Whatever your opinion, bullfighting has a prominent place in Mexican heritage and is even considered an essential element of the culture in Tijuana. The skill and bravery of matadors is closely linked with cultural ideals regarding machismo, and some of the world's best perform at Tijuana's two stadiums. The season usually runs from May through the first week of October, with events held Sundays at 4:30pm and at other scheduled times. Ticket prices range from $25 to $50 (the premium seats are on the shaded side of the arena) and can be purchased at the bullring or in advance from San Diego's **Five Star Tours** (© 619/232-5049 or 664/622-2203). **El Toreo** stadium (© 664/686-1510; www.bullfights.org; open only during performances) is 3.2km (2 miles) east of downtown on Bulevar Agua Caliente at Avenida Diego Rivera. **Plaza de Toros Monumental,** or Bullring-by-the-Sea (© 664/680-1808; www.plazamonumental.com), is 10km (6 miles) west of downtown on Highway 1-D (before the first toll station); it perches at the edge of both the ocean and the California border. You can take a taxi easily to El Toreo—fares are negotiable, and around $10 one-way from downtown should be fair. You can also negotiate a fare to Bullring-by-the-Sea, which will range anywhere from $12 to $25, depending on the bargaining mood of the taxi driver.

DOG RACING   There's satellite wagering on U.S. horse races at the majestic **Caliente Racetrack,** Bulevar Agua Caliente 12027, 4.8km (3 miles) east of downtown, but these days only greyhounds actually kick up dust at the track. Races are held daily at 7:45pm, and at 1pm on Sunday. General admission is free. For more information, call © 664/682-3110 or 619/231-1910 in San Diego.

SHOPPING

Tijuana's biggest attraction is shopping—ask any of the 44 million people who cross the border each year to do it. They come to take advantage of reasonable prices on a variety of merchandise: terra-cotta and colorfully glazed pottery, woven blankets and serapes, embroidered dresses and sequined sombreros, onyx chess sets, beaded necklaces and bracelets, silver jewelry, leather bags and huarache sandals, rain sticks (bamboo branches filled with pebbles that simulate the patter of raindrops), hammered-tin picture frames, thick drinking glasses, novelty swizzle sticks, Cuban cigars, and Mexican liquors such as Kahlúa and tequila. You're permitted to bring $400 worth of purchases back across the border (sorry, no Cuban cigars allowed), including 1 liter of alcohol or three bottles of wine per person.

When most people think of Tijuana, they picture **Avenida Revolución,** which appears to exist solely for the extraction of dollars from American visitors. Dedicated shoppers quickly discover that most of the curios spilling out onto the sidewalk look alike, despite the determined seller's assurances that their wares are the best in town. Browse for comparison's sake, but for the best souvenir shopping, duck into one of the many *pasajes,* or passageway arcades, where you'll find items of a slightly better quality and merchants willing to bargain. Some of the most enjoyable *pasajes* are on the east side of the street between calles 2 and 5; they also provide a pleasant respite from the quickly irritating tumult of Avenida Revolución.

An alternative is to visit **Sanborn's,** on Avenida Revolución between calles 8 and 9 (© **664/688-1462**), a branch of the Mexico City department store long favored by American travelers. It sells an array of regional folk art and souvenirs, books about Mexico in both Spanish and English, and candies and fresh sweet treats from the bakery—and you can have breakfast in the sunny cafe. It's open daily from 7:30am to 1am.

One of the few places in Tijuana to find better-quality crafts from a variety of Mexican states is **Tolán,** Avenida Revolución between calles 7 and 8 (© **664/688-3637**). In addition to the obligatory selection of standard Avenida Revolución souvenirs, you'll find blue glassware from Guadalajara, glazed pottery from Tlaquepaque, crafts from the Oaxaca countryside, and distinctive tilework from Puebla. Prices at Tolán are fixed, so you shouldn't try to bargain the way you can in some of the smaller shops and informal stands. Same goes for **Casa del Angel** at 1026 Revolución.

If a marketplace atmosphere and spirited bargaining are what you're looking for, head instead to **Mercado de Artesanías** (crafts market), Calle 2 and Avenida Negrete, where over 200 stalls of vendors selling pottery, clayware, clothing, and other crafts from throughout Mexico fill an entire city block.

A more sophisticated selection of Mexican handicrafts is found in the three stores featuring **Mexico Mexico Mexico** products. One of the largest distributors of goods crafted by artisans across Mexico, you'll find a broad selection of quality wares including Talavera ceramics from Puebla, Oaxacan black-clay pottery, Huichol bead art, hand-blown glassware from Tonalá, Day of the Dead curios, *alebrijes* (fantasy animal figurines), and works of art made from *milagros,* small silver religious offerings. Shop locations in Tijuana include **El Campanario,** Av. Revolución 952 (no phone), **El Girasol,** Av. Revolución between 3rd and 4th (© **664/685-8561**), and **H. Arnold,** Av. Revolución 1067 (no phone).

Shopping malls are as common in Tijuana as in any big American city; you shouldn't expect to find typical souvenirs there, but shopping alongside residents and other intrepid visitors is often more fun than feeling like a sitting-duck tourist. One of the biggest, and most convenient, is **Plaza Río Tijuana,** Paseo de los Héroes 96 at Avenida Independencia, Zona Río (© **664/684-0402**), an outdoor plaza anchored by

> **Tips** **Where to Park in Tijuana**
>
> Plaza Río Tijuana has ample free parking and is just across the street from the Cultural Center, where private lots charge $5 to $8 to park. Street parking is available along white curbs—curbs painted red, yellow, or green indicate no-parking zones, as do signs displaying an "E" with a red circle and slash through the center.

several department stores and featuring dozens of specialty shops and casual restaurants. **Plaza Agua Caliente,** Bulevar Agua Caliente 4558, Col. Aviación (© **664/681-7777),** is a more upscale shopping center, and in addition to fine shops and restaurants, it is known for its emphasis on health and beauty, with day spas, gyms, and doctors' offices in abundance here.

Other shopping malls are listed at **www.tijuanaonline.org/english/shopping/ index.htm**.

On the other side of Paseo de los Héroes from Plaza Río Tijuana is **Plaza del Zapato,** a two-story indoor mall filled with only *zapato* (shoe) stores. Though most are made with quality leather rather than synthetics, inferior workmanship ensures they'll likely last only a season or two. But with prices as low as $30, why not indulge?

For a taste of everyday Mexico, visit **Mercado Hidalgo,** 1 block west of Plaza del Zapato at avenidas Sánchez Taboada and Independencia, a busy indoor-outdoor marketplace where vendors display fresh flowers and produce, sacks of dried beans and chiles by the kilo, and a few souvenir crafts (including some excellent piñatas). Morning is the best time to visit the market, and you'll be more comfortable paying with pesos, since most sellers are accustomed to a local crowd.

WHERE TO STAY

When calculating room rates, always remember that hotel rates in Tijuana are subject to a 12% tax.

EXPENSIVE

Camino Real Tijuana 🐾🐾   The Camino Real is Tijuana's newest hotel, with the hallmark architectural style and use of bold colors that define this luxury Mexican hotel chain. It's popular especially with business travelers, and its location in the Zona Río makes it ideal for shopping or cultural excursions to the city. It's also close to the most sophisticated dining and nightlife in Tijuana. Rooms are both elegant and spacious. The sixth floor is dedicated to Camino Real Club Level rooms, which have a private reception, upgraded rooms, and a selection of amenities including complementary continental breakfast buffets and afternoon cocktails and appetizers. The contemporary lobby showcases renowned Mexican artists, and two restaurants offer both a casual and an upscale dining option. There are a variety of packages available, including weekend escape, seasonal bullfight, and honeymoon packages. Rooms, restaurants, and the lobby have been renovated and the gym currently is being renovated.

Paseo de los Héroes 10305, Zona Río, 22320 Tijuana, B.C. © **877/215-3051** in the U.S., or 664/633-4000 in Tijuana. Fax 664/633-4001. www.caminoreal.com/tijuana. 263 units. $175 double; $215 Grand Club rooms, $230–$450 suites. AE, MC, V. Free parking. **Amenities:** 3 restaurants; lobby bar; fitness room; concierge; business center; 24-hr. room service; babysitting; laundry and dry cleaning services. *In room:* A/C, TV, Wi-Fi, minibar, hair dryer, iron, safe.

Grand Hotel Tijuana ⭐ Popular with business travelers, visiting celebrities, and for society events, this hotel has some of the best-maintained public and guest rooms in Tijuana, which helps make up for what it lacks in regional warmth. You can see the hotel's 32-story mirrored twin towers from throughout the surrounding city. Modern and sleek in design, it opened in 1982—at the height of Tijuana's prosperity—under the name Fiesta Americana, a name locals (and many cab drivers) still use. Rooms have spectacular views of the city from the higher floors. The top three floors have been converted into the Grand Club Level, with VIP access, private reception, upgraded rooms, and a selection of amenities including DSL Internet access, fax machines in the room, and complementary continental breakfast buffets and after-noon appetizers and wine. A new Vegas-like lobby gives way to several ballrooms and an airy atrium that serves elegant international cuisine at dinner and weekend brunch. Next to the atrium is a casual Mexican restaurant, beyond which the Vegas resem-blance resumes with an indoor shopping arcade. The hotel offers a golf package for $82 per person—it includes 1 night's lodging with a welcome cocktail and a round of 18 holes (including cart) at the adjacent Tijuana Country Club.

Agua Caliente 4500, 22420 Tijuana, B.C. (P.O. Box BC, Chula Vista, CA 92012). ✆ **866/472-6385** in the U.S., or 664/681-7000 in Tijuana. Fax 664/681-7016. www.grandhoteltij.com.mx. 422 units. $135 double; $195 Grand Club room; $230–$750 suite. AE, MC, V. Free underground parking. **Amenities:** 2 restaurants; lobby bar; heated pool; tennis courts; fitness center; sauna; concierge; tour desk; business center; shopping arcade; 24-hr. room service; laundry and dry cleaning; sports and race book (off-track betting). *In room:* A/C, TV, high-speed Internet access, minibar, hair dryer, iron, safe.

MODERATE

Hacienda del Mar ⭐ If you prefer to keep a little distance between you and the hustle and bustle of downtown Tijuana, this clean, comfortable hotel in Tijuana's beach zone is an excellent value. It's just 15 minutes from the action in downtown TJ and is almost adjacent to the seaside bullring. Rooms, with carpeting, are clean and comfortable. Two suites have private Jacuzzis. The staff at this privately owned hotel is bilingual and very helpful. Special weekly rates are offered for families and patients of local clinics.

Paseo Playas 116, 22320 Playas de Tijuana, B.C. ✆ **888/675-2927** in the U.S., or 664/630-8603 to -06 in Tijuana. Fax 664/630-8603. www.ventanarosahotels.com. 60 units. $59–$72 double; $97–$110 junior suite. MC, V. Free secured parking. **Amenities:** Restaurant; bar; heated pool; concierge; laundry and dry cleaning. *In room:* A/C, TV, safe, nonsmoking rooms.

Hotel Lucerna ⭐ Once the most chic hotel in Tijuana, Lucerna now feels slightly worn, but the place still has personality. The flavor here is Mexican colonial—wrought-iron railings and chandeliers, rough-hewn heavy wood furniture, brocade wallpaper, and traditional tiles. The hotel is in the Zona Río, away from the noise and congestion of downtown, so a quiet night's sleep is easily attainable, and it's just 2 blocks from the Plaza Río Tijuana shopping center (see above). All the rooms in this five-story hotel have balconies or patios but are otherwise unremarkable. Sunday brunch is served outdoors by the swimming pool. The staff is friendly and attentive.

Av. Paseo de los Héroes 10902, Zona Río, Tijuana, B.C. ✆ **800/582-3762** in the U.S., or 664/633-3900. 168 units. $190 double; $360 suite. AE, MC, V. **Amenities:** 2 restaurants; 2 bars; swimming pool; fitness center; tour desk; car rental; airport transfers; business center; room service; laundry service. *In room:* A/C, satellite TV, high-speed Internet access, coffeemaker, hair dryer, iron, safe.

Residence Inn by Marriott Real del Mar ⭐⭐ If being in the center of down-town is a bit too much Tijuana for you, this hotel offers a location that is near enough to the city's action while also being in its own tranquil setting, complete with golf course. Real del Mar is a resort and residential development about 16km (10 miles) south of Tijuana, across the highway from the ocean. In addition to golf, it has an equestrian center, spa, and shopping. The Marriott brand is, of course, familiar to American travelers, and you can expect the same standards of quality and comforts in this one, though it's more upscale than most Residence Inns, and you have your choice of two room categories (studios or suites). All suites offer ocean views, fireplaces, living rooms, and small but complete kitchens—more closely resembling small apartments than hotel rooms. These units are ideal for families or extended stays in the area and are worth the splurge. Two restaurants are available for dining: El Patio Brasserie overlooks the golf course and is open for breakfast and lunch, while Rincon de San Roman, under the direction of a Paris-educated chef, serves Continental cuisine for lunch and dinner.

Carretera Escénica Tijuana-Ensenada Km 19.5, 22605 Tijuana, B.C. ℭ 800/803-6038 in the U.S., or 664/631-3670. Fax 664/631-3677. www.realdelmar.com.mx. 75 units. $119–$129 double or studio; $149–$159 suite. Rate includes wine and beer in the evening and breakfast in the morning. Golf and spa packages available. Complimentary on-site parking. Pets are welcome for a $75 one-time sanitation fee. AE, MC, V. **Amenities:** Pool; tennis court; exercise room; spa; tour desk; room service; babysitting; laundry service; grocery shopping service. *In room:* A/C, TV, high-speed Internet access, kitchen, fridge, microwave, coffeemaker, hair dryer, iron.

WHERE TO DINE
EXPENSIVE

Cien Años ★★★ MEXICAN   This is an elegant and gracious Zona Río restaurant offering artfully blended traditional Mexican flavors (tamarind, poblano chile, mango) in modern presentations. Try chiles rellenos stuffed with shrimp in lobster sauce, delicate *calabaza* (squash-blossom) soup, or chipotle oysters. The most adventurous diners can sample garlicky ant eggs or buttery *guisanos* (cactus worms). If you're interested in true haute cuisine, the buzz around Tijuana is all about this place.

Calle José María Velasco 1407. ℭ 888/534-6088 in the U.S., or 664/634-3039. Main courses $18–$30. MC, V. Sun–Fri 8am–11pm; Sat 8am–midnight.

La Cantina de los Remedios MEXICAN   This is one of Tijuana's most festive atmospheres, wildly popular with both Mexicans and Americans alike for its typical Mexican cuisine and courtyard atmosphere. Another highlight is its all-inclusive menu option, which has made it a hit in seven other cities throughout Mexico. For one price, guests can enjoy an appetizer, soup or salad, main course, dessert, and a cocktail. Here, the drink menu is extensive, inspiring the name *los remedios,* or the remedies.

Av. Diego Rivera 19 718, Zona del Río. ℭ 664/634-3065. All-inclusive meal $18–$137. MC, V. Mon–Thurs 1pm–1am; Fri–Sat 1pm–2am; Sun 1–10pm.

MODERATE
Hard Rock Cafe AMERICAN/MEXICAN   Had an overload of Mexican culture? Looking for a place with all the familiar comforts of home? Then head for the Tijuana branch of this ubiquitous watering hole, which promises nothing exotic; it serves the standard Hard Rock chain menu, which admittedly features an outstanding hamburger, in the regulation Hard Rock setting (dark, clubby, walls filled with rock-'n'-roll memorabilia). While the restaurant's street presence is more subdued than most Hard Rock locations, you'll still spot the trademark Caddie emerging from above the door. Prices are in line with what you'd see in the U.S.—and therefore no bargain in competitive Tijuana.

Av. Revolución 520 (near Calle 1), Zona Centro. ℭ 664/685-0206. Menu items $5–$10. AE, MC, V. Daily 11am–2am.

Finds   A Northern Baja Spa Sanctuary

One of Mexico's best-known spas is in northern Baja, just 58km (36 miles) south of San Diego. The **Rancho La Puerta** ✦✦, opened in 1940 as a "health camp," was among the pioneers of the modern spa and fitness movement. The location was chosen for its perfect climate. The rates at the time were $18 a week—but you had to bring your own tent.

Much has changed. Today, the ranch occupies 1,200 hectares (2,964 acres) of lush oasis surrounded by pristine countryside, which includes a 2.5-hectare (6-acre) organic garden and La Cocina Que Canta, a spa-cuisine cooking school. Cottages can accommodate up to 150 guests per week, and the ranch has a staff of almost 400. Each cottage has its own patio garden and is decorated with Mexican folk art. Inside the rooms are spacious living-room-sized seating areas, desks, CD players, hair dryers, robes, and safes, and most rooms have fireplaces.

Three swimming pools, four tennis courts, five hot tubs, saunas, steam rooms, and 11 gyms for aerobic and restorative classes are only a part of the facilities. Separate men's and women's health centers offer the full range of spa services. Hiking trails surround the resort, and there's even a labyrinth that is a full-size replica of the ancient labyrinth found in Chartres Cathedral, for moving meditation.

There are also several lounges and shared spaces, including the library, with thousands of books to browse and read, an evening movie lounge, recreation room, and for those who can't conceive of totally disconnecting, the E-center, with 24-hour access to e-mail and Internet.

Rancho La Puerta runs weeklong programs—Saturday through Saturday—emphasizing a mind/body/spirit philosophy, and certain weeks throughout the year are geared specifically to one topic. Specialty Week themes range from couples to Pilates and dance to meditation. Prices begin at $2,690 for the week most of the year, and at $2,780 for the week from March through May. Included in the rates are all classes, meals, evening programs, and use of facilities. Personal spa services are an extra charge. You may be able to book shorter stays (3 nights or more); and rates may be prorated on a nightly basis.

For reservations or to request a brochure, visit **www.rancholapuerta.com**; call **800/443-7565** in the U.S., or fax 858/764-5500. American Express, Master-Card, and Visa are accepted.

INEXPENSIVE

Cafe La Especial MEXICAN   Tucked away in a shopping *pasaje* at the bottom of some stairs (turn in at the taco stand of the same name), this restaurant is a well-known shopper's refuge and purveyor of home-style Mexican cooking at reasonable (though not dirt-cheap) prices. The gruff, efficient waitstaff carry out platter after platter of *carne asada* served with fresh tortillas, beans, and rice—it's La Especial's most popular item. Traditional dishes like tacos, enchiladas, and burritos round out the menu, augmented by frosty-cold Mexican beers. Park in the adjacent El Gigante lot.

Av. Revolución 718 (between calles 3 and 4), Zona Centro. © 664/685-6654. Menu items $4–$12. MC, V. Daily 9am–10pm.

Carnitas Uruapán 🐷🐷 MEXICAN   *Carnitas*—marinated pork roasted on a spit till falling-apart tender, then served in chunks with tortillas, salsa, cilantro, guacamole, and onions—is a beloved dish in Mexico and the main attraction at Carnitas Uruapán. It serves the meat by the kilo (or portion thereof) at long, communal wooden tables to a crowd of mostly locals. A half-kilo of carnitas is plenty for two people and costs around $12, including beans and that impressive array of condiments. It's a casual feast without compare, but vegetarians need not apply. This branch is in the fashionable Zona Río and serves seafood as well.

Bulevar Díaz Ordaz 12650 (across from Plaza Patria), La Mesa. © 664/681-6181. Menu items $2.50–$8. No credit cards. Sun–Thurs 8am–midnight; Fri–Sat 8am–2am.

TIJUANA AFTER DARK

Avenida Revolución is the center of the city's nightlife; many compare it with Bourbon Street in New Orleans during Mardi Gras—except here it's a regular occurrence, not a once-a-year blowout.

Zona Río and Plaza Fiesta are more geared toward late-night dining and dance clubbing than tequila swilling and bar hopping. Although the nightlife scene changes regularly, perhaps the most popular dance club is **Baby Rock,** 1482 Diego Rivera, Zona Río (© **664/634-2404**), a cousin to Acapulco's lively Baby O, which features everything from Latin rock to rap. It's near the Guadalajara Grill restaurant. It's open 9pm to 3am, with a cover charge of $12 on Saturdays.

Also popular in Tijuana are sports bars, featuring wagering on events from all over the United States as well as races from Tijuana's Caliente track. The most popular of these bars cluster in the **Pueblo Amigo** and **Vía Oriente** areas and around **Plaza Río Tijuana** in the Zona Río, a center designed to resemble a colonial Mexican village. Also in Zona Río is the chic club **Karma** (Paseo de los Héroes 954713; © **664/ 900-6063;** Wed–Sat 9pm–3am). Just beyond Zona Río you'll find **Tangaloo** (Av. Monterrey 3215; © **664/681-8091;** www.tangaloo.com; Thurs–Sun 9pm–4am), a hip club featuring DJs spinning electronic dance music, with a changing theme each Saturday night. Two of the town's hottest clubs, which are open until 4 or 5am on the weekends, **Rodeo de Media Noche** (© **664/682-4967;** cover $8) and **Señor Frogs** (© **664/682-4964;** no cover), are in Pueblo Amigo Plaza, which is just off of Paseo Tijuana. Pueblo Amigo Plaza is less than 3km (2 miles) from the border, a short taxi ride or—during daylight hours—a pleasant walk.

2 Rosarito Beach & Beyond: Baja's First Beach Resorts

55km (34 miles) S of San Diego; 29km (18 miles) S of Tijuana

Just a 20-minute drive south of Tijuana and a complete departure in ambience, Rosarito Beach is a tranquil, friendly beach town. It also gained early renown during the U.S. Prohibition, when the elegant Rosarito Beach Hotel catered to Hollywood stars. This classic structure still welcomes numerous guests, despite the fact that its opulence has lost some luster. Hollywood has likewise played a major part in Rosarito's recent renaissance—it was the location for the soundstage and filming of the Academy Award–winning *Titanic*. The Titanic Expo museum at **Foxploration!** here continues to draw fans of the film.

Two roads run between Tijuana and Ensenada (the largest and third-largest cities in Baja)—the scenic, coast-hugging toll road (marked CUOTA, or 1-D) and the free but slower-going public road (marked LIBRE, or 1). We strongly recommend starting out on the toll road (pay at each *caseta*, or toll booth; dollars are accepted and they give U.S. change), but use the free road along Rosarito Beach if you'd like to easily pull on and off the road to shop or look at the view. The beaches between Tijuana and Rosarito are also known for excellent surf breaks.

If you're not driving, you can take **Mexicoach** (© 664/685-1440; www.mexicoach. com) from San Ysidro to Rosarito, leaving your car on the U.S. side of the border, for $14 each way. Alternatively, board the bus shuttle service at the Border Station Parking (next to the San Diego Factory Outlet Center) or from the Trolley's last stop at the border (see "Getting There & Departing" on p. 149), and it will take you to the Tijuana Tourist Terminal, Av. Revolución, between calles 6 and 7, where you can continue on to Rosarito. The cost from the Tijuana Tourist Terminal to Rosarito is $9 each way. The Tijuana Tourist Terminal is open daily from 5:30am to 9pm. Mexicoach departs from San Ysidro to Tijuana every 30 minutes from 8am to 9pm and from Tijuana to Rosarito every 2 hours from 7am to 7pm, 365 days per year. Returns to the border leave from the same terminal.

VISITOR INFORMATION   Try **Baja California Tourism Information** (© 800/ 522-1516 in California, Arizona, or Nevada; 800/225-2786 in the rest of the U.S. and Canada, or 619/298-4105 in San Diego; www.baja.gob.mx). This office provides advice and makes hotel reservations throughout Baja California. You can also contact the local **Secretaria de Turísmo,** Carretera Libre Tijuana-Ensenada Km 28 (© 800/ 962-2252 in the U.S., 01-800/025-6288 toll-free in Mexico; www.rosarito.org). The office is open Monday through Friday from 8am to 8pm, and Saturday and Sunday from 9am to 1pm. Special **tourist aid** service is available by calling **078** from any phone.

SHOPPING

The dozen or so blocks north of the Rosarito Beach Hotel abound with the stores typical in Mexican border towns; curio shops, cigar and *licores* (liquor) stores, and *farmacias* (where drugs like Viagra, Retin-A, Prozac, and many more are available at low cost and without a prescription). Rosarito has also become a center for carved furnishings—plentiful downtown along Bulevar Benito Juárez—and pottery, best purchased at stands along the old highway, south of town. A reliable but more expensive furniture shop is **Casa Neri** (formerly Casa La Carreta), Km 29.5, on the old road south of Rosarito (© 661/612-2326; www.casaneri.com), where you can see plentiful examples of the best workmanship—chests, tables, chairs, headboards, cabinets, and cradles—and 35 years of family-run custom furniture.

The **Casa Torres Museum Store** (at the Rosarito Beach Hotel shopping center; © 661/612-1008) has been around since 1969 selling museum-quality handicrafts from throughout Mexico. Find carved wooden masks, beaded Huichol art, Day of the Dead curios, and more. An adjoining duty-free store sells perfumes, liquors, and cosmetics.

WHERE TO STAY

In the event you go to Rosarito Beach to drink and dance by night and to drink and sunbathe by day, plan to stay at the Festival Plaza Hotel (© 888/295-9669; www. festivalplazahotel.com). If a lobby that appears as though it could be hosed down gives

Rosarito Beach

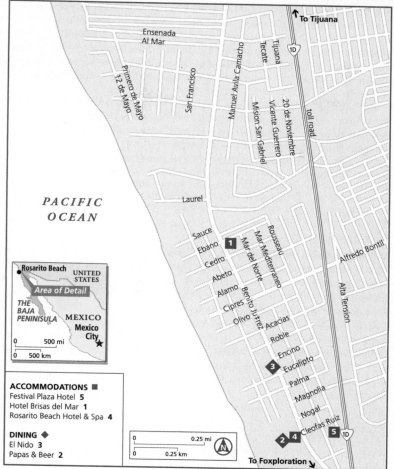

ACCOMMODATIONS ■
Festival Plaza Hotel **5**
Hotel Brisas del Mar **1**
Rosarito Beach Hotel & Spa **4**

DINING ◆
El Nido **3**
Papas & Beer **2**

any indication of party-ready quotient, Festival Plaza is off the charts. If you're look-ing for something more subdued, see the following recommendations.

Hotel Brisas del Mar *Value*   This clean, friendly hotel is close to everything in Rosarito and just a 3-minute walk to the beach. It's also a good value. The rooms in this two-story hotel are basic, but highlights of the hotel are its semichic lounge-style bar and the friendly, attentive staff. If you don't have to be on the beach, this is the best bet in town.

Bulevar Benito Juárez 22, 22710 Playas de Rosarito, B.C. ⓒ **888/871-3605** in the U.S., or 661/612-2546. www.ventanarosahotels.com. 71 units. $75–$115 double. MC, V. Free secured parking. **Amenities:** Restaurant; bar; heated pool and a separate kids' pool; heated Jacuzzi; laundry service. *In room:* A/C, TV, safe.

Rosarito Beach Hotel & Spa *Value*   Although this once-glamorous resort has been holding steady since its heyday, the vestiges of vacationing movie stars, a casino, and 1920s elegance have been all but eclipsed by the glaring nighttime neon and party mania that currently define the former retreat. Despite the resort's changed personality, unique features of artistic construction and lavish decoration remain, setting it apart from the rest along a wide stretch of a family-friendly beach. The hotel draws a mixed crowd. The stately onsite home of the original owners has been transformed into the full-service Casa Playa Spa, where massages and other treatments cost as much as they do in the U.S.

You'll pay more for an ocean view, and more for the newer, air-conditioned rooms in the tower; the older rooms in the poolside building may only have ceiling fans, but they prevail in the character department, with hand-painted trim and original tile. Although the rooms are slightly worn, they are large and comfortable.

Bulevar Benito Juárez, Zona Centro, 22710 Rosarito, B.C. (P.O. Box 430145, San Diego, CA 92143). Ⓒ **800/343-8582** or 1-866/ROSARITO in the U.S., or 661/612-0144. Fax 661/612-1125. www.rosaritohotel.com. 280 units. $132–$216 double Fri–Sat, $97–$132 double Sun–Thurs; $223–258 suite Fri–Sat, $146–$181 suite Sun–Thurs. 2 children under 12 stay free in parent's room. Packages available. MC, V. Free parking. **Amenities:** 2 restaurants; bar; 2 swimming pools; racquetball and tennis courts; playground; room service. *In room:* A/C (in some rooms), TV, high-speed Internet (in some rooms), minifridge (in some rooms).

WHERE TO DINE

While in Rosarito, you may want to try **Chabert's** (Continental) or the more casual **Azteca Restaurant** (Mexican), both in the Rosarito Beach Hotel. Early risers out for a stroll can enjoy fresh, steaming-hot tamales (with a variety of stuffings), a traditional Mexican breakfast treat sold from sidewalk carts for around 50¢ each.

El Nido 🐸🐸 MEXICAN/STEAKS   One of the first eateries in Rosarito, El Nido remains popular with visitors unimpressed by the flashier, neon-lit joints that pop up to please the college-age set. The setting here is Western frontier, complete with rustic candles and rusting wagon wheels; sit outside in the enclosed patio or opt for the dark, cozy interior warmed by a large fireplace and open grill. The mesquite fire is constantly stoked to prepare the grilled steaks and seafood that are El Nido's specialty; the menu also includes free-range (and superfresh) quail and venison from the owner's ranch in the nearby wine country. Meals are reasonably priced and generous, including hearty bean soup, American-style green salad, baked potatoes, and all the fresh tortillas and zesty salsa you can eat.

Bulevar Benito Juárez 67. Ⓒ **661/612-1430.** Main courses $6–$23. No credit cards. Daily 8am–11pm.

ROSARITO BEACH AFTER DARK

Because the legal drinking age in Baja is 18, the under-21 crowd from Southern California tends to flock across the border on Friday and Saturday nights. The most popular spot in town is **Papas & Beer** (Ⓒ **661/612-0444;** www.papasandbeer.com) on Rosarito Beach. It's a relaxed, bikini-and-board-shorts type club on the beach with blaring hip-hop music and umbrellas in the sand, just a block north of the Rosarito Beach Hotel. Even for those young in spirit only, it's great fun, with open-air tables and a bar surrounding a sand volleyball court. It's open daily all year long from 11am to 3am. Or choose from several other adjacent clubs, each offering booming music, spirited dancing, and all-night-long energy. Cover charges vary depending on the season, the crowd, and the mood of the staff. The **Salon Méxicano** (Ⓒ **661/612-0144**), in the Rosarito Beach Hotel, attracts a slightly more mature crowd, with a Mexican fiesta every Friday and Saturday night. The Fiesta Mexicana features folkloric dance performances, mariachis, and a buffet-style Mexican dinner.

3 Ensenada: Port of Call ⭐

135km (84 miles) S of San Diego; 110km (68 miles) S of Tijuana

It's almost as if the air gets lighter once you roll into Ensenada. A far cry from the fiesta-drenched Tijuana and Rosarito, Ensenada just feels different: more relaxed, more genuine. This classic town, situated on a rocky bay flanked by sheltering mountains and a busy port, has an unmistakable sincerity. Sure, many of the locals speak perfect English and frequently visit the U.S., but Ensenada has more Mexican charm than any of its neighbors to the north and, in fact, evokes the dual culture of a border town without the chaos. About 40 minutes from Rosarito, it's the kind of place that loves a celebration. Almost anytime you choose to visit, the city is festive—be it for a bicycle race or a seafood festival.

One of Mexico's principal ports of call, Ensenada welcomes half a million visitors a year who are attracted to its beaches, excellent sportfishing, nearby wineries, and surrounding natural attractions.

GETTING THERE   After passing through the final tollbooth, Highway 1-D curves sharply toward downtown Ensenada. Watch out for brutal metal speed bumps slowing traffic into town—they're far less forgiving on the average chassis than those in the U.S.

VISITOR INFORMATION   The **Tourist and Convention Bureau booth** (© **800/310-9687** in the U.S., or 646/178-8588 or 646/178-8578) is at the western entrance to town, where the waterfront-hugging Bulevar Lázaro Cárdenas—also known as Bulevar Costero—curves away to the right. The office is open daily from 9am till dusk and can provide a downtown map, directions to major nearby sites, and information on special events throughout the city. As in most of the commonly visited areas of Baja, one or more employees speak English fluently. Taxis park along the bustling López Mateos, or Avenida Primera (First Ave.).

EXPLORING ENSENADA

Ensenada is technically a "border town," but part of its appeal is its multilayered vitality born out of being concerned with much more than tourism. The bustling port consumes the entire waterfront—beach access is north or south of town—and the Pacific fishing trade and agriculture in the fertile valleys surrounding the city dominate the economy. Try not to leave Ensenada without getting a taste of its true personality; for example, stop by the indoor-outdoor fish market at the northernmost corner of the harbor where each day, from early morning to midday, merchants and housewives gather to assess the day's catch—tuna, marlin, snapper, plus many other varieties of fish and piles of shrimp from the morning's haul.

Ensenada is the perfect place to sample the culinary craze of Baja California, the Baja fish taco. Several stands prepare this local treat; strips of freshly caught fish are battered and deep fried, then wrapped in corn tortillas and topped with shredded cabbage, cilantro, salsa, and various other condiments. Although every local has a different opinion on the best fish taco in town, play it safe by going to the stands swarmed by locals. Fish tacos are delicious, cheap, and filling, and it's easy to see why surf bums and collegiate vacationers consider them a Baja staple.

Avenida Lopez Mateos is the hub of tourist activity in the city, and for a nice espresso, a "rocky road" mocha, or a quick e-mail check, head to one of Ensenada's first Internet cafes, **Uncle Sam's Espresso Bar,** where $1.50 gets you a shot of espresso and $2 gets you an hour of Internet access. The understated owner, Ricardo, and his regulars will tell you Ensenada's real stories if you ask, and they'll also hook you up with affordable Internet phone lines to the U.S.

Elsewhere in town, visit the **Bodegas de Santo Tomás Winery,** Av. Miramar 666 at Calle 7 (© **646/178-2509;** www.santo-tomas.com). While most visitors to Mexico are quite content quaffing endless quantities of cheap cerveza, even part-time oenophiles should pay a visit to this historic winery—the second oldest in Mexico (after Casa Madero in Coahuila). It uses old-fashioned methods of processing grapes, first cultivated from Spanish varietals in 1888, in the lush Santo Tomás Valley, where a Dominican mission of the same name was founded almost a century earlier. A 45-minute tour introduces you to low-tech processing machinery; hand-hammered wood casks; and cool, damp stone aging rooms. It culminates in an invitation to sample several Santo Tomás vintages, including an international-medal-winning cabernet and delightfully crisp sparkling blanc de blanc. The wood-paneled, churchlike tasting room is adorned with paintings of mischievous altar boys being scolded by stern friars for pilfering wine or ruining precious grapes. Anyone used to the pretentious, assembly-line ambience of trendier wine regions will relish the friendly welcome and informative tour presented here. Tours in English run every hour from 9am to 5pm Monday through Saturday and from 10am to 4pm Sunday. The tour is free, and if you wish to follow it up with a tasting, $5 gets you a sampling of six young or low-priced wines, and the $10 option includes six older or high-priced wines and two reserves.

Wines for sale cost $6.50 to $26 a bottle. *Note:* Most of the winery's product is exported for the European market.

Be sure to poke around Santo Tomás a bit after your tour concludes. The little modern machinery installed here freed up a cavernous space now used for monthly jazz concerts, and a former aging room has been transformed into La Embotelladora Vieja (The Old Aging Room) restaurant (see "Where to Dine," later). Across the street stands La Esquina de Bodegas (The Corner Wine Cellar), former aging rooms for Santo Tomás: The industrial-style building now functions as a gallery showcasing local art, with a skylit bookstore on the second level and a small cafe (punctuated by giant copper distillation vats) in the rear.

Ensenada's primary cultural center is the **Centro Cívico, Social, y Cultura,** Bulevar Lázaro Cárdenas at Avenida Club Rotario. The impressive Mediterranean building was formerly Riviera del Pacífico, a glamorous 1930s bayfront casino and resort frequented by Hollywood's elite. Tiles in the lobby commemorate "Visitantes Distinguidos 1930–1940," including Marion Davies, William Randolph Hearst, Lana Turner, Myrna Loy, and Jack Dempsey. Now used by the Rotary Club as offices and for cultural and social events, the main building is open to the public. Elegant hallways and ballrooms evoke bygone elegance, and every wall and alcove glows with original murals depicting Mexico's colorful history. Lush formal gardens span the front of the building, and there's a small art gallery on one side. Through the lobby, facing an inner courtyard, is Bar Andaluz, which is open to the public sporadically. It's an intimate, dark-wood place where you can just imagine someone like Papa Hemingway holding cocktail-hour court beneath that colorful toreador mural.

A NEARBY ATTRACTION

South of the city, a 45-minute drive along the rural Punta Banda peninsula, is one of Ensenada's major attractions: **La Bufadora,** a natural sea spout in the rocks. With each incoming wave, water is forced upward through the rock, creating a geyser whose loud

Ensenada

UNITED STATES
Ensenada
Area of Detail
THE BAJA PENINSULA
MEXICO
Mexico City

ACCOMMODATIONS ■
Estero Beach Resort **13**
Las Rosas Resort & Spa **1**

DINING ◆
El Charro **4**
El Rey Sol **11**
Hussong's Cantina **2**
La Embottelladora Vieja **6**
Manzanilla **10**
Papas & Beer **3**
Sanos **7**
Uncle Sam's Espresso Bar **8**

ATTRACTIONS ●
Bodegas de Santo Tomás Winery **5**
Centro Cívico, Social y Cultural **12**
Los Castillo jewelry store **9**

grunt gave the phenomenon its name (*la bufadora* means "buffalo snort"). Local fishermen who ply these waters have a much more lyrical explanation for this roaring blowhole. According to local legend, a mother gray whale and her calf were just beginning their migration from the safety of Baja's San Ignacio lagoon to Alaska. As they rounded Punta Banda, the curious calf squeezed into a sea cave, only to be trapped. The groan that this 21m-high (70-ft.) blowhole makes every time it erupts is the sound of the stranded calf still crying for his mother, and the tremendous spray is his spout.

From downtown Ensenada, take Avenida Reforma south (Carretera Transpeninsular) to Highway 23 west. It's a long, meandering drive through a semi-swamplike area untouched by development; look for grazing animals, bait shops, and fishermen's shacks along the way. La Bufadora is at the end of the road, and once parked ($2 per car in crude dirt lots), you must walk downhill to the viewing platform, at the end of a 540m (1,771-ft.) pathway lined with souvenir stands. In addition to running a gauntlet of determined vendors featuring the usual wares, visitors can avail themselves of inexpensive snacks at the sole restaurant there, including tasty fish tacos. Visitation is enormous, but longstanding plans to pave the dirt parking lots and build permanent restaurants and shops have yet to become a reality.

For a guided walking tour of downtown Ensenada, shopping tours, or tours to the wine country, you can also contact **Jatay Tours** (© **646/172-2246** or 646/107-4373).

SPORTS & OUTDOOR ACTIVITIES

Ensenada is home to a thriving adventure subculture: Off-road racers, climbers, surfers, kayakers, and more flock to Ensenada in search of their adrenaline fix.

FISHING Ensenada, which bills itself as "the yellowtail capital of the world," draws sportfishermen eager to venture out from the beautiful Bahía de Todos Santos (Bay of All Saints) in search of the Pacific's albacore, halibut, marlin, rockfish, and sea bass. A wooden boardwalk parallel to Bulevar Lázaro Cárdenas (Costero) near the northern entrance to town provides access to the sportfishing piers and their charter-boat operators. Open-party boats leave early, often by 7am, and charge around $35 per person, plus an additional fee (around $5) for the mandatory fishing license. Nonfishing passengers must, by law, also be licensed. Those disinclined to comparison shop the boats can make advance arrangements with San Diego–based **Baja California Tours** (© **800/336-5454** or 858/454-7166; www.bajaspecials.com). In addition to daily fishing excursions, it offers 1- to 3-night packages including hotel, fishing, some meals, and transportation from San Diego.

HIKING Ensenada is the gateway city to the **Parque Nacional Constitución de 1857.** On the spine of the Sierra de Juárez, the park was once a heavily used mining area, but most of the mines are now defunct. In contrast to the dry and sometimes desolate surroundings of much of the northern peninsula, the 5,000-hectare (12,350-acre) forest preserve averages about 1,200m (3,936 ft.) in altitude and is covered in places with pine forests. The most idiosyncratic thing, however, is the sight of a good-size lake in an alpine setting (the lake often is dry). The park has no developed trails other than a 10km (6.2-mile) one that circumnavigates the lake, Laguna Hanson, but there are endless opportunities for blazing your own. To get to the park, take Highway 3 south from Ensenada and exit at the graded dirt access road at Km 55. The park entrance road (35km/22 miles to the park entrance) is gravel and generally well maintained but can be really rough after a rainy year. If the entrance is staffed, you'll be asked for a modest entrance fee. For more information, contact the Baja California National Parks Service at © **686/554-5470** or pnconstitucion@conanp.gob.mx.

The **Parque Nacional Sierra San Pedro Mártir** is to Baja California what Yosemite is to Alta California. Almost 72,000 hectares (177,840 acres) of the highest mountains on the peninsula have been preserved here. The highest, Picacho del Diablo (Devil's Peak), rises to 3,095m (10,154 ft.) and draws hikers and backpackers eager to scale its two-pronged peak about 80 miles south of Ensenada. Views from the summit encompass both oceans and an immense stretch of land. Best of all, it's virtually unvisited, something that sets it apart from the normal national park experience in Los Estados Unidos. As such, consider taking a guide. **California Alpine Guides** (© **877/686-2546;** www.californiaalpineguides.com), out of Mammoth Lakes, California, is an adventure-tour operator with guides who know what they're doing in the unmarked Baja desert wilderness.

Farther south on Carretera Transpeninsular from Ensenada, you'll come to a signed turnoff for the park at Km 140, soon after you pass the little town of Colonet. The sign also says OBSERVATORIO. Fill up with gas in Colonet—there is no more until you exit this way again—and reset your trip odometer at the turnoff. In between, it's entirely possible to put on a gas-guzzling 242km (150 miles) of rugged driving. It's 76km (47 miles) to the park entrance.

You'll find a high alpine realm of flower-speckled meadows, soaring granite peaks, and year-round creeks. Official trails are few and far between, so wander at your own risk, but anyone who's good with a map and compass can have a great time hiking. Cow trails (yes, cows in a national park) are numerous. Four year-round creeks drain the park and make great destinations. Picacho del Diablo is a difficult but rewarding overnight hike and long scramble. Always remember that you're in one of the most rugged and remote places in all of Baja, and with the lack of marked trails, it's quite likely that if you get lost or hurt, nobody will come looking for you.

For other adventure tours in the region, contact **Expediciones de Turismo Ecológico y de Aventura,** Bulevar Costero 1094–14, Centro (© **646/178-3704;** www.mexonline.com/ecotur.htm), which runs hiking, mountain-bike, ATV, and other adventure tours in the region.

SEA KAYAKING The rocky coastline of Punta Banda is a favorite first trip for beginning ocean kayakers due to its several secluded beaches, sea caves, and terrific scenery. Many kayakers use La Bufadora as a launching point to head out to the Todos Santos Islands. It's about 11km (7 miles) from La Bufadora to the southern and larger of the two islands. The first 4.8km (3 miles) follow a rocky coast to the tip of Punta Banda. From here you'll need to size up the wind, the waves, and the fog. If the coast is clear, take a compass and begin the 6km (4-mile) open-water crossing. Bring water and camping gear to spend a night on the pristine island. **Dale's La Bufadora Dive Shop** (© **646/154-2092**) has kayak rentals and is open weekends or by prior reservation. **Expediciones de Turismo Ecológico y de Aventura,** Bulevar Costero 1094–14, Centro (© **646/178-3704;** www.mexonline.com/ecotur.htm), offers guided kayak trips, including a full kayak expedition through the Bay of Los Angeles.

SCUBA DIVING & SNORKELING La Bufadora is a great dive spot with thick kelp and wonderful sea life. Get underwater and zoom through lovely kelp beds and rugged rock formations covered in strawberry anemones and gypsy shawl nudibranchs. You may also spot spiny lobsters and numerous large fish. It's possible to swim right over to the blowhole (see "A Nearby Attraction," above), but use caution in this area—you don't want to end up like that mythical whale calf. **Dale's La Bufadora Dive Shop** (© **646/154-2092**) is onshore at the best entry point. The staff will set you up with fills (for air tanks) and advice.

Several dive shops in Ensenada, including **Almar,** Av. Macheros 149 (© **646/178-3013;** www.almardiveshop.com), will arrange boat dives to the Todos Santos islands, which sit at the outer edge of Todos Santos Bay. They also dive at Punta Banda, La Bufadora, San Miguel reef, and local fish camps. The diving here is similar to the diving at Catalina or the other California Channel Islands—lots of fish, big kelp, urchins, and jagged underwater rock formations. The visibility varies widely depending on the swell. It's $120 for a two-tank dive, with a minimum of five people.

SURFING   Only the best and boldest surfers challenge the waves off Islas de Todos Santos, two islands about 19km (12 miles) west of Ensenada, considered to be some of the best surf on the coast. Waves at the famous Killers break can reach 9m (30 ft.) in winter, and surfers must hire a *panga* to take them to the waves. You'll find gentler but still challenging waves at San Miguel and Salsipuedes. For local surf reports and gear rental, visit the **San Miguel Surf Shop,** Avenida López Mateos between Gastelum and Miramar (© **646/178-1007**). Longboards and shortboards rent for $25 a day, and for $5 extra, you get a wetsuit.

SHOPPING

Ensenada's slightly more refined equivalent of Tijuana's Avenida Revolución is the crowded Avenida López Mateos (or Av. Primera), which runs roughly parallel to Bulevar Lázaro Cárdenas (Costero); the highest concentration of shops and restaurants is between avenidas Ruiz and Castillo. Beggars fill this street, and sellers are less likely to bargain here than in Tijuana—many of the merchandise is of much higher quality than in the north, and the shopkeepers of lesser stores are used to gullible cruise-ship buyers in Ensenada. Compared to Tijuana, there is more authentic Mexican art- and craftwork in Ensenada, pieces imported from rural states and villages where different skills are traditionally practiced. Off the highway on the way into Ensenada is the can't-miss **Art & Stuff** in El Sauzal (© **949/202-5321** in the U.S., or 646/175-8859; Km 103 Carretera Tijuana-Ensenada). This unpretentious and eclectic gallery has a collection worthy of boastfulness and high prices, but the owner is endearingly humble. Local artist Señora Q is the showstopper here with her whimsical interpretations that hint at magical realism on found objects, canvases, and in sculptures.

For jewelry and fine silver adornments, nothing compares to **Los Castillo,** five specialty stores along Avenida Lopez Mateos (© **646/156-5274;** www.loscastillosilver.com). Owned for 39 years by the lovely Ensenada-raised jewelry designer Margarita MacFarland and operated by her gracious son and daughters, Los Castillo is the official outpost of Castillo family creations from Taxco, Mexico. For the uninitiated, the Castillos are some of Mexico's most renowned silver artisans and the patriarch, Antonio Castillo, educated Margarita MacFarland in the art of jewelry design. The elegant work of Emilia Castillo, Antonio's daughter, combines intricate sterling silver designs upon pristine porcelain to create original works of art on fine china, which also can be found at Neiman Marcus in the U.S. Emilia's brother, Wolmar Castillo, creates ornate sterling silver serving pieces and jewelry that can't be found anywhere else. If you've come to Ensenada to shop, Los Castillo should be at the tip-top of your list. A few doors down from Los Castillo, and at the opposite end of the spectrum, **Colores de Mexico** sells designer look-alike bags made of leather. For hand-crafted furnishings, **Fausto Polanco** (© **646/174-0336;** www.faustopolanco.com.mx), at Lopez Mateos and Castillo, sells fine hacienda-style furnishings at U.S. prices.

WHERE TO STAY

Casa Natalie ⟨★★★⟩ *Finds*   When it comes to luxury and service in Ensenada, this year-old outpost of understated opulence is unmatched. A guard-gated entrance to Casa Natalie's modern, adults-only sanctuary in El Sauzal, just north of downtown Ensenada, ensures supreme privacy—in fact, from the highway, it looks like anything but an elegant enclave. Once inside, the resort's intimate setting charms and delights. Undoubtedly Northern Baja's finest boutique hotel, Casa Natalie feels light and airy, with lounge-ready seagrass furniture and wispy white drapes that frame the floor-to-ceiling windows, which form a concave half moon to the outside. The living room, chef's kitchen, and dining area, all of which feel more like your own luxury home than an impersonal hotel, open up on a sleek infinity-edge pool, which pours toward the Pacific and is surrounded by teak sun beds with open-air canopies and white privacy curtains.

The resort's chef, Luis Carbajal, designs special menus according to guests' individual tastes and the restaurant is open all day. Seven master suites, all of which face or look down upon the pool and ocean, embody the casual sophistication so intrinsic to Baja and are named after the peninsula's indigenous plants. All beds are king-size and adorned in Westin's trademarked "Heavenly Bed" trimmings, so you know you'll sleep well, and each room's airy decor is comfortable as well as beautiful—beautiful enough, in fact, for repeat visitor Sandra Bullock and her Baja 1000-racer husband, Jesse James. At prices like these, you can't afford not to live like a movie star. ***Note:*** Casa Natalie is of no relation to Casa Natalia in San José del Cabo.

Carretera Tijuana-Ensenada Km 103.3, El Sauzal, 22760 Ensenada, B.C. ⓒ 888/562-8254 in the U.S., or 646/174-7373. www.casanatalie.com. 7 units. $252–$380 suite. Off season and midweek rates are about 10% less. **Amenities:** Restaurant; bar; heated swimming pool; full-service spa; hot tub; room service; laundry service; tour desk with tours to wine country. *In room:* A/C, satellite TV with premium channels, Wi-Fi, CD/DVD player.

Estero Beach Resort 🐾 *Kids*

About 10km (6¼ miles) south of downtown Ensenada, this sprawling complex of rooms, cottages, and mobile-home hookups has been popular with families and active vacationers since the 1950s. The bay and protected lagoon at the edge of the lushly planted property are perfect for swimming and launching sailboards; there's also tennis, horseback riding, volleyball, and a game room with Ping-Pong and billiards. The guest rooms are a little worn, but no one expects fancy here. The beachfront restaurant serves a casual mix of seasonal cuisine including seafood, sushi, Mexican fare, hamburgers, fried chicken, omelets, and even a special kids menu. Some suites and 5 of the 15 cottages have kitchenettes, and some can easily accommodate a whole family.

Estero Beach. (Mailing address: Apdo. Postal 86, Ensenada, B.C.) ⓒ 646/176-6225. www.hotelesterobeach.com. 100 units. $90–$160 double; $70–$130 cottage; $400–$500 suite. Mobile-home hookups range from $35–$45 per night and $360–$750 per month. From Ensenada, take Carretera Transpeninsular south; turn right at ESTERO BEACH sign. MC, V. **Amenities:** Restaurant; 2 bars; pool w/2 Jacuzzis; tennis, basketball, and volleyball courts; tour desk; beach club; game room; Mexican culture museum and shop; safety-deposit boxes. *In room:* TV.

Las Rosas Hotel & Spa 🌟🌟

One of the most modern hotels in the area, Hotel Las Rosas still falls short of most definitions of luxurious, yet this pink oceanfront hotel 3.2km (2 miles) north of Ensenada is the favorite of many Baja aficionados. It offers most of the comforts of an upscale American hotel—which doesn't leave room for much Mexican personality. The atrium lobby is awash in pale pink and sea-foam green, a color scheme that pervades throughout—including the guest rooms, sparsely furnished with quasitropical furniture. Some rooms have fireplaces and/or in-room whirlpools, and all have balconies overlooking the pool and ocean. One of the resort's main photo ops is the infinity swimming pool that overlooks and appears to merge with the Pacific Ocean beyond.

Carretera Transpeninsular, 3.2km (2 miles) north of Ensenada. (Mailing address: Apdo. Postal 316, Ensenada, B.C.) ⓒ 646/174-4310. 47 units. $126–$190 double. Extra child under 12 $16; extra adult $22. MC, V. **Amenities:** Restaurant; cocktail lounge; swimming pool; tennis and racquetball courts; basic workout room; clifftop hot tub; business center w/Internet; tour desk; room service; massage; laundry service. *In room:* A/C, TV.

WHERE TO DINE

Ensenada is staking its claim as Northern Baja's preeminent destination for those who love a fine meal and a nice glass of wine. Restaurants are popping up, changing hands, and reinventing themselves regularly, and still others haven't changed in 50 years.

El Charro (Kids) MEXICAN   You'll recognize El Charro by its front windows: Whole chickens rotate slowly on the rotisserie in one while a woman makes tortillas in the other. This little place has been here since 1956 and looks it, with charred walls, a ceiling made of split logs, and giant piñatas hanging from the walls above the concrete floor. The simple fare consists of such dishes as half a roasted chicken with fries and tortillas, or *carne asada* (grilled marinated beef) with soup, guacamole, and tortillas. Kids are welcome; they'll think they're on a picnic. Wine and beer are served, and beer is cheaper than soda.

Av. López Mateos 475 (between Ruiz and Gastellum). No phone. Menu items $5–$12; lobster $20. No credit cards. Daily 11am–2am.

El Rey Sol (★) FRENCH/MEXICAN   Opened by French expatriates in 1947, the family-run El Rey Sol has long been considered one of Ensenada's finest eateries. Decked out like the French flag, this red, white, and blue building is a beacon on busy López Mateos. Although El Rey Sol's cuisine and overall style are a little outdated, the charm is still there. Wrought-iron chandeliers and heavy oak farm tables create a country-French ambience, and the service is excellent. House specialties include an impeccable French onion soup with Gruyère toast; seafood puff pastry; baby clams steamed in butter, white wine, and cilantro; chicken in brandy and chipotle-chile cream sauce; tender grilled steaks; and homemade French desserts. Portions are generous and always feature fresh vegetables from the nearby family farm. Every table receives a complimentary platter of appetizers at dinnertime; lunch is a hearty three-course meal. Don't miss the almond croissant for breakfast.

Av. López Mateos 1000 (at Blancarte). © 646/178-1733. Reservations recommended for weekends. Main courses $9–$19. AE, MC, V. Daily 7:30am–10:30pm.

La Embotelladora Vieja (★★★) (Finds) FRENCH/MEXICAN   If you're planning to splurge on one fine meal in Ensenada, this should be the place to do it. Hidden on an industrial side street and attached to the Bodegas de Santo Tomás winery, it looks more like a chapel than the elegant restaurant it is. Sophisticated diners will feel right at home in the stylish setting, a former winery aging room now resplendent with red-oak furniture (constructed from old wine casks), high brick walls, and crystal goblets and candlesticks on linen tablecloths. The wine list is exemplary, featuring bottles from Santo Tomás and other Baja vintners, and the "Baja French" menu features dishes carefully crafted to include or complement wine. Look for such appetizers as abalone ceviche or cream of garlic soup followed by grilled swordfish in cilantro sauce, filet mignon in port wine–Gorgonzola sauce, or quail with tart sauvignon blanc sauce.

Av. Miramar 666 (at Calle 7). © 646/174-0807. Reservations recommended for weekends. Main courses $8–$20. AE, MC, V. Mon–Sat noon–10pm.

Manzanilla (★★)   Named for the kind of olives that speckle the surrounding countryside, Manzanilla is one of Ensenada's finest. Specializing in nouvelle Mexican cuisine, Manzanilla masters fresh-caught seafood, rice and pastas, smoked oysters, Sonoran beef, and locally grown produce, all impeccably paired with regional wines

Diving with Great White Sharks in Baja

For anyone who still draws a pause when they hear the theme from *Jaws,* read no further: This is no adventure for the faint of heart. Off the coast of Baja, one can go cage diving with great white sharks at Isla Guadalupe. More than an extreme sport, this activity actually supports shark science. **Absolute Adventures–Shark Diver** (© **888/405-3268,** 415/404-6144, or 415/235-9410 in the U.S.; www.sharkdiver.com) is led by Patric Douglas, an adventure guide who has teamed up with scientists in Baja Mexico and Southern California to fuse ecotourism with research. Dives take place at Isla Guadalupe, a 158-sq.-km (109-sq.-mile) island 242km (150 miles) off-shore from the Pacific coast of Mexico, roughly south of San Diego and west/northwest of Punta Eugenia on the Baja California peninsula. Sur-rounded by deep water, as much as 3,600m (11,808 ft.) between the island and the mainland, the island is home to a stunning array of wildlife, includ-ing one of the world's most accessible populations of great white sharks.

The great white shark *(Carcharodon carcharias)* occurs naturally in all temperate marine waters and is usually between 3 and 4m (10 and 13 ft.) long, although it can grow to 6.5m (21 ft.) and weigh over 1,800kg (2 tons). They are among the most feared predators in the world, known for their fearsome sudden attacks. Great whites typically surprise their prey by rush-ing from below and grasping the victim with a powerful, large bite. If the bite is not fatal, the prey is usually left to weaken or die through blood loss, at which time the white shark returns and consumes its prey. Shark diving allows shark enthusiasts to observe the world of great whites, as well as the array of other marine life in the area, in their natural environment. Absolute Adventures claims to use the largest shark cages in existence—4.5 to 9.3 sq. m (50 to 100 sq. ft) in size—which are used to create a discernable barrier that the sharks quickly recognize so divers may safely view and pho-tograph the sharks. The four-man shark cages are constructed using high-grade materials and a state-of-the-art fabrication process. The 5-day live-aboard cage-diving expeditions take place on one of their four full-time shark-diving vessels and cost $2,850 per person (all offer air-condi-tioned staterooms). The program supports large-scale research programs involving researchers from Mexico (Centro Interdisciplinario de Ciencias del Mar) and University of California–Davis, in Northern California.

in a chic environment of dark wood and skylights accented with stained-glass win-dows in the shape of olive leaves.

Riveroll #122 (off Lopez Mateos). © 646/175-7073. Reservations recommended. Main courses $10–$30. MC, V. Wed–Sat 1pm–2am.

Sanos   It doesn't get any better than this for passionate carnivores. Located close to the entrance to town, Sanos Steak House is just that: fine cuts of meat cooked to your fancy in a casual hacienda-style courtyard setting. Opened in 2002, Sanos is the brainchild of

John "Sano" Hussong Ortel, and aside from succulent meats, the restaurant also serves fresh salads, seafood, poultry, and pastas, all with a Baja-fabulous twist. Ask to take a peek at their wine list, which offers a wide selection of local wines.

Carretera Tijuana-Ensenada Km 108.5. ⓒ **646/174-4061**. www.sanosrestaurant.com. Main courses $12–$36. AE, MC, V. Daily 8am–11pm.

ENSENADA AFTER DARK

No discussion of Ensenada would be complete without mentioning **Hussong's Cantina,** Av. Ruiz 113, near Avenida López Mateos (ⓒ **646/178-3210**); just like the line from *Casablanca,* "everyone goes to Rick's," everyone's been going to Hussong's since the bar opened in 1892. Nothing much has changed in the last century plus—the place still sports Wild West–style swinging saloon doors, a long bar to slide beers along, and strolling mariachis bellowing to rise above the din of revelers. There's definitely a minimalist appeal to Hussong's, which looks as if it sprang from a south-of-the-border episode of *Gunsmoke.* Beer and tequilas at astonishingly low prices are the main order of business. Be aware that hygiene and privacy are a low priority in the restrooms.

While the crowd at Hussong's (a pleasant mix of tourists and locals) can really whoop it up, they're amateurs compared to those who frequent **Papas & Beer,** Avenida Ruiz near Avenida López Mateos (ⓒ **646/178-4231**), across the street. A tiny entrance leads to the upstairs bar and dance club, where the music is loud and the young crowd is definitely here to party. Happy patrons hang out of the second-story windows calling out to their friends and stop occasionally to eat *papas fritas* (french fries) accompanied by local beers. Papas & Beer has quite a reputation with the Southern California college crowd and has opened a branch in Rosarito Beach (see "Rosarito Beach After Dark" on p. 166). You've probably noticed bumper stickers for these two quintessentially Baja watering holes, but they don't just give them away. In fact, each bar has several souvenir shops along Avenida Ruiz.

4 The Valle de Guadalupe: Mexico's Wine Country

The secret's out that Baja's wine country is blossoming into something that potentially could be as big as Napa, but a visit to the Guadalupe Valley still feels like an off-the-beaten-path exploration.

A 29km (18-mile) drive northeast of Ensenada along Highway 3 toward Tecate will bring you to the Valle de Guadalupe (Guadalupe Valley), the heart of Mexico's small but expanding wine industry. Although more traditional connoisseurs may have been dismissive of Mexico's wine efforts in the past, in recent years the production and quality have made quantum leaps, and several Mexican vintages have earned international acclaim.

Spanish missionaries first introduced wine to Baja California in 1701, when a Jesuit priest, Father Juan de Ugarte, planted the peninsula's first grape vines. In 1791, the first vineyards were established in these fertile valleys at Misión Santo Tomás. In 1888, the Santa Tomás winery was established, giving birth to Baja's wine country.

It wasn't until the 1970s that commercial wineries entered the area, with the establishment of the Domecq and L.A. Cetto operations—two of Mexico's largest wine producers, which until recently specialized in inexpensive, mass-produced wines. It was the opening of the boutique winery **Monte Xanic** in the late 1980s that brought the culture of fine wines to the area.

Wine Country

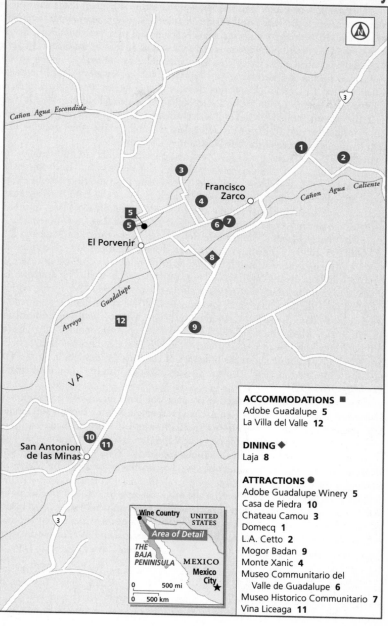

ACCOMMODATIONS ■
Adobe Guadalupe **5**
La Villa del Valle **12**

DINING ◆
Laja **8**

ATTRACTIONS ●
Adobe Guadalupe Winery **5**
Casa de Piedra **10**
Chateau Camou **3**
Domecq **1**
L.A. Cetto **2**
Mogor Badan **9**
Monte Xanic **4**
Museo Communitario del
  Valle de Guadalupe **6**
Museo Historico Communitario **7**
Vina Liceaga **11**

The Valle de Guadalupe is in the "world wine strip," a zone of lands with the climate and porous soil that result in ideal conditions for grape growing—similar to those found in Northern California, France, Spain, and Italy. Northern Baja's dry, hot summers and cool, humid winters added to a stream of cool ocean breezes make the conditions in Guadalupe Valley especially conducive for vineyards, similar to what you would find in the Mediterranean. The most common wines found here include Chenin Blanc, Colombard, Sauvignon Blanc, and chardonnay among the whites, and cabernet sauvignon, merlot, Barbera, Nebbiolo, and zinfandel among the reds. However, the region's limited rainfall and water supply will likely limit its growth, meaning it is likely to remain the picturesque place it is today rather than growing into a tourist-oriented culture in the way Napa Valley has evolved.

In 1905, the Mexican government granted political asylum to 100 families from Russia, who arrived in the Guadalupe Valley to cultivate wheat. They soon realized they could earn more for their small colony producing wine and thus became the pioneers of grape cultivation in the area. Although many of the families emigrated to Russian communities throughout the United States during the Cold War, to this day, many of the present-day residents are descendents of those Russian families. The lovingly maintained **Museo Comunitario del Valle de Guadalupe,** on Francisco Zarco (© **646/155-2030**), has displays and artifacts from this curious time of cultural conversion. Although the information is all in Spanish, museum administrator Alex Gallardo currently is developing English-language materials as well. The museum has a small adjoining restaurant that serves traditional Russian food and a wine tasting is included with the $2 donation to the museum, although we don't recommend the wine or food offered here. Just across the street is the **Museo Histórico Comunitario,** affiliated with Mexico's INAH (National Institute of Anthropology and History). Although small in scale, it has informative displays of the indigenous Kumiai culture of the region, and more about the influence of the Russian immigrants in the Valley of Guadalupe. The museum is open Tuesday through Sunday from 10am to 5pm (© **646/178-2531**).

If Baja's indigenous culture interests you, and you book far enough in advance, Alex Gallardo can set up excursions into native lands, where Kumiai Indians still reside, to view ancient cave paintings (© **646/155-2030;** mundovid@hotmail.com).

The best time to visit the Valle de Guadalupe is in late August, during Las Fiestas de la Vendimia (Harvest Festivals). Various vineyards schedule a multitude of activities during the festivals, including tastings, classical music concerts, and Masses celebrating the harvest.

Note that most of the roads in the Valle de Guadalupe are dirt-surfaced, so an SUV is the preferred vehicle to explore the area in. The area's only fully paved road is Highway 3 (to Tecate), which cuts through the valley. Most of the wineries and attractions are just off this scenic road, which is lined with vineyards and olive orchards.

WINERY TOURS

Winery tours are available at most of the region's wineries, with some having more structure than others. Especially if you visit the smaller wineries, you'll find you may be the only visitor, meaning you'll enjoy personal attention. But before you snap up cases of the vintages you taste, keep in mind that customs limits you to taking only three bottles back across the U.S. border.

Scheduled winery tours are offered by **Baja California Tours** (© **800/336-5454** or 858/454-7166 in the U.S.; www.bajaspecials.com). Tours include visits to several wineries, a historical overview of the valley, transportation from the border, and lunch. They also have overnight tours, including during the annual Harvest Festival.

I've listed below a few of the more popular wineries you may want to visit on your own, but the area is home to almost 20 wineries.

Bodegas de Santo Tomás is Baja's oldest winery. They offer daily tours and hourly wine tastings from 9am to 5pm Monday through Saturday and from 10am to 4pm Sundays for $5. They are in Ensenada, at Av. Miramar 666 (© **646/178-3333,** 646/174-0836, or 646/174-0829; www.santo-tomas.com).

Casa de Piedra offers free tours and wine tastings through its small but celebrated vineyard by appointment only. It's in Valle de Guadalupe, at Km 93.5, Highway 3 to Tecate (© **646/156-5268;** www.vinoscasadepiedra.com).

Chateau Camou offers three different wine-tasting tours, all of which include a souvenir glass, Monday through Saturday from 8am to 3pm and Sundays from 9am to 2pm. The Claret is a 30-minute tour, which includes four wines for $5. The 30-minute Bordeaux tour ends with a tasting of six wines and costs $10. I recommend the Magnum, a $40 reservations-required tour and comprehensive tasting led by the winemaker and capped off with lunch and a glass of wine. This winery has beautiful gardens and panoramic views of the valley. It's in Francisco Zarco, Valle de Guadalupe, just off Highway 3 to Tecate (© **646/177-2221** or 646/177-3303; www.chateau-camou. com.mx).

Domecq hosts free tours and wine tastings for $2.50 Monday through Friday 9:30am to 5pm and Saturdays from 10am to 1pm. They have a gift shop and picnic areas on premises. Domecq is in Valle de Guadalupe at Km 73.5, on Highway 3 to Tecate (© **646/155-2249;** www.vinosdomecq.com.mx).

L.A. Cetto, one of the largest and most commercial wineries in the region, offers free wine tastings and tours daily from 9am to 4pm. There are also a gift shop, gardens, and picnic areas onsite in Valle de Guadalupe at Km 73.5 on Highway 3 to Tecate (© **646/155-2264;** www.lacetto.com).

Mogor Badan, a boutique winery that produces one red and one white that are sold in fine-dining restaurants throughout the world, offers tours and wine tastings by advance appointment. E-mail is the best way to reach Mogor Badan, which is in Valle de Guadalupe, Rancho El Mogor, Km 86.5 on Highway 3 to Tecate (©/fax **646/177-1484;** abadan@cicese.mx).

Monte Xanic is a true jewel of a winery to visit, although they change their hours on a whim and can be difficult to reach. Wine tastings and tours (costing $2) are available by appointment Monday through Friday from 10am to 4pm and Saturdays from 9am to noon. These are considered by many to be Mexico's finest wines. The winery is in Francisco Zarco, Valle de Guadalupe, just off Highway 3 to Tecate (© **646/174-6769** or 646/174-6155; www.montexanic.com).

Vina Liceaga has by-appointment wine and grappa tastings and tours available on Saturdays and Sundays from 10am to 5pm. Don't miss their award-winning merlot. Still in Valle de Guadalupe, at Km 93.5 on Highway 3 to Tecate (© **646/155-3093** or 646/156-5313; www.vinosliceaga.com).

WHERE TO STAY

Adobe Guadalupe   Adobe Guadalupe is both an intimate inn and a boutique winery. The owners see to it that you don't forget it's a winery first and a hotel second, so don't expect a red carpet. Six basic bedrooms, a stunning interior courtyard, and picturesque stables comprise this lovely mission-style structure situated on 26 hectares

(65 acres) of vineyard. Owners Donald and Tru Miller grow cabernet sauvignon, merlot, Nebbiolo, cabernet Franc, Tempranillo, shiraz, and Viognier grapes, which they combine to create five blends named after archangels. The vineyards were started in 1998, and their first harvest was in 2000. The rooms pale in comparison to the well-appointed kitchen, living room, and dining room, but they make for a clean, comfortable place to rest after a day of horseback riding, traipsing through vineyards with the Millers' five Weimaraners, sampling wines, or lounging by the pool. Rates include a magnificent made-to-order Mexican breakfast, which is served in the kitchen from 8 to 10am daily. Dinner is at 7pm and costs $60 for a four-course meal served with Adobe Guadalupe wines. The wine is good and the food is hit-and-miss, but if you plan to have wine with dinner, it's worth it to stay on property and avoid the narrow, shoulder-less highway between Ensenada and the Guadalupe Valley after dark.

Hwy. 1-D, Km 77.5, Guadalupe Valley. (Mailing address: 416 W. San Ysidro Bulevar, Suite #L-732, San Ysidro, CA 92173.) ℰ 649/631-3098 in the U.S., or 646/155-2094. www.adobeguadalupe.com. 6 units. $168 double, includes breakfast. AE, MC, V. Once you've arrived in the town of Guadalupe along Hwy. 3, turn left just past the river into the town of Francisco Zarco. The pavement will soon end, but continue for about 5.6km (3½ miles), past the Monte Xanic and Chateau Camou wineries. At the stop sign (adjacent to the Unidad Médica Familiar building), turn right and continue .8km (a half-mile) more. Adobe Guadalupe will be on your right. **Amenities:** Dining room; heated swimming pool and Jacuzzi; concierge; massage services; horseback rides; tours to other wineries; picnic area. *In room:* A/C, TV, ceiling fan, no phone.

La Villa del Valle   ★★★ *(Finds)*   For the most exquisite take on wine-country accommodations, La Villa del Valle, formerly Las Brisas del Valle, is a delightful sanctuary on 28 hectares (70 acres) of lavender-studded hills in the Guadalupe Valley. You come here to relax, and relaxed you will be after one whiff of the fragrant air surrounding this six-room boutique hotel. No one said living off the land had to mean roughing it—owners Eileen and Phil Gregory incorporate the natural Mediterranean-style landscape to create a retreat of organic luxury: flowering herb gardens frequented by the hotel chef, homemade lavender-infused bath products, walls painted with natural minerals, handmade sinks, fresh olive oil made from on-property olive harvests; river-rock showers . . . the list goes on. A vegetable garden with produce ranging from artichokes to lemongrass supplies the restaurant with the freshest four-course dinners ($45 per person) in the valley; and 14-inch thick beds paired with overstuffed pillows and panoramic valley views make for heavenly guest rooms. At La Villa del Valle, all the details come together to create a place you'll never want to leave.

Rancho Ejido San Marcos Toros Pintos, Francisco Zarco, Ensenada, B.C. ℰ 646/183-9249. www.lavilladelvalle.com. 6 units. $175 double includes breakfast and evening glass of wine and appetizers. AE, MC, V. Just past Km 89 on Hwy. 3 toward Tecate, turn left onto the dirt-road exit for Ej. Porvenir, Delegación, and Rancho Sicomoro. Follow signs to La Villa del Valle, which is 2 miles down the dirt road. **Amenities:** Restaurant; heated swimming pool; yoga studio; massage and facial services; meditation labyrinth; Jacuzzi; concierge. *In room:* A/C, Wi-Fi, no phone.

WHERE TO DINE

Laja   ★★★ *(Finds)*   GOURMET MEXICAN   Under the direction of former Four Seasons chef Jair Tellez, this extraordinary gem of a gourmet restaurant, which has won accolades from the major Southern California publications, is reason enough to visit the valley. Set in a lovely adobe and stone building with picture windows overlooking the valley, Laja, with its own herb garden and small vineyard, serves a daily fixed menu of four to eight courses featuring local fresh produce and wines.

On Hwy. 3 Km 83, Francisco Zarco, Valle de Guadalupe. ℰ 646/155-2556. Reservations required. Main courses $25–$40. MC, V. Wednesday 1:30–3:30pm; Thurs–Sat 1:30–8:30pm.

5 San Felipe: Quiet Beach Village ★★

407.1km (253 miles) S of San Diego; 382km (237 miles) S of Tijuana

Unless you happen upon San Felipe during Spring Break, when thousands of college kids flee south to party at **El Rockodile** on the *malecón* (© **686/577-1219;** www. 4rockodile.com), or during Semana Santa—the week before Easter when Mexicans from throughout Baja make a break for the beach with tents and extended family in tow—nothing much happens in this teensy little beach town. And that's just what makes it so special.

Beyond the first impression of tranquillity in this popular camping destination, San Felipe seems to hold a special place in the hearts of the West Coast travelers who've known about it for decades. A survey of average So-Cal adults elicits childhood stories of family vacations spent camping on the beach in San Felipe, and the destination still retains an air of nostalgia. Although residential and resort development is winding its way through the surrounding area, those who haven't been back since their elementary-school days will be happy to know not much has changed in the center of town, at least.

Ask anyone what there is to do in San Felipe, and they'll probably say, "not much." If you're expecting anything more than a banana-boat ride ($5 per person, flag down the boat driver on the beach), a sportfishing excursion ($35–$45 per person for 5 hours; call **Jesús Meza** at © **686/215-4816;** or make a deal with the captains on the beach), some fish-taco-and-cerveza indulgence, and perhaps a few sunny highlights in your hair, San Felipe may not be for you. San Felipe is as low-key as Baja gets, and that makes it an important stopover for those seeking insight into the "Old Baja" of yore.

WHERE TO STAY & DINE

Promises of luxurious resorts and residential developments line the highway in the form of billboards, but for now, expect bare-bones accommodations and simple cuisine during your stay.

Stay at La Hacienda de la Langosta Roja (Calzada Chetumal no. 125; © **686/577-0483;** www.sanfelipelodging.com). It's right in the center of town, 1 block from the *malecón,* so the location can't be beat. The spare rooms are tidy as can be, the running water is hot, the cable TV works, and the first-floor restaurant is the closest thing to fine dining you can find in San Felipe. In fact, apart from great Italian food, it serves the best ceviche I've had anywhere in Baja, and the wine list has a decent selection of regional and international wines. You can't go wrong with the Red Lobster Hotel.

Some may prefer more classic San Felipe accommodations—the ubiquitous campground. For RV and tent campers alike, it doesn't get any better than **Pete's Camp** (© **951/694-6704** in the U.S., no local phone; www.petescamp.com), on the north beach of San Felipe. The lovely Navarro family owns and operates the 79-space campsite, which is open to families, RVs, and pets (on leashes), and the onsite restaurant serves Mexican and American favorites. Nightly rates are $15 per vehicle per site. Any vehicles more than 4.5m (15 ft.) in length must take two sites, at a rate of $30 per night.

For seafood, fish tacos, and margaritas that will rock your world, plan to spend an afternoon at Bajamar on the *malecón.* Not only are the shrimp tacos ($6) fried to perfection and the salsa extra fresh, the place is equal parts local families and festive tourists, so the air is celebratory. Bajamar even offers a healthy option on the menu: try the grilled seafood skewers for $13.

Appendix A:
Baja in Depth

The entire country of Mexico stretches nearly 3,220km (1,996 miles) from east to west and more than 1,600km (992 miles) north to south. Only one-fifth the size of the United States, its territory includes trackless deserts in the north, dense jungles in the south, thousands of miles of lush seacoast and beaches along the Pacific and Caribbean, and the central highlands, crisscrossed by mountain ranges.

The Baja peninsula was once a part of mainland Mexico, and perhaps its physical separation has helped contribute to the sense of cultural separation from the rest of its homeland. Although no matter where you go in Mexico the sense of national pride runs deep, in Baja there is also a close sense of kinship with its neighbor to the north—the U.S. state of California, which, of course, was once part of Mexico itself.

Today, many travelers to Baja claim this region feels more like an extension of Southern California than it does Mexico. This is especially true in the Los Cabos area, at the very tip of Baja, where a large and growing expatriate community of wealthy Americans and Canadians has taken up residence. There, English is as common as Spanish, and dollars are interchangeable with pesos. However, this isn't as prevalent in the mid- and northern parts of Baja, especially in the central rural areas.

Still, Baja has a cultural identity unique to itself. It has always been a rugged and often inhospitable land, and has been, through the years, as much a home to pirates, outlaws, and adventurers as to anyone. The ability to survive here has given rise to a sturdy soul in the inhabitants of this region, something that continues to be a source of pride.

No one knows much about the ancient inhabitants of the Baja peninsula other than that they left a remarkable collection of dramatic paintings on the walls of caves in central Baja's mountainous region. These mystical paintings of faceless human and animal forms, despite all that we now know, seem to defy interpretation. Although the date of these paintings, as well as their meaning, remains unclear, the art they left behind is a stunning expression of a rich and complex cosmological view.

There is also limited knowledge of the indigenous tribes who lived here at the time of the arrival of the Spanish explorers, but what is clear is that they were less than welcoming. The first known European ship to arrive to these shores was the *Concepción* in 1534, under sail by a group of mutineers who landed in La Paz. Natives killed the majority, and the few survivors brought back tales of caches of black pearls found on a rugged island. Hernán Cortez, who was leading the Spanish Crown's conquest of Mexico, organized further explorations, which ultimately ended in a similar fate. He finally succeeded in financing an expedition led by Captain Francisco de Ulloa that charted what is now known as the Sea of Cortez, establishing the fact that this was not an island but a peninsula.

For these reasons and more, Baja is an intriguing place. Most travelers to the area will be drawn to its cobalt-blue waters and desert landscapes, but for more adventurous souls, what will ultimately hold your attention is the vast and mysterious interior section of the peninsula and the strength of character it requires to survive and thrive there. This may no longer be the "no man's land" that once characterized it, yet Baja remains a rugged region (outside the resort areas), one that invites you to challenge yourself to test your personal limits.

1 The Land & Its People

SOCIAL MORES American, Canadian, and English travelers have often observed that Mexicans have a different conception of time—that life in Mexico obeys slower rhythms. This is true, and yet few observers go on to explain what the consequences of this are for the visitor to Mexico. This is a shame, because an imperfect appreciation of the difference causes a good deal of misunderstanding between tourists and locals.

On several occasions, Mexican acquaintances have asked me why Americans grin all the time. At first I wasn't sure what to make of the question and only gradually came to appreciate what was at issue. As the pace of life for Americans, Canadians, and others has quickened, they have come to skip some of the niceties of social interaction. When walking into a store, many Americans simply smile at a clerk and launch right into a question or request. The smile, in effect, replaces the greeting. In Mexico, it doesn't work that way. Mexicans misinterpret this American manner of greeting. After all, a smile when there is no context can be ambiguous; it can convey amusement, smugness, or superiority.

One of the most important pieces of advice I can offer travelers is this: Always give a proper greeting when addressing Mexicans. Don't try to abbreviate social intercourse. Mexican culture places a higher value on proper social form than on saving time. A Mexican must at least say *"¡Buenos días!"* or even a quick *"Qué tal?"* to show proper respect. When an individual meets up with and leaves a group, he will greet and say goodbye to each person separately, which can take quite a while. For us, the polite thing would be to keep our interruption to a minimum and give a general greeting or goodbye to all, but foregoing an introductory greeting in Mexico is in poor taste.

Mexicans, like most people, will consciously or subconsciously make quick judgments about individuals they meet. Most divide the world into the *bien educado* (well raised and cultured) and the *mal educado* (poorly raised). Unfortunately, many visitors are reluctant to try out their Spanish, preferring to keep exchanges to a minimum. Don't do this. To be categorized as a foreigner isn't a big deal. What's important in Mexico is to be categorized as one of the cultured foreigners and not one of the barbarians. Even an attempt at Spanish makes it easier to get the attention of waiters, hotel desk clerks, and people on the street.

TODAY'S BAJA CULTURE & PEOPLE The Baja peninsula was for years one of Mexico's least populated regions. With the exception of the stretch of coast between Tijuana and Ensenada, which began attracting spirited travelers from the U.S. during Prohibition with its more lenient liquor laws, only a small number of hardy souls resided in the central and southern parts of the peninsula working as ranchers or fishermen. Even La Paz, the capital of Baja, was considered a minor shell of a port, with a limited citizenry.

It wasn't until the Carretera Transpeninsular (Hwy. 1) was completed in 1973, connecting Tijuana with Cabo San Lucas, that opportunities for growth opened up. Prior to that, it took 10 days to travel the rugged dirt roads between Tijuana and La Paz (today—at a speed of 80kmph/50 mph, which is not always possible, and with limited rest stops—it would take 23 hr.). The population in the southern region exploded following this event, and the area has flourished ever since. This has been aided in large part by Fonatur's (Mexico's tourism infrastructure secretariat) focus on investing in the Los Cabos area to create another center of tourism for Mexico. The area south of Loreto, also known as Nopoló, has also been a focus of Fonatur investment efforts, recently revitalized with the Loreto Bay real-estate project.

Because Baja's geography created a natural barrier to growth for so many years, you'll find that many of Baja's inhabitants are transplants from the north or from other parts of Mexico, most a mix of foreign and indigenous ancestry. In addition to the European settlers, who included sea-weary sailors and English pirates who jumped ship, the early pioneers of Baja included Chinese immigrants brought here to work, a colony of Russian refugees granted political asylum who came to the Valle de Guadalupe, and French miners who settled in Santa Rosalía. Their descendents have greatly contributed to the come-one-and-all spirit of Baja.

However, there remains a sense of separatism to this culture, and as such, you may not find the bursting cultural pride of other parts of Mexico. What you will often encounter, though, is an eagerness by locals to share the natural treasures of Baja—the unique desert flora, the rich underwater life, or even basic survival skills in this challenging terrain. Most of Baja's long-term residents appear to be inherently respectful of the surrounding nature and, especially in the middle and southern reaches, grateful for its bountiful seafood, available work, and sunny weather.

BAJA'S GEOGRAPHY   The Baja peninsula is a long, narrow piece of land dominated by mountain ranges and desert terrain. The length of the peninsula extends 1,300km (806 miles) from the U.S.-Mexico border to its southernmost tip. Its widest point across land is at the border itself, which measures 193km (120 miles), while the narrowest part, near the southern tip, extends just 45km (28 miles) from the Bay of La Paz in the east to the Pacific Ocean in the west. Its total coastal area, including the Pacific Ocean, Sea of Cortez, and many coves and inlets, measures about 4,800km (2,976 miles) of shoreline. Throughout Baja, mountains rise up in a succession of ranges, with a total of 23 named ranges. The four primary ranges are the **Sierra de San Pedro Mártir, Sierra de Juárez, Sierra de la Giganta,** and **Sierra de la Laguna.** The highest peak in Baja is the **Picacho del Diablo (Devil's Peak),** which reaches an elevation of 3,095m (10,152 ft.). More than 65% of Baja's total land area is classified as desert, although—truly a land of contrasts—it also boasts pine (conifer) forests in its northern mountainous regions.

NATURAL LIFE & PROTECTED AREAS   There are two national parks in Baja, which are considered some of the most beautiful sites within the state. There also are two national marine parks; one is in Loreto and the more magnificent is in Cabo Pulmo. The **Parque Nacional Constitución de 1857** is within the Sierra de Juárez mountain range, in the extreme north of the peninsula, at an average altitude of 1,650m (5,412 ft.), with a surface area of 5,000 hectares (12,372 acres). In it, you'll find diverse pine forests with some trees growing to heights of over 30m (98 ft.), as well as Laguna Hanson, also known as Laguna de Juárez, a lake in the park's interior (note that due to diminished rainfall in recent years, the lake is currently dry). The area was declared a national park in 1962, and in 1983 it became a part of the country's protected natural areas. Within the park, you can enjoy hiking, mountain climbing, biking, bird-watching, stargazing, and other activities. Two Pro-Natura-designed roads allow you to admire the beauty of the park from elevated vantage points. Camping is available here, and there are a few rustic cabins for rent throughout the park system. Two ecotourism ranches, Rodeo del Rey and Los Bandidos, are also within the park, offering rustic rooms as well as campsites and related services. An information booth with maps is just past the entry point; a per-vehicle entry charge applies.

The **Parque Nacional Sierra San Pedro Mártir,** 210km (130 miles) southeast of Ensenada, has elevations that range from 1,000 to more than 3,048m (3,280–9,997 ft.). Its surface area covers 72,000 hectares (177,840 acres) of pine forests. The park is managed by the Baja California State Government and it is home to Mexico's National Astronomical Observatory, UNAM. Among the highlights of a visit here include a 2km (1.2-mile) hike up to the El Altar viewpoint, at a 2,888m (9,473 ft.) elevation, where both the Pacific Ocean and Sea of Cortez can be seen. In the southeast portion of the park is the highest peak in Baja, Picacho del Diablo (Devil's Peak), at an elevation of 3,095m (10,152 ft). It's a popular place for mountain climbing and rappelling. Snow is common here in the winter, and no services are available once you're inside the park, so it's essential to bring your own supplies. Camping areas, restrooms, and forest ranger services are available.

Within these parks, you'll see pine, fir, cypress, and poplar forests. Wild fauna found here may include ram, cougar, blacktailed deer, bobcats, royal eagles, owls, and the California condor.

Cabo Pulmo Marine Park, 64km (40 miles) from the Los Cabos International Airport, encompasses approximately 7,111 hectares (17,571 acres) of coral reefs, seamounts, wrecks, warm blue waters, and hundreds of species of fish. Stretching 11km (7 miles) from Bahía Las Barracas in the north to Bahía Los Frailes to the south, this Sea of Cortez haven is open to anyone but fishermen. Since 1995, when the Mexican government declared it a marine preserve, fishing has been prohibited, but snorkeling, which can be done right from the shore, scuba diving, freediving, and kayaking are all fair game. Aside from brightly colored coral, prepare to see anything from manta rays and giant grouper to seahorses and whale sharks. Beach camping is popular on Playa Los Arbolitos, and bungalows are available through Cabo Pulmo Beach Resort or through independent homeowners in this dusty cash-only town.

2 A Look at Mexico's Past

PRE-HISPANIC CIVILIZATIONS

The earliest Mexicans were Stone Age hunter-gatherers from the north, descendants of a race that had probably crossed the Bering Strait and reached North America around 12,000 B.C. They arrived in what is now Mexico by 10,000 B.C. It is likely that Baja was inhabited by human populations well before mainland Mexico, as Baja was the logical termination point for the coastal migration route followed by Asian groups crossing the Bering Strait. The San Dieguito culture migrated south into Baja somewhere between 7000 and 5000 B.C. Sometime between 5200 and 1500 B.C., in what is known as the **Archaic period,** they began practicing agriculture and domesticating animals.

THE PRE-CLASSIC PERIOD (1500 B.C.–A.D. 300) Eventually, agriculture improved to the point that it could support large communities and free some of the population from agricultural work. A

civilization emerged that we call the **Olmec**—an enigmatic people who settled the lower Gulf Coast in what is now Tabasco and Veracruz. Anthropologists regard them as the mother culture of Mesoamerica because they established a pattern for later civilizations in a wide area stretching from northern Mexico into Central America. The Olmec developed the basic calendar used throughout the region, established a 52-year cycle (which they used to schedule the construction of pyramids), established principles of urban layout and architecture, and originated the cult of the jaguar and the sanctity of jade. They may also have bequeathed the sacred ritual of "the ball game"—a universal element of Mesoamerican culture.

One intriguing feature of the Olmec was the carving of colossal stone heads. We still don't know what purposes these heads served, but they were immense projects; the basalt from which they were sculpted was mined miles inland and transported to the coast, probably by river rafts. The heads share a rounded, baby-faced look, marked by a peculiar, high-arched lip—a "jaguar mouth"—that is an identifying mark of Olmec sculpture.

The Maya civilization began developing in the Yucatán during the late pre-Classic period, around 500 B.C. Our understanding of this period is sketchy, but Olmec influences are apparent everywhere. The Maya perfected the Olmec calendar and, somewhere along the way, developed an ornate system of hieroglyphic writing and early architectural concepts. Two other civilizations began the rise to prominence around this time: the people of Teotihuacán, just north of present-day Mexico City, and the Zapotec of Monte Albán in the valley of Oaxaca.

In Baja, the San Dieguito culture either developed into, or was superseded by, the Yumano culture, believed to be the creators of the rock paintings and petroglyphs found on the central interior of the peninsula. The Yumanos made use of more sophisticated hunting equipment as well as fishing nets, and also created ceramics. Paintings also indicate a fundamental knowledge of astronomy and depict solstice celebrations. Descendants of this culture were the Indians found living here by the Spanish in the 16th century.

THE CLASSIC PERIOD (A.D. 300–900) The flourishing of these three civilizations marks the boundaries of this period—the heyday of pre-Columbian Mesoamerican artistic and cultural achievements. These include the pyramids and palaces in Teotihuacán; the ceremonial center of Monte Albán; and the

Dateline

- **10,000–1500 B.C.** Archaic period: hunting and gathering; later, the dawn of agriculture: domestication of chiles, corn, beans, avocado, amaranth, and pumpkin. Mortars and pestles in use. Stone bowls and jars, obsidian knives, and open-weave basketry developed. Possible dating of the cave paintings of central Baja, believed to have been created by nomadic indigenous tribes.
- **1500 B.C.–A.D. 300** Pre-Classic period: Olmec culture develops large-scale settlements and irrigation methods. Cities spring up. Olmec influence spreads over other cultures in the Gulf Coast, central and southern Mexico, Central America, the lower Mexican Pacific Coast, and the Yucatán. Several cities in central and southern Mexico begin the construction of large ceremonial centers and pyramids. The Maya develop several city-states in Chiapas and Central America.
- **A.D. 300–900** Classic period: Broad influence of Teotihuacán culture and the establishment there of a truly

stelae and temples of Palenque, Bonampak, and the Tikal site in Guatemala. Beyond their achievements in art and architecture, the Maya made significant discoveries in science, including the use of the zero in mathematics and a complex calendar with which the priests could predict eclipses and the movements of the stars for centuries to come.

The inhabitants of **Teotihuacán** (100 B.C.–A.D. 700), near present-day Mexico City, built a city that, at its zenith, is thought to have had 100,000 or more inhabitants. It was a well-organized city, covering 23 sq. km (9 sq. miles), built on a grid with streams channeled to follow the city's plan.

Farther south, the **Zapotec,** influenced by the Olmec, raised an impressive civilization in the region of Oaxaca. Their two principal cities were **Monte Albán,** inhabited by an elite community of merchants and artisans, and **Mitla,** reserved for the high priests.

THE POST-CLASSIC PERIOD (A.D. 900–1521)

Warfare was the most conspicuous activity of the civilizations that flourished in this period. Social development was impressive but not as cosmopolitan as the Maya, Teotihuacán, and Zapotec societies. In central Mexico, a people known as the **Toltec** established their capital at Tula in the 10th century.

They revered a god known as **Tezcatlipoca,** or "smoking mirror," who later became an Aztec god. The Toltec maintained a large military class divided into orders symbolized by animals. At its height, Tula may have had 40,000 people, and its influence spread across Mesoamerica. By the 13th century, however, the Toltec had exhausted themselves, probably in civil wars and in battles with the invaders from the north.

THE CONQUEST

In 1517, the first Spaniards arrived in what is today known as Mexico and skirmished with Maya Indians off the coast of the Yucatán Peninsula. One of the fledgling expeditions ended in shipwreck, leaving several Spaniards stranded as prisoners of the Maya. The Spanish sent out another expedition, under the command of **Hernán Cortez,** which landed on Cozumel in February 1519. Cortez inquired about the gold and riches of the interior, and the coastal Maya were happy to describe the wealth and splendor of the Aztec empire in central Mexico. Cortez promptly disobeyed all orders of his superior, the governor of Cuba, and sailed to the mainland.

Cortez arrived when the Aztec empire was at the height of its wealth and power. **Moctezuma II** ruled over the central and southern highlands and extracted tribute

---

cosmopolitan urbanism. Satellite settlements spring up across central Mexico and as far away as Guatemala. Trade and cultural interchange with the Maya and the Zapotec flourish. The Maya perfect the calendar and improve astronomical calculations. They build grandiose cities at Palenque, Calakmul, and Cobá, and in Central America.

■ **900** Post-Classic period begins: More emphasis is placed on warfare in central Mexico. The Toltec culture emerges at Tula and replaces Teotihuacán as the dominant city of central Mexico. Toltec influence spreads to the Yucatán, forming the culture of the Itzaés, who become the rulers of Chichén Itzá.

■ **909** This is the date on a small monument at Toniná

(near San Cristóbal de las Casas), the latest date yet discovered, symbolizing the end of the Classic Maya era.

■ **1325–1470** Aztec capital Tenochtitlán is founded; Aztecs begin military campaigns in the Valley of Mexico and then thrust farther out, subjugating the civilizations of the Gulf Coast and southern Mexico.

continues

from lowland peoples. His greatest temples were literally plated with gold and encrusted with the blood of sacrificial captives. Moctezuma was a fool, a mystic, and something of a coward. Despite his wealth and military power, he dithered in his capital at Tenochtitlán, sending messengers with gifts and suggestions that Cortez leave. Meanwhile, Cortez blustered and negotiated his way into the highlands, always cloaking his real intentions. Moctezuma, terrified by the military tactics and technology of the Spaniard, convinced himself that Cortez was, in fact, the god Quetzalcoatl making his long-awaited return. By the time the Spaniards arrived in the Aztec capital, Cortez had gained some ascendancy over the lesser Indian states that were resentful tributaries to the Aztec. In November 1519, Cortez confronted Moctezuma and took him hostage in an effort to leverage control of the empire.

In the middle of Cortez's dangerous game of manipulation, another Spanish expedition arrived with orders to end Cortez's authority over the mission. Cortez hastened to meet the rival's force and persuade them to join his own. In the meantime, the Aztec chased the garrison out of Tenochtitlán, and either they or the Spaniards killed Moctezuma. For the next year and a half, Cortez laid siege to

Tenochtitlán, with the help of rival Indians and a decimating epidemic of smallpox, to which the Indians had no resistance. In the end, the Aztec capital fell, and when it did, all of central Mexico lay at the feet of the conquistadors.

Cortez began his explorations of Baja California in 1532. Looking across from western Mexico, the Spanish believed Baja to be an island, and so declared the sea the Mar de Cortez (Sea of Cortez). The first explorations failed, succumbing to pirates. The first Spanish ship recorded to have reached Baja was in 1534 when the *Concepción,* under the leadership of a mutinous crew, landed at present-day La Paz, only to be attacked by indigenous inhabitants while refilling their water stocks. A few members of the crew returned to the ship and sailed back to the mainland, where they told Cortez of an island rich with black pearls, fueling his desires for further explorations. In 1539, one expedition, under the direction of Capt. Francisco de Ulloa, explored the entire perimeter of the Sea of Cortez, establishing the fact that Baja was not an island, but was a peninsula.

The Spanish Conquest started as a pirate expedition by Cortez and his men, unauthorized by the Spanish crown or its governor in Cuba. The Spanish king legitimized Cortez following his victory

---

- **1516** Gold found on Cozumel during aborted Spanish expedition of Yucatán Peninsula arouses interest of Spanish governor in Cuba, who sends Juan de Grijalva on an expedition, followed by another led by Hernán Cortez.
- **1519** Conquest of Mexico begins: Hernán Cortez and troops make their way along

Mexican coast to present-day Veracruz.
- **1521** Conquest is complete after Aztec defeat at Tlatelolco.
- **1521–24** Cortez organizes Spanish empire in Mexico and begins building Mexico City on the ruins of Tenochtitlán.
- **1532** Cortez launches the first exploration to Baja, then

believed to be an island. The expedition is unsuccessful, with ships intercepted by pirates.
- **1534** The *Concepción* makes landfall near present-day La Paz, under charge of a group of mutineers; most are killed by the indigenous inhabitants of the area.
- **1539** Capt. Ulloa explores the entire perimeter of the

over the Aztec and ordered the forced conversion to Christianity of this new colony, to be called **New Spain.** Guatemala and Honduras were explored and conquered, and by 1540, the territory of New Spain included possessions from Vancouver to Panama. In the 2 centuries that followed, Franciscan and Augustinian friars converted millions of Indians to Christianity, and the Spanish lords built huge feudal estates on which the Indian farmers were little more than serfs. The silver and gold that Cortez looted made Spain the richest country in Europe.

THE MISSION PERIOD

Among the subsequent expeditions sent by the Spanish crown, many included Catholic priests seeking to establish missions for converting the native cultures to Christianity. Padre Juan Maria Salvatierra was the first to succeed in establishing a permanent settlement on the Baja peninsula, when he founded the mission Nuestra Señora de Loreto in 1697, at the site of present-day Loreto. This began the Jesuit Mission period in Baja, which lasted until 1767, during which 20 missions were established, stretching from the southern tip of Baja into central Baja near present-day Cataviña. The mission system worked by offering protection to the natives by the Church and the Spanish crown, in exchange for submitting to religious instruction. If they were not in agreement, they were generally punished or massacred. Those who did agree assisted in the building of the mission, which became a place of refuge. In addition to religious instruction, natives also learned European farming techniques and other trades. Unlike their counterparts on the mainland, none of the Jesuit priests operating in Baja ever produced a text recording the indigenous languages. During the mission years, repeated epidemics of smallpox, syphilis, and measles, combined with those who lost their lives in rebellions, decimated the local populations, leaving Baja primarily to the new European settlers. The Jesuit missions were followed by missions established by the Franciscans and Dominicans, leading to a more diverse population of European cultures. By the end of the 18th century, it was estimated that the native population in Baja numbered fewer than 5,000.

THE COLONIAL PERIOD

Back on the mainland, Hernán Cortez set about building a new city upon the ruins of the old Aztec capital. To do this he collected from the Indians the tributes once paid to the Aztec emperor, many of these rendered in labor. This arrangement, in one form or another, became the basis for the construction of the new colony. But

---

Sea of Cortez, establishing that Baja is not an island, as believed, but a peninsula.
- **1541** Cortez is recalled to Spain, never to return to Mexico.
- **1565** Trade routes between Acapulco and Manila are established, with Baja becoming an important stopping point along this route, which lasted more than 250 years. It was also the site of ongoing pirating, which becomes an embarrassment to the Spanish crown.
- **1535–1821** Viceregal period: 61 viceroys appointed by King of Spain govern Mexico. Control of much of the land ends up in the hands of the Catholic Church and the politically powerful.
- **1697–1767** Jesuit Mission period of Baja, during which 20 missions were established for the purpose of converting the indigenous populations to Christianity.
- **1810–21** War of Independence: Miguel Hidalgo starts movement for Mexico's independence from Spain but is executed within a year; leadership and goals change during the war years, but Agustín de Iturbide outlines a

continues

diseases brought by the Spaniards decimated the native population over the next century and drastically reduced the pool of labor.

Cortez soon returned to Spain and was replaced by a governing council, and, later, the office of viceroy. Over the 3 centuries of the colonial period, 61 viceroys governed Mexico while Spain became rich from New World gold and silver—chiseled out by Indian labor. The colonial elite built lavish homes in Mexico City and in the countryside. They filled their homes with ornate furniture, had many servants, and adorned themselves in imported velvets, satins, and jewels.

A new class system developed. Those born in Spain considered themselves superior to the *criollos* (Spaniards born in Mexico). Those of other races and the *castas* (mixtures of Spanish and Indian, Spanish and African, or Indian and African) occupied the bottom rungs of society. It took great cunning to stay a step ahead of the avaricious Crown, which demanded increasing taxes and contributions from its fabled foreign conquests. Still, wealthy colonists prospered enough to develop an extravagant society.

However, discontent with the mother country simmered for years over social and political issues: taxes, royal monopolies, the bureaucracy, Spanish-born citizens' advantages over Mexican-born subjects, and restrictions on commerce with Spain and other countries. In 1808, Napoleon invaded Spain and crowned his brother Joseph king in place of Charles IV. To many in Mexico, allegiance to France was out of the question; discontent reached the level of revolt.

INDEPENDENCE

The rebellion began in 1810, when **Father Miguel Hidalgo** gave the *grito,* a cry for independence, from his church in the town of Dolores, Guanajuato. The uprising soon became a full-fledged revolution, as Hidalgo and Ignacio Allende gathered an "army" of citizens and threatened Mexico City. Although Hidalgo ultimately failed and was executed, he is honored as the Father of Mexican Independence. Another priest, José María Morelos, kept the revolt alive with several successful campaigns through 1815, when he, too, was captured and executed.

After the death of Morelos, prospects for independence were rather dim until the Spanish king who replaced Joseph Bonaparte decided to make social reforms in the colonies. This convinced the conservative powers in Mexico that they didn't need Spain after all. With their tacit approval, Agustín de Iturbide, then commander of royalist forces, changed sides

compromise between monarchy and republic.

- **1822** First Empire: Iturbide ascends throne as Emperor of Mexico, loses power after a year, and loses life in an attempt to reclaim throne.
- **1824–64** Early Republic period, characterized by almost perpetual civil war between federalists and centralists, conservatives and

liberals, culminating in the victory of the liberals under Juárez.

- **1833–47** Mexican-American War results in the loss of huge amounts of territory to the U.S. by Mexico. In 1847 Mexico City falls to U.S. troops. The Treaty of Guadalupe Hidalgo was signed in 1848, in which Mexico conceded not only

the Río Grande area of Texas but part of New Mexico and all of California for a payment of U.S. $25 million and the cancellation of all Mexican debt.

- **1849** The California Gold Rush lures many Mexicans and Indians from the Baja peninsula to seek their fortunes in California, reducing Baja's already scarce population, and transforming it into a and declared Mexico independent and himself emperor. (Spain, already losing its imperial power due to conflicts in Europe, could no longer hang onto Mexico, nor could the new king afford to wage war.) Before long, however, internal dissension brought about the fall of the new emperor, and Mexico was proclaimed a republic.

Political instability engulfed the young republic and Mexico waged a disastrous war with the United States and lost half its territory. A central figure was **Antonio López de Santa Anna,** who assumed the leadership of his country no fewer than 11 times and was flexible enough in those volatile days to portray himself variously as a liberal, a conservative, a federalist, and a centralist. He probably holds the record for frequency of exile; by 1855 he was finally left without a political comeback and ended his days in Venezuela.

Political instability persisted, and the conservative forces, with some encouragement from Napoleon III, hit upon the idea of inviting in a Habsburg to regain control (as if that strategy had ever worked for Spain). They found a willing volunteer in Archduke Maximilian of Austria, who accepted the position of Mexican emperor with the support of French troops. The ragtag Mexican forces defeated the French force—a modern, well-equipped army—in a battle near Puebla (now celebrated annually as **Cinco de Mayo**). A second attempt was more successful, and Ferdinand Maximilian Joseph of Habsburg became emperor. After 3 years of civil war, the French were finally induced to abandon the emperor's cause; Maximilian was captured and executed by a firing squad near Querétaro in 1867. His adversary and successor (as president of Mexico) was **Benito Juárez,** a Zapotec Indian lawyer and one of the great heroes of Mexican history. Juárez did his best to unify and strengthen his country before dying of a heart attack in 1872; his impact on Mexico's future was profound, and his plans and visions bore fruit for decades.

THE PORFIRIATO & THE REVOLUTION

A few years after Juárez's death, one of his generals, **Porfirio Díaz,** assumed power in a coup. He ruled Mexico from 1877 to 1911, a period now called the Porfiriato. He stayed in power by imposing repressive measures and courting the favor of powerful nations. Generous in his dealings with foreign investors, Díaz became, in the eyes of most Mexicans, the archetypal *entreguista* (one who sells out his country for private gain). With foreign investment came the concentration of great wealth in few hands, and social conditions worsened.

---

haven for outlaws, pirates, and renegades.

■ **1864–67** Second Empire: The French invade Mexico in the name of Maximilian of Austria, who is appointed Emperor of Mexico. Juárez and the liberal government retreat to the north and wage war with the French forces. The French finally abandon Mexico and leave Maximilian to be defeated and executed.

■ **1872–76** Juárez dies, and political struggles ensue for the presidency.

■ **1877–1911** Porfiriato: Porfirio Díaz, president/dictator of Mexico for 33 years, leads country to modernization by encouraging foreign investment in mines, oil, and railroads. Mexico witnesses the development of a modern economy and a growing disparity between rich and poor.

Social conditions, especially in rural areas, become desperate.

■ **1911–17** Mexican Revolution: Francisco Madero drafts revolutionary plan. Díaz resigns. Leaders jockey for power during period of great violence, national upheaval, and tremendous loss of life.

■ **1920** U.S. Prohibition, in which the manufacture, sale,

continues

In 1910, Francisco Madero called for an armed rebellion that became the **Mexican revolution** (*La Revolución* in Mexico; the revolution against Spain is the *Guerra de Independencia*). Díaz was sent into exile; while in London, he became a celebrity at the age of 81, when he jumped into the Thames to save a drowning boy. He is buried in Paris. Madero became president but was promptly betrayed and executed by **Victoriano Huerta.** Those who had answered Madero's call responded again— to the great peasant hero **Emiliano Zapata** in the south, and to the seemingly invincible **Pancho Villa** in the central north, flanked by Alvaro Obregón and Venustiano Carranza. They eventually put Huerta to flight and began hashing out a new constitution.

For the next few years, the revolutionaries Carranza, Obregón, and Villa fought among themselves; Zapata did not seek national power, though he fought tenaciously for land for the peasants. Carranza, who was president at the time, betrayed and assassinated Zapata. Obregón finally consolidated power and probably had Carranza assassinated. He, in turn, was assassinated when he tried to break one of the tenets of the Revolution—no reelection. His successor, Plutarco Elias Calles, learned this lesson well, installing one puppet president after another, until **Lázaro Cárdenas** severed the puppeteer's strings and banished him to exile.

Until Cárdenas's election in 1934, the outcome of the revolution remained in doubt. There had been some land redistribution, but other measures took a back seat to political expediency. Cárdenas changed all that. He implemented massive redistribution of land and nationalized the oil industry. He instituted many reforms and gave shape to the ruling political party (now the **Partido Revolucionario Institucional,** or PRI) by bringing a broad representation of Mexican society under its banner and establishing mechanisms for consensus building. Most Mexicans practically canonize Cárdenas.

MODERN MEXICO

The presidents who followed were noted more for graft than for leadership. The party's base narrowed as many of the reform-minded elements were marginalized. Economic progress, a lot of it in the form of large development projects, became the PRI's main basis for legitimacy. In 1968, the government violently repressed a democratic student movement. Police forces shot and killed an unknown number of civilians in the Tlatelolco section of Mexico City. Though the PRI maintained its grip on power, it lost all semblance of being a

---

and consumption of alcoholic beverages is made a federal offense, is a boon to Baja, with Americans rushing across the border into Tijuana and northern Baja to buy liquor and drink in cantinas. It also initiates an era of organized crime and sees the establishment of casinos and brothels.

■ **1917–40** Reconstruction: Present constitution of Mexico

is signed; land and education reforms are initiated and labor unions strengthened; Mexico expropriates oil companies and railroads. Pancho Villa, Zapata, and presidents Obregón and Carranza are assassinated.

■ **1940** Mexico enters contemporary period of political stability and makes steady economic progress. Quality of life improves, although

problems of corruption, inflation, national health, and unresolved land and agricultural issues continue.

■ **1952** The Territory of Northern Baja California becomes Mexico's 29th state.

■ **1973** Carretera Transpeninsular (Hwy. 1) opens, connecting Tijuana to Cabo San Lucas. This leads to serious growth in Baja, and the following year, Baja California progressive party. In 1985, a devastating **earthquake in Mexico City** brought down many of the government's new, supposedly earthquake-proof buildings, exposing shoddy construction and the widespread government corruption that fostered it. The government's handling of the relief efforts also drew heavy criticism.

In 1994, a political and military **uprising in Chiapas** focused world attention on Mexico's great social problems. A new political force, the Ejército Zapatista de Liberación Nacional, or EZLN (Zapatista National Liberation Army), has skillfully publicized the plight of the peasant. Adding to the troubles of that year, Luis Donaldo Colosio, the PRI's popular presidential candidate, was shot to death while campaigning in Tijuana in March 1994. In the ensuing investigation, top-ranking party officials, including standing president Carlos Salinas's brother, Raul, were implicated, bringing to light the extent of interparty power struggles within the PRI.

In the years that followed, opposition political parties grew in power and legitimacy. Facing pressure and scrutiny from national and international organizations, and widespread public discontent, the PRI had to concede defeat in state and congressional elections throughout the '90s. The party began choosing its candidates through primaries instead of through appointment. But in the presidential elections of 2000, Vicente Fox, candidate for the opposition party PAN, won by a landslide. In hindsight, there was no way that the PRI could have won in a fair election. For most Mexicans, a government under the PRI was all that they had ever known.

Since then, Mexico has been sailing into the uncharted waters of coalition politics. The three main parties, PRI, PAN, and PRD, have grown into their new roles within a more open, more transparent political system. To their credit, the sailing has been much smoother than many observers predicted. In 2006, the PAN party again took the vote with Felipe Calderón, but the process was not as smooth. Andrés Manuel López Obrador, former Mexico City mayor and working-party favorite, and his supporters challenged the results with marches, protests, and acts of civil disobedience so zealous that, among other things, they led President Fox to relocate to Dolores Hidalgo, Guanajuato, for the annual Independence Day "grito," which usually takes place in the capital. Although election results were initially contested (and heavily protested), a September 5, 2006, tribunal declared the election fair and Calderón assumed the presidency on December 1 of the same year.

Sur becomes Mexico's 30th state.

- **1994–97** Mexico, Canada, and the United States sign the North American Free Trade Agreement (NAFTA). An Indian uprising in Chiapas sparks countrywide protests over government policies concerning land distribution, bank loans, health, education, and voting and human rights.

- **2000** Mexico elects Vicente Fox, of the PAN party, president.

- **2006** Conservative party candidate, Felipe Calderón is elected president. Labor party candidate Andrés Manuel López Obrador contests the election results, spawning protests in the capital and in southern Mexico. Nonetheless, the Federal Electoral Tribunal rules Calderón the victor.

3 Art & Architecture 101

PRE-HISPANIC FORMS

Mexico's **pyramids** were truncated platforms crowned with a temple. Many sites have circular buildings, such as El Caracol at Chichén Itzá, usually called the observatory and dedicated to the god of the wind. El Castillo at Chichén Itzá has 365 steps—one for every day of the year. The Temple of the Magicians at Uxmal has beautifully rounded and sloping sides. Evidence of building one pyramidal structure on top of another, a widely accepted practice, has been found throughout Mesoamerica.

Throughout Mexico, carved stone and mural art on pyramids served a religious and historic function rather than an ornamental one. **Hieroglyphs,** picture symbols etched on stone or painted on walls or pottery, functioned as the written language of the ancient peoples, particularly the Maya. By deciphering the glyphs, scholars allow the ancients to speak again, providing us with specific names to attach to rulers and their families, and demystifying the great dynastic histories of the Maya. For more on this, read *A Forest of Kings* (Morrow, 1990), by Linda Schele and David Freidel, and *Blood of Kings* (George Braziller, 1986), by Linda Schele and Mary Ellen Miller. Good hieroglyphic examples appear in the site museum at Palenque.

Pre-Hispanic cultures left a wealth of fantastic painted **murals and cave paintings,** most of which are remarkably preserved, in the central mountain region concentrated in the San Francisco de la Sierra and Santa Martha mountains. Most depict a combination of faceless human forms and animal forms, in apparent depictions of ritualistic ceremonies. Their origin remains a mystery. Over 300 cave paintings are concentrated in an area known as the Great Wall, in the San Francisco de la Sierra—it's the largest concentration of ancient rock paintings in the world.

SPANISH INFLUENCE

With the arrival of the Spaniards, new forms of architecture came to Mexico. Many sites that were occupied by indigenous groups at the time of the conquest were razed and in their place appeared Catholic churches, public buildings, and palaces for conquerors and the king's bureaucrats. In the Yucatán, churches at Izamal, Tecoh, Santa Elena, and Muná rest atop former pyramidal structures. Indian artisans, who formerly worked on pyramidal structures, were recruited to build the new buildings, often guided by drawings of European buildings. Frequently left on their own, the indigenous artisans implanted traditional symbolism in the new buildings: a plaster angel swaddled in feathers, reminiscent of the god Quetzalcoatl, and the face of an ancient god surrounded by corn leaves. They used pre-Hispanic calendar counts—the 13 steps to heaven or the nine levels of the underworld—to determine how many florets to carve around church doorways.

To convert the native populations, New World Spanish priests and architects altered their normal ways of teaching and building. Often before a church was built, an open-air atrium was constructed to accommodate large numbers of parishioners for services. *Posas* (shelters) at the four corners of churchyards were another architectural technique unique to Mexico, again to accommodate crowds. Because of the language barrier between the Spanish and the natives, church adornment became more explicit. Biblical tales came to life in frescoes splashed across church walls. Christian symbolism in stone supplanted that of pre-Hispanic ideas as the natives tried to make sense of it all. Baroque became even more baroque in Mexico and was dubbed **churrigueresque** or **ultrabaroque.** Exuberant and complicated, it combines Gothic, baroque, and plateresque elements.

Almost every major town in the Baja peninsula has the remains of a **mission** nearby. Many were built in the 17th century following the early arrival of Jesuit friars. Prime examples include the **Misión Nuestra Señora de Loreto,** the first mission in the Californias, started in 1699. The catechization of California by Jesuit missionaries was based from this mission and lasted through the 18th century. About 2 hours from Loreto, in a section of the old Camino Real used by Spanish missionaries and explorers, is **Misión San Francisco Javier,** one of the best-preserved, most spectacularly set missions in Baja—high in a mountain valley beneath volcanic walls. Founded in 1699 by the Jesuit priest Francisco María Píccolo, it was the second mission established in California, completed in 1758. The original building of the **Misión Santa Rosalía de Mulegé,** founded in 1706 by Father Juan de Ugarte and Juan María Basaldúa, was completed in 1766, but in 1770, a flood destroyed nearly all the common buildings, and the mission was rebuilt on the site it occupies today, on a bluff overlooking the river. Although not the most architecturally interesting of Baja's missions, it remains in excellent condition and still functions as a Catholic church, although mission operations halted in 1828. Inside, there is a perfectly preserved statue of Santa Rosalía and a bell, both from the 18th century.

When Porfirio Díaz became president in the late 19th century, the nation's art and architecture experienced another infusion of European sensibility. Díaz idolized Europe, and he commissioned a number of striking European-style public buildings, including many opera houses. He provided European scholarships to promising young artists who later returned to Mexico to produce Mexican-subject paintings using techniques learned abroad.

In Baja, Díaz granted the Compañía de Boleo (part of the Rothschild family holdings) a 99-year lease to the rich deposits of copper in the area surrounding Santa Rosalía in exchange for the company building a town, the harbor, and public buildings, and establishing a maritime route between the port and Guaymas, meant to create employment for Mexican workers. The architectural influence of Santa Rosalía is decidedly European, and nowhere more so than in its church, the **Iglesia de Santa Barbara,** a structure of galvanized steel designed by Gustave Eiffel (of Eiffel Tower fame) in 1884. It was originally created for the 1889 Paris World Expo, where it was displayed as a prototype for what Eiffel envisioned as a sort of prefab mission. The structure eventually made its way to Santa Rosalía in 1897, where its somber gray exterior belies the beauty of the intricate stained-glass windows viewed from inside.

THE ADVENT OF MEXICAN MURALISM

As the Mexican Revolution ripped the country apart between 1911 and 1917, a new social and cultural Mexico was born. In 1923, Minister of Education José Vasconcelos was charged with educating the illiterate masses. As one means of reaching people, he invited **Diego Rivera** and several other budding artists to paint Mexican history on the walls of the Ministry of Education building and the National Preparatory School in Mexico City. Thus began the tradition of painting murals in public buildings, which you will find in towns and cities throughout Mexico.

4 Religion, Myth & Folklore

Mexico is predominantly Roman Catholic, a religion introduced by the Spaniards during the conquest of Mexico. Despite its preponderance, the Catholic faith in many places in Mexico (Chiapas and Oaxaca, for example) has pre-Hispanic undercurrents. You need only visit the *curandero* section of a Mexican market (where you can purchase copal, an incense agreeable to the gods; rustic beeswax candles, a traditional offering; the native species of tobacco used to ward off evil; and so on) or attend a village festivity featuring pre-Hispanic dancers to understand that supernatural beliefs often run parallel with Christian ones in Mexico.

Mexico's complicated mythological heritage from pre-Hispanic religion is full of images derived from nature—the wind, jaguars, eagles, snakes, flowers, and more—all intertwined with elaborate mythological stories to explain the universe, climate, seasons, and geography. Most groups believed in an underworld (not a hell), usually containing nine levels, and a heaven of 13 levels—which is why the numbers 9 and 13 are so mythologically significant. The solar calendar count of 365 days and the ceremonial calendar of 260 days are significant as well. How one died determined one's resting place after death: in the underworld (*Xibalba* to the Maya), in heaven, or at one of the four cardinal points. For example, men who died in battle or women who died in childbirth went straight to the sun. Everyone else first had to make a journey through the underworld.

5 Recommended Books & Films

BOOKS

HISTORY & CULTURE For an overview of pre-Hispanic cultures, pick up a copy of Michael D. Coe's *Mexico: From the Olmecs to the Aztecs* (Thames & Hudson, 1994) or Nigel Davies's *Ancient Kingdoms of Mexico* (Penguin, 1991). Richard Townsend's *The Aztecs* (Thames & Hudson, 2000) is a thorough, well-researched examination of the Aztec and the Spanish conquest. For the Maya, Michael Coe's *The Maya* (Thames & Hudson, 2005) is probably the best general account. For a survey of Mexican history through modern times, *A Short History of Mexico* by J. Patrick McHenry (Doubleday, 1970) provides a complete, yet concise account.

For contemporary Mexican culture, start with Octavio Paz's classic, *The Labyrinth of Solitude* (Grove Press, 1985), which still generates controversy among Mexicans. For those already familiar with Mexico and its culture, Guillermo Bonfil's *Mexico Profundo: Reclaiming a Civilization* (University of Texas Press, 1996) is a rare bottom-up view of Mexico today.

Lesley Byrd Simpson's *Many Mexicos* (University of California Press, 1966) provides a comprehensive account of Mexican history with a cultural context.

A classic on understanding the culture of this country is *Distant Neighbors,* by Alan Riding (Vintage, 1989).

Books on the history of mainland Mexico abound, but **Baja's history** is just as fascinating, although worlds apart. Check out Harry W. Crosby's *The Cave Paintings of Baja California* (Sunbelt Publications, 1997), a book that delves into the history and mystery of indigenous people long forgotten.

Miraculous Air (Milkweed Editions, 2007), a fictionlike travel memoir by C.M. Mayo, takes the reader on a journey through the history, culture, economics, and lifestyle of the entire Baja peninsula. John Steinbeck's *The Log from the Sea of Cortez* (Penguin Classics, 1951), while technical in spots, also is a must for those impassioned by Baja's sea. And for those looking for a whimsical take on Baja life, plus regional recipes, it doesn't get any better than Ann Hazard's *Cooking with Baja Magic Dos* (Renegade Enterprises, 1995), the sequel to her first cookbook of the same name.

ART & ARCHITECTURE *Art and Time in Mexico: From the Conquest to the Revolution,* by Elizabeth Wilder Weismann (Harper & Row, 1985), covers religious, public, and private architecture. *Casa Mexicana,* by Tim Street-Porter (Stewart, Tabori & Chang, 1989), takes readers through the interiors of some of Mexico's finest homes-turned-museums, public buildings, and private homes.

Folk Treasures of Mexico, by Marion Oettinger (Harry N. Abrams, 1990), is the fascinating story behind the 3,000-piece Mexican folk-art collection amassed by Nelson Rockefeller over a 50-year period.

Maya Art and Architecture, by Mary Ellen Miller (Thames & Hudson, 1999) showcases the best of the artistic expression of this culture, with interpretations into its meanings.

For a wonderful read on the food of the Yucatán and Mexico, pick up *Mexico, One Plate at a Time,* by celebrity chef and Mexico aficionado Rick Bayless (Scribner, 2000).

NATURE *A Naturalist's Mexico,* by Roland H. Wauer (Texas A&M UP, 1992), is a fabulous guide to birding. Norman C. Roberts' *Baja California Plant Field Guide* (Longitude Books, 1989) is a fascinating illustrated guide to everything that grows in Baja.

MOVIES

The 2003 blockbuster *Frida,* starring Salma Hayek and Alfred Molina, is not only an entertaining way to learn about two of Mexico's most famous personalities, Frida Kahlo and Diego Rivera, but also of its history. The exquisite cinematography perfectly captures Mexico's inherent spirit of magic realism.

Que Viva México is a little-known masterpiece by Russian filmmaker Sergei Eisenstein, who created a documentary of Mexican history, politics and culture, out of a series of short *novellas,* which ultimately tie together. Although Eisenstein's budget ran out before he could complete the project, in 1979, this film was completed by Grigory Alexandrov, the film's original producer. It's an absolute must for anyone interested in Mexico or Mexican cinema.

Mexico's contemporary filmmakers are creating a sensation lately, and none more so than director Alfonso Cuarón. One of his early and highly acclaimed movies is the 2001 classic *Y Tu Mamá También (And Your Mother, Too),* featuring current heartthrobs Gael Garcia Bernal and Diego Luna. This sexy, yet compelling, coming-of-age movie not only showcases both the grit and beauty of Mexico, but the universality of love and life lessons.

Like Water for Chocolate is the 1993 film based on the book of the same name by Laura Esquivel, filmed by the author's husband, acclaimed contemporary Mexican director Alfonso Arau. Expect to be very hungry after watching this lushly visual film, which tells the story of a young woman who suppresses her passions under the watchful eye of a stern mother, and channels them into her cooking. In the process, we learn of the traditional norms of Mexican culture, and a great deal of the country's culinary treasures.

Appendix B:
Useful Terms & Phrases & a Guide to Mexico's Food & Drink

1 Basic Vocabulary

Most Mexicans are very patient with foreigners who try to speak their language; it helps a lot to know a few basic phrases. I've included simple phrases for expressing basic needs, followed by some common menu items.

ENGLISH-SPANISH PHRASES
BASIC PHRASES

English	Spanish	Pronunciation
Good day	**Buen día**	bwehn *dee*-ah
Good morning	**Buenos días**	*bweh*-nohss *dee*-ahss
How are you?	**¿Cómo está?**	*koh*-moh ehss-*tah?*
Very well	**Muy bien**	mwee byehn
Thank you	**Gracias**	*grah*-syahss
You're welcome	**De nada**	deh *nah*-dah
Good-bye	**Adiós**	ah-*dyohss*
Please	**Por favor**	pohr fah-*vohr*
Yes	**Sí**	see
No	**No**	noh
Excuse me	**Perdóneme**	pehr-*doh*-neh-meh
Give me	**Déme**	*deh*-meh
Where is . . . ?	**¿Dónde está . . . ?**	*dohn*-deh ehss-*tah?*
the station?	**la estación?**	lah ehss-tah-*syohn*
a hotel?	**un hotel?**	oon oh-*tehl*
a gas station?	**una gasolinera?**	*oo*-nah gah-soh-lee-*neh*-rah
a restaurant?	**un restaurante?**	oon res-tow-*rahn*-teh
the bathroom?	**el baño?**	el *bah*-nyoh
a good doctor?	**un buen medico?**	oon bwehn *meh*-dee-coh
the road to . . . ?	**el camino a/ hacia . . . ?**	el cah-*mee*-noh ah/*ah*-syah
To the right	**A la derecha**	ah lah deh-*reh*-chah
To the left	**A la izquierda**	ah lah ees-*kyehr*-dah
Straight ahead	**Derecho**	deh-*reh*-choh

English	Spanish	Pronunciation
I would like	**Quisiera**	key-*syeh*-rah
I want . . .	**Quiero . . .**	*kyeh*-roh
to eat.	**comer.**	koh-*mehr*
a room.	**una habitación.**	*oo*-nah ah-bee-tah-*syohn*
Do you have . . . ?	**¿Tiene usted . . . ?**	tyeh-neh oo-*sted*?
a book?	**un libro?**	oon *lee*-broh
a dictionary?	**un diccionario?**	oon deek-syow-*nah*-ryo
a pen?	**una pluma?**	oon ah *ploo*-mah
How much is it?	**¿Cuánto cuesta?**	*kwahn*-toh *kwehss*-tah?
When?	**¿Cuándo?**	*kwahn*-doh?
What?	**¿Qué?**	keh?
There is (Is there . . . ?)	**(¿)Hay (. . . ?)**	eye?
What is there?	**¿Qué hay?**	keh eye?
Yesterday	**Ayer**	ah-*yer*
Today	**Hoy**	oy
Tomorrow	**Mañana**	mah-*nyah*-nah
Good	**Bueno**	*bweh*-noh
Bad	**Malo**	*mah*-loh
Better (best)	**(Lo) Mejor**	(loh) meh-*hohr*
More	**Más**	mahs
Less	**Menos**	*meh*-nohss
Enough	**Bastante**	bahs-*tahn*-tay
No smoking	**Se prohibe fumar**	seh proh-*ee*-beh foo-*mahr*
Postcard	**Tarjeta postal**	tar-*heh*-ta pohs-*tahl*
Insect repellent	**Repelente contra insectos**	eh-peh-*lehn*-te *cohn*-trah een-*sehk*-tos

MORE USEFUL PHRASES

English	Spanish	Pronunciation
Do you speak English?	**¿Habla usted inglés?**	*ah*-blah oo-*sted* een-*glehs*?
Is there anyone here who speaks English?	**¿Hay alguien aquí que hable inglés?**	eye *ahl*-gyehn ah-*kee* keh *ah*-bleh een-*glehs*?
I speak a little Spanish.	**Hablo un poco de español.**	*ah*-bloh oon *poh*-koh deh ehss-pah-*nyohl*

English	Spanish	Pronunciation
I don't understand Spanish very well.	**No (lo) entiendo muy bien el español.**	noh (loh) ehn-*tyehn*-doh mwee byehn el ehss-pah-*nyohl*
The meal is good.	**La comida está buena.**	lah koh-*mee*-dah *eh-stah bweh-nah*
What time is it?	**¿Qué hora es?**	keh *oh*-rah ehss?
May I see your menu?	**¿Puedo ver el menú (la carta)?**	*pueh*-do vehr el meh-*noo* (lah *car*-tah)?
The check, please.	**La cuenta, por favor.**	lah *quehn*-tah pohr fa-*vorh*
What do I owe you?	**¿Cuánto le debo?**	*kwahn*-toh leh *deh*-boh?
What did you say?	**¿Mande?** (formal)	*mahn*-deh?
	¿Cómo? (informal)	*koh*-moh?
I want (to see) . . .	**Quiero (ver) . . .**	*kyeh*-roh (vehr)
a room . . .	**un cuarto** or **una habitación . . .**	oon *kwar*-toh, *oo*-nah ah-bee-tah-*syohn*
for two persons.	**para dos personas.**	*pah*-rah dohss pehr-*soh*-nahs
with (without)	**con (sin)**	kohn (seen)
bathroom.	**baño.**	*bah*-nyoh
We are staying here only . . .	**Nos quedamos aquí solamente . . .**	nohs keh-*dah*-mohss ah-*kee* soh-lah-*mehn*-teh
one night.	**una noche.**	*oo*-nah *noh*-cheh
one week.	**una semana.**	*oo*-nah seh-*mah*-nah
We are leaving . . .	**Partimos (Salimos) . . .**	pahr-*tee*-mohss (sah-*lee*-mohss)
tomorrow.	**mañana.**	mah-*nya*-nah
Do you accept . . . ?	**¿Acepta usted . . . ?**	ah-*sehp*-tah oo-*sted*
traveler's checks?	**cheques de viajero?**	*cheh*-kehss deh byah-*heh*-roh?
Is there a Laundromat . . . ?	**¿Hay una lavandería . . . ?**	eye *oo*-nah l ah-*vahn*-deh-*ree*-ah
near here?	**cerca de aquí?**	*sehr*-kah deh ah-*kee*
Please send these clothes to the laundry.	**Hágame el favor de mandar esta ropa a la lavandería.**	*ah*-gah-meh el fah-*vohr* deh mahn-*dahr* ehss-tah *roh*-pah a lah lah-*vahn*-deh-*ree*-ah

NUMBERS

1	**uno** (*oo*-noh)	17	**diecisiete** (dyess-ee-*syeh*-teh)
2	**dos** (dohss)	18	**dieciocho** (dyess-ee-*oh*-choh)
3	**tres** (trehss)	19	**diecinueve** (dyess-ee-*nweh*-beh)
4	**cuatro** (*kwah*-troh)	20	**veinte** (*bayn*-teh)
5	**cinco** (*seen*-koh)	30	**treinta** (*trayn*-tah)
6	**seis** (sayss)	40	**cuarenta** (kwah-*ren*-tah)
7	**siete** (*syeh*-teh)	50	**cincuenta** (seen-*kwen*-tah)
8	**ocho** (*oh*-choh)	60	**sesenta** (seh-*sehn*-tah)
9	**nueve** (*nweh*-beh)	70	**setenta** (seh-*tehn*-tah)
10	**diez** (dyess)	80	**ochenta** (oh-*chehn*-tah)
11	**once** (*ohn*-seh)	90	**noventa** (noh-*behn*-tah)
12	**doce** (*doh*-seh)	100	**cien** (syehn)
13	**trece** (*treh*-seh)	200	**doscientos** (do-*syehn*-tohs)
14	**catorce** (kah-*tohr*-seh)	500	**quinientos** (kee-*nyehn*-tohs)
15	**quince** (*keen*-seh)	1,000	**mil** (meel)
16	**dieciseis** (dyess-ee-*sayss*)		

TRANSPORTATION TERMS

English	Spanish	Pronunciation
Airport	**Aeropuerto**	ah-eh-roh-*pwehr*-toh
Flight	**Vuelo**	*bweh*-loh
Rental car	**Arrendadora de autos**	ah-rehn-da-*doh*-rah deh *ow*-tohs
Bus	**Autobús**	ow-toh-*boos*
Bus or truck	**Camión**	ka-*myohn*
Lane	**Carril**	kah-*reel*
Direct	**Directo**	dee-*rehk*-toh
Baggage (claim area)	**Equipajes**	eh-kee-*pah*-hehss
Intercity	**Foraneo**	foh-rah-*neh*-oh
Luggage storage area	**Guarda equipaje**	*gwar*-dah eh-kee-*pah*-heh
Arrival gates	**Llegadas**	yeh-*gah*-dahss
Originates at this station	**Local**	loh-*kahl*
Originates elsewhere	**De paso**	deh *pah*-soh
Stops if seats available	**Para si hay lugares**	*pah*-rah see eye loo-*gah*-rehs
First class	**Clase primera**	*klah*-seh pree-*meh*-rah
Second class	**Segunda clase**	seh-*goon*-dah *klah*-seh
Nonstop	**Sin escala**	seen ess-*kah*-lah
Baggage claim area	**Reclamo de equipajes**	*reh*-klah-moh deh eh-kee-*pah*-hehs
Waiting room	**Sala de espera**	*sah*-lah deh ehss-*peh*-rah

English	Spanish	Pronunciation
Toilets	**Sanitarios**	sah-nee-*tah*-ryohss
Ticket window	**Taquilla**	tah-*kee*-yah

POSTAL GLOSSARY

Airmail   **Correo Aéreo**

Customs   **La aduana**

General delivery   **Lista de correos**

Insurance (insured mail)   **Seguro (correo asegurado)**

Mailbox   **Buzón**

Money order   **Giro postal**

Parcel   **Paquete**

Post office   **Oficina de correos**

Post office box (abbreviation)   **Apdo. Postal**

Postal service   **Correos**

Registered mail   **Registrado**

Rubber stamp   **Sello**

Special delivery, express   **Entrega inmediata**

Stamp   **Estampilla** or **timbre**

2 Menu Glossary

Achiote   Small red seed of the *annatto* tree.

Achiote preparado   A Yucatecan-prepared paste made of ground *achiote,* wheat and corn flour, cumin, cinnamon, salt, onion, garlic, and oregano.

Agua fresca   Fruit-flavored water, usually watermelon, cantaloupe, chia seed with lemon, hibiscus flower, rice, or ground melon-seed mixture.

Antojito   Typical Mexican supper foods usually made with *masa* or tortillas and having a filling or topping such as sausage, cheese, beans, and onions; includes such things as tacos, tostadas, *sopes,* and *garnachas.* Often served as appetizers or snacks.

Atole   A thick, lightly sweet, hot drink made with finely ground corn and usually flavored with vanilla, pecan, strawberry, pineapple, lemon, or chocolate.

Botana   An appetizer.

Buñuelos   Round, thin, deep-fried crispy fritters dipped in sugar.

Carnitas   Pork deep-cooked (not fried) in lard and then simmered and served with corn tortillas for tacos.

Ceviche   Fresh raw seafood marinated in fresh lime juice and garnished with chopped tomatoes, onions, chiles, and sometimes cilantro. Often served with tortilla chips *(totopos).*

Chayote   A vegetable pear or mirliton, a type of spiny squash boiled and served as an accompaniment to meat dishes or to flavor soups and broths.

Chiles en nogada   Poblano peppers stuffed with a mixture of ground pork and beef, spices, fruits, raisins, and almonds. It's traditionally served cool or at room temperature, covered in walnut-cream sauce, and sprinkled with pomegranate seeds.

Because this dish highlights the colors of the Mexican flag—red, white, and green—chiles en nogada is Mexico's official Independence Day dish.

Chiles rellenos   Usually poblano peppers stuffed with cheese, potatoes, or spicy ground meat with raisins, rolled in a batter, and fried.

Churro   Tube-shaped, breadlike fritter, dipped in sugar and sometimes filled with *cajeta* (goat-milk-based caramel) or chocolate.

Cochinita pibil   Pork wrapped in banana leaves, pit-baked in a *pibil* sauce of *achiote*, sour orange, and spices; most common in the Yucatán.

Damiana   The small yellow flower, indigenous to Baja, known for its aphrodisia-cal, fertility-enhancing properties. Liqueur of the same name, made from the blossoms, is served on ice after dinner or as a secret ingredient in margaritas.

Enchilada   A tortilla dipped in sauce, usually filled with chicken or white cheese, and sometimes topped with *mole* (*enchiladas rojas* or *de mole*); tomato sauce and sour cream (*enchiladas suizas*—Swiss enchiladas); covered in a green sauce (*enchiladas verdes*); or topped with onions, sour cream, and guacamole (*enchiladas potosinas*).

Escabeche   A lightly pickled sauce used in Yucatecan chicken stew.

Frijoles refritos   Boiled pinto beans, mashed and cooked with lard.

Garnachas   A thickish small circle of fried *masa* with pinched sides, topped with pork or chicken, onions, and avocado, or sometimes chopped potatoes and tomatoes.

Gorditas   Thick, fried corn tortillas, slit and stuffed with choice of cheese, beans, beef, or chicken, with or without lettuce, tomato, and onion garnish.

Horchata   Refreshing lightly sweetened drink made of ground rice or melon seeds, ground almonds, and cinnamon.

Huevos mexicanos   Scrambled eggs with chopped onions, hot green peppers, and tomatoes.

Huitlacoche   Sometimes spelled "cuitlacoche." A mushroom-flavored black fungus that appears on corn in the rainy season; considered a delicacy.

Manchamantel   Translated, means "tablecloth stainer." It's a stew of chicken or pork with chiles, tomatoes, pineapple, bananas, and jicama.

Masa   Ground corn soaked in lime, it's the basis for tamales, corn tortillas, and soups.

Mixiote   Rabbit, lamb, or chicken cooked in a mild chile sauce (usually chile ancho or pasilla) and then wrapped like a tamal and steamed. It is generally served with tortillas for tacos, with traditional garnishes of pickled onions, hot sauce, chopped cilantro, and lime wedges.

Pan de muerto   Sweet bread made around the Days of the Dead (Nov 1–2) in the form of mummies or dolls, or round with bone designs.

Pan dulce   Lightly sweetened bread in many configurations, usually served at breakfast or bought in any bakery.

Papadzules   Tortillas stuffed with hard-boiled eggs and seeds (pumpkin or sun-flower) in a tomato sauce.

Pibil   Pit-baked pork or chicken in a sauce of tomato, onion, mild red pepper, cilantro, and vinegar.

Pipián   A sauce made with ground pumpkin seeds, nuts, and mild peppers.

Poc chuc   Slices of pork with onion marinated in a tangy sour-orange sauce and charcoal-broiled; a Yucatecan specialty.

Pozole   A pre–Colombian-era soup made of hominy, meat, chile, and other seasonings. Often served for breakfast with garnishes ranging from cilantro to radishes.

Pulque   A drink made of fermented juice of the maguey plant; best in the state of Hidalgo and around Mexico City.

Quesadilla   Corn or flour tortillas stuffed with melted white cheese and lightly fried.

Queso relleno   Translated as "stuffed cheese," this dish consists of a mild yellow cheese stuffed with minced meat and spices; it's a Yucatecan specialty.

Rompope   Delicious Mexican eggnog, invented in Puebla, made with eggs, vanilla, sugar, and rum.

Salsa verde   An uncooked sauce using the green tomatillo puréed with spicy or mild hot peppers, onions, garlic, and cilantro.

Sopa de flor de calabaza   A soup made of chopped squash or pumpkin blossoms.

Sopa de lima   A tangy soup made with chicken broth and accented with fresh lime; popular in Yucatán.

Sopa de tortilla   A traditional chicken broth–based soup, seasoned with chiles, tomatoes, onion, and garlic, served with crispy fried strips of corn tortillas. Also called *sopa azteca.*

Sopa tlalpeña (or *caldo tlalpeño*)   A hearty soup made with chunks of chicken, chopped carrots, zucchini, corn, onions, garlic, and cilantro.

Sopa tlaxcalteca   A hearty tomato-based soup filled with cooked *nopal* cactus, cheese, cream, and avocado, with crispy tortilla strips floating on top.

Sope   Pronounced "*soh*-peh." An *antojito* similar to a *garnacha* except spread with refried beans and topped with crumbled cheese and onions.

Tacos al pastor   Thin slices of flavored pork roasted on a revolving cylinder dripping with onion slices and the juice of fresh pineapple slices. Served in small corn tortillas, it's topped with chopped onion and cilantro.

Tamal   Often incorrectly called a tamale (*tamal* is singular; *tamales* is plural), this dish consists of a meat or sweet filling rolled with fresh *masa* wrapped in a corn husk or banana leaf and steamed.

Tequila   Distilled alcohol produced from the *A. tequilana* species of agave (known as Blue Weber agave) in and around the area of Tequila, in the state of Jalisco. Mezcal, by contrast, comes from various parts of Mexico and from different varieties of agave and is considered less sophisticated than tequila (and more easily detected on the drinker's breath).

Tikin xic   Also seen on menus as "tik-n-xic" and "tikik chick," it is a charbroiled fish brushed with *achiote* sauce.

Tomatillo   Small, tart green tomatoes that come wrapped in delicate, sticky husks. The base for most green salsas, and also used fresh in some salads.

Torta   A sandwich, usually on *bolillo* bread, typically with sliced avocado, onions, tomatoes, and a choice of meat and often cheese.

Totopos   Fried tortilla chips.

Xtabentun Pronounced "shtah-behn-*toon*," this is a Yucatecan liquor made of fermented honey flavored with anise. It comes *seco* (dry) or *crema* (sweet).

Zacahuil Pork leg tamal, packed in thick *masa*, wrapped in banana leaves, and pit-baked, sometimes pot-made with tomato and *masa*; it's a specialty of mid- to upper Veracruz.

3 Food

Authentic Mexican food differs dramatically from what is frequently served in the United States under that name. For many travelers, Mexico will be new and exciting culinary territory. Even grizzled veterans will be pleasantly surprised by the wide variation in specialties and traditions offered from region to region.

Despite regional differences, some generalizations can be made. Mexican food usually isn't pepper-hot when it arrives at the table (though many dishes have a certain amount of piquancy, and some home cooking can be very spicy, depending on a family's or chef's tastes). Chiles and sauces add heat and flavor after the food is served; you'll never see a table in Mexico without one or both of these condiments. Mexicans don't drown their cooking in cheese and sour cream, a la Tex-Mex, and they use a great variety of ingredients. But the basis of Mexican food is simple—tortillas, beans, chiles, onions, squash, and tomatoes—the same as it was centuries ago, before the Europeans arrived. Although geographically separated from the mainland, Baja's culinary customs mirror those of the mainland in this regard.

For information on food and drink safety, see "Treating & Avoiding Digestive Trouble" on p. 25. For information on food and dining etiquette, see "Etiquette & Customs" on p. 43.

MEALTIME

MORNING The morning meal, known as *el desayuno,* can be something light, such as coffee and sweet bread, or something more substantial: eggs, beans, tortillas, bread, fruit, juice, and maybe even *pozole* soup or tacos. It can be eaten early or late and is always a sure bet in Mexico. The variety and sweetness of the fruits on offer is remarkable, and you can't go wrong with Mexican egg dishes.

MIDAFTERNOON The main meal of the day, known as *la comida* (or *almuerzo*), is eaten between 2 and 4pm. Some stores and businesses still close for the meal so people can eat at home with their families, but in places like Los Cabos, where tourism is the number-one industry, the traditional *comida* may be cut short. The first course is the *sopa,* which can be either soup *(caldo)* or rice *(sopa de arroz)* or both; then comes the main course, which ideally is a meat or fish dish prepared in some kind of sauce and served with beans, followed by dessert.

EVENING Between 8 and 10pm, most Mexicans have a light meal called *la cena.* If eaten at home, it is something like a sandwich, bread and jam, or perhaps a couple of tacos made from some of the day's leftovers. At restaurants, the most common thing to eat is *antojitos* (literally, "little cravings"), a general label for light fare. *Antojitos* include tostadas, tamales, tacos, and simple enchiladas, and are big hits with travelers. Large restaurants offer complete meals as well. In Baja, popular *antojitos* include *menudo* (a thick soup of cow's feet and stomachs, seasoned with chiles, oregano, and chopped onion), *huaraches* (a flat, thick oval-shaped tortilla, topped with fried meat and chiles), and *chalupas* (a crisp whole tortilla, topped with beans, meat, and other toppings).

EATING OUT: RESTAURANTS, *TAQUERIAS* & TIPPING

First of all, I feel compelled to debunk the widespread myth that the cheapest place to eat in Mexico is in the market. Actually, this is almost never the case. You can usually find better food at a better price without going more than 2 blocks out of your way. Why? Food stalls in the marketplace pay high rents, they have a near-captive clientele of market vendors and truckers, and they get a lot of business from many Mexicans for whom eating in the market is a traditional way of confirming their culture. However, Baja is a little bit different in that many traditional markets have given way to supermarket box stores such as Comercial Mexicana (Mega), Soriana, and Costco.

Most towns—resorts and nonresorts—have one or two restaurants (sometimes one is a coffee shop) that are social centers for a large group of established patrons. These establishments over time become virtual institutions and change comes very slowly. The food is usually good, standard fare cooked as it was 20 years ago, and the decor is simple. The patrons have known each other and the staff for years, and the *charla* (banter), gestures, and greetings are friendly, open, and unaffected. If you're curious about Mexican—or expatriate—culture, eating and observing the goings-on in one of these places will be fun for you.

During your trip, you're sure to see many *taquerías* **(taco joints)** and **taco stands,** which function as Mexican fast-food joints. These are generally small places with a counter or a few tables set around the cooking area; you get to see exactly how the cooks make their tacos before deciding whether to order. Most tacos come with a little chopped onion and cilantro but not tomato and lettuce. Find one that seems popular with the locals and where the cook performs with brio (a good sign of pride in the product). Sometimes there will be a woman making the tortillas right there (or working the *masa* into *gorditas, sopes,* or *panuchos* if these are also served). You will never see men doing this—this is perhaps the strictest gender division in Mexican society. Men may do all other cooking and kitchen tasks, and work with prepared tortillas, but they will never be found working *masa*. In Baja, taco stands hold court on popular thoroughfares, such as banks and intersections. While the food—tacos, burritos, hot dogs, and hamburgers—can be downright delicious, it's best to avoid them after rain, for sanitary reasons.

For lunch, the main meal of the day, some restaurants offer a multicourse blue-plate special called *comida corrida* or *menú del día*. This is the least expensive way to get a full meal.

In Mexico, you need to ask for your check; it is generally considered inhospitable to present a check to someone who hasn't requested it. If you're in a hurry to get somewhere, ask for the check when your food arrives.

The **tipping** situation is about the same as in the United States, though you'll sometimes find a 15% **value-added tax** on restaurant meals, which shows up on the bill as "IVA." This is a boon to arithmetically challenged tippers, saving them from undue exertion.

To summon the waiter, wave or raise your hand, but don't motion with your index finger, which is a demeaning gesture that may even cause the waiter to ignore you. Or if it's the check you want, you can motion to the waiter from across the room using the universal pretend-you're-writing gesture.

Most restaurants do not have **nonsmoking sections;** when they do, we mention it in the reviews. But Mexico's wonderful climate allows for many open-air restaurants, usually set inside a courtyard of a colonial house, or in rooms with tall ceilings and plenty of open windows.

Index

See also Accommodations and Restaurant indexes, below.

— I don't speak sign language.

A hotel can close for all kinds of reasons.
Our Guarantee ensures that if your hotel's undergoing construction, we'll let you know in advance. In fact, we cover your entire travel experience. See www.travelocity.com/guarantee for details.

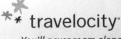

You'll never roam alone.

There's a parking lot where my ocean view should be.

 À la place de la vue sur l'océan, me voilà avec une vue sur un parking.

 Anstatt Meerblick habe ich Sicht auf einen Parkplatz.

 Al posto della vista sull'oceano c'è un parcheggio.

 No tengo vista al mar porque hay un parque de estacionamiento.

 Há um parque de estacionamento onde deveria estar a minha vista do ocean

 Ett parkeringsområde har byggts på den plats där min utsikt över oceanen borde vara.

 Er ligt een parkeerterrein waar mijn zee-uitzicht zou moeten zijn.

 هنالك موقف للسيارات مكان ما وجب ان يكون المنظر الخلاب المطل على المحيط .

 眼前に広がる紺碧の海・・・じゃない。窓の外は駐車場

 停车场的位置应该是我的海景所在。

— I'm fluent in pig latin.

Hotel mishaps aren't bound by geography.
Neither is our Guarantee. It covers your entire travel experience, including the price. So if you don't get the ocean view you booked, we'll work with our travel partners to make it right, right away. See www.travelocity.com/guarantee for details.

 travelocity
You'll never roam alone.

©2007 Travelocity.com LP CST # 2056372-50